SPANISH DRAWINGS

in the Princeton University Art Museum

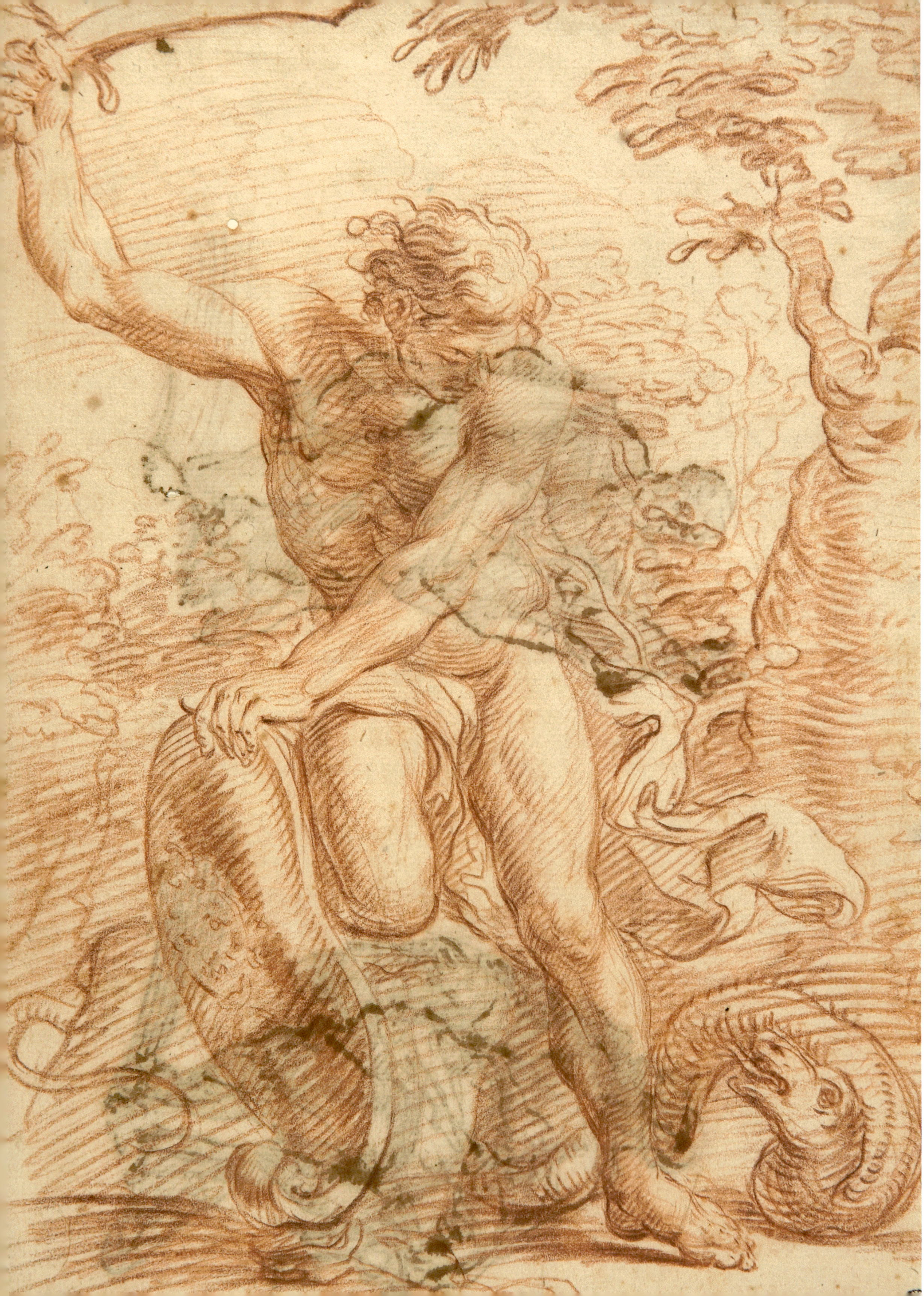

SPANISH DRAWINGS
in the Princeton University Art Museum

Lisa A. Banner

with contributions by Jonathan Brown, Robert S. Lubar, and Pierre Rosenberg

Princeton University Art Museum
Distributed by Yale University Press, New Haven and London

Supported by the Center for Spain in America

Spanish Drawings in the Princeton University Art Museum is published by the Princeton University Art Museum and distributed by Yale University Press, New Haven and London.

Princeton University Art Museum
Princeton, New Jersey 08544-1018
artmuseum.princeton.edu

Yale University Press
P.O. Box 209040
302 Temple Street
New Haven, Connecticut 06520-9040
yalebooks.com/art

Support for this publication has been provided by the Center for Spain in America.

CSA
CENTER FOR SPAIN
IN AMERICA

Associate Editor: Janet S. Rauscher
Photographer and Digital Imaging Specialist: Jeff Evans
Copy Editor: Melissa Duffes
Publications Assistant: Amanda Gannaway
Proofreader: David A. Auerbach
Designer: Bruce Campbell
Typesetter: Mary Gladue
Printer: Brilliant Graphics, Exton, Pennsylvania

Library of Congress Control Number:
2012948086

ISBN: 978-0-300-14931-9

Illustrations:
front cover: Jusepe de Ribera, *Studies of Male Head in Profile*, ca. 1622, detail (cat. 4)
frontispiece: Unknown Artist, Portuguese?, *Cadmus Killing the Dragon*, late 17th–early 18th century, detail (cat. 81)

CONTENTS

FOREWORD AND ACKNOWLEDGMENTS

Among the Princeton University Art Museum's hidden jewels is the collection revealed here, a group of Spanish drawings that may not be among the nation's largest but is one of subtle masterworks and intimate pleasures. This catalogue takes its place in two important contexts: the first, a growing list of titles dedicated to the world's most arresting collections of Spanish drawings; the second, a rich roster of tomes dedicated to discrete areas among the nearly universal holdings of the Museum, including past volumes dedicated to Greek and Roman sculpture and to American drawings and watercolors as well as future titles that will explore ancient glass and Italian drawings.

In the second context, this publication is intended to be neither comprehensive nor the last word on our extensive holdings of Spanish drawings. Instead, it is really the *first* word—publishing many of the drawings contained herein for the first time and significantly advancing our understanding of those that have been published but are largely understudied. Much more remains to be considered by future generations, and we are pleased to bring the collection to the attention of scholars, invite their probity, and look forward to advancing future scholarly developments.

Long-term projects of this kind are inevitably the fruit of the labors of many, and by naming those who have been instrumental to this publication I risk either misattributing emphasis or omitting a key player or two. I can only fairly begin, however, by recognizing Jonathan Brown as the guiding spirit behind this undertaking. We have long been fortunate to count Jonathan, a scholar of Spanish art of universally recognized importance, as a member of the Museum's Advisory Council, as one of Princeton's most distinguished alumni, and as a longtime habitué of Marquand Library. Without Jonathan's enduring advocacy for this volume, which long predates my arrival as director in 2009, I am certain that we would not be where we are today.

Likewise, I must thank each of the key contributors to the volume, beginning with Lisa Banner as its primary author; Rob Lubar, for his contributions in respect to the modern drawings; and Pierre Rosenberg for his introductory text. Each adds much to our understanding of both the most essential drawings in the collection and those that demand continued investigation. Several key members of the Museum's staff also contributed to our understanding of these drawings, including Laura Giles, Heather and Paul G. Haaga Jr., Class of 1970, Curator of Prints and Drawings; Calvin Brown, Associate Curator of Prints and Drawings; Betsy Rosasco, Research Curator of European Painting and Sculpture (most especially for her translation from the French of Pierre Rosenberg's essay); and Cathryn Goodwin, Manager of Collection Information and Access.

Both on staff and on the team assembled for this project, we have been blessed by the talents of many. Jill Guthrie, our former Managing Editor, brought to the project her usual rigorous standards and high expectations. Associate Editor Janet Rauscher came to this project early in her as-yet short tenure here in Princeton but proved her mettle immediately by leaping in with both feet to contribute as both a scholar and an accomplished editor. Without her stalwart efforts, this book would remain an engaging amalgam of ideas but would fall far short of the product you now hold in your hands. I likewise thank and recognize Jeff Evans, Photographer and Digital Imaging Specialist, for nearly all of the photography contained here; Norman Muller, Conservator, for the betaradiographs of watermarks; Betty Fiske, paper conservator; Bruce Campbell, who created the book's handsome design; Mary Gladue, for her careful typesetting; Bob Tursack, Dustin Tursack, and Brilliant Graphics, who printed the volume; Melissa Duffes, copy editor; David Auerbach, proofreader; and Amanda Gannaway, interim publications assistant.

For research assistance, guidance, and generous sharing of their own research, resources, and knowledge with Lisa Banner, we also acknowledge Kevin Groome, Henry Fountain and Savannah Walker, Susan Grace Galassi, Isabel Ortega, Isabel Clara García-Toraño Martínez, Álvaro Molina, Mary Zuber, George Goldner, Juliet Wilson-Bareau, Janis Tomlinson, Stephanie Stepanek, Frederick Ilchman, Marcus Burke, Priscilla Muller, Margaret Connors McQuade, Constancio del Álamo, Patrick Lenaghan, John O'Neill, Edwin Rolón, Miriam Stewart, Francesc Quílez, Cristina Mendoza, Ascensión Ciruelos, Julian Brooks, Imma Socias, Cocó Alcalá, Miguel Falomir Faus, Aruna d'Souza, Titia Hulst, Daniel Silva, Constancio Del Álamo, Suz Massen, Elizabeth Lane, Sarah Miró, William Ambler, Molly Ott Ambler, Virginia Lladó-Buisán, Richard Mulholland, Ann Baldwin, Clara de la Peña McTigue, Philippe Ávila, Mark Morosse, Arielle Dorlester, Elizabeth Pergam, Mark McDonald, Zahira Véliz, David Bomford, José Manuel de la Mano, José Manuel Matilla, Laura Stirton-Aust, Suzanne Boorsch, Adela Espinós, Benito Navarrete Prieto, Fuensanta García de la Torre, Alta Berri, Jan Leja, J. D. Calder, Nancy Minty, Rebecca Tucker, Christopher Smith, Luis Méndez Rodríguez, Gabriele Finaldi, Marijn Schapelhouman, Esther López Sobrado, Erika Dolphin, Nigel Glendinning, Christopher Linnane, Ignacio Cano, Agnes Tabbellion and Javi Martínez, Jennifer Belt, Sarah Wittman, Xavier Bray, Ronda Kasl, Juan Antonio Yeves Andrés, Bonaventura Bassegoda, Javier Portús, Carlos Saguar Quer, María Cruz de Carlos, Peter Cherry, Gridley McKim Smith, Mark McDonald, Julian Brooks, Maite Alvarez, Jesús Escobar, Ellen Prokop, Ilona Katzew, Dagmar Korbacher, Andrea Bayer, *mis tres reyes*, and numerous others.

Finally, I thank José Luis Colomer, without whose critical commitment of funds from the Center for Spain in America this project would have remained an unfulfilled aspiration. Throughout what became an extended process, and what might have seemed at times an endless succession of moving targets, José Luis has been a collaborator of generosity and spirit. The wider field of Spanish drawings and we here at Princeton alike are fortunate for his passionate dedication.

James Christen Steward
Director
Princeton University Art Museum

SPONSOR'S PREFACE

Spanish drawings have been an unchartered territory for many years compared to their counterparts from other European nations. It was generally assumed that drawing was uncommon among Spanish artists, and that the few who cared to undertake such preparations for their works were exceptions in a land of improvisers who preferred *alla prima* virtuosity to the studiousness of draftsmanship. Fortunately, our views on the use and function of graphic arts in Spain are rapidly changing as systematic research progresses and catalogues raisonnés are published, providing new evidence to refute the notion of a non-cultivated art among the Spaniards. The long-standing attitude regarding the dearth of drawings is at last being challenged and revised, and now exhibitions of Spanish drawings from American and European museums demonstrate growing attention to this national school as a field in which many exciting discoveries are still possible.

The Center for Spain in America (CSA) promotes advanced study and public awareness in the United States of Spanish art and culture. Its aims and objectives include programs in collaboration with universities, libraries, and museums; fostering the development of research in Spanish drawings; and encouraging the compilation of scholarly catalogues that are jointly supported with its sister entity in Madrid, the Centro de Estudios Europa Hispánica (CEEH). Indeed it is an honor to continue the series by publishing this volume in association with the Princeton University Art Museum. I am very grateful to Jonathan Brown for suggesting the possibility of a complete catalogue of this collection of Spanish drawings, providing dissemination and enjoyment of the holdings he helped shape in collaboration with Mathias Polakovits. Special thanks go to Lisa Banner, the main author of this catalogue, which has benefitted from her previous experience as a research fellow at the Hispanic Society of America and her co-curatorship of the exhibition *The Spanish Manner* at The Frick Collection, New York. I would also like to extend my gratitude to James Steward, Director of the Princeton University Art Museum, and the Museum's Department of Prints and Drawings, for making this project part of their program. I hope that this publication will stimulate further interest from students and scholars in Spanish drawings as our Center promotes other studies and public displays of these works in the United States.

José Luis Colomer
Director
Center for Spain in America

A NOTE ON COLLECTOR MATHIAS POLAKOVITS

For a long time I kept a scrap of newspaper on which was written the telephone number of Jackie Onassis—Jackie Kennedy. I no longer remember the exact circumstances, surely social, in New York, in which Mathias introduced us. He was a friend of the Kennedys, especially Robert Kennedy, and was with him when he was assassinated on June 5, 1968. Mathias was a member of an international jet set that he had seduced and conquered by his charm, his intelligence, his vitality, his volubility. Mathias's charm was only one facet of the attractive personality of this seducer with a sonorous, theatrical voice that hadn't entirely lost the accent he cleverly exploited.

Mathias Polakovits was born in 1921 in Budapest, to a family in comfortable circumstances. He studied in Switzerland and England. In 1949 he managed to escape Hungary, hidden, he claimed, in a train's toilet compartment with false walls. His first years in Paris were not easy. How to support himself? He thought of becoming a singer, and in 1952 was heard on the radio and at the Cannes Casino under the name of Mathias Palco (with a repertory of Schubert, Menotti, Martinu). It was as a journalist, however, that he made his name: *Paris-Match*—to which he was recommended by Philippe de Rothschild—took him on in 1952. That year he wrote on the Egyptian revolution, meeting Colonel Neguib, and then, in 1956, Colonel Nasser. The same year, he covered the Hungarian revolution along with the photographer Jean-Pierre Pedrazzini, who was fatally wounded beside him by Soviet bullets. New York was next, still for *Paris-Match*, where he was named bureau head in 1960, a position he occupied until his voluntary departure in 1969.

I am looking at a photograph in which Mathias can be recognized in a rich costume. He accompanies Philippine de Rothschild, disguised as the young girl with a shuttlecock in the famous painting by Chardin. The occasion was a costume ball organized by Marie-Laure de Noailles at her Parisian townhouse on Place des États-Unis. The ball took place on February 23, 1956, and the Hungarian revolt began a few months later. Mathias was able to bring his mother from Hungary to France that year. By October 1955, he had become a French citizen.

I met Mathias in the winter of 1966–67. I had published an article on the drawings of Claude Vignon (1593–1670) in the third issue of *Master Drawings* for the year 1966. Vignon's drawings, which had sunk into anonymity, are much rarer than his paintings, which are easy to recognize. My article brought together a core of works whose attribution could not be challenged. Mathias wrote to me, inviting me to come see—at 799 Madison Avenue, in a well-located but shabby apartment—his "Vignon." This drawing (for which no one to the present day has suggested a convincing attribution) had nothing to do with Vignon. At the time, Mathias only owned a few sheets, purchased randomly when he fell for them, or given to him by friends. The visit was stormy. Mathias knew nothing. He confused techniques—red chalk, black chalk—couldn't distinguish a drawing from its counterproof, and did not know any more about the drawings collections of the Metropolitan Museum than he did about publications on drawings by Berenson, Friedländer, and Blunt. The straw that broke the camel's back was "Lugt." Mathias had never even heard of this indispensable publication, which allows scholars to identify the successive owners of a drawing. It was a shock to him.

Mathias set to work with tenacity, voracity, with his immense curiosity. He wanted to learn, he wanted to be an art historian. He read assiduously everything that came to hand— articles, monographs, exhibition catalogues. He frequented drawing cabinets in New York, Paris, and London, and visited, with the modesty of a neophyte, established drawings collectors in those cities. Above all, he became a habitué of the sales rooms at Drouot, Sotheby's, and Christie's, began to buy, and bought abundantly. Seated in the first row during sales, he rarely gave up something he wanted. When he ended his activity as a journalist, which allowed him a comfortable retirement, it was above all to devote himself full-time to his collection—a devotion that continued for all of the years that remained to him. It was his reason to live. He died of AIDS, an illness that was still seldom discussed in Paris in 1987.

Mathias collected drawings of every school—including Spain, which I did not know—but hardly strayed beyond 1800. He bought mainly at public sales, at a time when the price of drawings—especially anonymous ones—remained low, incredibly low. He loved sheets by minor artists, artists who had known an hour of glory but whom posterity had forgotten. He loved landscapes and figure drawings (*académies*), from which Princeton profited greatly. He loved above all French drawings, which he classified not alphabetically but chronologically, in large black boxes in his dark apartment at 8 Boulevard de La Tour-Maubourg. His dream drawing was the preparatory study, hitherto wrongly attributed, for a painting by a minor artist. He worked—the word may seem surprising—with determination, tirelessly, drawing on his friends, whether Parisian or passing through Paris, in what was sometimes a difficult ordeal, wringing from them the attribution he hadn't found himself but which he dreamed of finding.

For Mathias, a drawing was not an object of delectation; it should instruct, advance our knowledge. We all learned much thanks to Mathias's collection. At his death, he gave his three thousand French drawings to the École nationale supérieure des Beaux-Arts in Paris. One can easily consult them there in the Cabinet Jean Bonna, recently and felicitously installed. To return to Lugt, Mathias's own collector's mark, a PM enclosed in an oval, bears the Lugt number 3561. One wonders about the mark's significance. Paul Mathias? *Paris-Match*? Or Pierre-Jean Mariette, the great eighteenth-century drawings connoisseur?

To return for a moment to Jackie Kennedy: she was a draftswoman, and had given him one of her gouaches, a rearing horse. Mathias, in turn, gave it to the Franco-American Museum of the Château of Blérancourt, in Aisne. A whole journey. An exemplary collector? An exceptional example of a collector.

Pierre Rosenberg

INTRODUCTION

In the arena of European old master drawings, a collection comprising some eighty sheets and focused on a national school does not seem to be noteworthy. Thousands upon thousands of drawings were created. In fact, with relative ease—and despite recent inflation in prices—a respectable collection of this size still could be gathered by a wealthy individual. An exception is drawings by the old masters of Spain. As has long been recognized, early Spanish drawings—those executed between 1450 and 1700—are much more difficult to find than drawings by Italian, French, or Netherlandish artists of this period. Students of Spanish drawings have long been cognizant of this circumstance and have formulated various hypotheses to explain the anomaly.

One of these rests on the observation that three of the best-known painters—El Greco, Velázquez, and Zurbarán—made few drawings, preferring to work directly on the canvas, a technique known as *alla prima*. Their preference for this technique, it is argued, suggests that drawing was not regarded as a tool of the trade as practiced in Spain. This hypothesis is inconsistent with the evidence. The practice of drawing as the foundation of great art was preached by the two leading theorists of the time—Vicente Carducho and Francisco Pacheco—and there is every reason to believe that their views were widely known and shared by painters of the epoch. Drawings are routinely listed in *almonedas* (estate sales) and in inventories of possessions made after the death of the owner. These sources testify to drawings' presence in the workshops and town houses of Madrid.

If it is accepted that Spanish painters were avid draftsmen, there should be many more of their drawings in existence. (The largest catalogue of an individual draftsman, Antonio del Castillo, lists 190 sheets; the tally drops precipitously to Murillo, Alonso Cano, Carducho, and Ribera, to each of whom roughly 100–120 sheets are attributed.) The most persuasive argument for this paucity has been prompted by the often-poor condition of the sheets. This characteristic feature has led scholars to propose that drawings were mostly acquired by painters, who utilized them as models in the workshop; drawings were used, not just perused. Regarded as functional tools of the profession, drawings were endowed with intrinsic artistic value only by other practitioners—and collectors were not disposed to pick up the slack. With rare exceptions, the amateur of drawings up to about 1750 is documented only in Seville.

From that point forward, the production and preservation of drawings by contemporary artists in Spain achieved par with other European countries. Goya is a striking example; around one thousand of his drawings are preserved. However, such court painters as Francisco Bayeu and Mariano Salvador Maella also were highly productive draftsmen, and hundreds of their drawings survive in the Prado and other collections, public and private. At the same time, collectors of old master drawings entered the scene. Unfortunately, they were a little too late; the numbers of drawings produced in the Golden Age, in one way or another, had been drastically diminished.

Nevertheless, collections of drawings by the Spanish masters still could be assembled. Collectors liked to mount them in albums, a few of which still exist intact.

This practice is personified by Juan Agustín Ceán Bermúdez (1748–1829), rightly called Spain's first art historian. Although his collection of prints and drawings was dispersed prior to 1869, it probably was mounted into albums; an extant example can be seen in the so-called the Alcubierre Album (now in the possession of Juan Abelló, Madrid), which was assembled in Seville by Miguel de Espinosa Saavedra Tello de Guzmán, second Conde del Águila (1715–1784).[1]

The Alcubierre album once contained 108 sheets, with an understandable emphasis on the artists of Seville. (The album has been dismantled by its current owner.) English gentlemen who, for one reason or another, had taken up residence in Seville were also avid buyers. They acted as *marchands amateurs* and sold to collectors from France as well as England. Today, these sheets form the core of the collections of the Musée du Louvre, the British Museum, and the Hamburger Kunsthalle.

With the dawn of the twentieth century, the study of drawings moved from the salon to the seminar: the art historians had arrived. Spanish drawings got off to a spectacular start in an opulent picture book authored by the leading German Hispanist August L. Mayer: *Die Handzeichnungen spanischer Meister. 150 Skizzen und Entwurfe vom 16 bis 19. Jarhundert* (Leipzig, 1915). This ambitious project never left the launching pad, as far as its impact on the field is concerned. The other major publication dedicated to Spanish drawings is *Dibujos españoles*, compiled by Francisco Javier Sánchez Cantón and published in 1930 in five small tomes.[2] It was the author's intention to make available a compendium of this unfamiliar material. Of the 435 drawings in the preface, no fewer than 337 were claimed to be unpublished. Unfortunately, the decision was made to limit the entries to the identification of the artist and the location and subject of each drawing. In hindsight, it can be seen that the collecting and study of Spanish drawings was almost a self-defeating enterprise. There was no critical mass; the field seemed very small, the number of drawings attributable to important artists too few to attract the attention of eager young or even senior scholars.

It was not until the 1950s that the practices of modern connoisseurship were applied to Spanish drawings. One of the leaders was Professor Harold E. Wethey (University of Michigan), who devoted his attention to the drawings of Alonso Cano and his followers in Madrid and Granada.[3] A major turning point occurred with the initiation of what was planned to be a corpus of Spanish drawings from 1400 to 1800, compiled by Diego Angulo Iñiguez and his disciple, Alfonso Pérez Sánchez. In the event, their reach exceeded their grasp. Four volumes appeared, covering the period of the fifteenth century to about 1600 in Castile (vol. 1, 1975); Madrid, 1600–1650 (vol. 2, 1982); Seville, 1600–1650 (vol. 3, 1985); and Valencia, 1600–1700 (vol. 4, 1988).[4] Five additional volumes were planned but, owing to Angulo's death, never appeared. Whatever the shortcomings of this enterprise (chiefly the lapidary entries), there is no doubt that for the images alone, it has become the standard reference for those with a serious interest in old Spanish drawings. The gaps were partially filled in 1986 by Pérez Sánchez in one of the standard references, which provides a broad overview of the history of Spanish drawings.[5]

I hope it will not be taken amiss if I mention two of my contributions, which have specific ties to Princeton. (I am a graduate alumnus of the class of 1964 and was a member of the faculty of the Department of Art and Archaeology from 1965 to 1973.) They are catalogues of the drawings and prints of Jusepe de Ribera (Princeton University Art Museum, 1973) and Bartolomé Murillo (first edition, Princeton University Art Museum, 1976; revised edition, Yale University Press, 2012).[6] My hope was that a monographic approach would offer a needed alternative to the strictly chronological and regional framework employed by Angulo and Pérez Sánchez.

Although it may be early days, it is safe to say that we are now enjoying a Golden Age for the study of Spanish old master drawings. Supported by Spanish foundations and study centers, catalogues raisonné of the drawings of many of the leading painters have been published or are underway. At the same time, catalogues of the principal public collections are coming to fruition. This is where the present catalogue, of the collection at the Princeton University Art Museum, comes into play.

Returning to the opening paragraph of this essay, I hope that it will be apparent that the importance of the collection of Spanish drawings in the Princeton University Art Museum is belied by its size. In the United States, the collection is numerically surpassed by those of the Metropolitan Museum of Art and the Hispanic Society of America, both in New York, as well as the Fogg Art Museum, Harvard University. (The major holdings in European museums, which are considerably larger than any to be found on these shores, are in the Museo Nacional del Prado, the Biblioteca Nacional de España, and the Real Academia de Bellas Artes de San Fernando, all in Madrid; the Galleria degli Uffizi, Florence; the Musée du Louvre, Paris; the British Museum, London; and the Hamburger Kunsthalle.) Although not one of the larger collections, Princeton's is notable for the wide range of coverage; in other words, it offers a representative sample of important moments in the history of Spanish draftsmanship. Murillo, Ribera, and Goya are present and accounted for. Artists of the seventeenth century whose drawings are little-known but of excellent quality are Francisco de Herrera the Elder, Sebastián de Herrera Barnuevo, and Jerónimo Jacinto de Espinosa. Spanish drawings of the eighteenth century are coming into clearer focus. The Princeton collection contains a double-sided sheet by Francisco de Goya, which once formed part of Album B, the second of the eight so-called private albums. Less well known is Antonio González Velázquez, a key figure in the transmission of mid-eighteenth-century Roman painting to the court in Madrid.

As far as the nineteenth century is concerned, Princeton owns several fine drawings from the later nineteenth century by painters whose careers are amply discussed in the catalogue: Eugenio Lucas, Daniel Urrabieta Vierge, and Mariano Fortuny. It will not be a surprise that there are drawings by such major figures of the twentieth century as Salvador Dalí, Joan Miró, and Pablo Picasso, all prolific graphic artists.

Mention should be made, however briefly, of the collector who is in large measure responsible for the ascent of the Princeton collection into the higher reaches of Spanish drawings: Mathias Polakovits. His eventful life and ebullient personality are evoked in the essay by his friend and tutor, Pierre Rosenberg. I met Mathias in 1972, while I was doing research on the drawings of Ribera. As it happened, he owned two, one of which, I believe, is among the finest drawings the artist ever made. After his retirement, Mathias became an obsessed collector of drawings and, in time, as sharp a connoisseur as I have ever known. Spanish drawings took a backseat to his passion for the artists of France and Italy; I sometimes believe that he purchased them just to test and improve my knowledge of the subject. His unfailing instinct for quality and variety more than compensated for his casual interest in Spanish drawings. Without his willingness to take risks in acquiring unidentified drawings and his unbounded interest in identifying a "hand," Princeton would be just another of the many drawings collections into which the odd Spanish drawing had strayed.

Even a casual glimpse at the catalogue reveals that there is still much research to done; the same might be said of the field in general. However, the author of this catalogue, Lisa A. Banner, Class of 1985, has taken a big step forward in advancing our knowledge and has made many important discoveries, providing the Art Museum with a catalogue worthy of its reputation.

Jonathan Brown

1 Navarrete Prieto and Pérez Sánchez 2009.

2 Sánchez Cantón 1930.

3 Wethey 1952; and Harold E. Wethey, "Discípulos granadinos de Alonso Cano," *Archivo Español de Arte* 27 (1954): 25-34. For an up-to-date study, see Véliz 2011.

4 Angulo Íñiguez and Pérez Sánchez 1975–1988.

5 Pérez Sánchez 1986.

6 Princeton 1973; Princeton 1976–1977; and Brown 2012.

CATALOGUE

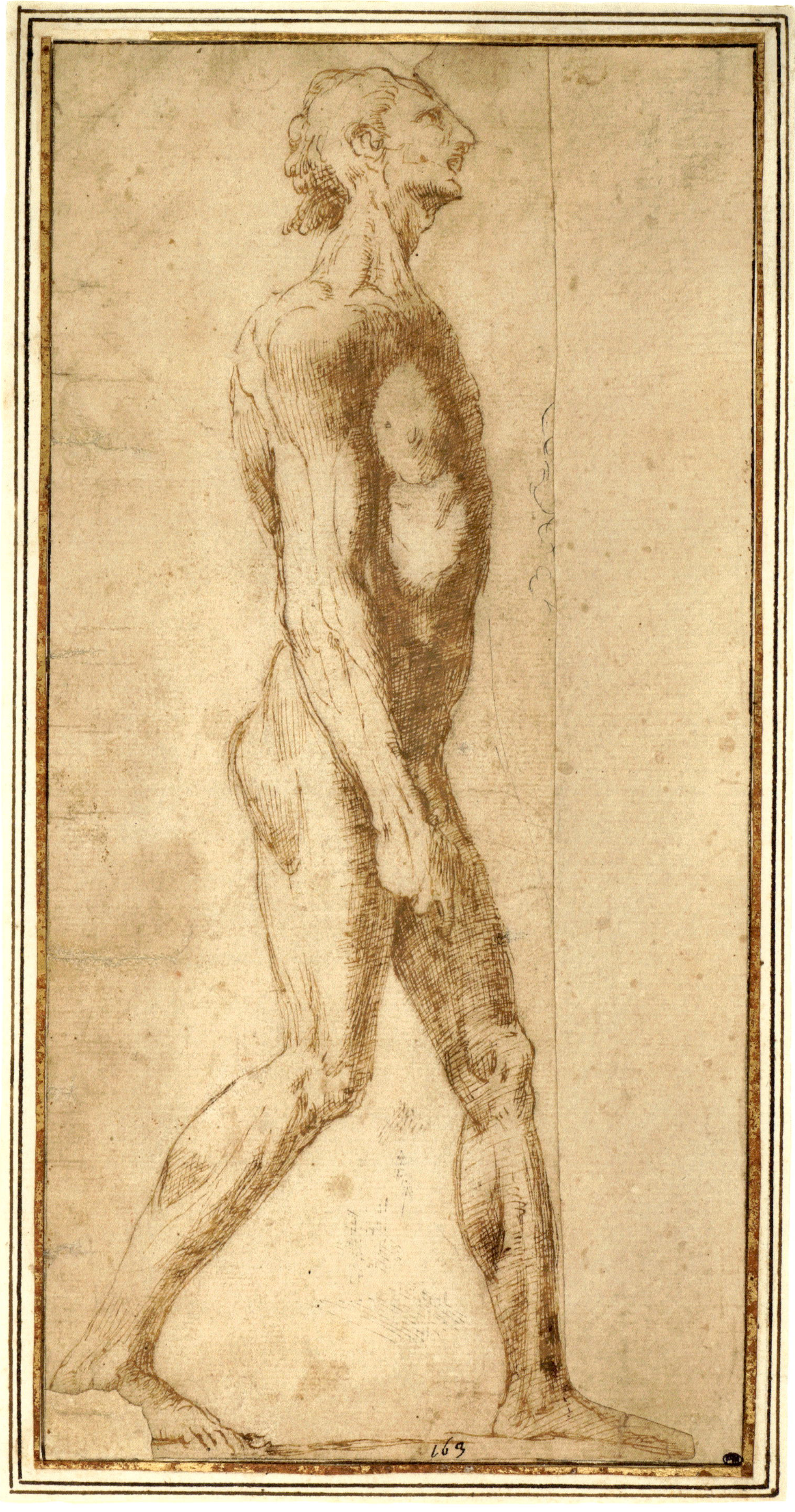

1. *Striding Male Nude*

Pen and brown ink with traces of pen and black ink on tan laid paper, pieced and lined

29.7 x 15.2 cm. (11¹¹⁄₁₆ x 6.0 in.)

Inscribed in pen and brown ink, lower center: *163*; verso, in graphite, lower left: *Ribera*; lower right: *Zingaro – Solaro*

WATERMARK: Partial circle with letters *FB* in the primary sheet

PROVENANCE: Mathias Polakovits, Paris and New York, stamp (Lugt 3561) lower right, in black

REFERENCE: Princeton 2003, 118, 115 ill., as "Circle of Alonso Berruguete"

EXHIBITION: Princeton 2001, as "Circle of Berruguete"

Museum purchase, Laura P. Hall Memorial Fund and Fowler McCormick, Class of 1921 Fund
2002-85

This sheet displays characteristics of the best drawings by such sixteenth-century Spanish masters as Juan de Juanes (ca. 1510–1579) and Alonso Berruguete (1486–1561), whose drawings share many attributes. When the drawing first entered Princeton's collection, an attribution to the circle of Berruguete was proposed; however, as the work does not relate directly to any of Berruguete's known commissions, this attribution cannot be established with certainty. The drawing shares several characteristics with the graphic style of Valencian artist Juan de Juanes seen in works at the Courtauld Institute and is close in treatment and technique to the studies for open-mouthed, striding figures found in his study for *Saint Stephen Taken to His Execution*, part of the important altarpiece commissioned for the Valencian Church of Saint Stephen (ca. 1562) (fig. 1.1).[1]

With short pen strokes and his characteristic treatment of feet and hands, Juanes left telltale clues to his authorship of the Madrid sketch. The hand dangles from an elongated arm, in which the bone structure is apparent. The striding feet are flattened, with slender, carefully defined ankles and simple, short downward flicks of the pen indicating toes. The hand is in the form of a closed fist, with two fingers visible. The same dangling fingers and closed fist are found in the Courtauld drawing, on Saint Stephen and on the figures of the accompanying rabble who carry the stones later used to murder the saint (fig. 1.2).

In the Princeton drawing, a strong neck, with ligaments holding the head like a stalk, emerges from the figure's large shoulders and barrel-shaped chest. The small, sharp chin juts forward and is contoured from below, outlined with tiny, close strokes that form a shadow. With short, quick hatching at the lower part of a bulging muscle mass, the artist isolated the buttocks and the muscle in the calf, giving shape to the slender leg. The emphasis on the buttocks, with slight downward strokes along the outside flank and heavy cross-hatching in the shadowed leg, also resemble the way that shadow is described on the figures in the Juanes studies at the Courtauld. Further,

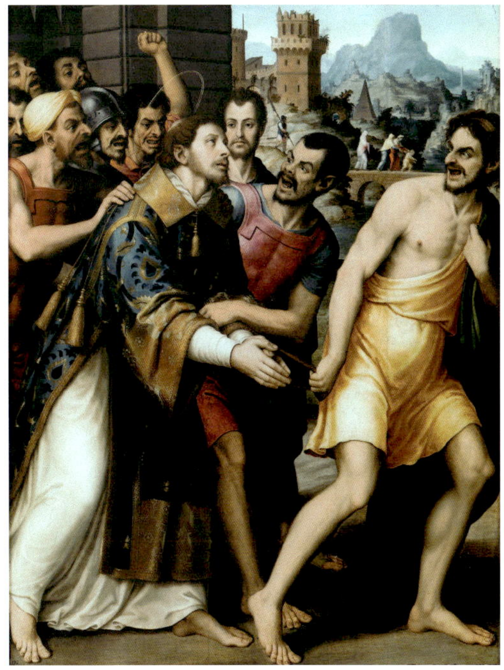

Fig. 1.1 Juan de Juanes, Spanish, ca. 1510–1579: *Saint Stephen Taken to His Martyrdom.* Oil on board, 160 x 123 cm. Museo Nacional del Prado, Madrid (P00840).

the distinctive frieze-like presentation of the figure in the Princeton drawing can be compared with the same disposition of figures in the Courtauld example, which has two sketches of the composition on one sheet. In the Courtauld drawing, musculature is emphasized, especially on the arms of the figure gripping

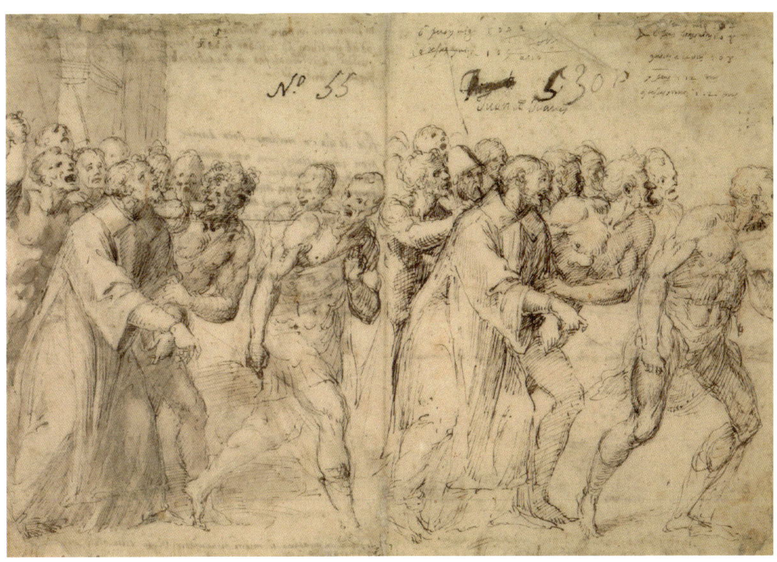

Fig. 1.2 Juan de Juanes, Spanish, ca. 1510–1579: *Two studies for* Saint Stephen Taken to His Martyrdom. Pen and ink on paper, 21.7 x 31.5 cm. The Samuel Courtauld Trust, The Courtauld Gallery, London (D.1963.WF.4730).

Saint Stephen. A thin and muscled arm ends in a knobby elbow. The bicep on the *Standing Figure* at Princeton is emphasized with delicate vertical strokes, giving extra emphasis to the length of the arm and defining the bone structure that runs its length.

However, several aspects of the drawing also point to the hand of Berruguete, as seen, for example, in a drawing at the Hispanic Society recently attributed to him.[2] This drawing, a large sketch of a kneeling leg, is directly related to Michelangelo's studies of a man's leg in the same pose, and Berruguete is known to have studied with Michelangelo in his studio.

The drawing has been trimmed and laid down onto another support. There is a partial watermark at the edge of the sheet where it has been cut around the figure. This appears to be in the primary drawing support, although the sheet has been pasted down onto secondary support. Notations on the original mat refer to the artists Jusepe de Ribera (1591–1652), who worked mostly in Naples, and an earlier artist active in Naples, Antonio da Solaro (ca. 1382–1445), called "il Zingaro," or the Gypsy. Neither of these attributions is acceptable.

Sixteenth-century studies of male nudes survive from the hands of Juan de Arfe (1535–1603), Gaspar Becerra (ca. 1520–1570), and Alonso Berruguete and are more common among artists who trained or studied in Italy. Berruguete, for example, habitually copied Masaccio's frescoes in the Brancacci chapel (ca. 1425, Santa Maria del Carmine, Florence) and might have copied the humiliated figure of Adam fleeing Paradise with Eve.[3] Nude studies of this sort are generally thought to be rare in Spanish art of the sixteenth and seventeenth centuries, especially for subjects that do not involve the dead Christ; *Study of a Nude Man* by Juan Gómez (ca. 1550–1597), who worked "in the manner of Berruguete," was, however, included in the Lefort collection.[4] The drawing's subject was not further described or illustrated, and the work has been lost since its publication. LAB

1 Véliz 2012, 50–53.
2 Madrid 2006–7a, 24–28.
3 Boubli 1994, 18.
4 Lefort 1869. About the drawings of Juan Gómez, see Angulo Íñiguez and Pérez Sánchez 1975–88, vol. 1, 43. Juanes made use of the Hospital General's anatomy lessons, as reported by Jusepe Martínez (see Martínez 1988). The anatomy faculty in Valencia, created in 1549, was the first in Spain and performed up to twenty-five dissections for anatomy lessons every year (González García 1999, 54 n. 107). Spanish drawings from live models and cadavers survive from the sixteenth and seventeenth centuries—for example, the drawings and prints of Juan de Arfe y Villafañe (1535–1603) and José García Hidalgo (1645–1717). Earlier examples of Spanish drawings of the nude include such extraordinary studies as Gaspar Becerra's (ca. 1520–1570) fragmentary *Final Judgment*, copied from Michelangelo's drawings for the fresco while Becerra studied in Italy. (Museo Nacional del Prado, F.A.2).

ANDRÉS DE MELGAR

Benavente, ca. 1500–ca. 1557, Santo Domingo de la Calzada

Andrés de Melgar's early life and formation remain obscure. He was born in Benavente around 1500 and spent his youth in Sahagún.[1] Melgar studied with Alonso Berruguete at Valladolid from 1523 to 1526, when he served as a witness in favor of Berruguete.[2] By 1530 the artist was a resident of Santo Domingo de la Calzada.[3] Between 1531 and 1533, Melgar completed nine paintings depicting the life of Santo Domingo de la Calzada for the cathedral.[4] The years 1533 to 1538 are not well documented, although during this time Melgar might have returned to the workshop of Berruguete in Valladolid. In 1538 he traveled with sculptor Damián Forment to review alabaster quarries and was back in Santo Domingo de la Calzada in 1539 to polychrome and gild Forment's sculptures for the main altarpiece.

In 1540, Melgar submitted papers in Valladolid for a patent of nobility and was determined to be an "*hijodalgo.*" It is evident from signed documents that Melgar was at Santo Domingo de la Calzada from 1544 to 1546 and again in 1548.[5] An evaluation of his work for the cathedral occurred in 1553, and final payments were made in 1554.[6] Based on archival records of his activity, Melgar lived until about 1557.[7]

2. *Grotesque Design*, possibly for Santo Domingo de la Calzada: *Two Vertical Columns of Figures and Floral Motifs*, ca. 1540–54

Verso: *Grotesque Designs*, possibly for Santo Domingo de la Calzada: *Decorative Motifs and Frieze of Figures*, ca. 1540–54

Pen and brown ink over traces of black chalk and metalpoint, lined

33.6 x 25.0 cm. (13½ x 9¹³⁄₁₆ in.)

Inscribed in pen and brown ink, lower left: *-8;* upper right: *33*

Watermark: Center right, countermark. (The watermark resembles sixteenth-century watermarks of assembled letters beginning with D, especially Briquet #9387 and Briquet #9388) (see appendix)

Provenance: Frank Jewett Mather Jr., Princeton

Exhibitions: Princeton 1995; Princeton 1997

Gift of Frank Jewett Mather Jr.
x1947-162

This double-sided sheet of grotesques, ornamental borders, and small figurative scenes has remained unattributed until now. It was donated to the Museum by Frank Jewett Mather Jr. as a mid-sixteenth-century Italian drawing and was reclassified as Spanish after 1962, when Janos Scholz suggested on the mat that it might be by the same hand as the twenty-two sheets and fragments of grotesques with Spanish inscriptions in the Metropolitan Museum of Art that Janet Byrne later called "a riddle waiting to be solved" (acc. nos. 52.570.314–335 [some double-sided]).[8] An additional double-sided sheet is in the collection of the Museum of Art, University of Michigan (1960/2.19).[9] Nicole Dacos has attributed those drawings to Andrés de Melgar and related them to documented commissions to Melgar for the Cathedral of Santo Domingo de la Calzada, along the Camino de Santiago in northern Spain.[10] Comparison of the Princeton sheet to those published by Dacos, the sheets at the Metropolitan Museum, and the painted decoration created by Melgar for Santo Domingo de la Calzada suggest that this drawing is also by the hand of Andrés de Melgar.

The style of the drawing supports this hypothesis, as it owes much to Julio de Aquilis, who brought the grotesque technique to Spain. After learning the technique in the studios of Raphael and Giovanni da Udine in Rome, Julio de Aquilis arrived in Valladolid with Flemish artist Alexander Mayner in 1533 to appraise Berruguete's altarpiece at San Benito and to decorate the palace of Francisco de los Cobos, secretary to Charles V.[11] Drawings by Melgar in other collections have autograph inscriptions that include the name "Julio," suggesting that Melgar copied drawings by Julio de Aquilis, perhaps from sketchbooks in Berruguete's studio.[12]

Another word that is inscribed on several drawings, "flamenco" (Spanish for "Flemish"), might reflect the influence of Flemish artists or refer to Flemish artist Alexander Mayner, who came with Julio to Valladolid. Some of Julio's grotesque drawings are preserved in the Lázaro Galdiano Museum, Madrid (Ms. 15110), in an album with drawings by Berruguete and Melgar.[13] Those drawings might be related to Julio's documented work from 1533 to 1536 at the palaces of Francisco de los Cobos in Valladolid and Úbeda as well as the palace of Charles V at the Alhambra, where he and Mayner worked from 1537 to 1542 and where Julio worked again in 1545.[14] Mayner was active in Spain from 1533 until his death before 1545.[15] It is unclear whether Melgar met the artists during their stay in Valladolid or collaborated with them on decorations for Francisco de los Cobos, but it is apparent that he studied their grotesque drawings.

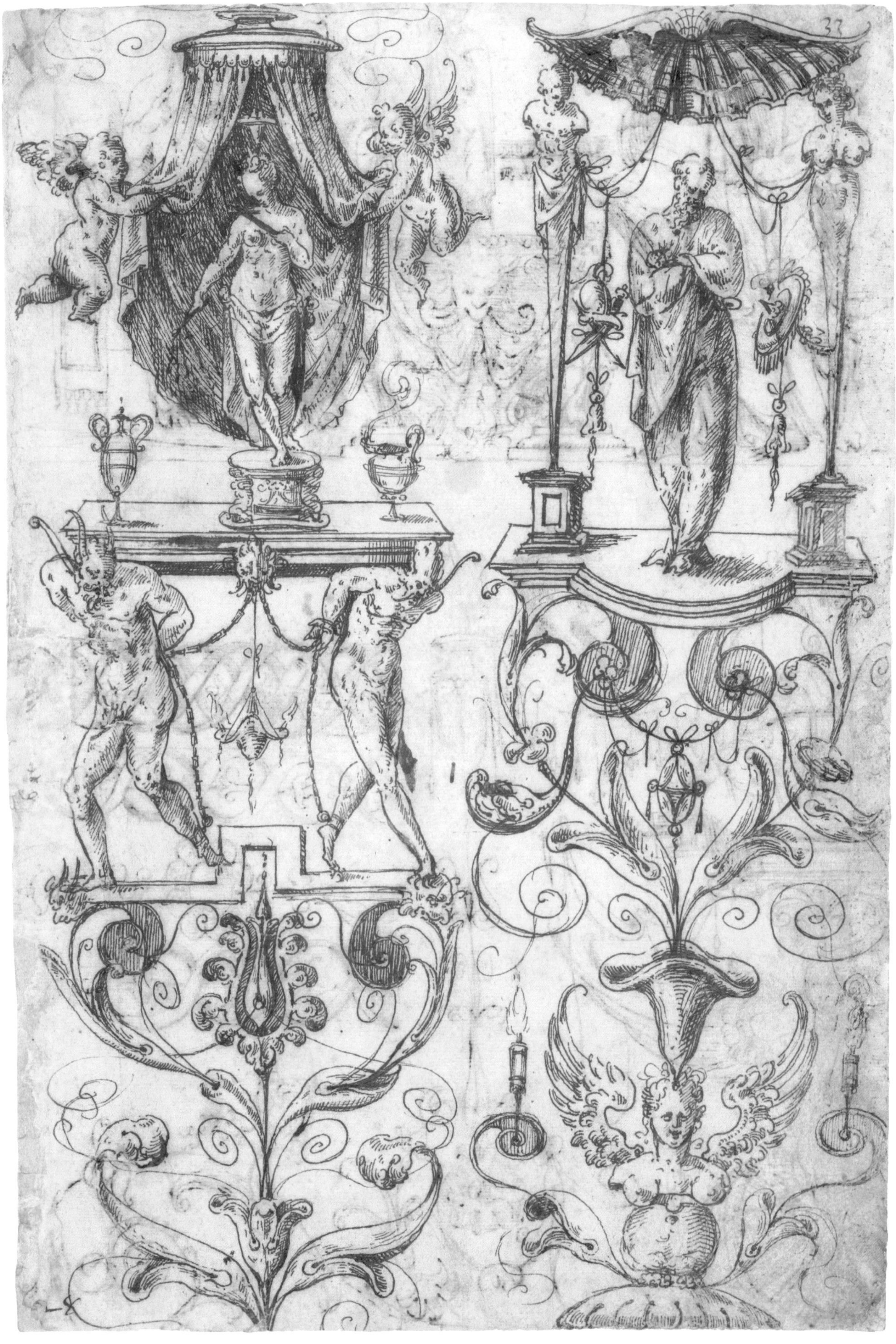

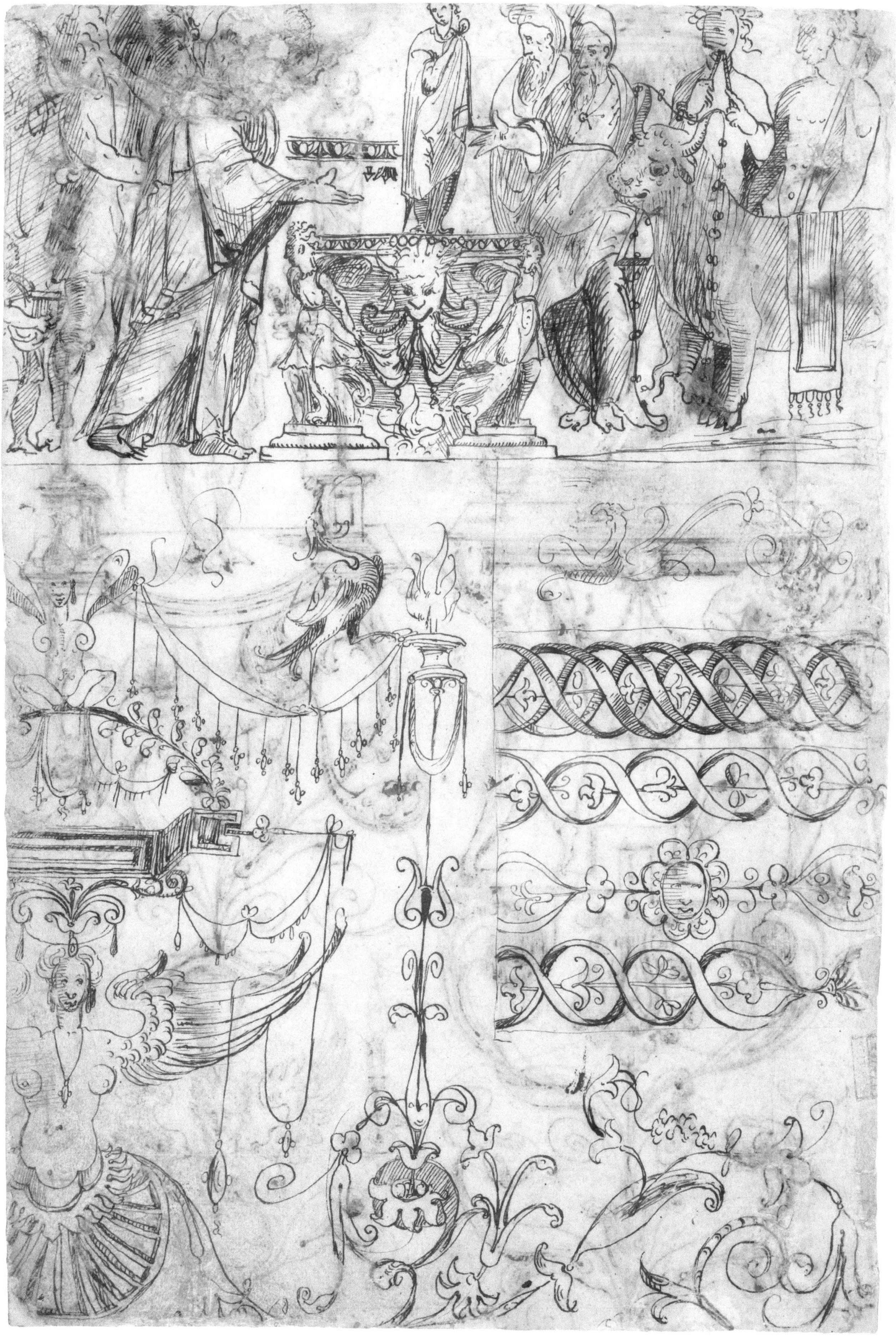

Verso cat. 2

Nicole Dacos and, later, María del Carmen Heredia Moreno have distinguished the hand of Andrés de Melgar among drawings in several collections.[16] By identifying his drawings and separating them from those of Julio and Berruguete, these scholars have shed light on the career of Andrés de Melgar and identified the distinctive qualities of his work.[17] Dacos especially noted print motifs in drawings inscribed "flamenco." Melgar's use of motifs like those created by Cornelis Floris around 1540, distributed through prints after his work by Cornelis Bos from around 1546, assist scholars in dating his work.[18]

This sheet reveals the influence of Julio in the use of fantastic birds, urns, and spirals. Its composition, juxtaposing unrelated elements and filling every spare space on the sheet, implies that the sections may have been copied. Putti, herms, horned men, female winged busts, urns, seashells, and floral designs cover both sides of the drawing.[19]

The recto has a design in two columns. Similar columns of figures painted by Melgar in the niche behind the statue of St. Dominic on the main altar at Santo Domingo de la Calzada suggest that drawings like this served as models.[20] On the verso at top a procession of male figures with a bull and an altar with a mask recall pagan paintings from ancient Roman grottoes. Below are two sections, one showing a winged bust supporting a platform under a smaller winged bust, connected to the next discrete section with a scrolling floriated design. The twisting helix found on the right lower section of the verso might have been copied from a frieze design and was used by Melgar as a border on the garments of polychrome sculpted figures at Santo Domingo de la Calzada. Although Melgar painted grotesques in gold on a colored ground, detailed color descriptions on some of his drawings might refer to painted grotesque border friezes copied from the walls of the palace of Francisco de los Cobos, now lost.[21]

Melgar's drawings, while skillful, show more attention to two-dimensional effects of line built up with short flicks of the pen than to shadow contours, seen for instance on the horned men on the recto of this drawing or the wings on the bird and figures on the verso. The same technique is evident in his decorations at Santo Domingo de la Calzada, where linear effects predominate. Rather than the swelling volumes shaped by close hatching and the layering of different strokes found in Julio's drawings, or the confident and sculptural fluid lines found in Berruguete's masterful renderings of horses, Melgar's grotesques are less refined and demonstrate less understanding of the body. The legs of the figures at the altar on the verso are heavy and unresolved within their drapery; their awkward hands are characteristic of Melgar's drawings and painted grotesques.

The inscription "33" on the upper right corner of the recto, seemingly in the same pen and dark brown ink as the rest of the sheet, implies a sequence of drawings to which this sheet belonged and suggests that it might once have been part of a sketchbook. The inscription "-8" at the lower left corner of the recto could be related to an inventory valuation, perhaps denoting eight *reales*, or it could refer to the pagination of a series of drawings.

The watermark in Princeton's sheet is similar to one of assembled letters (Briquet #9388 from ca. 1569), suggesting that this sheet can be dated to after 1540, when Melgar made a trip to Valladolid, and must have been completed before 1554, when the artist received final payment from the Cathedral of Santo Domingo de la Calzada.[22] At least one of the sheets of grotesques now attributed to Melgar at the Metropolitan Museum (acc. 52.570.325) also bears a mid-sixteenth-century watermark (figs. 2.1, 2.2).[23]

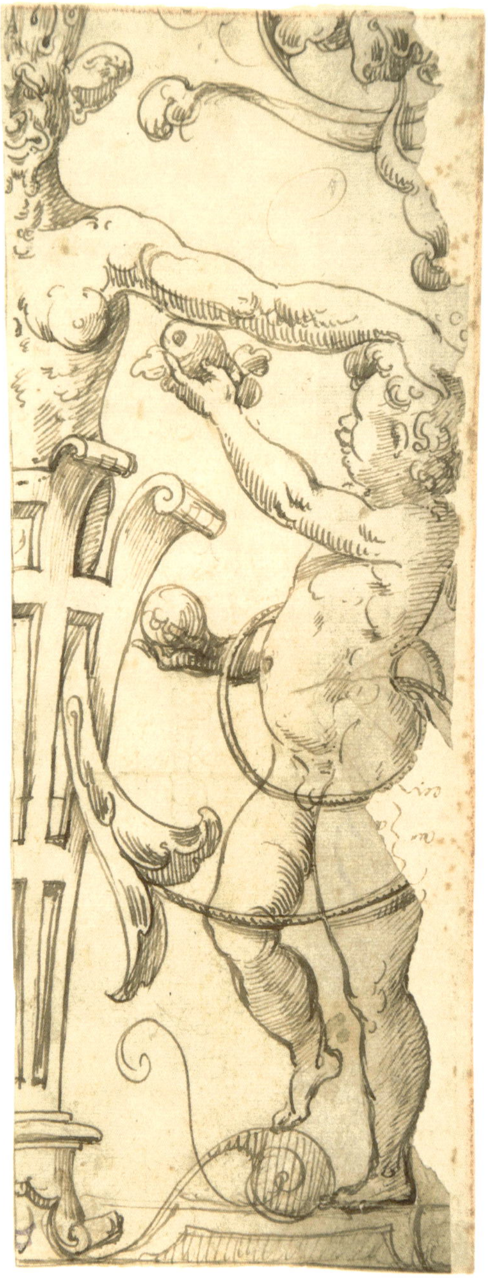

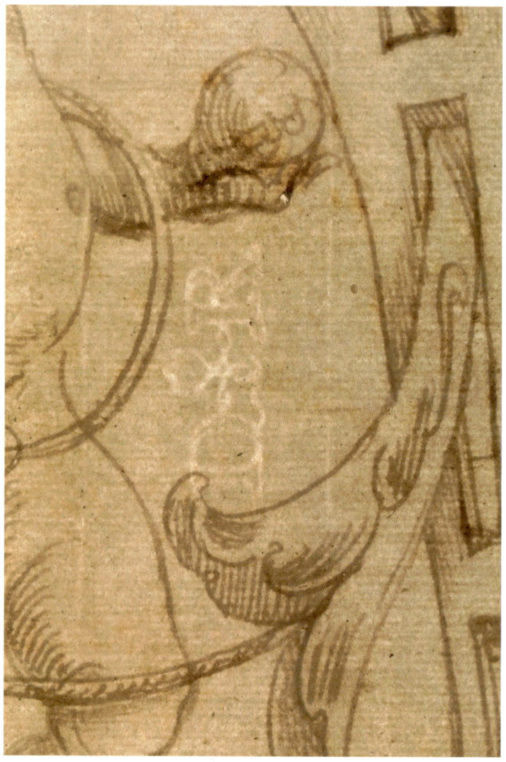

Fig. 2.1 Attributed to Andrés de Melgar, Spanish, ca. 1500–ca. 1557: *Strapwork Term with Arm Extended onto Head of Putto Offering Fruit.* Pen and dark brown ink, and some brush and brown wash, 26.1 x 10.4 cm. The Metropolitan Museum of Art, The Elisha Whittelsey Collection, The Elisha Whittelsey Fund, 1952 (52.570.325); fig. 2.2 watermark detail of fig. 2.1.

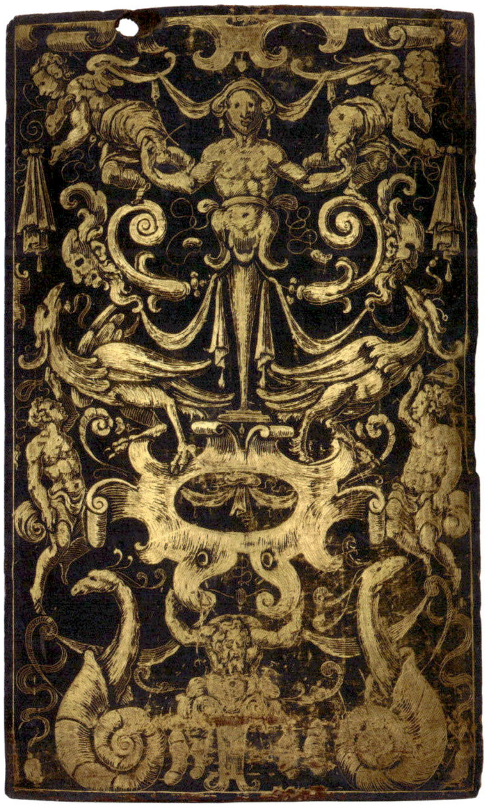

Fig. 2.3 Andrés de Melgar, Spanish, ca. 1500–ca. 1557: *Grotesques with Birds, Putti, and Snails,* ca. 1540. Pine panel with *sgraffito* designs on gold leaf and blue tempera, 51.6 x 31.3 cm. Private collection.

Unlike the Princeton sheet, the double-sided sheet at the University of Michigan Museum of Art features extensive writing, including directions about background colors and types of grotesque figures to be used, similar to inscriptions on the drawings at the Metropolitan Museum. Like the Princeton example, this double-sided sheet is also numbered, although in this case the numeration appears at the lower left corner of the recto, "36," indicating that perhaps this and the Princeton sheet were together in a sequence of at least thirty-six sheets.

Finally, a group of three wooden panels can be added to the small but growing catalog of Melgar's work. They include grotesques painted in gold on blue backgrounds; on the verso of one of the three an inscription in pen and brown ink describes how the panel should be painted (fig. 2.3). The writing is in the same hand as the inscriptions on the Metropolitan Museum of Art drawings and on the drawing in Michigan. While Princeton's drawing has no writing, the numbering of the sheet on the recto suggests that the drawings were kept together as a sort of reference tool in developing grotesque designs for the decoration of a major commission, like that of the main altarpiece at Santo Domingo de la Calzada, painted on polychromed wood.

The artistic personality of Andrés de Melgar is still emerging, but with the addition of the Princeton sheet more than forty grotesque designs have been attributed to his hand in the Metropolitan Museum of Art, the University Art Museum in Ann Arbor, the École des Beaux Arts, and the Lázaro Galdiano Museum in Madrid.[24] Surprisingly, despite few archival records of his life, his drawings have been connected with well-known and documented commissions and contracts for extant work at Santo Domingo de la Calzada. LAB

1 Echeverría Goñi 1995, 217.
2 Dacos 1997, 27; Heredia Moreno 2005, 137; and Echeverría Goñi 1995, 217.
3 Sáenz Terreros 1981–82, 405.
4 Ibid., 398.
5 Ibid., 407–8; and Ramírez Pascual 1995, 64–66.
6 Sáenz Terreros 1981–82, 405–6.
7 Echeverría Goñi 1995, 217.
8 Byrne 1981, 13, 64. Metropolitan Museum of Art accession numbers 52.570.314–335. The provenance of the Metropolitan Museum of Art sheets is G. Piancastelli (1845–1926); Mary and Edward Brandegee, Boston, after 1906; Janos Scholz (1904–1993), New York, from 1939; and gift by Janos Scholz to the Metropolitan in 1952.
9 1960/2.19 recto and verso, attributed to Follower of Nicoletto Rosex da Modena, Spanish 16th century. *Ornamental Sketch,* recto and verso, 13 1/8 x 8 15/16 in. (33.7 x 22.9 cm.), University of Michigan Museum of Art, 1960/2.19.
10 Dacos 1997, 30–31; and Parrado del Olmo 1998, 260–61.
11 Véliz 1986, 57; and López Torrijos 1987, 174.
12 Heredia Moreno 2005, 137.
13 Ibid., 132–43.
14 López Torrijos 1987, 174–75.
15 Ibid.
16 Ibid., 176; Dacos 1997, 26–32; and Heredia Moreno 2005, 141–42.
17 Boubli 1994, 11–32; Dacos 1997, 26–32; and Heredia Moreno 2005, 137ff.
18 Byrne 1981, 13, 64, 66; Dacos 1997, 30; and Heredia Moreno 2005, 142.
19 Dacos 1997, 28, 31.
20 Echeverría Goñi 1995, 223 ill.; and Dacos 1997, 29–31 ill.
21 Heredia Moreno 2005, 137, 140, 142.
22 Sáenz Terreros 1981–82, 407–8; and Parrado del Olmo 1998, 256–57.
23 The watermark is similar to Briquet 9388.
24 The drawing at the University of Michigan came from the Miniscalchi collection, Verona, also known as the Miniscalchi-Erizzo collection. The last male heirs of the family died in the 1950s, and the Michigan sheet was purchased from Matthiesen Gallery, London, in 1960. The drawings at the Museo Lázaro Galdiano that have been attributed to Melgar are included in Ms. 15110, along with drawings by Berruguete.

BARTOLOMÉ CARDUCHO

Florence, ca. 1560–1609, Madrid

Bartolomé Carducho, also known as Bartolomeo Carducci, studied in his native city with Bartolommeo Ammanati and later with Federico Zuccaro, whom he assisted on the cupola frescoes of Santa Maria del Fiore in Florence before moving with him to Rome. When Zuccaro was called to work for Philip II at the Escorial, Carducho accompanied him. Once established there, Carducho had the opportunity to copy the paintings by Titian in Philip II's collection, and he improved his style with a more robust understanding of volume and color. Few drawings by Carducho survive, making attributions difficult, and his paintings—many commissioned for religious institutions in Spain—have suffered from abrasion and damage. His most important work for Philip II survives at the Escorial.

Attributed to Bartolomé Carducho

3. *Standing Apostle*, ca. 1600

Black chalk with white heightening on blue laid paper, lined

35.0 x 18.8 cm. (13¾ x 7⅜ in.)

Provenance: Mathias Polakovits, Paris and New York, stamp (Lugt 3561) recto, lower right, in black

Reference: Princeton 2003, 115, as "Spanish, Anonymous, 17th century"

Exhibitions: Princeton 1995; Princeton 1997

Museum purchase, Laura P. Hall Memorial Fund and Fowler McCormick, Class of 1921, Fund 2002-103

The figure's pose and upward gaze suggest that this work is a study for a standing Saint John the Evangelist at the Crucifixion, similar to the figure in a painting of *Crucifixion with Thieves* now attributed to Bartolomé Carducho.[1] While the figure in Princeton's study is more animated than that in the painting, the work is executed in a manner that is similar to other studies Carducho created while working at the Escorial in the 1580s, many of which are also executed in chalk on blue paper. His preference for small heads atop elongated, heavy-limbed bodies is seen in such works as preparatory studies for the Saint Lawrence paintings in the upper cloister of the Escorial, completed in 1589 (Museo del Prado, Madrid, F.A.5, F.A.4). These drawings offer details that can be compared with *Standing Apostle.* White chalk highlighting on the Princeton drawing creates tonal values in some of the shaded areas of the drapery and is used in painterly fashion, as on the sleeves and drapery of the standing figure at the right in *Saint Lawrence Ordained Deacon by Saint Sixtus* (Prado F.A.5). That figure gathers a fold of his robe in front of him in a pose and gesture similar to those of other standing figures in Carducho's *Saint Lawrence* series, seen here in the bulky fall of drapery under the apostle's elbow. The straight nose of Princeton's *Standing Apostle,* with flared nostril, resembles that feature on the face of the kneeling Saint Lawrence, as does the cup-like rendering of the ear, seen from the side. Isolated figures—like Carducho's drawing of *Penitent Saint Jerome* (Courtauld Institute, London, no. 3779) or *Figure of a Monk* (Biblioteca Nacional, Madrid, 7281), Carducho's drawing after Tibaldi's fresco of 1589—are robed in heavy drapery, like the present figure.[2] There are also similarities in the pose of this figure and that of the heavy-limbed Christ in *The Arrest,* a painting completed by Carducho for the Duke of Lerma at the Monasterio de la Ascensión de Nuestro Señor, Lerma.

Princeton's *Standing Apostle* appears to be in motion, with his right foot planted and the left slightly raised, with toes resting on the ground, as if the figure were striding toward the object of his gaze. We do not know where Mathias Polakovits acquired this striking drawing. Until a more concrete provenance can be established, a more exact attribution remains unattainable. LAB

1 Sotheby's, *Old Master and 19th Century European Art,* auction cat., Jan. 28, 2011, New York, lot 15.

2 Because Carducho restored Tibaldi's 1589 frescoes in 1608, this study may have been executed as part of the restoration effort of the paintings in the cloister of El Escorial. See Angulo Íñiguez and Pérez Sánchez 1975–88, vol. 1, 33, no. 103.

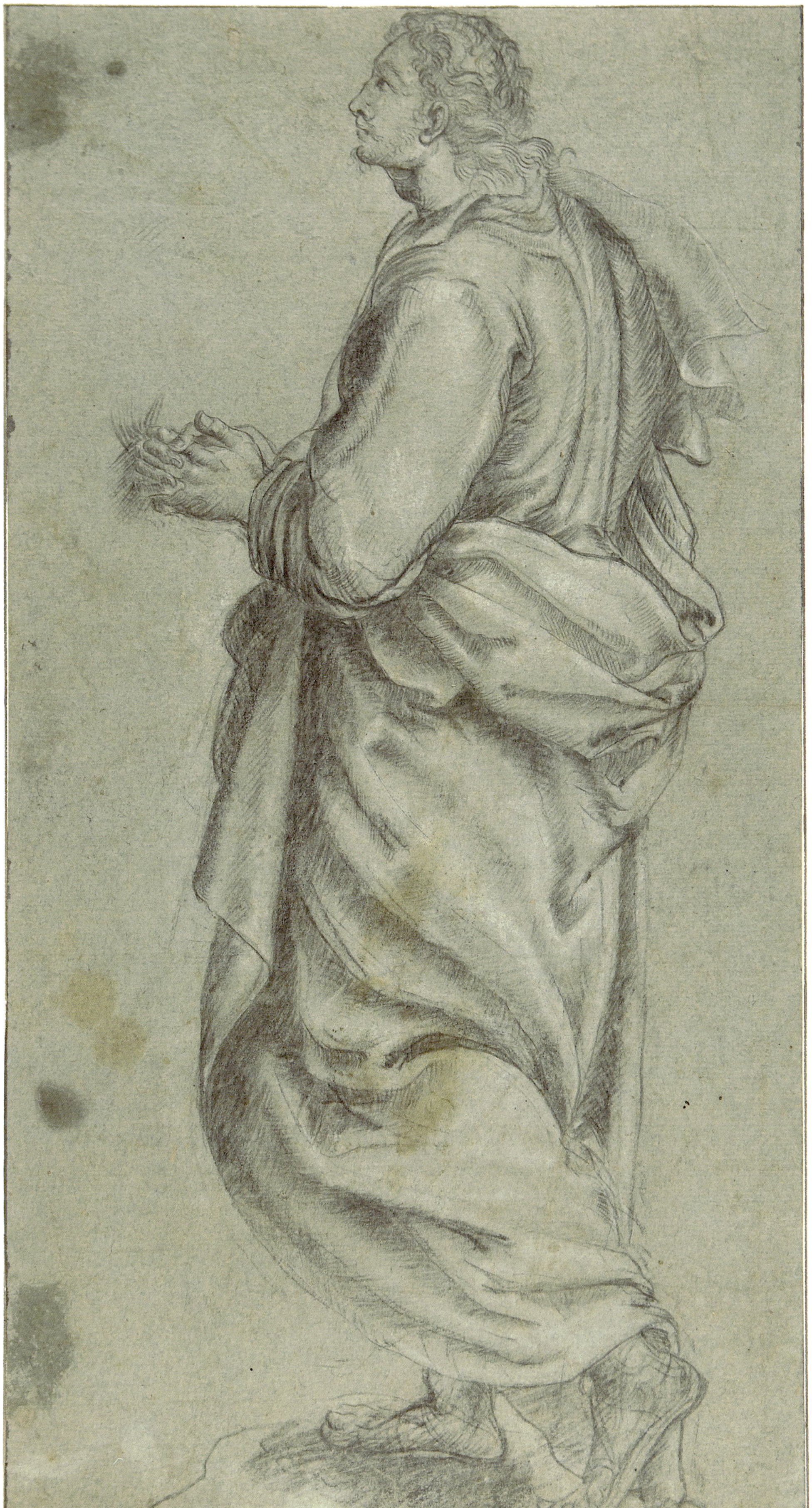

JUSEPE DE RIBERA

Játiva, 1591–1652, Naples

Jusepe de Ribera was a painter, draftsman, and printmaker known for his work in the tenebrist (from the Italian *tenebroso*, for "dark") tradition, also called dramatic illumination. By as early as 1609 he had left his native Valencia to study in Italy, the site of his true artistic formation.[1] The artist is documented at the Farnese court in Parma as early as 1610–11 and in Rome by June 5, 1612.[2] He traveled in Italy during the next few years and was documented in Parma in 1613–15 before returning to Rome.[3] During his time in Rome after 1615, Ribera lived on the Via Margutta, where it is thought that he associated with other expatriate painters working under the influence of Caravaggio, such as Gerrit van Honthorst (1592–1656) and Hendrik ter Brugghen (1588–1629). By 1616, Ribera was in Naples, then a Spanish territory, where he settled and spent the rest of his career, working mostly for Spanish clients,[4] sending work to Spain through the viceroys, and serving local religious and aristocratic patrons. Some early drawings, connected to paintings commissioned but now lost, were sent back to Madrid in this way and entered Spanish collections.[5] Ribera's 1630s commissions came from Philip IV as well as from the Duke of Alcalá and the Count of Monterrey, both viceroys of Naples. In 1638 the artist began a series of paintings for the Certosa di San Martino, including a large Communion of the Apostles, which was only finished in 1651, shortly before the artist's death.[6] A period of ill health reduced his ability to work from about 1644, and so paintings and drawings from the late period from his own hand (distinct from his workshop, which continued to flourish), are less common.

Along with the prevalence of shadows in paintings from throughout his career, Ribera's work is marked by a love of color, often emerging startlingly from the gloom. Like Goya would nearly two hundred years later, he often delighted in subjects of horror and the reality of human cruelty, favoring a sense of truth and reportage over idealism in depictions of scenes from mythology as well as of the martyrdom of the saints and of social outcasts—a preference that enhanced his popularity in his lifetime and his reputation after his death. Artists such as Salvator Rosa (1615–1673) and Luca Giordano (1634–1705) were among his most important followers. Ribera was probably the most influential Spanish printmaker before Goya, producing about eighteen prints, largely in the 1620s.

More than one hundred drawings have been identified as by Ribera's hand; these are now in collections throughout the world.[7] His works range from polished academic studies to hasty sketches, and the diversity of his graphic style as well as his constant experimentation with form, technique, and media make the artist's oeuvre the subject of continuing fascination. Ribera was a masterful draftsman in many techniques, including red chalk, pen and ink, and ink with brush and wash. Some of the earliest sheets that survive by Ribera's hand are in red chalk, a technique often used by artists who were preparing to transfer designs for prints, and several of those drawings are directly related to his signed and dated etchings. Other Ribera drawings that survive are unrelated to either prints or paintings, however, suggesting that the artist frequently drew from his imagination, creating bizarre and often fantastic scenes for his own enjoyment or that of a collector.[8]

4. *Studies of Male Head in Profile*, ca. 1622

Red chalk on cream laid paper lightly toned with brush and gray wash

25.1 x 20.6 cm. (9⅞ x 8⅛ in.)

Inscribed in pen and brown ink, lower right: *Spaenioletti*

Watermark: Fleur-de-lis within a circle

Provenance: Mathias Polakovits, Paris and New York, stamp (Lugt 3561) recto, lower right, in black

References: Brown 1972, 7 n. 3; Princeton 1973, 153–54; Princeton 2007, 271 ill.; New York 2010–11, no. 4, 28–29

Exhibitions: Princeton 1973, no. 1 ill.; Princeton 1995; Princeton 1997; Princeton 2001; "An Educated Eye: Princeton University Art Museum Collections," Princeton University Art Museum (Feb. 23–Aug. 3, 2008); New York 2010–11, 28, no. 4 ill.

Museum purchase, Laura P. Hall Memorial Fund and Fowler McCormick, Class of 1921, Fund 2002-97

Jonathan Brown has dated this stunning red chalk study to the early 1620s, based on its relationship to the etching of ears that Ribera signed and dated 1622.[9] A complex meditation on the different qualities of a male face, Ribera's study focuses on intense observation of the head and details of the facial features seen from several angles.

Ribera's extraordinary observation of the sculptural quality of the ear, for example, is repeated at the top and right sides of the sheet. Although one might be tempted to see the lower ear study as a simple amplification of the upper ear study, looking closely one finds that it is a different ear, with different bumps on the lobe and a different formation of the exterior. Even the hair that parts over the ear at the bottom is rendered differently than

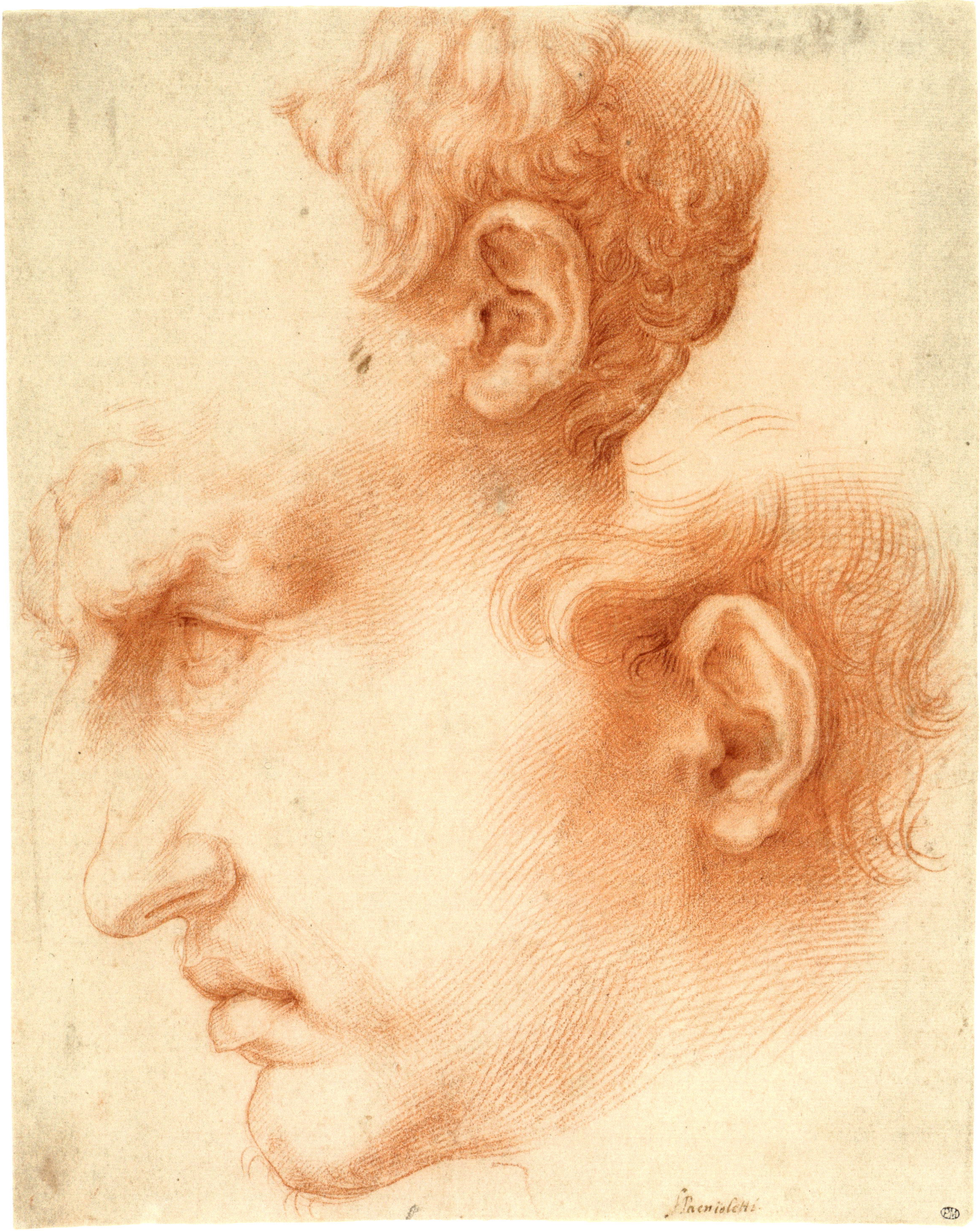

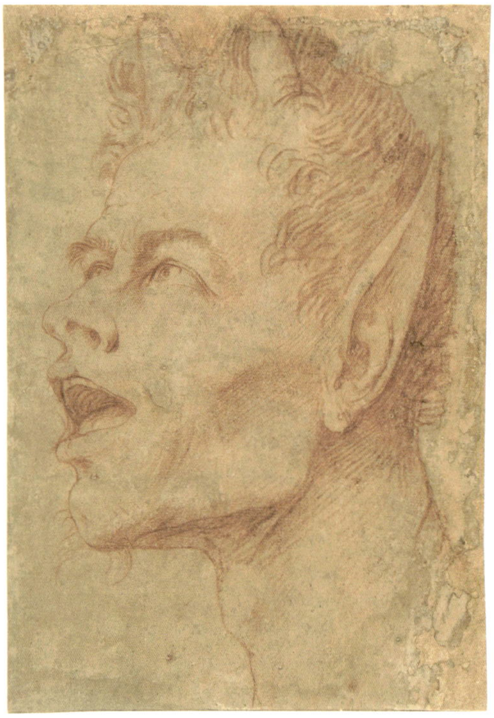

Fig. 4.1 Jusepe de Ribera, Spanish, 1591–1652: *Head of a Satyr Facing Left.* Red chalk on brownish paper, 30.5 x 21.3 cm. The Metropolitan Museum of Art, The Elisha Whittelsey Collection, The Elisha Whittelsey Fund, 1954 (54.2).

the close-cropped curls that surround the ear at top.

The brow, rendered at the center left side of the sheet, seems furrowed and is separated from the rest of the face that appears below, although the two sketches seem to share the eye. The upper lip and chin appear to be observed from life, as there are straggling hairs around the upper lip and stray hairs stick out from the front. The carefully crossed hatching at the center and along the lower jaw of the largest sketch seems to connect the disparate smaller studies into a cohesive whole.

The head studies might relate to a painting—perhaps *Saint Thomas* (ca. 1612, Foundation Roberto Longhi, Florence)—but no painting with a close relationship to this drawing, suggesting that the work is preparatory, has yet been identified.[10] Likely, the artist was simply studying the ear and the strong profile—with chiseled nose, thin nostril, full lips, and sculpted chin—in order to work out the features of the profile head. Details like the hairs on the chin connect this sheet with preparatory drawings by Ribera that demonstrate the same whimsical touch, such as *Head of a Satyr* at the Metropolitan Museum of Art (fig. 4.1).

A collector has annotated the drawing with his attribution at the lower right in pen and dark brown ink: *Spaenioletti.* The spelling of the artist's nickname varied according to collectors' whims, but in most cases collectors who referred to Ribera as "Spagnoletto" or "Spanioletti" were Italian. Although the provenance of this drawing before Polakovits is unknown, the annotation suggests that the sheet, like many other Ribera drawings, was once in an Italian collection.

5. *Martyrdom of Saint Sebastian,* ca. 1630

Verso: *Sketch of Male Head and smudges of red chalk*

Red chalk on cream laid paper

24.7 x 16.4 cm. (9 11/16 x 6 7/16 in.)

Inscribed in pen and brown ink, upper right corner: [illegible]; inscribed and cancelled in pen and brown and black ink, lower right: *1 real;* in pen and brown and black ink, along lower edge: [illegible], *4 reales* [cancelled] and *1 R*

WATERMARK: Fleur-de-lis (partial)

PROVENANCE: Frank Jewett Mather Jr.

REFERENCES: Florence 1967, 26–27, no. 32; Brown 1972, 2–7, fig. 1; Princeton 1973, 166, no. 19 ill.; Konečný 1985, 226–28, fig. 52 ill.; New York 1992, 208; Madrid 1992, 433–34, cat. D23 ill.; Finaldi 2005, 29–30; Copenhagen 2006, 60–61; Poitiers 2006–7, 56

EXHIBITIONS: Princeton 1973, no. 19 ill.; New York 1992 and Museo Nacional del Prado, Feb. 27, 1992–Aug. 9, 1992; Madrid 1992–93; "Jusepe de Ribera: 1591–1652," Certosa di San Martino, Castel Sant'Elmo, Naples (Feb. 27–May 17, 1992); Princeton 1995; Princeton 1997

Gift of Frank Jewett Mather Jr.
x1952-176

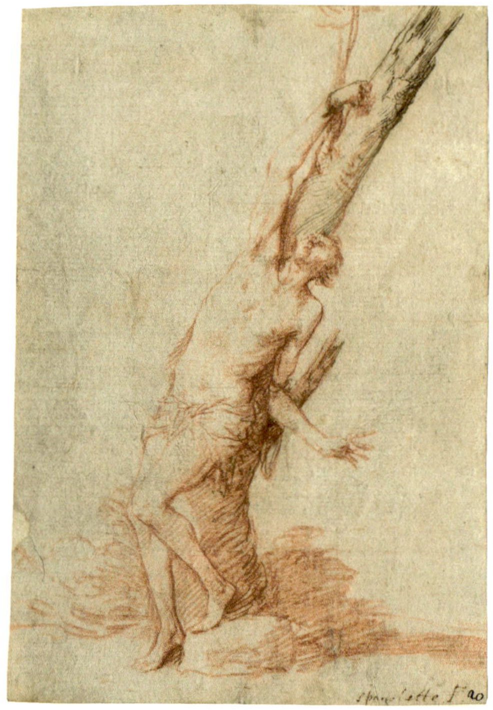

Fig. 5.1 Jusepe de Ribera, Spanish, 1591–1652: *Saint Sebastian,* 1626–1630. Red chalk with pen and brown ink, 17.3 x 12.4 cm. The Cleveland Museum of Art, Delia E. Holden Fund (1997.53).

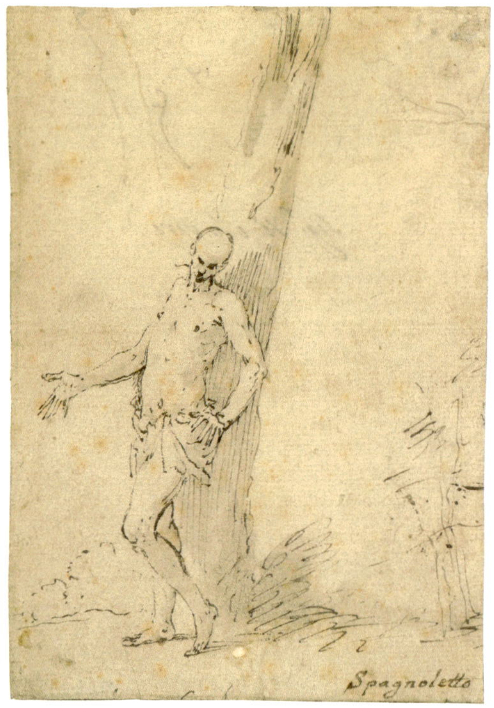

Fig. 5.2 Jusepe de Ribera, Spanish, 1591–1652: *Man Tied to a Tree.* Pen and gray wash on paper. Musée des Beaux-Arts, Rouen (AG1975.4.506).

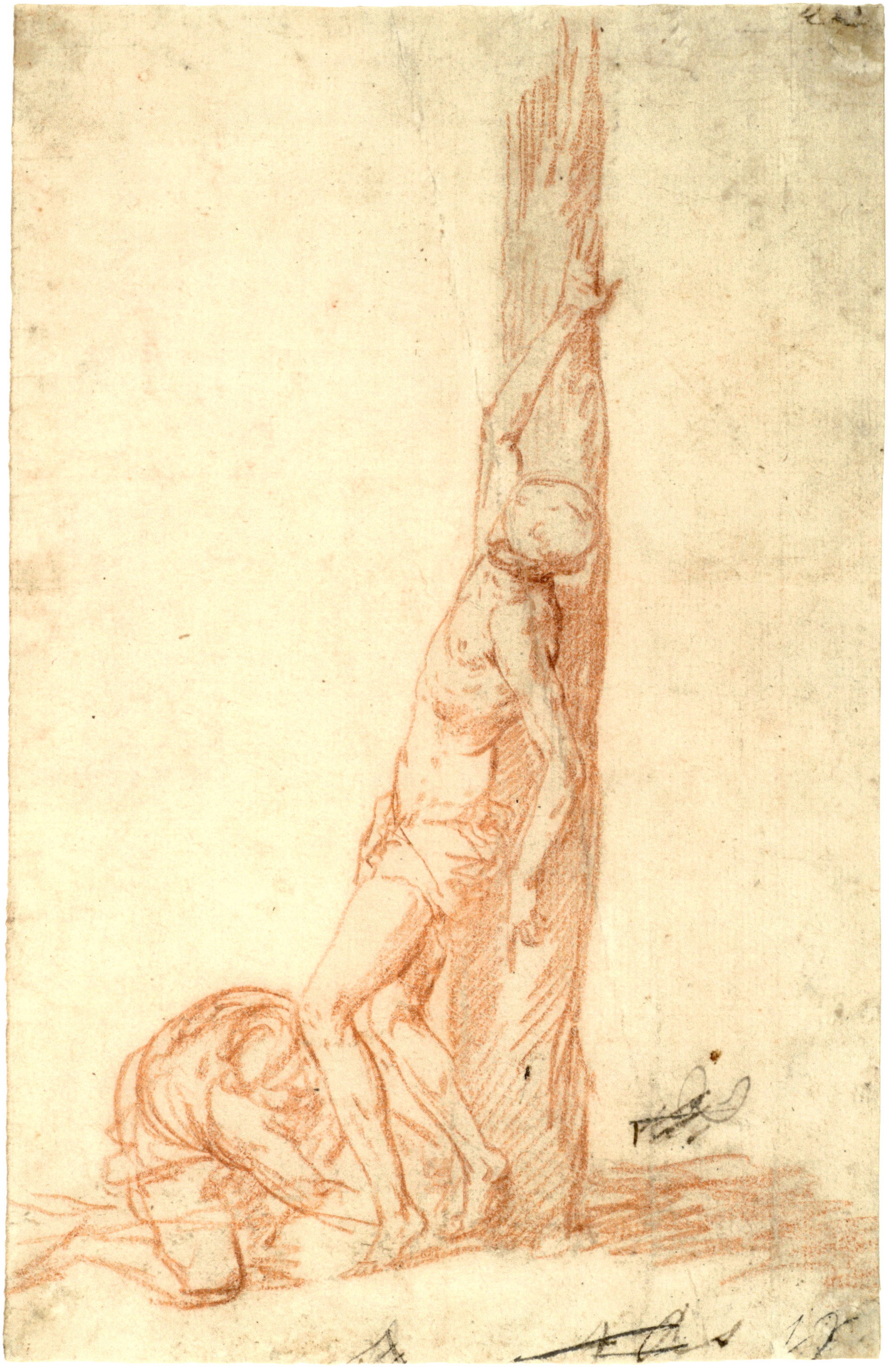

Verso cat. 5

Originally classified as anonymous Italian, this elegant red chalk sketch was attributed to Ribera by Jacob Bean in 1962.[11] Ribera's mastery of chalk is apparent in the rapid, yet suggestive, description of the body of his subject. The scene represents Saint Sebastian being tied to a tree, prior to being shot with arrows. The saint is bound with invisible rope and there are no arrows yet piercing his slender body. For this reason, Manuela Mena has connected Princeton's drawing with the Courtauld's red chalk *Saint Bartholomew*. The apostle Bartholomew was martyred by being tied to a tree and flayed alive. He is usually represented as an older, bearded man. Princeton's sketch is likely the youthful Saint Sebastian, a subject that Ribera drew many times.[12]

Like several other red chalk studies of Saint Sebastian by Ribera, this sheet demonstrates a more free technique than the drawings related to etchings of the 1620s, suggesting a dating closer to 1630.[13] Vitzthum, Brown, and Lubomír Konečný dated Princeton's sheet based on its comparison with the *Saint Sebastian* in the Cleveland Museum of Art (fig. 5.1). A dating from the late 1620s to around 1630 is also accepted by Finaldi,[14] who noted that Ribera's practice of reinforcing a drawing with touches of pen and brown ink is not singular to this sheet but is found on several drawings of this type, including the Cleveland drawing. Lizzie Boubli specifically compared the abbreviated traits of the figure on Princeton's sheet to Ribera's drawing of the *Man Tied to a Tree*, which is annotated "Spagnoletto" (fig. 5.2).[15] Support for a date of about 1630 also can be taken from comparison to the drawing of Saint Bartholomew now in the Courtauld, dated ca. 1634–39 based on its relationship to paintings around those dates.[16]

Originally, the drawing was valued at "1 *real*," just behind the trunk of the tree at right, and later revalued at the lower right: "4 *reales*."[17] Values in seventeenth-century Spanish currency frequently were written directly on sheets by an appraiser, perhaps when a drawing changed hands after a collector's death; it is also common to find Spanish drawings marked with several values. At times, these values were cancelled and new ones were added. The values generally adhere to coinage denomination, that is, ½ *real*, 1 *real*, 4 *reales*, 8 *reales*, and so on. Higher prices were annotated on drawings through the eighteenth century, as seen on Princeton's drawing by Murillo (cat. 9).

6. *Five Men in Oriental Costume*, ca. 1637

Verso: *Figure in Clouds with Arms Outstretched, with Additional Sketch of Right Arm Holding Staff*, ca. 1637

Red chalk on cream laid paper, edge mounted to cream wove paper

22.3 x 21.8 cm. (8¹³⁄₁₆ x 8⁹⁄₁₆ in.)

Provenance: Lt.-Col. William Stirling of Keir, later Sir William Stirling-Maxwell; his sale Sotheby & Co., London, Oct. 21, 1963, lot 23 (to J. S. Crawley); Mathias Polakovits, Paris and New York, stamp (Lugt 3561) recto, lower right, in black

References: Jonathan Brown, "The Prints and Drawings of Ribera," in Fort Worth 1982–83, 82 ill. (recto); Princeton 2003, 122

Exhibitions: Princeton 1995; Princeton 1997; Princeton 2001

Museum purchase, Laura P. Hall Memorial Fund and Fowler McCormick, Class of 1921, Fund 2002-98

Mathias Polakovits acquired this drawing in 1963 from the sale of the Stirling Maxwell collection.[18] The red chalk sketch on the verso is a preliminary idea for the figure of Apollo in Ribera's *Apollo Flaying Marsyas* of 1637 (Musées Royaux des Beaux-Arts, Brussels) and is published here for the first time.[19]

Although previously dated to the 1620s, when many of Ribera's finest red chalk studies were made, the verso might now be dated just prior to 1637, the year that Ribera completed the painting.[20] On that side, the delicate rendering of a hovering figure occupies the left side of the sheet while in the lower right a partial rendering of a hand holding what appears to be a stick reaches toward the figure. Both painting and drawing relate the story of the satyr Marsyas, who dared to question the authority and superiority of Apollo's lyre and invited him to a musical contest. The painting, also seen as a metaphor for one who questions the artistic ability of a master, shows Apollo punishing the prone satyr on the ground.[21] The final painting includes a discarded flute behind Marsyas's head. In the drawing, Ribera first drew the flute in a hand, depicting a moment just prior to Apollo's gruesome punishment of Marsyas, and depicted the flying drapery in an inspired flourish around the figure at left. The sketch of an angel flying in from the left might also have been used for *Saint Francis of Assisi in the Portiuncola* (also known as *Saint Francis of Assisi in the Brambles*) (Palacio Real de El Pardo, Patrimonio Nacional, Madrid).[22]

On the recto, the exceptional delicacy of the rendering of the foremost man, leaning on a stick, is achieved with a finely sharpened chalk and thin lines applied in outline, including those around the man's extended hand and finger. The figure in the background stands with his eyes closed just to the left of the central foreground figure. No known painting by Ribera directly relates to the recto of the sheet, but it might have been a preliminary sketch for the elders in a *Christ Among the Doctors* or a scene in a temple or synagogue, where bearded men traditionally are depicted standing together in a group.[23]

Another possible use for these faintly sketched studies is as a preliminary figure study for the prophets and patriarchs that Ribera painted between 1638 and 1643 in the Certosa di San Martino, Naples.[24] The face on the extreme left, silhouetted at the back of the group, resembles the face of Ribera's Ezekiel, and the one to his right wears a turban that recalls the headdress on Abdias. A smooth-headed, or bald, figure at the center right, behind the foremost figure, could be a study for a prophet. Ribera first painted the subject of *Christ Among the Doctors* (Cathedral of St. Mammès, Langres) around 1613–18.[25] LAB

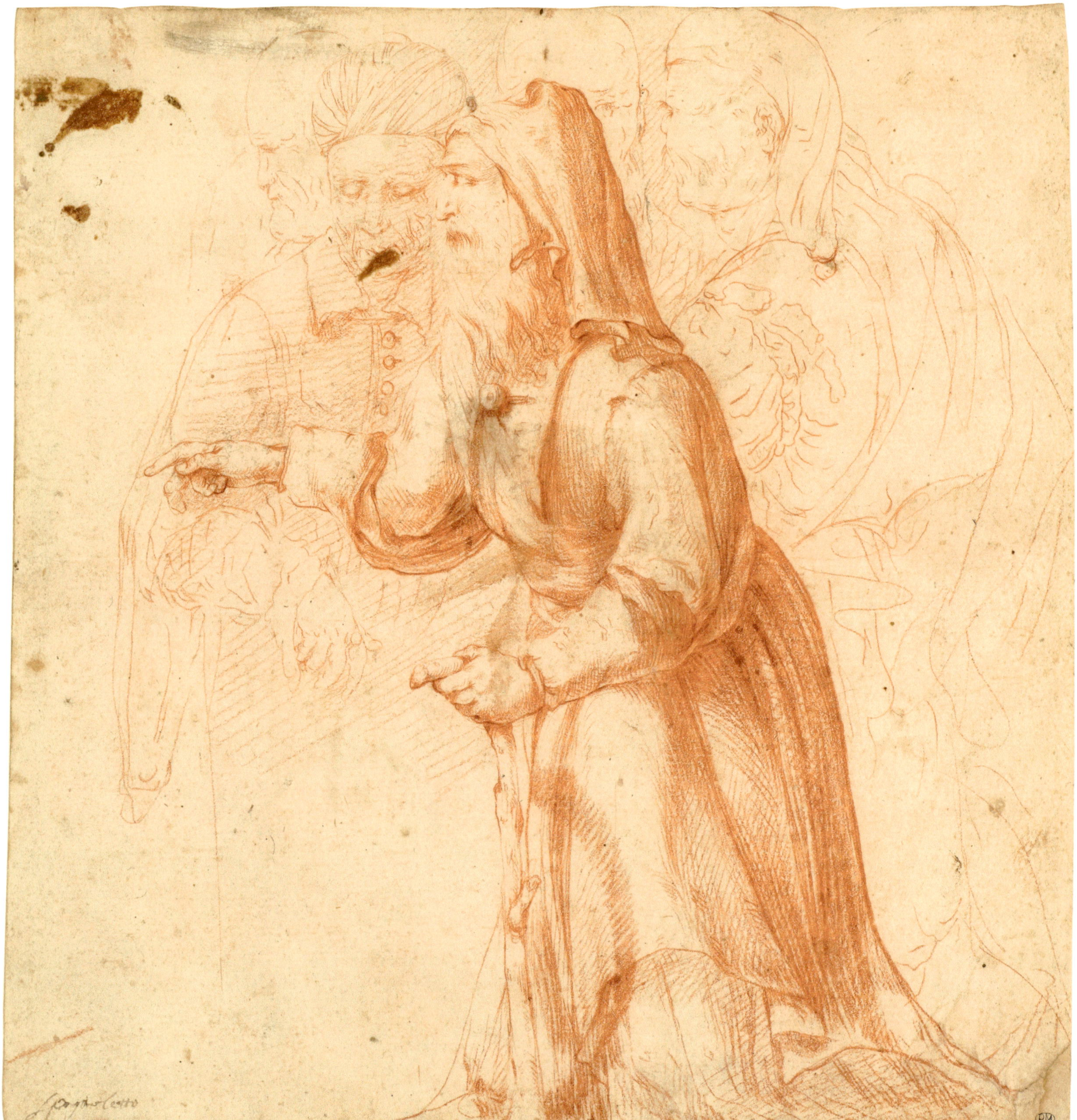

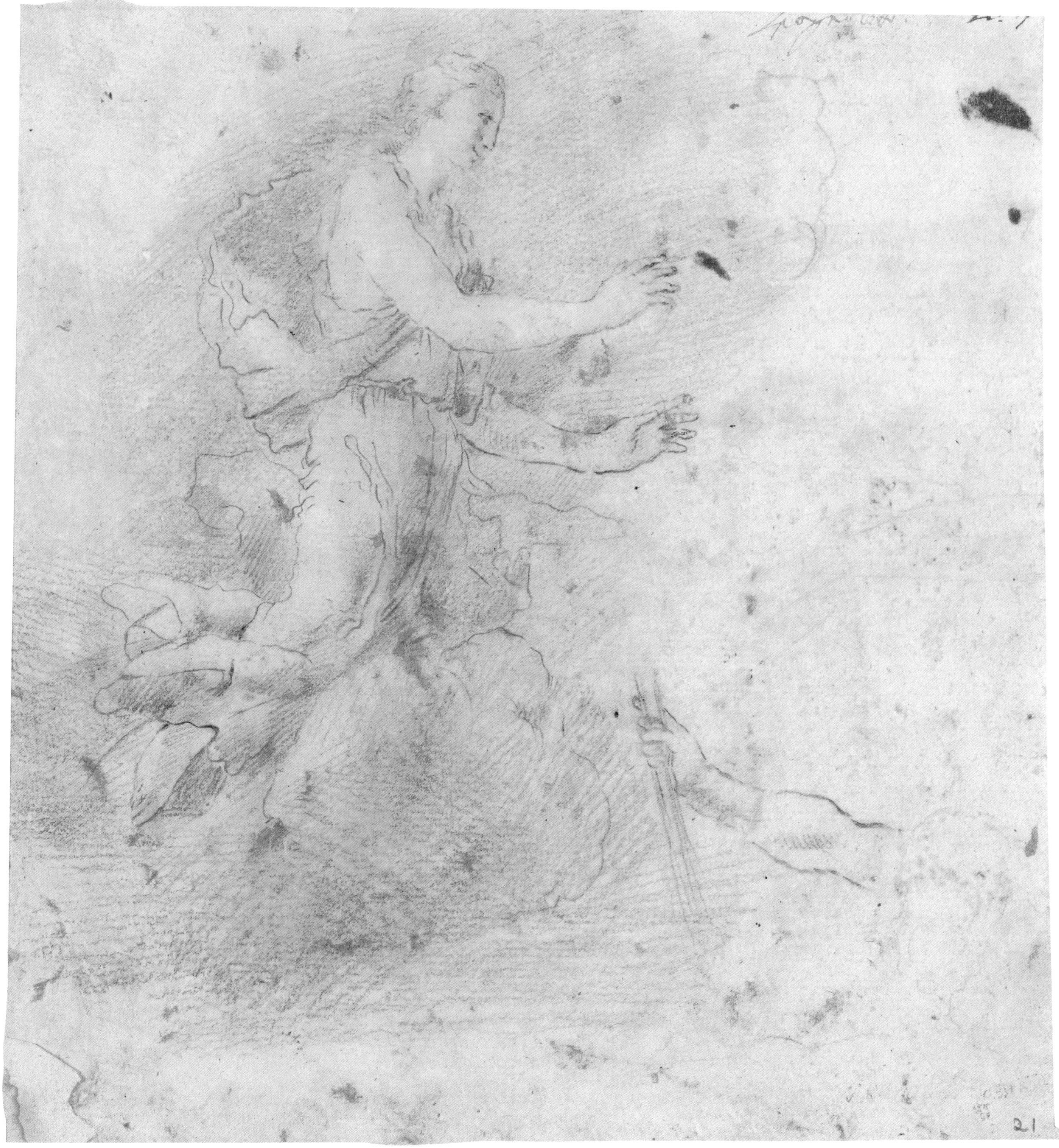

Verso cat. 6

1 Ribera's baptism was in 1591, generally assumed to be the year of his birth, making him about eighteen years old in 1609. The document placing Ribera in Rome as early as 1609 was traced by Danesi Squarzina and alludes to painters by the names of Giuseppe, Pietro, and Francesco "who were living on via Ferratina, in the house of M. Francesca." Danesi Squarzina 2006, 246.

2 Ibid., 244–51.

3 Madrid 2011b; and Papi 2007, 16–17.

4 Danesi Squarzina 2006, 246.

5 Madrid 2006–7a, 120–22.

6 Los Angeles 1997, 284.

7 The most important resources for Ribera's drawings are Princeton 1973, New York 1992, Madrid 1992–93, and Finaldi 2005.

8 Finaldi 2005.

9 Princeton 1973, 153–54; and Brown 1972, 7 n. 3.

10 Spinosa 2008, 312, A. 16. Included in the exhibition *El Joven Ribera* (2011), the painting is now dated to ca. 1612. The Saint Thomas figure, who, like the man in the drawing, is young, faces left. The figure has a scant goatee, and his hair and ear resemble the drawing at Princeton. The set of the mouth, with the lip curled down, and the strongly defined chin are also features of the painting. A relationship between the painting and drawing would effect our understanding of Ribera's early red chalk drawings.

11 Princeton 1973.

12 Drake and Drake 1971, q.v. "Saint Sebastian of Rome."

13 A drawing by Ribera from the Crozat collection, now in the Moravian Gallery in Brno, Czech Republic, demonstrates just this technique. For the discussion of the dating, see Konečný 1985, 226. Konečný discusses the Princeton drawing as a comparable sheet in technique.

14 Finaldi 2005, 29–30.

15 Lizzie Boubli entry in Poitiers 2006–7, 56, no. 19.

16 Konečný 1985, 226; and "Spanish Drawings from the Witt Collection, London," University of London Courtauld Institute Galleries, Mar.–May 1978 (exh. cat., 9, no. 13). Also see Princeton 1973; and Véliz 2012, 226–28, no. 79..

17 Although *ducati* were used in Naples, the drawing was evaluated in *reales*, implying a Spanish provenance.

18 *Catalogue of Important Old Master Drawings, Including the Property of Lt.-Col. William Stirling of Keir, etc. . . . and from the collection of the late Francis Matthiesen*, Oct. 21, 1963, 9, lot 23. Dimensions are given there as 8⅝ inches x 8½ inches, or 222 mm. x 215 mm. Hammer price $42 or £15, sold to J. S. Crawley.

19 Of the two paintings that Ribera completed of Apollo and Marsyas, the Brussels picture is closer to this drawing. The other version, signed and dated 1637, in the Museo Nazionale di San Martino, Naples, has Apollo gazing serenely at the prone figure of Marsyas, who is experiencing excruciating pain as Apollo begins to flay his foot. Two other pictures of the scene are known to Ribera scholars but have not been located, including one for Gaspar Roomer painted in or before 1630. Madrid 1992–93, 306–7. An additional pen and ink sketch of the scene, with more elongated and less precisely drawn figures, is in Rome (Istituto Nazionale per la Grafica, inv. no. 124851 F.C.)

20 It seems likely that the sketch was executed closer to the time of the 1637 painting in Brussels.

21 Ovid, *Metamorphoses*, trans. Charles Martin, intro. Bernard Knox (New York: Norton, 2005), 589, bk. 5, v. 574.

22 Madrid 1992–93, 214, no. 25, or Spinosa 2008, 361, A. 95. A copy of the *Saint Francis of Assisi in the Brambles*, noted by Spinosa, was recently found in the pictures among the former Museo de la Trinidad, Prado, inv. no. 3281. Madrid 1992–93, 216.

23 Madrid 2011b, 116–19, no. 7.

24 Madrid 1992–93, 57ff.

25 Danesi Squarzina 2006, 245, fig. 1.

FRANCISCO DE HERRERA THE ELDER

Seville, ca. 1590–ca. 1656, Madrid

Francisco de Herrera the Elder, known as Herrera el Viejo, was a contemporary of Francisco Pacheco (1564–1644) and a student with him in the studio of Luis Fernández (fl. 1542–1582).[1] Herrera's style reflects a vigorous naturalism in painting and drawing, and both reed pen and brush and wash drawings survive from his hand. His earliest known work is an engraved frontispiece for the *Constituciones del Arzobispado de Sevilla*, published in 1609, and the title page of *Relación de la Fiesta que se hizo en Sevilla a la Beatificación del Glorioso San Ignacio fundador de la Compañía de Jesús*, dated 1610. After 1610 there is additional documentation of his work as a painter as well as an engraver.

Herrera the Elder was admitted to the painter's guild in Seville in 1619, apparently following contentious discussion with his judges.[2] Among his best-known works are the series painted for the Franciscan College of Saint Bonaventure in Seville, including *Saint Bonaventure Enters the Franciscan Order* (1627–29, Prado). Another important commission, contracted on November 3, 1638, is the altarpiece of Saint Basil for the College of Saint Basil, Seville, a total of ten completed pictures, including *The Vision of Saint Basil* (1638, Museo de Bellas Artes, Seville) and *Saint Basil Dictating His Rule* (1639, Louvre).[3]

From Seville, Herrera went to Madrid at some point after 1640, according to Palomino, and seems to have stayed there until his death.[4] As John S. Thacher discovered, the only period for which there are documented dates for Herrera the Elder is 1610–1648, and his last known signed and dated painting is *Saint Joseph and the Christ Child* (1648, Lázaro Galdiano Museum, Madrid). Most scholars now agree that Herrera the Elder died in Madrid in 1654, and his will was resolved in 1657 in Seville.[5]

7. *Old Testament Prophet Gesturing to His Left*, ca. 1640

Brush and black ink with gray wash on cream laid paper, laid down on cream laid paper, edge mounted to tan wove card

15.1 x 11.1 cm. (5 15/16 x 4 3/8 in.)

Inscribed recto, in graphite, lower right corner on mount: *9;* inscribed verso, in black crayon, lower center on mount: *583*

Provenance: Frank Hall Standish (Catalogue, Paris, 1842); King Louis-Philippe, his sale, Paris, December 6, 1852, lot 583, as "École de Francisco Herrera"; Mathias Polakovits, Paris and New York, stamp (Lugt 3561) recto, lower right, in black

References: Paris 1852, 60, lot 583; Princeton 2003, 122, as "Francisco de Herrera the Elder or Francisco de Herrera the Younger, called 'El Mozo'"

Exhibitions: "Spanish Drawings," The Art Museum, Princeton University, Mar. 20–Apr. 22, 1984, as "attributed to Francisco de Herrera the Younger"; Princeton 1995; Princeton 1997; Princeton 2001, as "possibly Francisco de Herrera the Younger"

Museum purchase, Laura P. Hall Memorial Fund and Fowler McCormick, Class of 1921, Fund 2002-92

8. *Old Testament Prophet Holding a Staff*, ca. 1640

Brush and black ink with gray wash on cream laid paper, laid down on cream laid paper, edge mounted to tan wove card

15.6 x 11.3 cm. (6 1/8 x 4 7/16 in.)

Inscribed recto, in graphite, lower right corner on mount: *98;* inscribed verso, in black crayon, lower center on mount: *583*

Provenance: Frank Hall Standish (Catalogue, Paris, 1842); King Louis-Philippe, his sale, Paris, December 6, 1852, lot 583, as "École de Francisco Herrera"; Mathias Polakovits, Paris and New York, stamp (Lugt 3561) recto, lower right, in black

References: Paris 1852, 60, lot 583; Princeton 2003, 120, as "Francisco de Herrera the Elder or Francisco de Herrera the Younger, called 'El Mozo'"

Exhibitions: "Spanish Drawings," The Art Museum, Princeton University, Mar. 20–Apr. 22, 1984, as attributed to Francisco de Herrera the Younger"; Princeton 1995; Princeton 1997

Museum purchase, Laura P. Hall Memorial Fund and Fowler McCormick, Class of 1921, Fund 2002-91

These two drawings are closely related to a group at the Louvre also mounted onto secondary supports.[6] Lizzie Boubli noted that this mount is the same type found on several other drawings by the elder Herrera, all of which share provenance to the Louis Philippe sale of December 6, 1852, lot 583, which comprised sixteen pieces. A large "583" is scrawled at the lower center, verso, of the secondary support of each of the two Princeton drawings, indicating that these were included in the same lot. The drawings in the lot are described as "various studies of half-figures of men."[7] Although no dimensions are listed, the drawings also can be traced to the catalogue of artworks that Frank Hall Standish gave to King Louis Philippe in 1842, in which they are attributed to Herrera the Elder and School of Herrera.[8] Their earlier provenance is unknown, although Martínez Ripoll cited an 1832 publication indicating that Julian Williams, vice-consul of Great Britain in Seville, owned some Herrera drawings[9] and Standish is known to have acquired his Herrera drawings from Vice-consul Williams.[10]

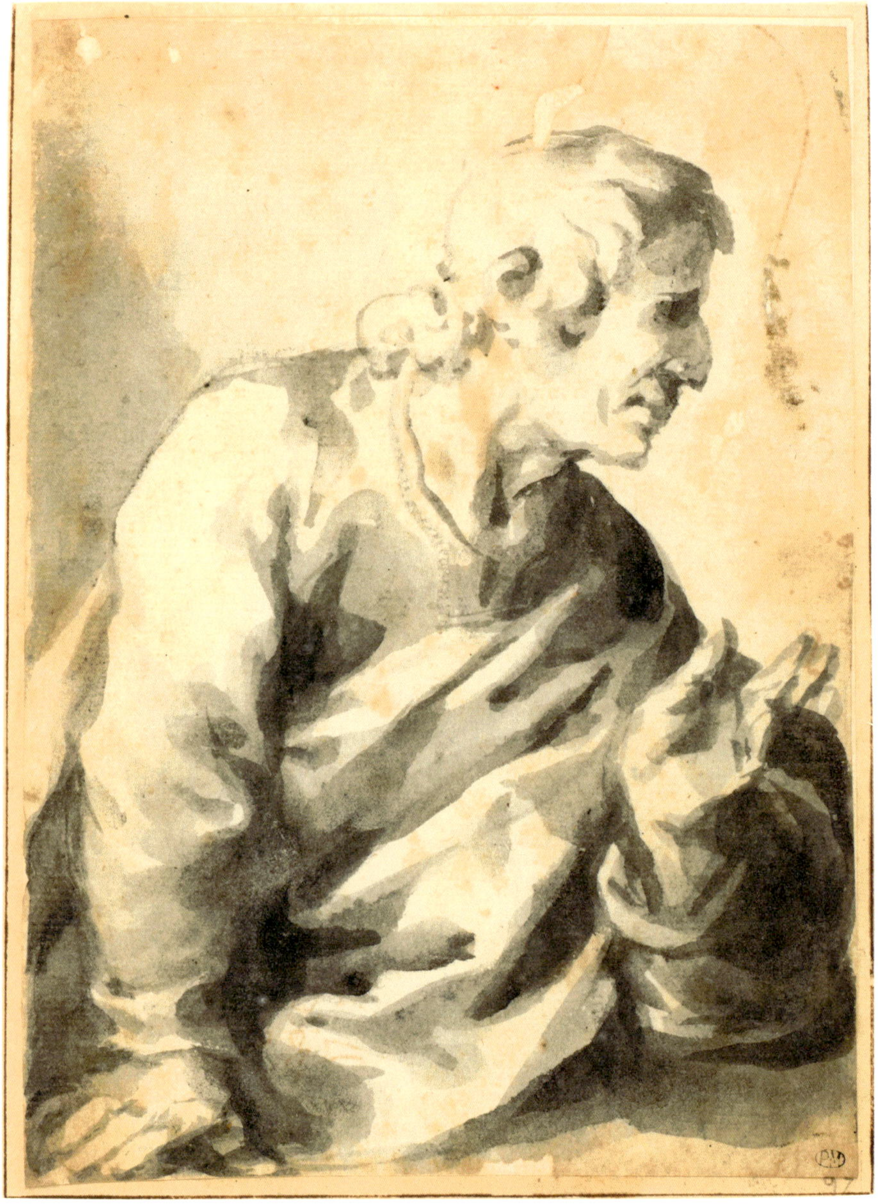

There are now about twenty known sheets by Herrera the Elder in the brush and gray wash technique, of approximately the same size, thought to represent an extended series of saints.[11] Several are horizontal and contain two half-length figures, suggesting that they might form a discrete series. Their measurements are approximately double the width of the sheets depicting single figures, the majority of which wear robes and are set against an empty background. The largest group of the single-figure sheets in brush and wash is at the Hamburger Kunsthalle; Martínez Ripoll indicated in 1978 that these drawings were likely related to a lost series of paintings of saints or apostles.[12] Several half-length paintings by Herrera the Elder in the Museo de Bellas Artes, Córdoba, may be the closest parallels to these drawings, as noted by Boubli following Pérez Sánchez.[13] Both the Hamburg drawings and the Córdoba paintings are attributed to Herrera based on comparison with signed and dated works, such as *The Miracle of the Loaves and Fishes* at the Archbishop's Palace in Madrid.[14] These paintings demonstrate similar handling of drapery and facial features, strengthening the traditional attribution to Herrera the Elder.[15] The close relationship of the drawings in Hamburg to the paintings at Córdoba reinforces the idea of Herrera providing drawings to his studio assistants.[16]

Two distinct drawing techniques were used by Herrera the Elder: reed pen and brown ink for the group of standing full-length apostles and brush and wash for the half-length figures.[17] A well-known series of apostles made with a reed pen and brown ink is dispersed among several museum collections, including

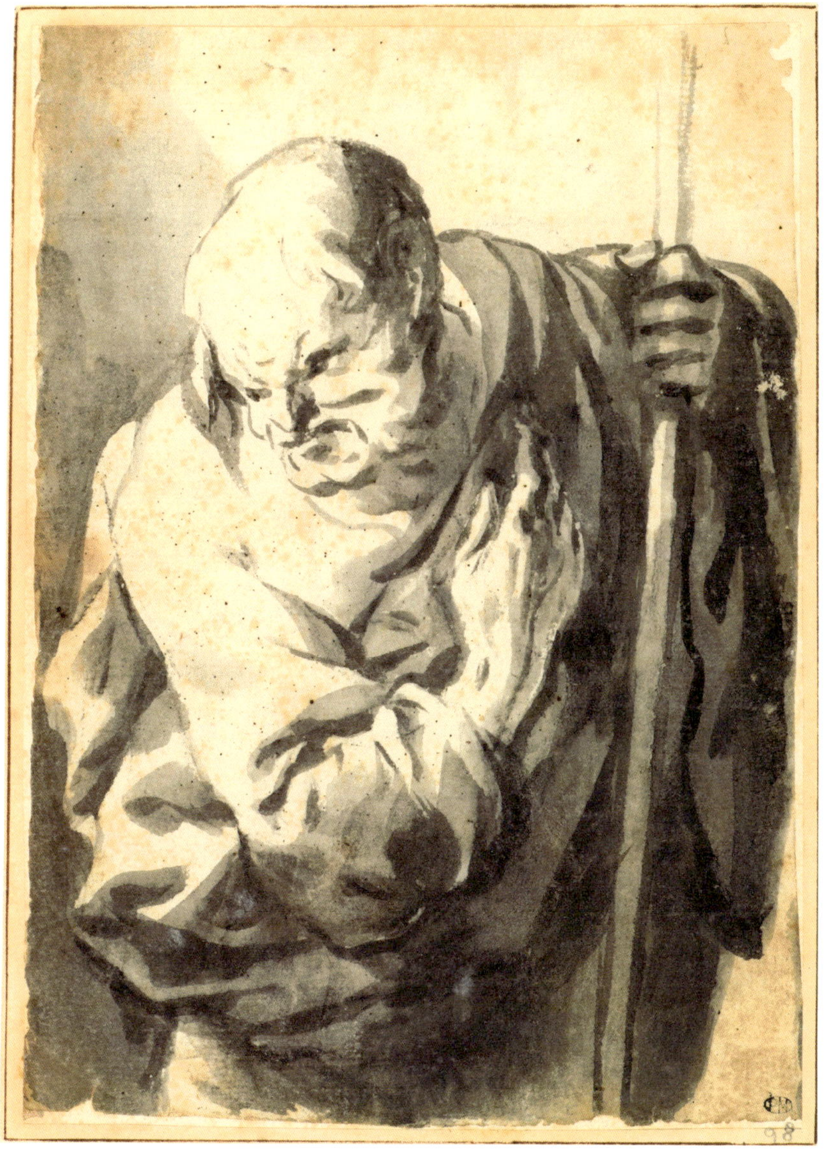

the Hispanic Society of America in New York, the British Museum in London, the Ashmolean Museum in Oxford, and the Biblioteca Nacional in Madrid; eight of these signed and dated drawings are known.[18] The standing apostles, each identified by his attributes and at times by an inscription with his name, are described with firm lines and cross-hatching, and most of the sheets are signed and dated 1642. Another series, formerly in the collection of the Instituto Jovellanos de Gijón, was attributed to Herrera the Elder, although they were lost in a fire during the Spanish Civil War.[19] Those were executed in pen and ink, with annotations *"F. Herrera"* and *"Franco de Herrera"* and measurements of 130 x 110 mm. Martínez Ripoll dated that group to about 1615–20, using surviving photographs. Because not all later scholars have accepted the Instituto Jovellanos group as by the hand of Herrera the Elder, however, they can only be regarded as a point of reference, rather than a control group.

Based on the date of the series of reed pen and ink drawings by Herrera the Elder, the drawings at Princeton likely date to about 1640. The Hamburg drawings have been dated by Pérez Sánchez and Navarrete Prieto to 1640–45,[20] and the figure types relate to the reed pen series, signed and dated 1642. Similarities in the vacant, deep-set eyes of the figures and their flowing hair strengthen a dating around 1640 for the Hamburg drawings and thus the two Princeton sheets.[21] The two drawings at Princeton can thus be added to approximately twenty known sheets of this type, all with similar dimensions, in the Hamburger Kunsthalle, the Metropolitan Museum of Art, the National Gallery of

Canada, and the Musée du Louvre, Paris, and formerly in the collection of Stanley Moss, Riverdale-on-Hudson, New York.[22] Most recently, the Biblioteca Nacional in Madrid acquired one of the drawings, which is of the same dimensions as the rest of the series, and is mounted on a similar secondary support (BN, Dib/18/1/9212).[23]

In 1978, Antonio Martínez Ripoll argued for the identification of some of the figures in these brush and wash drawings as apostles, but most are represented without attributes. Jonathan Brown, supported by Pérez Sánchez in 1985, hypothesized that the group instead represents a series of saints.[24] Traditionally, the drawings have been referred to as apostles, but with twenty related sheets, the known drawings number more than an *apostolado* and appear to have been made at the same time, on similar sized sheets. Pérez Sánchez also suggested that the figures may represent prophets, an identification that is convincing based on the number of drawings and their lack of attributes.[25] Four major and twelve minor Old Testament prophets are represented, and if this group is conceived as a group of prophets, then the group of sixteen sheets listed in the Louis Philippe catalogue can be seen a series of Old Testament prophets. The repetition of some of the figures, or the fluid interpretation of other prophets, might explain the larger number of sheets of this type known today, but the inclusion of Moses, Samuel, Elijah, and Elisha would also account for the representation of twenty figures.[26] Biblical exegesis often explains the prophecies of the Old Testament as prefigurations of the new covenant expressed in the books of the evangelists, but the prophets were rarely represented in series like the apostles.

Nonetheless, the figures share generalized broad features depicted with wide brushstrokes. Some hold books or staffs. Darker ink strokes laid down over lighter wash indicate that the artist painted over the figures several times to sharpen contrast in the drapery folds indicated on the robes, adding depth and shadow to otherwise broadly brushed figures. The homogeneous character of the sheets and the similarity of their dimensions and technique reinforce the idea that they were made as a series, perhaps one of prophets, or, as argued elsewhere, a series of famous historical and legendary men.[27] LAB

1 Ceán Bermúdez 1800, 274 ff.
2 Thacher 1937, 334.
3 Ibid., 367.
4 Palomino 1987, 127; and Thacher 1937, 333.
5 Lisa Banner in New York 2010–11, 51–57, nos. 13–14.
6 Boubli 2002, nos. 79 and 80.
7 Paris 1852, 60, lot 583.
8 Paris 1842, nos. 391–396 and 397–411. Navarrete Prieto and Pérez Sánchez 2009, 14.
9 Martínez Ripoll 1978, D. 17, and Herrera Dávila 1832, 87.
10 Seville 1995–96, 120.
11 Boubli 2002, 91–93.
12 Martínez Ripoll also discusses what he considered in 1978 to be the group of *dibujos perdidos*, or lost drawings, only known through mention in the Standish collection and presumed lost, Martínez Ripoll 1978, 244–46, Dp. 26–40. These seem to correspond with the drawings at Hamburg and elsewhere; also see Seville 1995–96, 120ff.
13 Seville 1995–96, 120ff. The paintings entered the Córdoba collection in 1868 from the Convent of Santa Clara de Priego. Pérez Sánchez and Navarrete Prieto 1996, 373.
14 Although the paintings at Córdoba were previously assigned to Juan Luis Zambrano (1598–ca. 1639), Pérez Sánchez and Navarrete Prieto have convincingly attributed them to Herrera. Pérez Sánchez and Navarrete Prieto 1996, 373. Also see Enrique Valdivieso, "Una adoración de la Eucaristía de Francisco de Herrera el viejo," *Laboratorio de Arte* (2001): 401–4.
15 Seville 1995–96, 133.
16 Madrid 2006–7, 115.
17 Boubli 2002, 91
18 Seville 1995–96, 100; and Madrid 2006–7a, 114–17.
19 Angulo Íñiguez and Pérez Sánchez 1975–88, 25; and Pérez Sánchez and Lafuente Ferrari 2003, 300–315.
20 Pérez Sánchez and Navarrete Prieto 1996, 377.
21 Lawrence 1974, 43–44, no. 21. McKim-Smith also argued for a date in the first half of the seventeenth century for Herrera the Elder's brush and wash drawings.
22 Seville 1995–96, 120–21ff.
23 The drawing at the Biblioteca Nacional is referred to as an apostle who holds a book in his left hand and points to the left with his right hand. It measures 155 x 108 mm., on a secondary support of 161 x 112 mm., and has a graphite inscription on the front lower edge: "101." The drawing was purchased in 2005 from Galería Artur Ramon, Barcelona. The drawings at Princeton seem to have been part of the same album at some point, as they have inscriptions of "97" (2002-92) and "98" (2002-91) on the secondary support, at the lower right corner, like the drawing at the Biblioteca Nacional.
24 Angulo Íñiguez and Pérez Sánchez 1975–88, vol. 3, 19.
25 Seville 1995–96, 120. Also see, Curatorial Files, Biblioteca Nacional, Madrid. My thanks to Isabel García-Toraño and Isabel Ortega for further information about the drawing and its provenance and for making the drawing available for study.
26 The four major prophets are: Daniel, Ezekiel, Isaiah, and Jeremiah. The twelve minor prophets are: Amos, Habakkuk, Haggai, Hosea, Joel, Jonah, Malachi, Micah, Nahum, Obadiah, Zeccariah, and Zephaniah. Sometimes, Elijah, Elisha, Moses, and Samuel are included in the tally of prophets, depending on the biblical scholar's interpretation; this would make twenty drawings in total, if the group with Moses were included.
27 Seville 1995–96, 120. Madrid 2006–7a, 114–17. New York 2010–11, 51–57.

BARTOLOMÉ ESTEBAN MURILLO

Seville, 1617–1682, Seville

Murillo, one of the finest Spanish draftsmen, is also among the best known, in part because so many of his drawings survive in major museum collections. Baptized on January 1, 1618, the artist spent the entirety of his career in Seville, working for ecclesiastic and noble patrons, with the exception of a brief visit to Madrid in 1658. During that trip, recounted by Palomino and Ceán Bermúdez, the artist was permitted by Velázquez to copy paintings in the royal collection.[1]

Palomino reported Murillo's early training with Juan del Castillo (ca. 1590–ca. 1657) in his native city and later in Cádiz.[2] His formative years were also marked by commissions from religious patrons, including the decoration of the small cloister of the convent of San Francisco (1644–45) and, later, the painting *Vision of Saint Anthony of Padua* at the Seville Cathedral (1656). Murillo's decoration of the church of Santa María la Blanca was completed in 1665. Another important group of paintings was commissioned by Miguel de Mañara for the Hospital de la Caridad in Seville (1668–72); a large series of nineteen canvases for the Capuchinos of Seville is also well documented.[3] Murillo's last work was an altarpiece for the Capuchinos in Cádiz, contracted in 1680. Drawings related to that commission survive, demonstrating Murillo's use of a remarkable rapid pen and ink drawing style, in addition to a fluid wash style, later in his life. Knowledge of Murillo's patrons and their commissions has added a great deal to our understanding of this artist. In particular, Jonathan Brown has enriched knowledge of Murillo with a detailed study of the album that contained Murillo's drawings.[4]

In addition to his many large commissions, Murillo was a painter of portraits and genre scenes, which were appreciated and collected widely in the eighteenth and nineteenth centuries, especially by French and English travelers to Spain, who promoted the fashion for collecting Murillo's work in their home countries. Among those who owned important paintings and drawings by Murillo were the Comte de Saint-Morys, Maréchal Soult, Baron St. Helens, Frank Hall Standish, King Louis Philippe, William Richardson Jr., and Sir William Stirling Maxwell; many of the drawings that formed their collections are now in museums.

9. *Christ on the Cross*

Pen and brown ink with brush and brown wash, over black chalk, on cream laid paper, lined

33.7 x 23.6 cm. (13¼ x 9⁹⁄₁₆ in.)

Inscribed in pen and brown ink, upper left corner: *14*; in lower left corner: *Barto.*^{c} *Muri.*^{o} *f.*^{t}; in lower right corner: *400*^{rs}; inscribed on verso in graphite, lower left: *J982*

PROVENANCE: John Rushout, second Earl of Northwick (1770–1859); George Rushout, third Earl of Northwick (1811–1859); Lady E. A. Rushout; E. G. Spencer-Churchill (Sotheby's, Nov. 1–4, 1920, lot 318); Sir Bruce S. Ingram, stamp (L. 1405a) on former mount, in black; H. Shickman Gallery, New York (vendor to Museum in 1972)

REFERENCES: *Catalogue of a Portion of the Famous and Important Collection of Drawings by Old Masters the Property of the Late John, Lord Northwick, Including Many Choice Examples by Well-known Masters of the Italian, Dutch, French, Spanish & British Schools*, Sotheby, Wilkinson & Hodge, London (Nov. 1–4, 1920), 57, no. 318 ill.; Sánchez Cantón 1930, vol. 5, pl. 418; "Exhibition of Old Master Drawings at the H. Shickman Gallery," New York, 1968 (exh. cat., no. 60 ill.); Brown 1973a, fig. 1; Lawrence 1974, no. 30, pl. 30; Princeton 1976–77, 136, no. 54; Los Angeles 1976, no. 227; Mayor 1977, 185; New York 2010–11, 72–73, no. 19; Santander 2012, 58–59, no. 37 ill.; Brown 2012, 152–53, no. 53 ill.

EXHIBITIONS: Lawrence 1974, no. 30, pl. 30; Princeton 1976, 136, no. 54; Los Angeles 1976, no. 227 ill.; Princeton 1995; Princeton 1997; New York 2010–11, no. 19; Santander 2012, no. 37 ill.

Museum purchase, Laura P. Hall Memorial Fund x1972-40

The second Lord Northwick, John Rushout, owned a prized collection of art, which was bequeathed to his nephew, George Rushout, who succeeded his uncle as head of the family.[5] After the third Lord Northwick's death, the majority of the collection, which included twenty-five Spanish drawings, was sold and dispersed. Princeton's Murillo drawing entered the collection of E. G. Spencer-Churchill, who was the heir to the third Lord Northwick's estate. Later, it became the property of Sir Bruce Ingram, whose stamp of ownership was on a former mount.

The painterly use of brush and wash to create this drawing adds to the atmospheric effect of the Crucifixion set against a troubled sky. Executed with thinly applied washes over chalk, Murillo's drawing is a fine example of the *vaporoso* style, or what Jonathan Brown has termed "in effect monochromatic painting."[6] Several other drawings in this style, executed with refined wash treatment, may have been intended as whole compositions

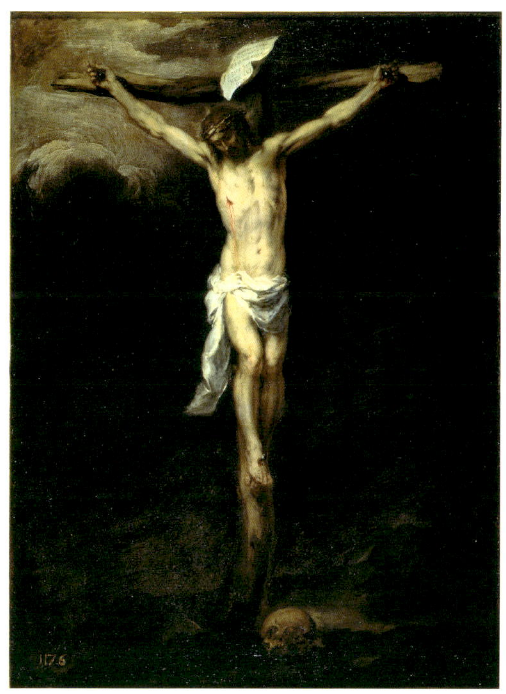

Fig. 9.1 Bartolomeo Esteban Murillo, Spanish, 1617–1682: *Crucified Christ*, ca. 1677. Oil on canvas, 71 x 54 cm. Museo Nacional del Prado, Madrid (P00967).

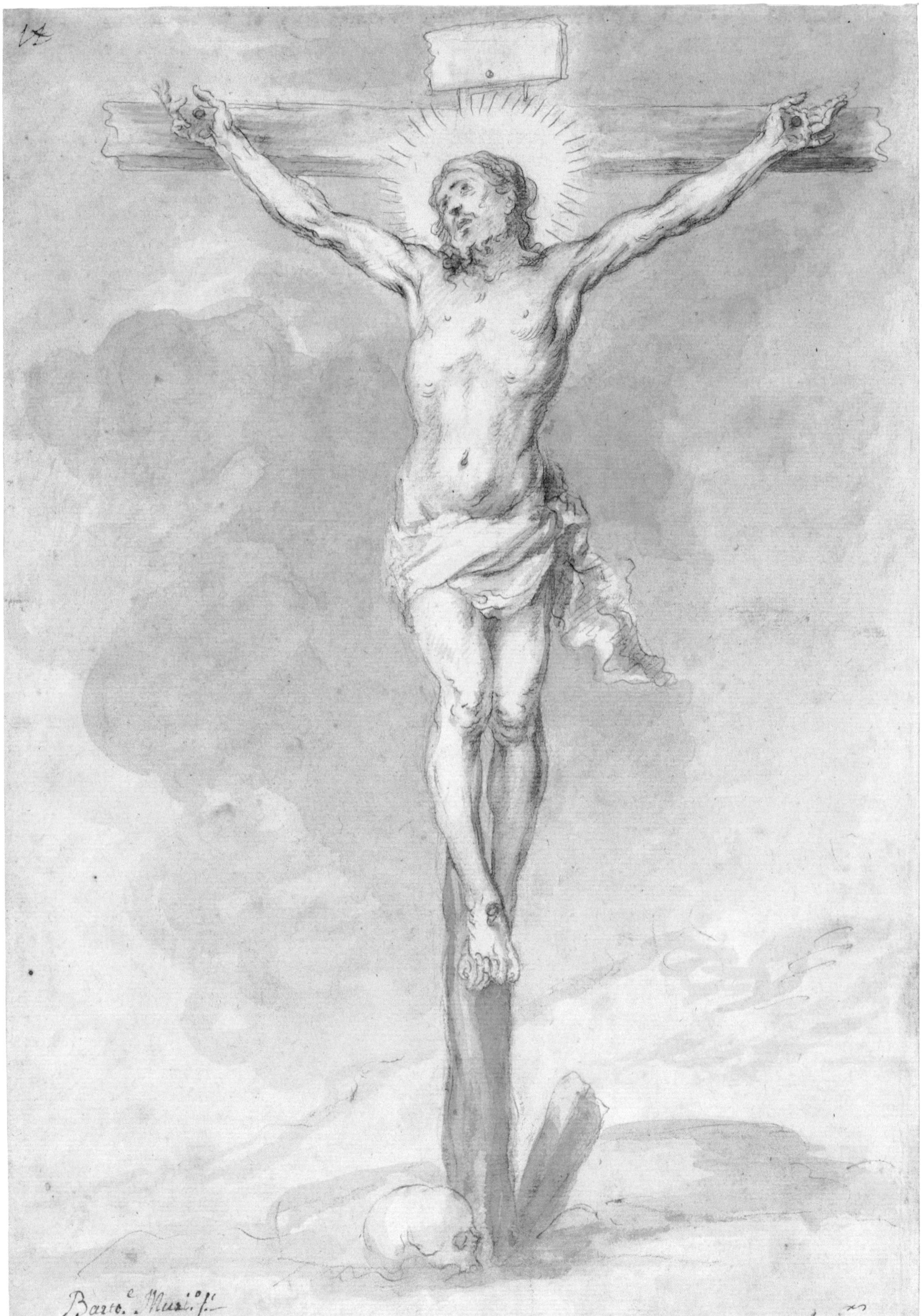

appreciated for their own sake rather than as preludes to a painting.

Princeton's drawing has not been connected with a known painting, despite the fact that Murillo painted the subject of the Crucifixion many times, varying the composition slightly by adding landscape to the background and raising or turning the head of the dying Christ. A version from the royal collection, dated 1677, includes a skull at the foot of the cross; Christ's arms are taut and pulled straight by the weight of his body, as in Princeton's drawing, but in other details it differs. Another such painting, also entitled *Christ on the Cross*, was sold in the sale of the Marquis de las Marismas, who died in 1842; the city of Jerusalem was visible in the background.[7] While the landscape component is not part of this composition, the low horizon line creates the sense that the viewer is looking up at the figure on a hill. A billowing cloud of wash fills the background, and a skull at the foot of the cross symbolizes triumph over death.

A close copy of Princeton's drawing was published by Sánchez Cantón in 1930, but its present whereabouts are unknown.[8] Another *Christ on the Cross* is executed in red and black chalk on buff paper and was once owned by the Conde del Águila.[9] A further drawing of the subject by Murillo belonged to Louis Philippe. Entitled *Le Christ en Croix. Dessin à la plume et lave*, it was included in the 1852 catalogue and, unlike many of the other drawings by Murillo, was not acquired by the Louvre.[10] No dimensions are given in the brief description and, because Princeton's drawing is no longer on its original mount, it is impossible to tell whether this drawing might be the one described in the 1852 catalogue.

Manuela Mena has dated this drawing to about 1670, based on its relationship to Murillo's paintings of Christ on the Cross, particularly that in the Timken Museum of Art (San Diego), in which the drapery flutters to the left and Christ's face is lifted to the right.[11] Mena noted that in Princeton's drawing the drapery over Christ's loins flutters to the right and his uplifted face is turned to the left; in many of the other compositions, the drapery and Christ's head are inclined to the same side.[12] LAB

10. *Studies of a Head and Ear*

Red and black chalk on beige laid paper

18.4 x 15.2 cm. (7¼ x 6.0 in.)

Provenance: Mathias Polakovits, Paris and New York, stamp (Lugt 3561) recto, lower right, in black

References: Brown 1983a, 161 and 163, pl. 32; New York 2010–11, 76–77, no. 21 ill.; Brown 2012, 232, no. A 3

Exhibitions: Princeton 1995; Princeton 1997; New York 2010–11, 76–77, no. 21 ill.

Museum purchase, Laura P. Hall Memorial Fund and Fowler McCormick, Class of 1921, Fund 2002-96

Murillo's drawings in red and black chalk play an important role in the artist's repertory as a draftsman. Some are sketch-like; others are highly finished and depict only the principal figure of composition. This combination of media is rarely found in the drawings of Murillo's predecessors in Seville, and there is reason to believe that he had seen examples by Peter Paul Rubens, which would have been made available to him during his one and only visit to Madrid in 1659–60.

The earliest datable drawing in red chalk is a finished study (Hamburger Kunsthalle) related to the *Mystic Marriage of St. Catherine* (fig. 10.1), which can be precisely dated by an autograph inscription: "Jan. 29, 1655 (En[er]o, 29 de 1655)." It has been suggested that the drawing was done after the painting, in which case it would be classified as a *ricordo*, not as a *modello*. In any event, the drawing provides an anchor for other finished drawings in the medium of chalk.

Murillo's characteristic combination of red-and-black chalk is visible in a partial study of the head of the Virgin Mary (British Museum, London), which is a preparatory study of the head of the *Virgin Mary Weeping* (Museo Nacional del Prado, Madrid). The drawing in pen and brown ink in the upper register is a study for the putti of the so-called *Immaculate Conception of La Loja* (Meadows Museum, Southern Methodist University, Dallas). The fragmentary study anticipates Murillo's use of this medium in the more finished drawings, using red chalk for the flesh tone, black for the drapery.

Another key piece is the detail of three angels connected to an unidentified Virgin of the Immaculate Conception (Hamburg Kunsthalle, 38596), which bears an autograph inscription of the date: "October 17, 1660 (17 de otubre [*sic*] 1660)." Executed solely in red chalk, the drawing evinces all of the characteristics of the finished chalk drawings. The touch is varied; pockets of shadows are created by blurred lines, and loose parallel hatching serves to separate the figure from the ground.

The Princeton drawing belongs to this category of partial studies for known compositions. This study focuses on the treatment of

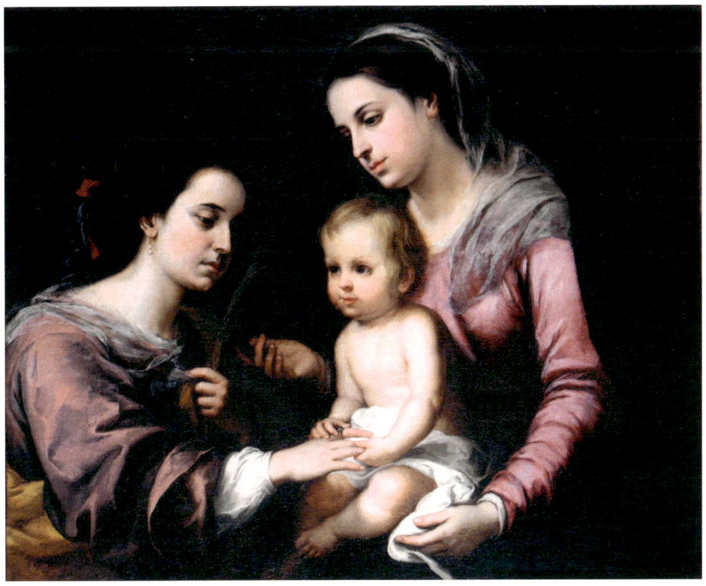

Fig. 10.1 Bartolomé Esteban Murillo, Spanish, 1617–1682: *Mystic Marriage of St. Catherine.* Oil on canvas, 76.5 x 94.5 cm. Museu Nacional de Arte Antiga, Lisbon, Portugal.

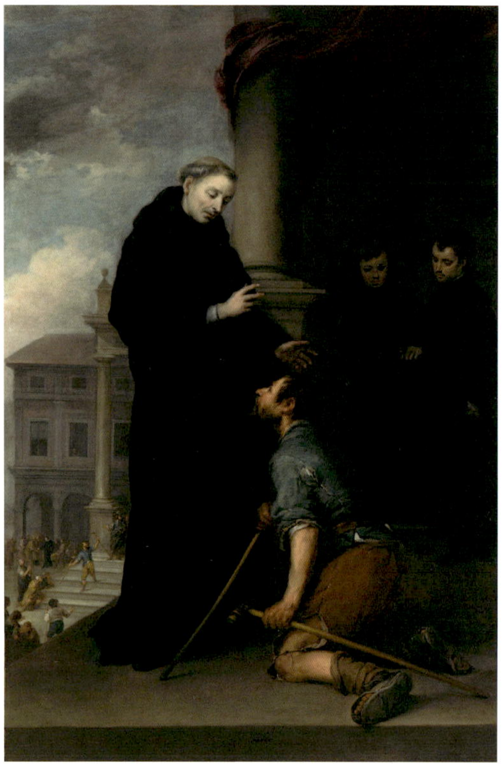

Fig. 10.2 Bartolomé Esteban Murillo, Spanish, 1618–1682: *St. Thomas of Villanueva Curing a Lame Man.* Oil on canvas, 220.8 x 48.7 cm. Alte Pinakothek, Munich (52).

the ear of the crippled beggar in the painting *St. Thomas of Villanueva Curing a Lame Man,* now in the Alte Pinakothek, Munich (fig. 10.2). The painting was part of an altarpiece commissioned for the Cavaleri Chapel, San Agustín, Seville, datable to 1665–70. Murillo first drew the head, using a combination of choppy stokes of red and black chalk to define the hollow cheeks of the poor man. The position of the head—tilted back, imploring the saint for relief from suffering—is a splendid example of the so-called "lost profile (*profile perdu*)." Bold strokes of parallel hatching in black chalk economically define the hair. By contrast, the facial features are meticulously drawn. In the lower register, Murillo carefully renders an alternate angle of vision for the ear alone, which he decided not to use.

Murillo completed a number of other highly finished drawings in red and black chalk, many of which are closely related to known paintings. They focus on the main figure, while the background is only summarily noted. The authenticity of these drawings has often been questioned, if not rejected. A close study of the securely dated Princeton drawing, however, leaves little room to doubt Murillo's mastery of the technique and the important role it played in his creative process. JB

1 Palomino 1987, 280–86; Ceán Bermúdez 1800, vol. 2, 48–65; and Madrid 2006–7a, 161–69.
2 Palomino 1987, 280–86; Ceán Bermúdez 1800, vol. 2, 48–65; and Stratton-Pruitt et al. 2002. Also see Sofia Sanabrais, "The Influence of Murillo in New Spain," *Burlington Magazine* 147, no. 1226 (May 2005): 327–30.
3 Princeton 1976–77; and Brown 2012.
4 Navarrete Prieto and Pérez Sánchez 2009, 24–26; and Brown 2012, 32–33.
5 *Catalogue of the paintings the property of J. R. Baron Northwick* 1859.
6 Jonathan Brown in New York 2010–11.
7 Charles Boyd Curtis, *Velázquez and Murillo: A Descriptive and Historical Catalogue of the Works. . .* (New York: J. W. Bouton, 1883), 203, no. 219e. The city is visible in a painting entitled *Christ on the Cross,* ca. 1675, at the lower right background (Prado, P0096).
8 Sánchez Cantón 1930, vol. 5, pl. 418.
9 Brown 1976–77, 138, cat. 56; and Navarrete Prieto and Pérez Sanchez 2009, 15, fig. 4. That drawing is in the Ford Family collection. It was connected by Angulo to the painting on copper of *Crucifixion with the Virgin Mary and Saints John and Mary Magdalene* (Meadows Museum, Dallas). Angulo Íñiguez 1974, 104.
10 Paris 1852, 61, lot 603.
11 Angulo Íñiguez and Pérez Sánchez 1975–88, vol. 3, pl. 398.
12 Santander 2012, 58–59 ill. The painting in the Timken is illustrated in Angulo Íñiguez and Pérez Sánchez 1975–88, vol. 3, pl. 398, and vol. 2, cat. 268.

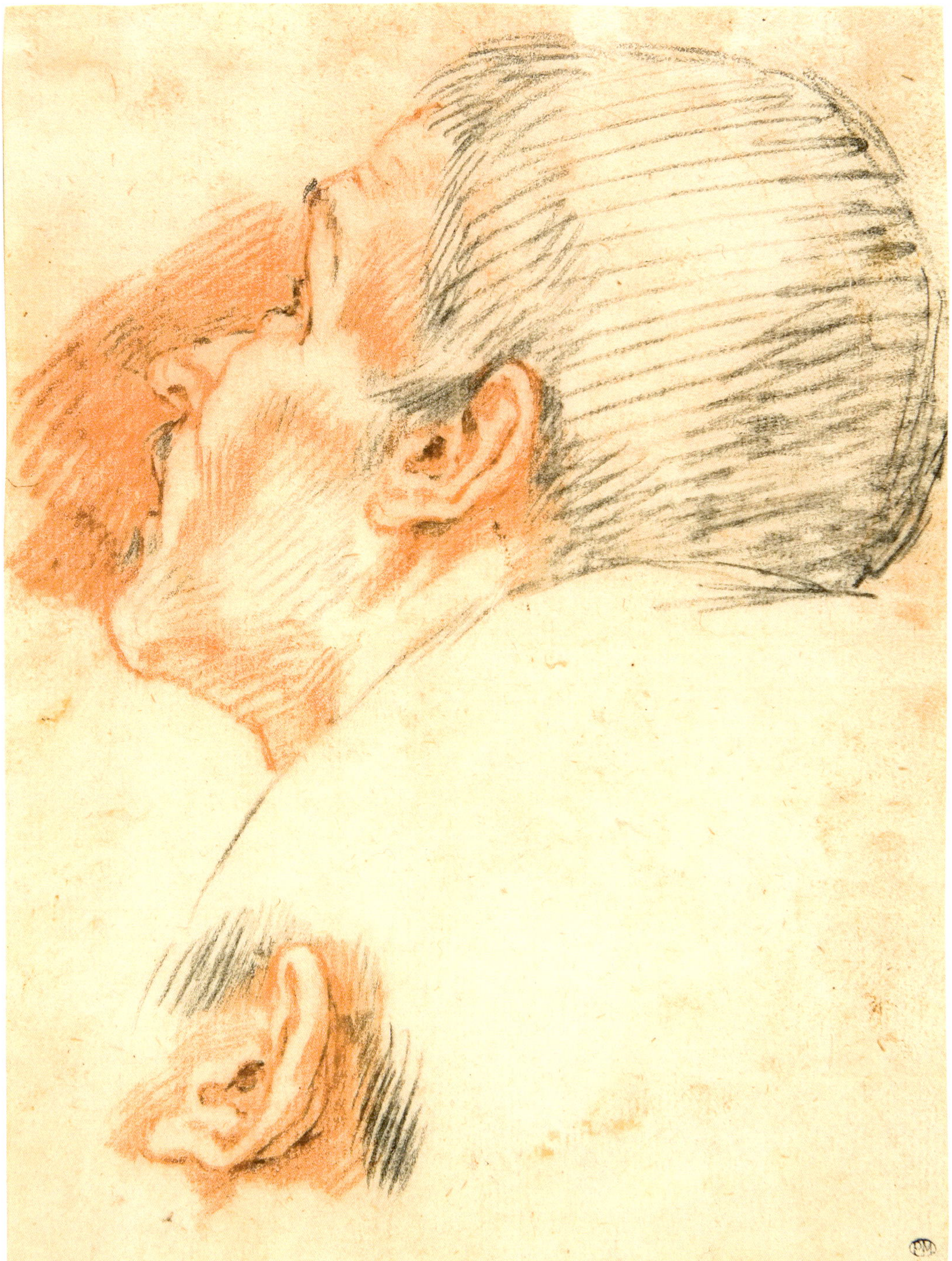

FRANCISCO HERRERA THE YOUNGER, CALLED "EL MOZO"

Seville, 1627–1685, Madrid

Francisco de Herrera e Hinestrosa, the son of Francisco de Herrera the Elder, was known as the Younger and sometimes called "el Mozo." The artist referred to himself as Don Francisco de Herrera y Aguilar and signed some of his work with that name.[1] Herrera the Younger studied with his father in Seville, joining the painters' guild there before 1648, just prior to departing for Rome, where he made engravings from about 1647 to 1650. He is documented in Madrid on February 7, 1650, presumably after his return from Rome. In 1653 he contracted to paint the high altarpiece of Saint Hermengild for the Carmelites in Madrid and then went to Seville to settle his father's estate; a lengthy legal process kept him in the city for several years, allowing him to reestablish a career there.

On December 19, 1655, Herrera joined the Confraternity of the Santísimo Sacramento del Sagrario at the Cathedral of Seville and was awarded several commissions thereafter. On January 11, 1660, as co-president with Bartolomé Esteban Murillo, the artist founded the academy of drawing and painting in Seville. He remained in Seville until August 3, 1660, when the Inquisition requested a picture of an auto-da-fé that occurred on April 13, 1660. He lost the commission because of the high price he demanded and returned to Madrid by November of that year. In 1663, Herrera secured several important commissions from Philip IV, including the cupola of the Church of Nuestra Señora de Atocha (destroyed), completed by 1665. Documents place him in Madrid in 1670, as *pintor de su majestad*, but in 1671 he was again in Seville, working on projects for the canonization of Ferdinand III, including designs for a reliquary urn to hold the saint's remains and for the etchings in a commemorative book by Fernando de la Torre Farfán. Once again in Madrid in 1672, Herrera designed stage sets for a performance of Vélez de Guevara's *Los celos hacen estrellas* for the queen's birthday, for which several detailed drawings survive (Österreichische Nationalbibliothek, Vienna).

Later that year, Herrera was appointed painter to Charles II (*pintor del rey*); in July 1677 he was promoted to Master of the Royal Works, a post he held until his death and one that determined a change in his artistic direction. In 1679 he oversaw decorations for the arrival of María Luisa de Orléans to wed Charles II and began work on a new design for the cathedral of Nuestra Señora del Pilar in Zaragoza. On July 18, 1680, a delegation of Spanish painters petitioned the king for a Spanish Academy to be established in Rome, appointing Herrera as the head of the academy in Madrid. His response to that petition (Biblioteca Nacional, Madrid) demonstrates his preference for an academy of architecture rather than painting, reflecting the change in his work at the end of his life. From April 1680 to 1682, Herrera was in Zaragoza, where he directed work on the Basilica of Nuestra Señora del Pilar. He returned to Madrid and died on August 25, 1685, at seventy-three.

FOLLOWER OF FRANCISCO HERRERA THE YOUNGER, CALLED "EL MOZO"

11. *Coronation of the Virgin*

Pen and brown ink with brush and brown wash, over black chalk, on beige laid paper, lined

28.4 x 19.2 cm. (11³⁄₁₆ x 7⁹⁄₁₆ in.)

Inscribed in blue pencil on verso: *323*

PROVENANCE: Mathias Polakovits, Paris and New York, stamp (Lugt 3561) recto, lower right, in black

REFERENCE: Princeton 2003, 122

EXHIBITIONS: Princeton 1995; Princeton 1997

Museum purchase, Laura P. Hall Memorial Fund and Fowler McCormick, Class of 1921, Fund 2002-93

This drawing appears to be a design for an oval ceiling painting; the figures are presented *di sotto in sù*, as if the viewer is meant to see the Virgin's coronation from below. Her right leg is especially foreshortened, with the foot thrusting forward on the edge of the cloud. Putti below are also foreshortened, adding to this effect, which was often employed by Francisco de Herrera the Younger in his major commissions, including *Triumph of San Hermengild* (Prado) and *Stigmatization of Saint Francis* (Seville Cathedral). Although many of the artist's paintings are lost, we have some records through contemporary accounts by Díaz del Valle and commission documents.

A similar drawing was lost in the destruction of the Instituto Jovellanos during the Spanish Civil War.[2] Because that drawing is known solely through photographs taken prior to 1936, it offers only a point of reference for such compositions among artists working in Madrid in the mid-seventeenth century. The iconography is the same as that of Princeton's drawing: God the Father and Christ hold two sides of a crown that they extend above the Virgin's head as she crosses her hands across her chest. Wash is freely applied on the Princeton drawing in a confident manner, emphasizing the movement of the figures, reinforcing the clouds upon which the Virgin rises, and suggesting an artist with academic training. Subtle differences in the composition, more likely due to a different hand than simply a different composition, point to a follower or pupil of Herrera the Younger as the author of the Princeton sheet, although it cannot be connected at this time with the work of his immediate circle or contemporaries. LAB

1 According to Spanish tradition, he could have used the name Herrera e Hinestrosa, after his father's and mother's surnames, but instead chose to use only his father's surname. Kinkead 1982a, 12.

2 Banner 2003; Banner 2006; and Pérez Sánchez and Lafuente Ferrari 2003.

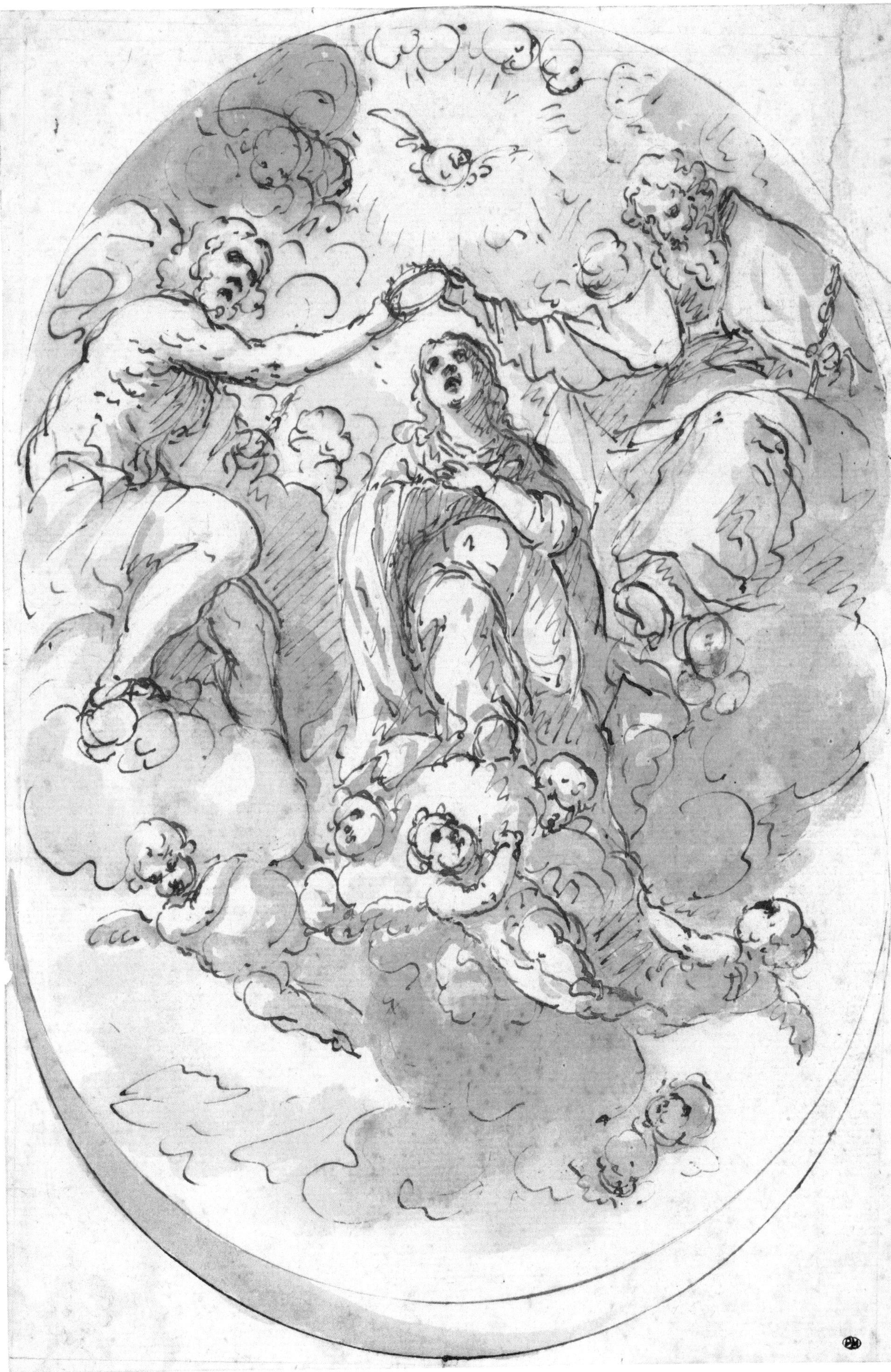

JERÓNIMO JACINTO ESPINOSA

Cocentaina, 1600–1667, Valencia

Born in 1600 in the Cocentaina region, Jerónimo Jacinto Espinosa was the son of a painter and the contemporary of some of the most renowned Spanish artists of the Golden Age: Ribera (born 1591), Zurbarán (born 1598), Velázquez (born 1599), and Alonso Cano (born 1601).[1] Espinosa frequently has been termed a "Valencian Zurbarán" for the simplicity of his compositions and the weighty naturalism of his figures.[2]

In 1915–16, Blasco Tramoyeres published most of the important dates of Espinosa's life from the study of archival documents.[3] Espinosa moved with his family to Valencia around 1612 and was enrolled in the Colegio de Pintores by 1616.[4] Jusepe Martínez suggested that Espinosa's formation and career, unlike those of Ribera, were entirely Valencian.[5] The period from 1640 to 1647, from which we have neither signed paintings nor documents recording his presence in Valencia, has prompted speculation of a possible trip to court, where he might have met Velázquez, or further travel to Seville, where he might have encountered Zurbarán or other contemporaries. Ceán Bermúdez posited a trip to Italy for Espinosa, but this is problematic and unlikely.[6]

In 1647, during an outbreak of the plague in Valencia, Espinosa made a pledge to San Luis Beltrán, and by 1655 the artist had completed a series of paintings for the chapel of San Luis Beltrán, as he promised to do if cured of illness. Espinosa's will was recorded on February 20, 1667, and his burial was noted in the church of Santo Domingo the next day.[7]

12. *Annunciation with Kneeling Donor*, 1658–60

Black chalk heightened with lead white (partially discolored), on laid paper prepared with brown opaque watercolor wash, incised with vertical and horizontal lines through center, lined

32.7 x 22.7 cm. (12⅞ x 8¹⁵⁄16 in.)

Inscribed in pen and brown ink, lower left: *Geronimo espinosa*

Provenance: Frank Jewett Mather Jr.

References: Vey and Salas 1965, 265; Pérez Sánchez 1972, 30; Lawrence 1974, 42, no. 19 ill.; Adela Espinós Díaz, *Catálogo de dibujos, Museo de Bellas Artes de Valencia, I (siglos XVI–XVII)* (Madrid, 1979), 53–84; Alfonso E. Pérez Sánchez, *Historia del dibujo español* (1986), 199–200 ill.; Angulo Íñiguez and Pérez Sánchez 1975–88, vol. 4, 29, no. 79, pl. XXIX; Valencia 2000, 82 ill. (reports that the drawing is in University of Pennsylvania [*sic*])

Exhibitions: Lawrence 1974, no. 19, ill.; Princeton 1995; Princeton 1997

Gift of Frank Jewett Mather Jr.
x1953-102

Espinosa repeatedly made use of the familiar composition shown here—of a kneeling donor experiencing a religious vision—in preparatory drawings for some of his most important paintings. As Alfonso Pérez Sánchez remarked, the Princeton drawing, with its stiff and formal composition, shares some aspects with the painting of the *Mass of Saint Gregory* (Museo del Prado, Madrid).[8] The figure of an angel descending at the right side of Princeton's sheet recalls the contorted descent of the angel in that painting, and, as a result, Pérez Sánchez has dated this drawing to an early period in the artist's career: 1624–34.[9] Espinosa repeated the descending angel again in a similar pose in an altarpiece of the *Sacrifice of Isaac* (Royal Parish of San Andrés, Valencia). The artist also depicted a similar figure of God the Father, again surrounded by angels, in *The Mass of Saint Gregory* and in the *Holy Family with Saint Joachim and Saint Anne* (Museo de Bellas Artes, Valencia).[10]

This important sheet can be compared to a signed drawing of the *Apparition of Christ to Saint Ignatius* in the Biblioteca Nacional, Madrid. The painting for which that drawing is preparatory is now in the Museo de Bellas Artes, Valencia, dated by Pérez Sánchez to 1658.[11] The final painting differs slightly from the signed preparatory drawing, but the similarity of the compositions and the signatures offer a point of comparison for the Princeton sheet and suggest a possible dating for this sheet to about 1658–60.

Best known for his religious compositions and altarpieces, Espinosa also painted a number of portraits of prominent Valencians, including the *Portrait of Dominican Fray Jerónimo Mos* (ca. 1627) at the Museo de Bellas Artes, Valencia. The kneeling figure of the donor at the right of the Princeton drawing appears to be a specific individual. The order of Montesa visible on the right side of the donor's cape indicates his membership in that order, but his identity has yet to be deciphered.[12] LAB

1 Valencia 2000, 19.
2 Many more drawings by Espinosa can be securely attributed. Those by Zurbarán are few in number and cannot be securely attributed.
3 Luis Tramoyeres Blasco, "El Pintor Jerónimo Jacinto de Espinosa," *Archivo de Arte Valenciano* 1, no. 4 (1915): 127–41; and 2, no. 1 (1916): 3–15; also Valencia 2000, 20–21.
4 Pérez Sánchez 1972, 14.
5 Valencia 2000, 22–23. Also see Martínez 1988.
6 Pérez Sánchez 1972, 16.
7 Valencia 2000, 67.
8 Ibid., 82.
9 Ibid., 82, no. 5.
10 Illustrated in ibid., 114.
11 Pérez Sánchez 1972, pl. 86.
12 Lawrence 1974, 42; Angulo Íñiguez and Pérez Sánchez 1975–88, vol. 4, 29, no. 79.

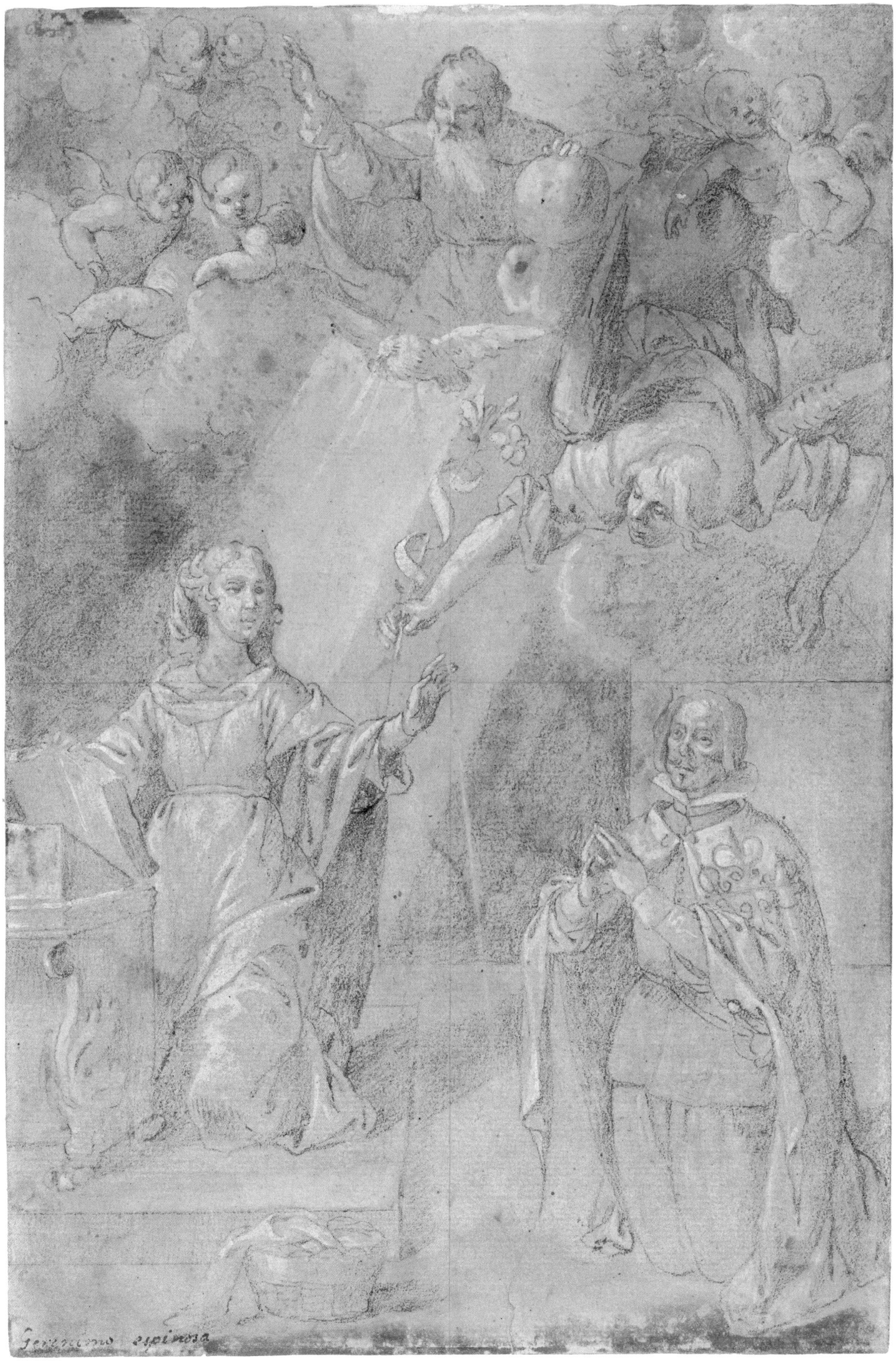

VICENTE SALVADOR GÓMEZ

Valencia, 1637–ca. 1680, Valencia

Vicente Salvador Gómez spent his career in Valencia, primarily engaged with religious commissions. Numerous drawings by the artist are known, including one in the Metropolitan Museum of Art, two at Ottawa, seven at the Prado, two at the British Museum, two at the Biblioteca Nacional, and several in the Museo de Bellas Artes, Valencia. All are in pen and ink with a similar herringbone cross-hatching technique; very few have wash added over the pen and ink drawing. Signed and dated drawings from the 1670s, including *Immaculate Conception* (s.d. 1674) and *Saint Embracing the Crucified Christ* (s.d. 1675), form a core group to which further attributions can be compared.[1] Although much of Salvador Gómez's work was religious, he also completed a commissioned pair of portraits of Alfonso V of Aragón and Juan II of Aragón for the Capilla de los Reyes in the Convento de los Predicadores (Convent of Saint Dominic, Valencia).[2]

Marco Antonio de Orellana's (1731–1813) biography of Valencian artists (first published in 1930) suggests that the artist studied drawing in the studio of Jerónimo Jacinto Espinosa, whose signed drawing *Annunciation with a Kneeling Donor* is also in Princeton's collection (cat. 12).[3] Salvador Gómez later worked for the Dominicans and the Jesuits in Valencia, completing religious commissions. Orellana also noted that a drawing of Delilah cutting Samson's hair was signed with the artist's profession: "Académico Mayor de la Academia de Santo Domingo"—establishing that the artist was a professor at the Academy of Saint Dominic in Valencia.

Salvador Gómez designed the frontispiece of *Montesa Ilustrada* (1669), a book published in Valencia with engravings by Pedro de Villafranca. The artist was noted absent from Valencia in documents of December 19, 1668, and April 16, 1669, and a hypothetical trip to Madrid could have occurred during this time.[4] An often-hypothesized trip to Italy may also have occurred but there is no definitive proof.[5]

In 1673, Salvador Gómez acquired books, prints, drawings, and models from the estate of Alonso Cano.[6] The following year he published *Cartilla y fundamentales reglas de Pintura*, which was intended as a training tool for artists.[7]

13. *Hercules in a Niche*

Pen and brown ink on lunette-shaped cream laid paper, laid down on cream laid paper prepared with light orange-pink wash

10.7 x 5.0 cm. (4 3/16 x 1 15/16 in.) (shown at 125% of actual size)

PROVENANCE: Mathias Polakovits, Paris and New York, stamp (Lugt 3561) recto, lower right in black

REFERENCE: Princeton 2003, 119

EXHIBITIONS: Princeton 1995; Princeton 1997; Princeton 2001

Museum purchase, Laura P. Hall Memorial Fund and Fowler McCormick, Class of 1921, Fund 2002-90

Drawings attributed to Salvador Gómez can be compared to those that are signed and dated: *The Immaculate Conception* (Museo del Prado, F.D. 1682) and *Saint Bernard Embracing Christ on the Cross* (British Museum, London, 1846-5-9-185).[8] *Saint Joseph and the Christ Child* (National Gallery of Canada, Ottawa, no. 18193) and *Virgin and Child Seated on a Cloud* (The Metropolitan Museum of Art, 1975.131.277), as well as *Saint Joseph and the Christ Child* (University of Michigan Museum of Art, 1960/2.14), are among the few other drawings by this artist in North America; all date to the 1670s.[9] Salvador Gómez's drawings are distinctive, with repeated intersecting diamond or herringbone patterns of hatching, as seen in this small sheet. Hercules stands naked except for the skin of the Nemean lion, which drapes over one shoulder and around his lower midriff, held in place by his right hand against his thigh. The lion's tail falls behind Hercules's leg, formed with two single, delicate lines that end in the tail's tuft. Over his shoulder Hercules holds the rough, bumpy club with which he killed the lion.

The border line around the composition and outlining are traits of the artist that are also seen in a pair of drawings in the Prado

(F.D. 1070 a and b). The way the foot of Hercules comes over the edge of the plinth on which he stands is similar to the way the puttis' feet dangle over the balustrade edge in *Saint Joseph and the Christ Child* (National Gallery of Canada, 18193), creating the illusion that the figure's foot intrudes into the viewer's space.

The subject of Princeton's drawing, Hercules, suggests that there may have been a royal connection for this small sketch. In 1634, Philip IV commissioned Zurbarán to decorate the Hall of Realms (Salón de Reinos) with the Labors of Hercules to commemorate his heroic feats and battles. In most cases, Zurbarán based his compositions on northern prints, especially those of Cornelis Cort.[10] The theme of Hercules and his Labors appears frequently in royal commissions for the Habsburgs, as they were considered to be descended from Hercules, legendary founder of Spain. Thus, the exploits of the demigod served as allegories for the antiquity of their dynasty.[11]

LAB

1 Brown 1973, 377 and 379 n. 23. The artist's death date has now been shown to be 1678, based on documentation of Salvador Gómez's last testament, burial, and post-mortem inventory. See Salort Pons, López Azorín, and Navarrete Prieto 2001.
2 Marco García 2006, 36.
3 Ibid., 32–33.
4 Ibid., 38.
5 Salort Pons, López Azorín, and Navarrete Prieto 2001, 393–424.
6 Marco García 2006, 88. Also see Véliz 2012, 238–41.
7 Brown 1973, 377.
8 Marco García reads the date as October 22, 1675; see Marco García 2006, 43.
9 Brown 1973, 377.
10 Brown 1991, 20–21.
11 Marie Tanner, *The Last Descendant of Aeneas: The Hapsburgs and the Mythic Image of the Emperor* (New Haven: Yale University Press, 1993), 288 n. 34.

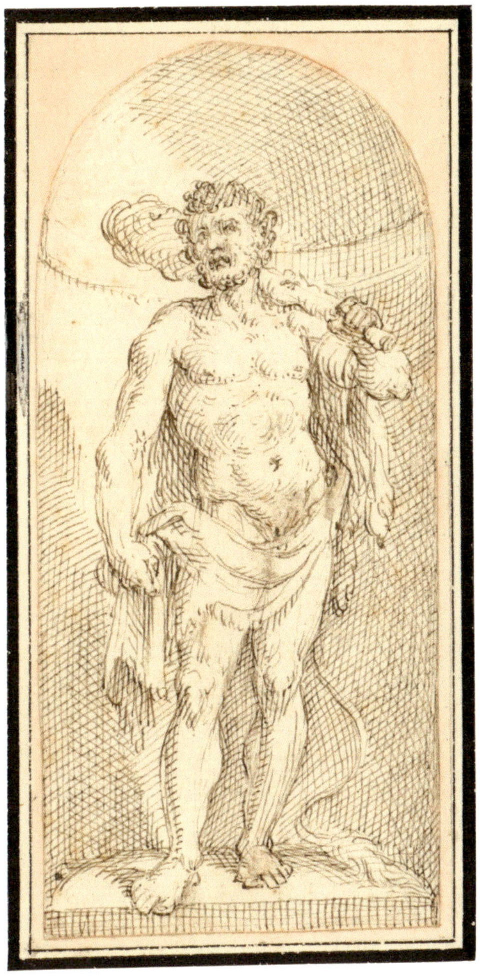

SEBASTIÁN DE HERRERA BARNUEVO

Madrid, 1619–1671, Madrid

A son of the sculptor Antonio Herrera (fl. 1621–d. 1646), Sebastián de Herrera Barnuevo was deeply influenced by the Andalusian artist Alonso Cano (1601–1667), who came to Madrid in 1638. Herrera Barnuevo collaborated with Cano on many projects, including royal commissions; as a result, several of the drawings that Cano made were once attributed to Herrera Barnuevo and vice versa.[1] Pérez Sánchez has remarked on the tendency to confuse drawings by the two artists, noting that Herrera Barnuevo's graceful and fluid use of wash and invention made his works similar to Cano's in some respects.[2] The artist also worked on several collaborations at court with Francisco Rizi (1608–1685), including preparations for Philip IV's 1649 marriage to his niece, Mariana of Austria, and in 1664 provided an *Allegory of the Death of Philip IV* (fig. 14.1) a frontispiece for a book of exequies to mark the sovereign's death.[3]

Herrera Barnuevo held many court posts in Madrid and at the Escorial, succeeding Juan Bautista Martínez del Mazo and preceding Juan Carreño de Miranda as *pintor de cámara*, or painter to the king. Documentary evidence survives concerning several of his commissions for Philip IV and later for Charles II, including the Heavenly and Earthly Trinities (Church of San Isidro, Madrid) and the main altarpiece of the church of the Agustinos Recoletos (Madrid), from which the central painting, *Triumph of Saint Augustine* (Museo del Prado, Madrid, on loan to San Francisco el Grande), survives.[4] His drawings for sculpture, as much as for architectural designs, are strong and distinctive, especially in the use of wash, and frequently include stylized female figures with long fingers.

Paintings and sculpture by the artist remain in situ in various churches in Madrid; many of the preparatory drawings for these commissions also survive, including distinctive drawings of *Saint Stanislaus Kostka* (Uffizi,

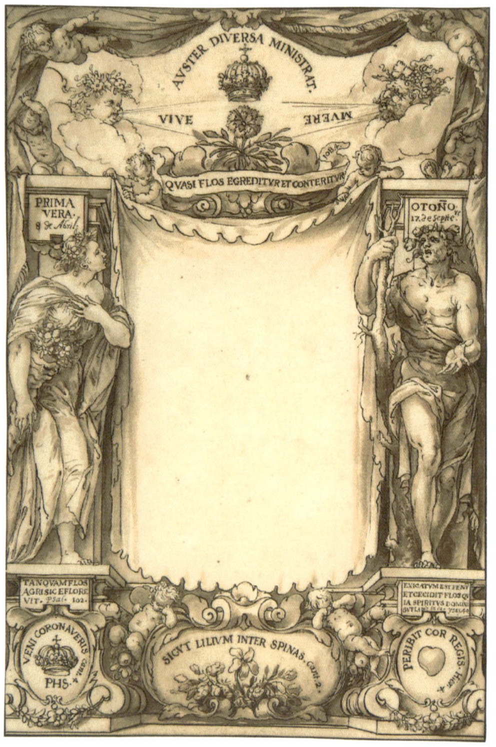

Fig. 14.1 Sebastián de Herrera-Barnuevo, Spanish, 1619–1671: *Allegory of the Death of Philip IV.* Pen and brown ink with brush and brown wash over traces of black chalk underdrawing, 24.3 x 15.9 cm. The Metropolitan Museum of Art, bequest of Harry G. Sperling, 1971 (1975.131.221).

Florence, inv. 10480S), the *Baldachin of San Isidro* (Biblioteca Nacional, Madrid), the *Virgin del Carmen*, and the *Ark of the Covenant* (Museo del Prado, Madrid). In 1653, Herrera Barnuevo completed an altarpiece dedicated to the Virgin of Guadalupe that is still in situ at the Descalzas Reales (Madrid) and for which many of the preparatory drawings of heroic women from the Old Testament survive, providing an ample body of work to which other drawings can be compared. Important sheets by the artist are found in the collections of the Metropolitan Museum of Art, the British Museum, the Musée du Louvre, the Biblioteca Nacional, the Museo Nacional del Prado, Fundación Lázaro Galdiano, the National Gallery of Canada, and elsewhere.

14. *Saint Nicholas of Tolentino*, ca. 1665

Pen and brown ink with brush and brown wash, over black chalk and traces of graphite (?), with incising, on beige laid paper, edge mounted

19.3 x 15.3 cm. (7 9/16 x 6 1/16 in.)

Inscription in the drawing on the book held by the central figure, spelled in reverse: "*PREC/EPTA/PARIS/MEI/SER/VAYI*"

WATERMARK: Unidentified lozenge shape, closed tulip flower or bud with leaves (see appendix)

PROVENANCE: Mathias Polakovits, Paris and New York, stamp (Lugt 3561) recto, lower right, in black

EXHIBITIONS: Princeton 1995; Princeton 1997

Museum purchase, Laura P. Hall Memorial Fund and Fowler McCormick, Class of 1921, Fund 2002-82

Saint Nicholas of Tolentino is represented here with a starburst on his breast, treading on the orb of the world and holding a book in one hand and a flowering crucifix in the other. An Augustinian saint, Nicholas of Tolentino was revered in Spain for his intercession on behalf of souls in purgatory. The souls at the bottom of the Princeton drawing are loosely based on Flemish print sources—for example, the frontispiece of Cornelius Curtius's life of Saint Nicholas of Tolentino, published in Antwerp in 1637 and based on the life of that saint written by Pietro da Monterubbiano.[5] Similar half-nude female and devil figures were later used in a frontispiece engraved by Pedro Villafranca (ca. 1615–1684), showing the allegorical triumph by Juan José de Austria over heresy.

In this allegorical rendering, the saint is represented triumphant and interceding on behalf of souls. The two figures chained to the globe at bottom represent souls enslaved in purgatory, still tied to the sins of the world.

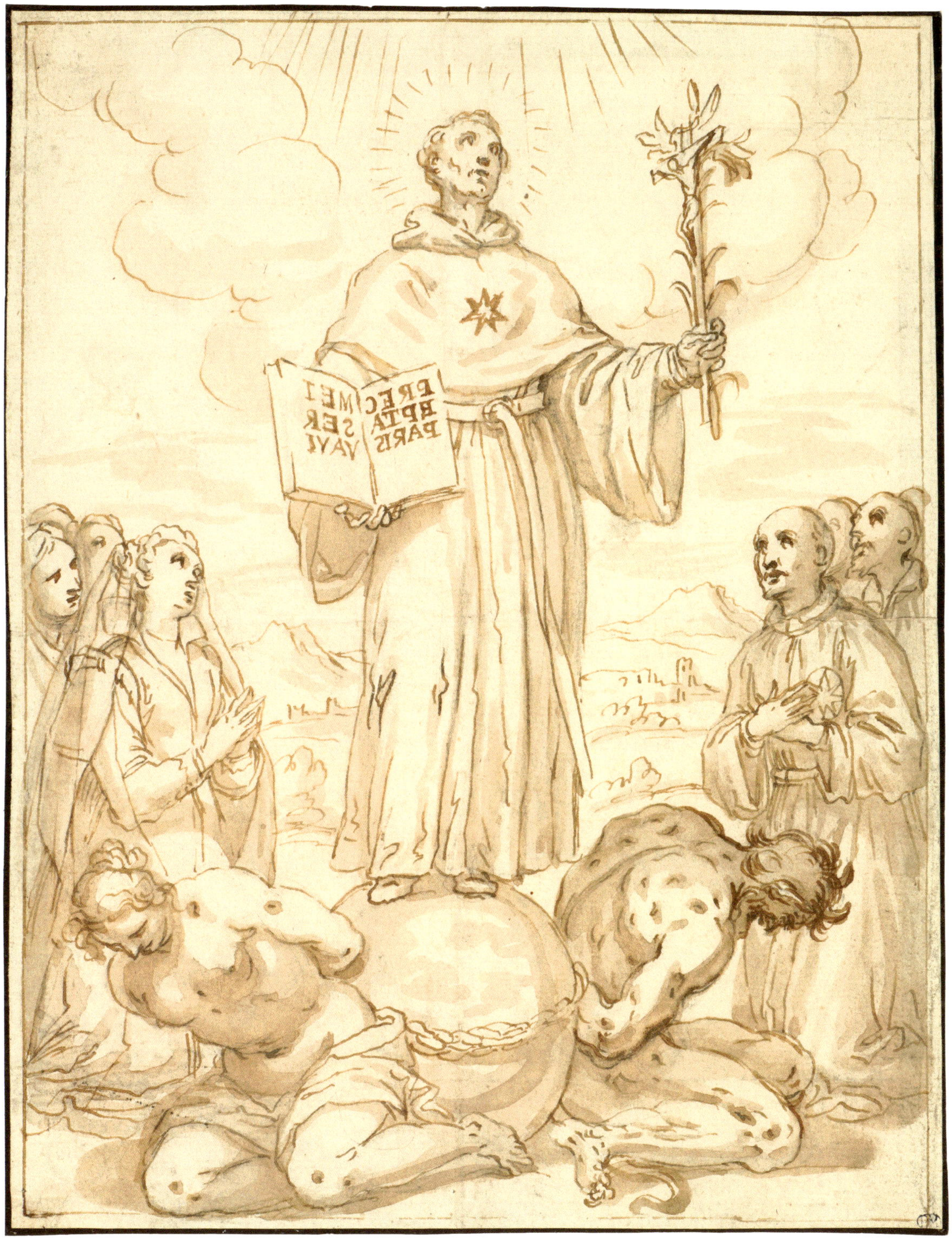

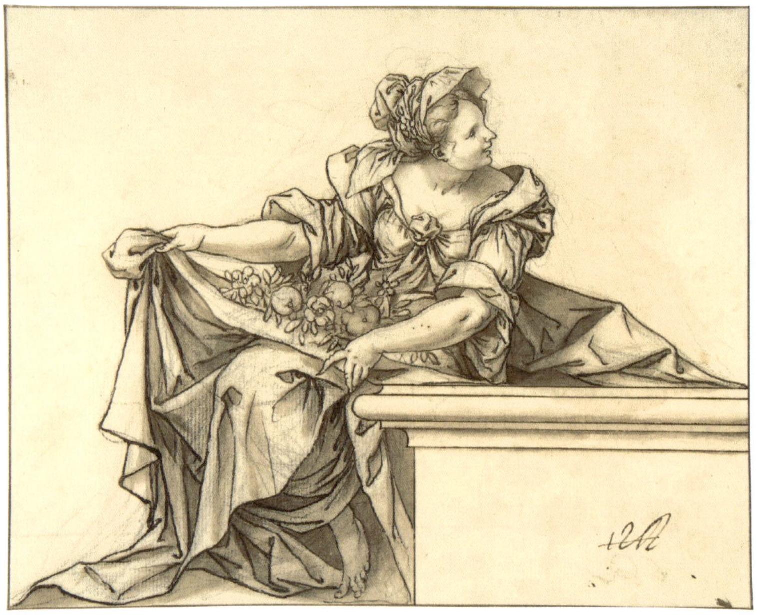

Fig. 14.2 Sebastián de Herrera Barnuevo, Spanish, 1619–1671: *Female Personification of Summer or Abundance.* Pen and brown ink with brush and brown wash over black chalk underdrawing on off-white paper, 21.3 x 26.8 cm. The Metropolitan Museum of Art, bequest of Harry G. Sperling, 1971 (1975.131.222).

Both figures have the same kind of dimpled flesh, indicated with short flicks, and small dots of wash on knees, elbows, and clavicles as well as all over the man's back, a technique used by Herrera Barnuevo in other drawings to show puckering of flesh at a joint or depression under the skin. The characteristic spread toes of the female figure at left can be compared to those of *Female Personification of Abundance* (fig. 14.2), a more finished drawing for a documented commission.

Sebastián de Herrera Barnuevo's allegorical frontispiece design for the book of exequies for Philip IV was completed in 1666 and engraved by Pedro de Villafranca y Malagón. Because of Saint Nicholas of Tolentino's intercession on behalf of souls in purgatory, Princeton's drawing may also have been designed for a book of exequies, or Augustinian sermons, perhaps dating from around the time of the king's death; a completed project relating to Princeton's drawing has not yet been found.

Typical of Herrera Barnuevo, the highly finished quality of this drawing in wash over black chalk suggests that the artist prepared designs for printmaking as works of art in their own right. This drawing shows evidence that it was likely made for a print, as the writing appears backward, incising is visible with raking light along some lines, and the verso of the sheet has been blackened for transfer, suggesting that this drawing was used, although no print after the drawing is known at present.

A watermark in the center of the sheet, in the form of a bud or tulip shape with two leaves, is unidentified. While the borderline around the composition was likely drawn for the technical reference to the size of the plate onto which the drawing would be transferred, it is also used to finish this composition. Drawn with a straight edge, the borderline in pen and brown ink is broken at top right to allow for rays of divine light to enter the space and surround Nicholas of Tolentino's head, adding Herrera Barnuevo's own innovation to the composition.

LAB

1 Véliz 2011. See Pérez Sánchez 1986, 252–58, for historiography on the artist. Herrera Barnuevo was so close to Cano that the younger man was named in Cano's will, signed in 1667. Madrid 2006–7a, 170–71. Ceán Bermúdez 1800, vol. 2, 286–88. Agulló y Cobo 1987, 12, 19, 24 n. 16.

2 Pérez Sánchez 1986, 252–58. Also see New York 2010–11, 42–50; and Madrid 2006–7a, 170–74.

3 Pascual Chenel 2009, 4ff. New York 2010–11, 104–5. Véliz 2012, 104–5. Navarrete Prieto, Zapata Fernández de la Hoz, and Martínez Ripoll 2008, 114–15.

4 New York 2010–11, 47. Ceán Bermúdez 1800, vol. 2, 286–88.

5 Cornelis Cort, *S. Nicolaus Tolentinus aliique aliquot eiusdem oedinis beati* (Antwerp: Joannes Cnobbarus, 1637). A copy of this book was included in the exhibition at Villanova University in 2005: *Thomas of Villanova—450 Years and Nicolas of Tolentine—700 Years: An Exhibit Commemorating Two Augustinian Saints.* Falvey Memorial Library, Villanova University, Villanova, Penn., Aug. 15–Sept. 30, 2005. Pascual Chenel 2009, 4–26, no. 82.

JOSÉ JIMÉNEZ DONOSO

Consuegra, ca. 1638(?)–1690, Madrid

José Jiménez Donoso went to Madrid early in his career, as an apprentice to Francisco Fernández (1605–1646), an obscure pupil of Vicente Carducho (1576/78–1638). According to Antonio Palomino, when Fernández died in 1646 the young Donoso went to Rome, where he studied in the academies.[1] The artist left Rome by 1657, and no documentation of his activity in Spain from 1657 to 1666 has surfaced.[2] In a document dated June 17, 1678, Donoso asserted that he was a resident of Madrid and "forty years of age, more or less," suggesting a 1638 date for his birth.[3]

Known as both a painter and an architect, Donoso specialized in decorative wall paintings and frescos, many of which are no longer extant. One of the few surviving documented fresco commissions is *Foundation of the Lateran Basilica* (Museo de Bellas Artes, Valencia), completed about 1666 for the Valencian Order of Mercy's chapel of San Juan de Letrán.[4] Donoso likely returned to Madrid in the 1670s, when he worked with Juan Carreño (1614–1685) to perfect his technique and later with Claudio Coello (1642–1693) on several fresco commissions in Toledo and Madrid.[5] With Coello and Matías de Torres (1635–1711), Donoso was commissioned to decorate the queen's apartments in the royal palace according to designs by Francisco de Herrera the Younger.[6] He and Coello also signed several legal documents together regarding payment for ephemeral decorations for the queen's entry into Madrid in 1680.[7] Another of Donoso's few extant commissions that remain in situ is the painted grand staircase at the Monasterio de las Descalzas Reales, Madrid. Of the drawings known by the artist, those that are securely by his hand have been connected with documented commissions. Perhaps the best known is the sketch for *Our Lady of Victory*, a preparatory drawing for the church of the convent of Saint Francis de Paul in Madrid (1682).[8]

ARTIST UNKNOWN, MADRID SCHOOL, FOLLOWER OF JOSÉ JIMÉNEZ DONOSO

15. *Hagar and Ishmael Visited by the Angel*

Pen and brown ink over black chalk on cream laid paper, lined

17.9 x 13.6 cm. (6 15/16 x 5 5/16 in.)

PROVENANCE: Possibly Paul Lefort, Paris; Dal Zotto, Venice (according to Janos Scholz, who identified this provenance based on the heavy black border mount); Frank Jewett Mather Jr.

REFERENCES: Lefort 1869, 12, no. 4, as "Anonyme. *Agar dans le désert.* Joli dessin à la plume, lavé de bistre, h. 20 c; l. 14 c."; Gibbons 1977, no. 893, as "Venetian, Eighteenth century"

EXHIBITIONS: Princeton 1995; Princeton 1997

Gift of Frank Jewett Mather Jr.
X1947-135

This drawing was long considered to be Venetian, with attributions to Giovanni Battista Pittoni (1687–1767) and Gaspare Diziani (1689–1767), and was catalogued as such by Felton Gibbons.[9] Prior to its acquisition by Frank Jewett Mather Jr., the drawing may have been in the collection of the prominent French collector of Spanish drawings, Paul Lefort.[10] Although the Lefort drawing was described as being of pen and ink and wash, the Princeton drawing does not have wash; a glossy transparent coating, however, gives the appearance of wash as described in the Lefort catalogue. The edges were cut at some point after the Lefort sale, slightly reducing the drawing to its current size without altering its vertical orientation.

In style, the drawing resembles both the rapid pen and ink drawings attributed to Pedro Atanasio Bocanegra (1638–1689) and drawings attributed to Jiménez Donoso.[11] Bocanegra was an accomplished follower of Alonso Cano (1601–1667); his *Saint Jerome Visited by an Angel with a Trumpet* (Uffizi, Florence, inv. no. 10103 S.) is reproduced frequently and provides a sense of his energetic and loose penmanship.[12] In composition, however, Princeton's sheet has more in common with *The Dream of Saint Joseph* (fig. 15.1)

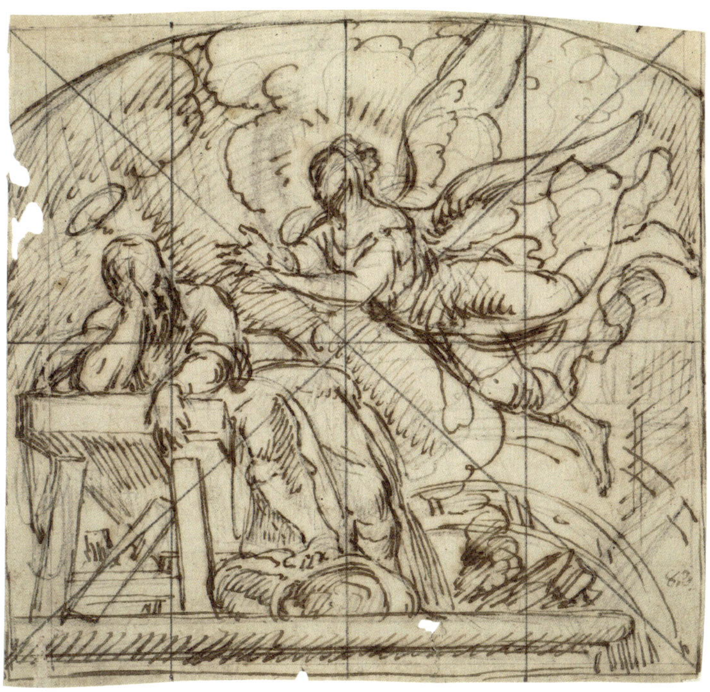

Fig. 15.1 Attributed to José Jiménez Donoso, Spanish, ca. 1638(?)–1690: *Design for a Ceiling Fresco: The Dream of Saint Joseph.* Pen and brown ink over graphite, squared for transfer in graphite, 16.7 x 17.9 cm. Museum of Fine Arts, Boston, Harvey D. Parker Collecction (97.651).

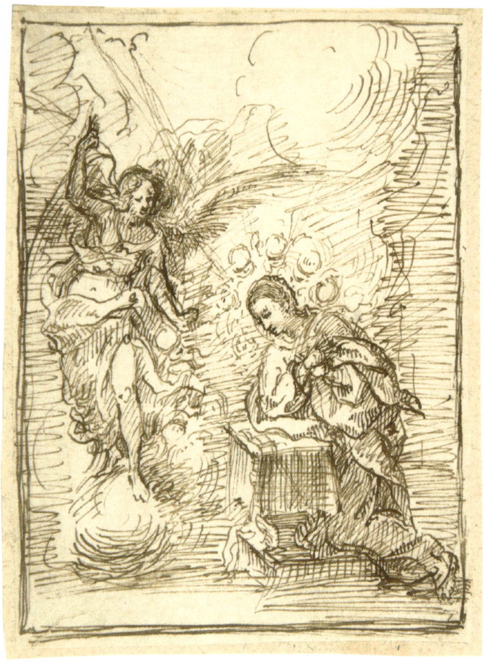

Fig. 15.2 Spanish, School of Seville: *The Annunciation*, 17th century. Pen and dark brown ink; composition outlined in the same, by the artist. On off-white paper, 14.5 x 10.7 cm. The Metropolitan Museum of Art, gift of Mr. and Mrs. William B. Jaffe, 1956 (56.235.13).

attributed to Jiménez Donoso, in which a flying heavenly figure visits a seated one; here, the treatment of the clouds and the fluid understanding of bodies beneath drapery more closely resembles the draftsmanship in Princeton's drawing than in Bocanegra's work. Donoso's pen style is more open and loose than that of Bocanegra, who modeled his handling of pen and ink closely on drawings by Alonso Cano, used dark brown ink, and frequently added brown wash to his figures.

In Princeton's *Hagar and Ishmael Visited by the Angel*, the angel's pose, with a twisting body, raised arm, and bent knees, demonstrates an understanding of the soaring pose of Saint Hermengild in Herrera the Younger's masterpiece for the Carmelites of San Hermenegildo in Madrid (Museo del Prado, Madrid, inv. no. P00833), completed in 1654, suggesting that the artist might have been familiar with that painting and thus was active in Madrid after the mid-seventeenth century.[13] The torsion of the angel, the overall sketchy pen quality, and the light brown ink also appear to be influenced by Herrera el Mozo's electric and rapid drawings. A number of artists in the academy of Seville, founded by Murillo and Herrera el Mozo, executed drawings in this style (fig. 15.2), copying elements from Murillo's composition of the *Annunciation*, especially the vertically descending angel. A similar descending angel with a raised arm appears in Donoso's drawing at the Hispanic Society.[14] LAB

1 Véliz 2012, 116. Palomino 1987, 286–89.
2 Véliz 2012, 116. Palomino 1987, 287.
3 Agulló y Cobo 2006, 150–51.
4 Ceán Bermúdez 1800, vol. 6, 8–13.
5 Madrid 2006–7a, 191.
6 Zapata Fernández de la Hoz 2010, 488.
7 Agulló y Cobo 2006, 85.
8 Véliz 2012, 116. Ponz, 1947, vol. 5, 491. Madrid 2006–7a, 191.
9 Gibbons 1977, no. 873. In 1980, Mary Cazort first suggested the drawing might be Spanish, and the attribution was changed to follower of Francisco de Herrera the Younger on the advice of Jonathan Brown in 1993.
10 Although its attribution was uncertain at the time, the subject, which was quite unusual in Spanish drawings, the dimensions, and the description suggest that this is the same drawing. As indicated by the conservation report, the drawing's edges have been cut down, explaining the slight difference from the dimensions recorded in Lefort.
11 Florence 1972, 86, no. 92, 69 ill., "Bocanegra, San Girolamo."
12 Ibid.
13 Brown 1998, 194–95 ill., *Triumph of Saint Hermengild.*
14 The drawing is a promised gift to the Hispanic Society. See Madrid 2006–7a, 191–95. The Academy, and the influence of Murillo's drawing style, is discussed in Peter Cherry, "Murillo's Drawing Academy," in Stratton-Pruitt et al. 2002, 47–60. Also see Brown 2012, 27–29.

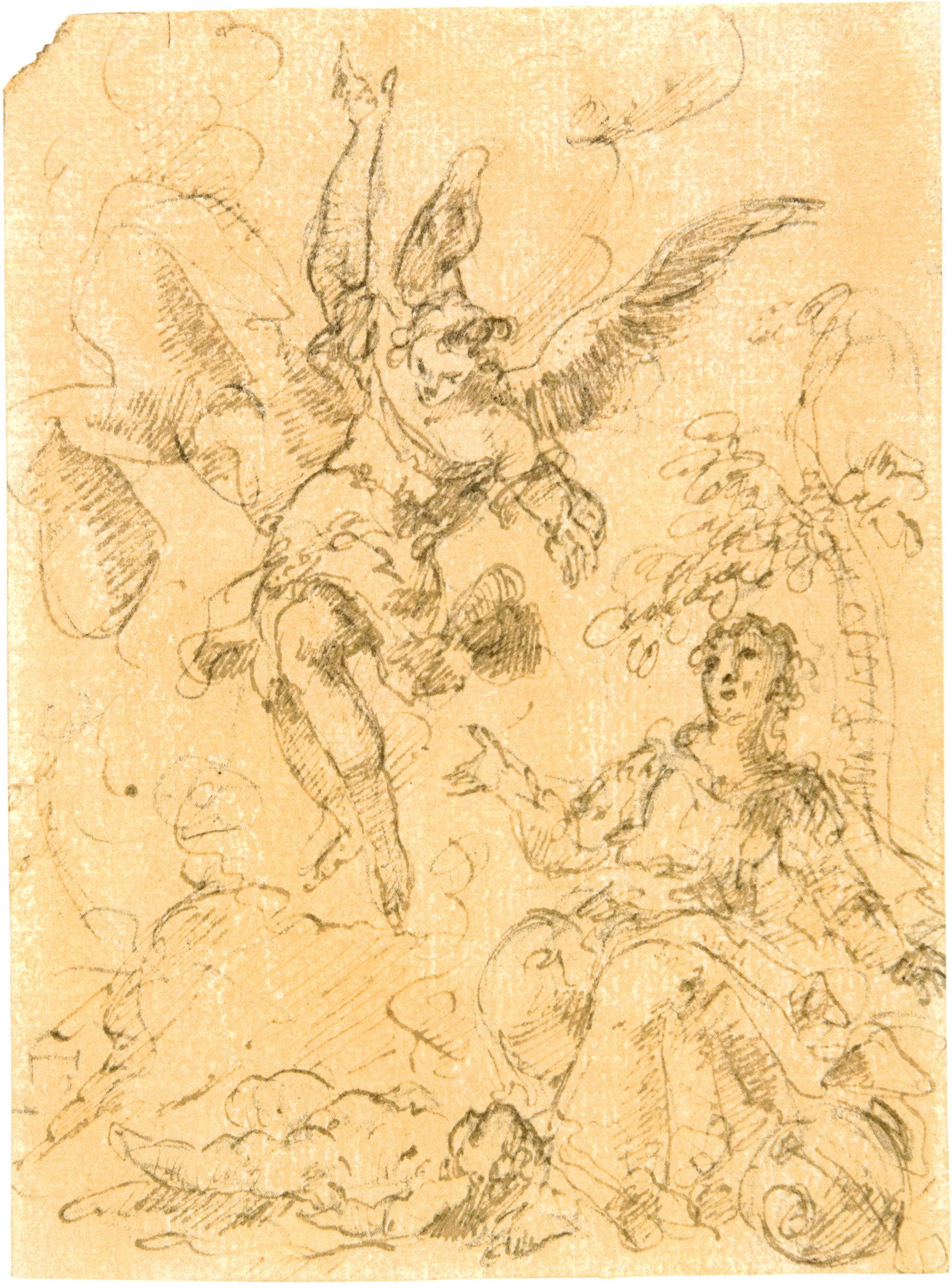

FELIPE GÓMEZ DE VALENCIA

Granada, ca. 1634–ca. 1694, Granada

What little is known of Felipe Gómez de Valencia's biography comes from Antonio Palomino's *Lives*, and our understanding of him as a draftsman is based on a handful of signed and inscribed drawings, which have formed the basis for further attributions to Gómez and informed our knowledge of his technique. He was a student of Miguel Jerónimo de Cieza (1611–1685), a painter from Granada who was in turn a pupil of Alonso Cano (1601–1667). Apparently Gómez worked and painted for most of his career in Granada, particularly for the church of San Antón.

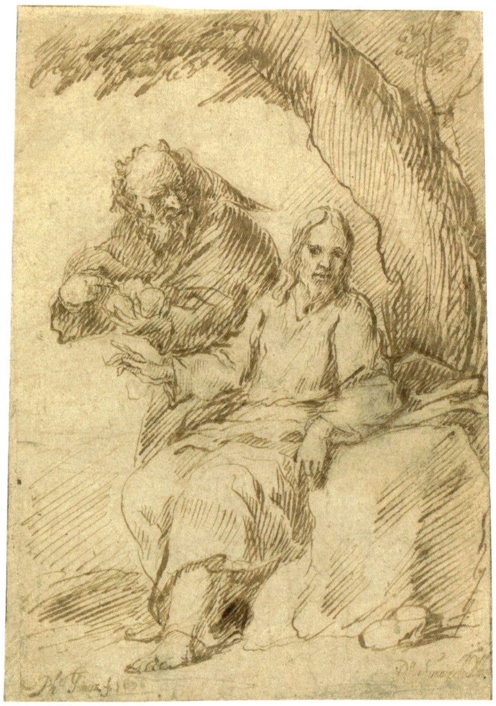

Fig. 16.1. Felipe Gómez de Valencia, Spanish, ca. 1634–1694: *The Temptation of Christ in the Desert*, probably 1676. Pen and brown ink on laid paper, 21.9 x 15.8 cm. National Gallery of Art, Andrew W. Mellon Fund (1977.34.1).

16. *Saint Francis of Assisi*, ca. 1675

Pen and brown ink over black chalk and graphite on beige laid paper, pieced

21.4 x 18.0 cm. (8 7/16 x 7 1/16 in.)

Inscribed in pen and brown ink, lower left corner: *Phelipe Gomes f.*

PROVENANCE: Mathias Polakovits, Paris and New York, stamp (Lugt 3561) recto, lower right, in black

EXHIBITIONS: Princeton 1995; Princeton 1997; Princeton 2001

Museum purchase, Laura P. Hall Memorial Fund and Fowler McCormick, Class of 1921, Fund 2002-89

Few drawings—those with a signature and often a date—can be securely attributed to Felipe Gómez de Valencia. Despite his name, Gómez seems to have first studied in Granada rather than in the Levant. The artist emulated the draftsmanship of other Andalusian artists of the same period, using a reed pen and similar techniques.[1] The secure drawings of Gómez loosely resemble those of Francisco Herrera the Elder (ca. 1590–ca. 1656), whose pen and brown ink and distinctive hatching technique were widely copied by his followers.[2] Notable characteristics of this work include the use of reed pens of varying thickness, the combination of light and darker brown inks, and a layering technique of hatching that forms folds and shadows. Among the secure drawings, several are inscribed with Gómez's name, in what appears to be a signature; in some cases, this is paired with an inscription or dedication line of sorts: "Pa. Simon de Llanes" (fig. 16.1) and "P.a Dionisio Sanchez" (Kupferstichkabinett, Berlin, KdZ 27666).

The drawing at Princeton has undergone restoration at the lower left corner, where the artist's name is inscribed, making discussion and attribution of this sheet problematic, as the inscription seems to have been torn and repaired. Lighter, shorter strokes of hatching along the folds of drapery were likely made with a reed pen. There are also reinforced herringbone hatch marks, which darken the shadows beside the figure and at the upper left corner. The lightly rendered hatching, visible along the bottom of the figure and in the cord on his robe, resembles the finely wrought hatching on other drawings by Gómez's hand and is also drawn in a lighter color of brown ink. Princeton's sheet has been reworked, however, at the top left corner in particular, perhaps obscuring an earlier idea in red chalk. Throughout the drawing, there is evidence of correction in a different, darker ink. The artist worked over passages drawn previously with a pen and light brown ink, then reinforced lines in darker ink that mixes gray and brown tonalities. The drawing bears the mark of the artist's self-correction, as if he were mastering the hatching and reconsidering his composition.

Other drawings by Gómez vary in the handling of pen and ink, suggesting an evolution in the artist's style and use of media. For example, the simple pen and ink with wash drawing at Berlin is signed "Ph.e Gomez f. 1674" and "Pa. Dionisio Sanchez," but the rest of the attributed drawings, one of which is dated 1676 and two of which are dedicated to Simón de Llanes, are executed in a technique using parallel strokes.[3] LAB

1 The use of the reed pen was studied by Elizabeth du Gué Trapier in Trapier 1942. Also see Véliz 2012, 214–21.

2 See the discussion on the followers in Angulo Íñiguez and Pérez Sánchez 1975–88, vol. 3, 18–31.

3 Nothing is currently known about Dionisio Sánchez or Simón de Llanes, who may have been fellow artists, collectors, or simply friends of the artist.

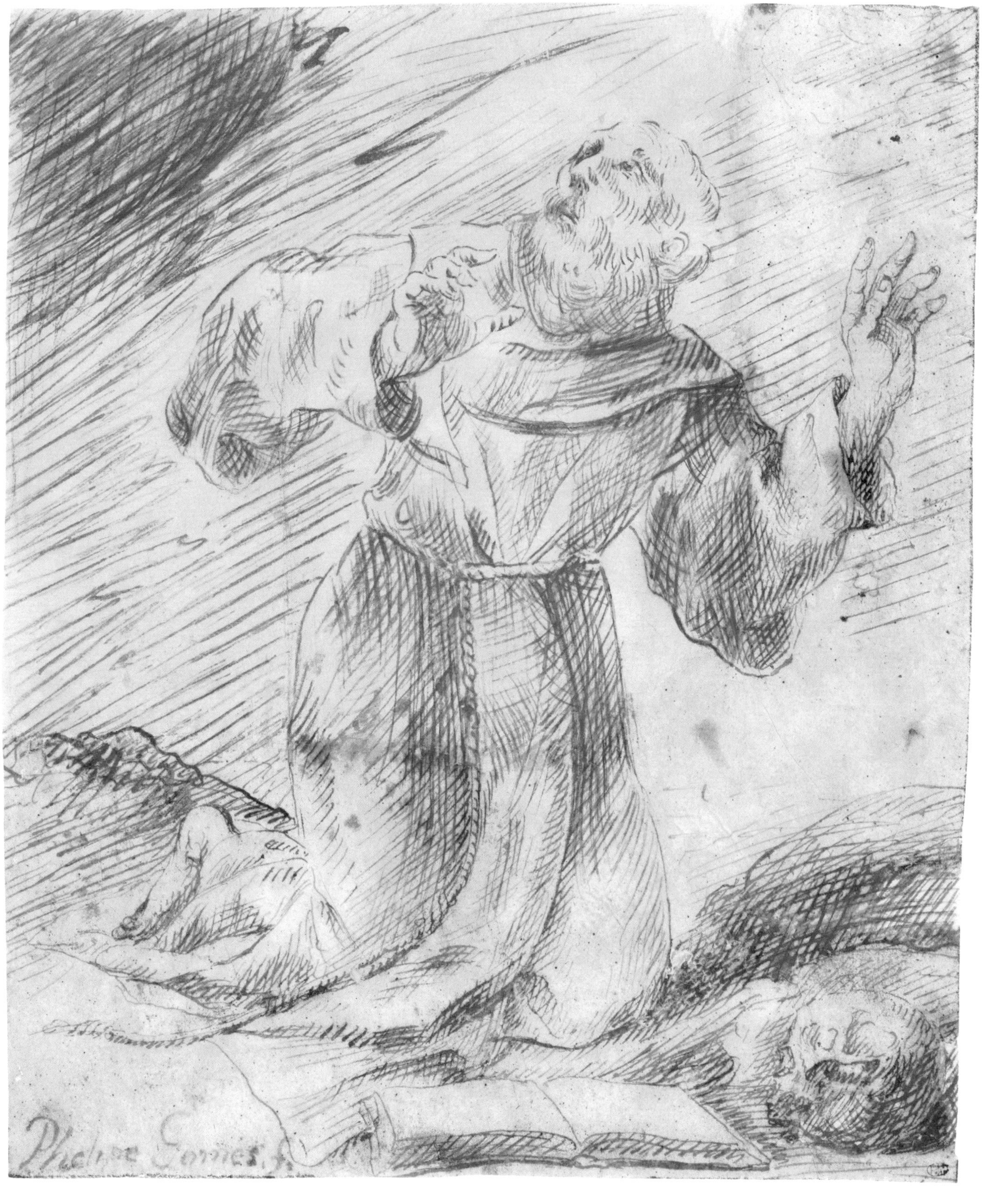

MATÍAS DE ARTEAGA Y ALFARO

Villanueva de los Infantes, Ciudad Real, 1633–1703, Seville

Matías de Arteaga y Alfaro, a painter and engraver, studied with Juan Valdés Leal (1622–1690) in Seville, engraved the paintings of both Herrera the Younger and Valdés Leal, and copied their drawings for engravings.[1] Working with these artists in 1671 and 1672, Arteaga y Alfaro engraved prints for the festival book of Torre Farfán, *Fiestas de la Santa Iglesia Metropolitana y Patriarcal de Sevilla al Nuevo culto del Señor Rey San Fernando el Tercero de Castilla y de León.*[2] Ceán Bermúdez also noted more than fifty-eight prints by Arteaga of the life of San Juan de la Cruz (Biblioteca Nacional, Madrid), which include such colorful scenes from the saint's life as the *Miracle of the Asparagus.*

From 1660 to 1673, Arteaga was among the artists in the Seville Academy, serving as secretary in 1666 and consul in 1669.[3] In addition to the founding members Murillo, Valdés Leal, Herrera the Younger, and Arteaga, others documented as members include Jerónimo Bobadilla (1619–1709), Francisco Meneses Osorio (ca. 1640–1721), and Ignacio de Iriarte (1620–1685).[4] According to Ceán Bermúdez, Arteaga was enamored of perspectival views of architecture and frequently included "temples, palaces, streets or gardens" in his paintings.[5] Most of his work remains in Seville, some in situ, including the series of nine paintings of the Eucharist that Arteaga completed in 1690 for the Sacramental Brotherhood of the Sacristy (Hermandad Sacramental del Sagrario) of the Cathedral.[6]

Because of his involvement with Valdés Leal's projects, Arteaga's drawings have at times been confused with those of the older artist. Recent reexamination of the artistic personality of Valdés Leal, his drawings, and his relationship to other artists active in Seville has subtly separated his drawings from those of his immediate circle, collaborators, and followers.[7] Drawings attributed to Arteaga are in the collections of the Courtauld Gallery (D.52.RW.35), the Hispanic Society (LA413), the Musée du Louvre (inv. RF42641), and the Real Academia Española).[8] The Louvre's drawing, considered the most secure work by his hand, has served as the touchstone for the other attributions.[9]

ATTRIBUTED TO MATÍAS DE ARTEAGA Y ALFARO OR HIS IMMEDIATE CIRCLE

17. *Adoration of the Shepherds*

Pen and brown ink with brush and brown wash, on beige laid paper, lined

15.6 x 13.3 cm. (6⅛ x 5¼ in.)

Inscribed in pen and brown ink, center right, above two shepherds: *A*; in graphite, lower right corner: *1183*; inscribed on verso in graphite at center: *J. de las Roelas Spanish / Coll Hone*; in pen and brown ink, lower right: *SW 264*

WATERMARK: Letters, V or A (possibly on secondary support)

PROVENANCE: Nathaniel Hone (d. 1784), stamp (Lugt 88a) recto, lower right, in black; Connecticut private collection; sale, Kende Galleries, Inc., New York, May 5, 1950, 10, lot 37

REFERENCE: *Old Master Drawings of the XV–XIX Century, The Property of a Connecticut Private Collector,* Kende Galleries, Inc., New York (exh. cat., 10, no. 37)

EXHIBITIONS: Princeton 1995; Princeton 1997

Museum purchase
x1950-24

When it was acquired by the Princeton University Art Museum in 1950, this drawing was attributed to Juan de las Roelas (1558–1625), as was another drawing obtained at the same time.[10] Paintings by Juan de las Roelas are often complex religious allegories, filled with figures, and only one drawing—completely different from the careful and slender figures executed here—is currently attributed to his hand. The slender figures instead are characteristic of Arteaga's drawing style.

On Princeton's sheet, the inclusion of two naked shepherds among the group approaching the Christ child is unusual and suggests an artist who was concerned with correct anatomy, even if his slope-shouldered figures did not quite achieve a post-renaissance ideal. At the far right, the upper body of the shepherd who is bent at the waist is exactly as long as his lower body, and the tiny feet do not seem capable of supporting this willowy figure. An "A" inscribed at center right marks the vanishing point, demonstrating that this is the work of a draftsman interested in architecture and setting, perhaps to the detriment of his rendering of figures.[11] If the drawing is indeed by Arteaga's hand, the "A" marking the vanishing point might also be the artist's monogram.

Of the drawings attributed to Arteaga, that in the Louvre (inv. RF42641) is cited for comparison most frequently. Arteaga's drawings often feature slender figures with long torsos and short legs, placed within an architectural setting, rendered in wash, and then reinforced with pen and ink. Often the architectural background is shaded only in wash so that it appears to recede.

The resemblance to Juan Valdés Leal is seen in the nine drawings attributed to that artist in the Louis Philippe sale of 1852; an additional six drawings were attributed there to his son, Lucas de Valdés, among a heavy representation of Seville School artists.[12] Distinguishing one hand from the other is complicated by the fact that Lucas de Valdés used his father's drawings to prepare compositions that the older artist was unable to complete.[13] Valdés Leal frequently depicted small figures with long torsos punctuated by the navel, relatively short legs, and small feet, a conceit that focuses on the expression and action in the upper body. His technique often combined brush and brown wash with pen and ink drawing. The delicacy of Princeton's drawing and the lightness of the application of wash also suggest an artist closer to the technique of Valdés Leal and the last third of the seventeenth century.

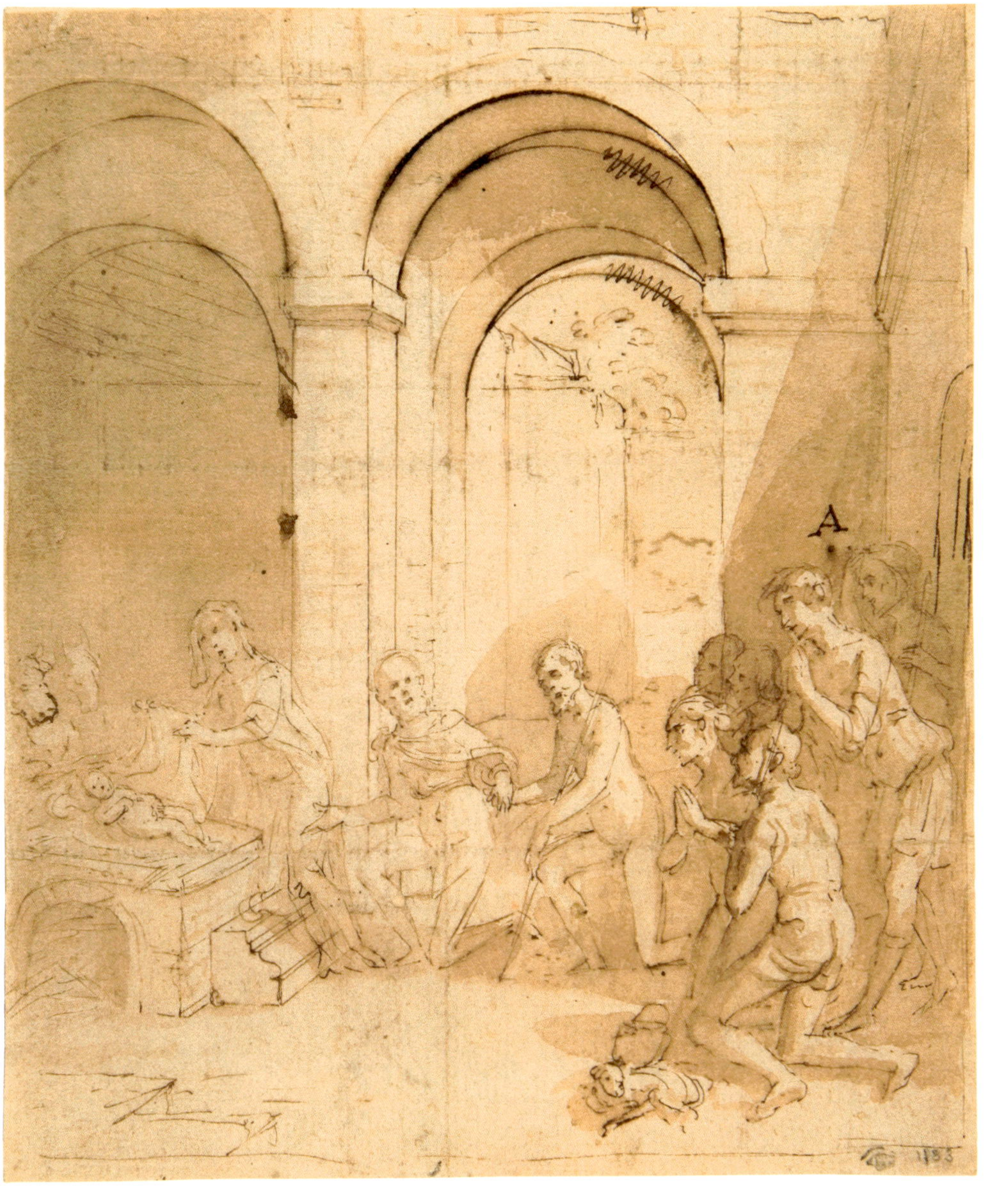

An architectural setting making use of ruled lines and extensive detail is characteristic of the few drawings currently attributed to Arteaga, including one at the Louvre, one at the Real Academia Española (Madrid, former Rodríguez Moñino-Brey collection), and one at the Hispanic Society (LA413). On the verso of the Princeton sheet are two inscriptions: one attributes the drawing to "J. de las Roelas/ Spanish/Coll. Hone" and the other is a combination of letters and numbers, "SW 264," written in a delicate hand in pen and brown ink. The second does not correlate with any mark currently listed in Lugt.[14] LAB

1 Ceán Bermúdez 1800, vol. 1, 77–78.
2 Madrid 2006–7a, 211ff.
3 Ceán Bermúdez 1800, vol. 1, 77–78; and Madrid 2006–7a, 211–12. Muller cites different dates for Arteaga's involvement in the Academy. Ceán Bermúdez explicitly reports 1666 and 1669. Brown 2012, 27–29. Peter Cherry, "Murillo's Drawing Academy," in Stratton-Pruitt et al. 2002, 47–60.
4 Pérez Sánchez 1986, 298–99.
5 Ceán Bermúdez 1800, vol. 1, 77–78. Brown 1983b, 407.
6 Madrid 2006–7a, 211–12.
7 Zapata Fernández de la Hoz 2010, 482–97; Madrid 2006–7a, 211–15; and Véliz 2012, 158–60. Among the followers were Arteaga y Alfaro, Francisco Meneses Osorio (ca. 1640–1721), and Valdés Leal's son, Lucas Valdés (1622–1725), who had similar working methods and collaborated with Valdés Leal on projects.
8 Madrid 2002a, fig. 72.
9 Brown 1983c, 407, no. 21. Also see Kinkead 1982b, 257–58.
10 The second drawing, x1950-25, has been reattributed to Andrea Boscoli by Laura Giles. The Kende catalogue noted "Four sepia wash drawings" in lot 37. Those acquired by Princeton included three other drawings: one attributed to Polidoro de Renzi and a pair mounted on one support and attributed to Cristoforo Rocalli. See Gibbons 1977, nos. 695, "After Pietro Buonaccorsi, called Perino del Vaga," and 769 and 770, now considered "Genoese or Roman, late 16th century."
11 My thanks to Egbert Haverkamp-Begemann for this astute observation.
12 Paris 1852. Also see Seville 1995–96, 244ff.
13 See Seville 1995–96, 244ff. Several of these drawings remain in French collections, including the preparatory drawing for the *Council of Nicea*, Musée du Louvre, Cabinet de Dessins, no. 18473.
14 I also have consulted with Rhea Blok at the Fondation Custodia about this inscription, and it does not match any collector's writing currently in their database.

JUAN ANTONIO CONCHILLOS Y FALCÓ

Valencia, 1641–1711, Valencia

Juan Antonio Conchillos y Falcó was a prolific and vigorous draftsman. Conchillos studied with Esteban March (1610–1668) in his native Valencia before making a trip to Madrid, where he met Palomino in 1697.[1]

According to Palomino, fellow Valencian José García Hidalgo gave Conchillos a commission for two compositions intended for a series of the life of Saint Eloy in the sacristy of the parish church of San Salvador, Madrid.[2] Several battle scenes by Conchillos and two depictions of the Conversion of Saint Paul, one of which is dated 1699, demonstrate Conchillos's dependence on northern prints, as well as on drawings by Esteban March.[3]

Several other paintings by Conchillos were described by Palomino, but only one altarpiece commission by the artist survives in situ: the series related to the Veronica veil reliquary, completed around 1680 for the Church of the Convent of the Clarisas of the Santa Faz, in the town of the same name, near Alicante.

As only a few of his paintings survive, Conchillos is better known through his drawings. Of the several altarpiece commissions reported by Palomino, the two canvases for the Life of San Benito (signed in 1703), originally in the Monasterio de Tabernes de Valldigna, now survive in the Museo de Bellas Artes, Valencia.[4] In addition to his son, Juan Antonio Conchillos, who inherited his father's studio contents and "innumerable" drawings in 1711, Conchillos had other students.[5]

18. *Seated Male Nude*, 1691–99

Black chalk, heightened with white chalk, on green laid paper, lined

21 x 14.3 cm. (8¼ x 5¼ in.)

Dated in black and white chalk, lower left: *En 16 de Novre 1691* [corrected in pen and brown ink to 1699]; inscribed in pen and black ink on verso of mount, upper right center: *AS*

Provenance: Mathias Polakovits, Paris and New York, stamp (Lugt 3561) recto, lower right, in black

Reference: Princeton 2003, 119

Exhibitions: Princeton 1995; Princeton 1997

Museum purchase, Laura P. Hall Memorial Fund and Fowler McCormick, Class of 1921, Fund 2002-87

Palomino describes the academy that Conchillos ran in his home in Valencia for many years, where the artist completed one drawing in charcoal every evening.[6] Surviving in great numbers, especially in Spanish collections, these large nude or seminude academic studies are the most readily identifiable works by his hand.[7] Nearly all of the surviving examples note the date, month, and year of execution (between 1691 and 1704), and most are rendered on a dark greenish gray paper with charcoal or greasy black chalk highlighted with white chalk. The flexibility and friability of charcoal made it an ideal medium for such studies, on which small changes could be rubbed or stumped away. At times, Conchillos seems to have made drawings of the model in a similar pose several nights in succession. This unusual procedure allows us to see the artist's working method and the development of certain poses.

In this example, the partially draped model sits on a low support while leaning his weight on his right hand, resting his left hand on his upper thigh. The large figure fills the paper, with the left knee outside the borders of the sheet, compelling the artist to work on the pose of the left hand and knee at the upper right corner of the sheet.

Princeton's sheet has a date of November 16, 1691, which has been corrected in pen and brown ink to read 1699. Conchillos often reworked his compositions, which perhaps explains why the drawing's date, written first in black chalk, was altered. Adding highlights or changing the date noted on a drawing was a common practice for the artist. For example, a drawing at the Real Academia de Bellas Artes de San Fernando (fig. 18.1) includes a pen and brown ink inscription of numbers above the date written in black chalk at lower center.[8] LAB

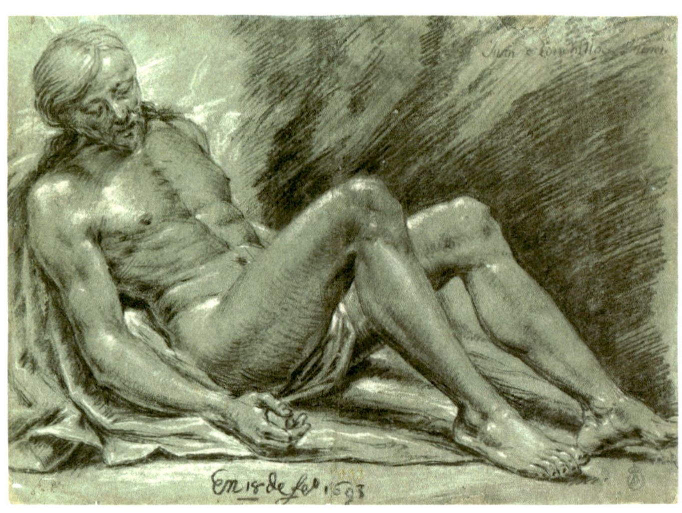

Fig. 18.1 Juan Antonio Conchillos y Falcó: *Dead Christ*. Real Academia de Bellas Artes de San Fernando (D-2186).

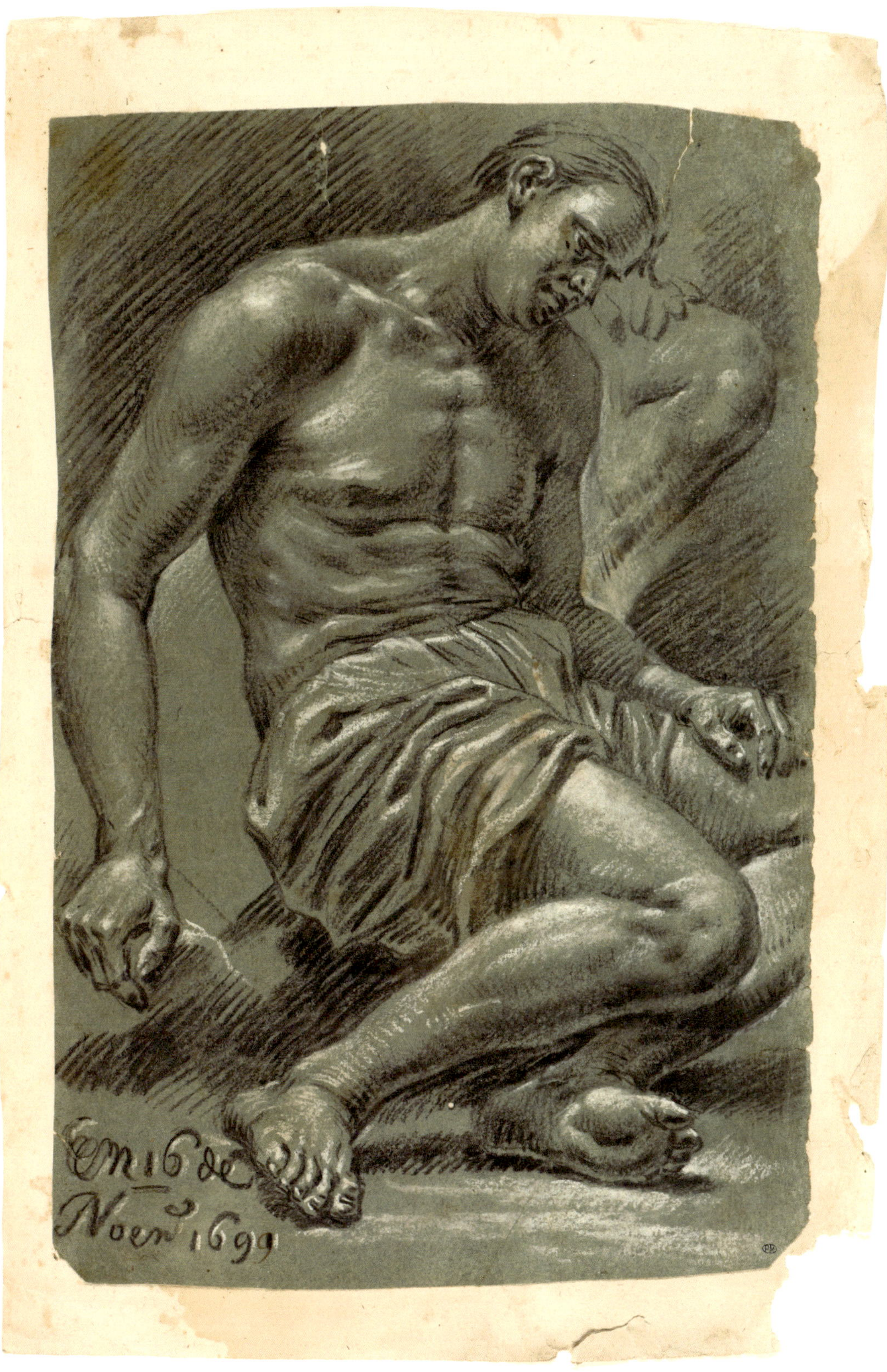

Noev 1699

19. *Vision of Saint Anthony of Padua*, ca. 1695

Verso: *Sketches of Saints, Immaculate Conception, Drapery*

Pen and brown ink with brush and opaque gray wash, over black chalk, on tan laid paper; verso: pen and brown ink over red chalk

28.2 x 23.3 cm. (11 1/16 x 9 3/16 in.)

Inscribed on verso in pen and brown ink, center: 1 *carto*

Provenance: Mathias Polakovits, Paris and New York, stamp (Lugt 3561) recto, lower right, in black

References: Angulo Íñiguez and Pérez Sánchez 1975–88, vol. 4, 21, no. 16, pl. 8; Princeton 2003, 119

Exhibitions: Princeton 1995; Princeton 1997

Museum purchase, Laura P. Hall Memorial Fund and Fowler McCormick, Class of 1921, Fund 2002-120

This drawing was first published by Diego Angulo Íñiguez and Alfonso Pérez Sánchez, who related it to the commissioned high altarpiece for the Convent of Capuchinos in Murcia, financed by the Conde del Valle de San Juan.[9] Pérez Sánchez accepted the attribution with reservation, however, because he had only seen the drawing in a photograph. The drawing is neither signed nor dated, although including both a signature and a date was a standard practice for Conchillos.

The Princeton *Vision of Saint Anthony of Padua* can be most closely compared to the series of pen and wash drawings divided between the Museo de Bellas Artes, Valencia, and the Museo del Prado, published by Adela Espinós Díaz in 1997.[10] Those drawings are thought to be preparatory studies for a series of paintings from the cloister of the now-destroyed convent of Nuestra Señora del Socorro, built over the ruins of an Augustinian convent outside the walls of Valencia.[11] Some of the ten drawings are inscribed with descriptive titles in pen and brown ink.[12] Where the name "Conchillos" appears it may have been written later by a collector.[13]

The drawing of *Saint Thomas of Villanueva on His Deathbed* (fig. 19.1) offers the best comparison to the Princeton sheet; both are executed in pen and brown ink with gray wash. The use of architectural elements in the background of the Princeton drawing is similar to the perspective rendering employed on the sheets in Valencia. The artist's technique in preparing this series—using black chalk border lines to frame the composition before drawing in light brown ink and shading with light gray wash—was also similar. Afterward, the artist reinforced some of the shadows with darker gray wash, adding depth and contrast to the figures and the columns. The use of a dotted line to render details, including those on the collar of the man at lower right in *Saint Thomas of Villanueva on His Deathbed*, and of small, short strokes to connote halos, appear in the Princeton drawing and the Valencia sheets.[14]

The drawing at Princeton represents Saint Anthony kneeling in prayer at an altar, with a vision of the infant Christ, seated on a cloud supported by putti, appearing to him. The small drawings on the verso of the Princeton sheet, studies of San Isidro and the Virgin rendered in pen and dark brown ink and red chalk, shed no further light on the authorship of the recto of the sheet and seem to be by a different hand.[15]

In style and execution, the sheet can be compared to Conchillos's undated drawing *Dormition of the Virgin*, in pen and ink with wash, and *Presentation of Jesus at the Temple*, dated by the artist May 27, 1695, at the Museo de Bellas Artes, Valencia.[16] Both of these drawings share a similar pen and wash technique although, unlike the Princeton sheet, both are executed on blue-tinted paper.

Adela Espinós Díaz has recently suggested that the series of drawings divided between the Prado and Valencia may be by the hand of Juan Antonio Conchillos's son, Manuel, whose drawings were not as accomplished as those of his father. Further research is needed to clarify the relationship of these drawings to the Juan Antonio Conchillos y Falcó known to Palomino, to whom the Princeton drawing was originally attributed by Alfonso Pérez Sánchez. According to Espinós Díaz, Manuel Conchillos is known to have completed a set of paintings for the cloister of the Convent of Nuestra

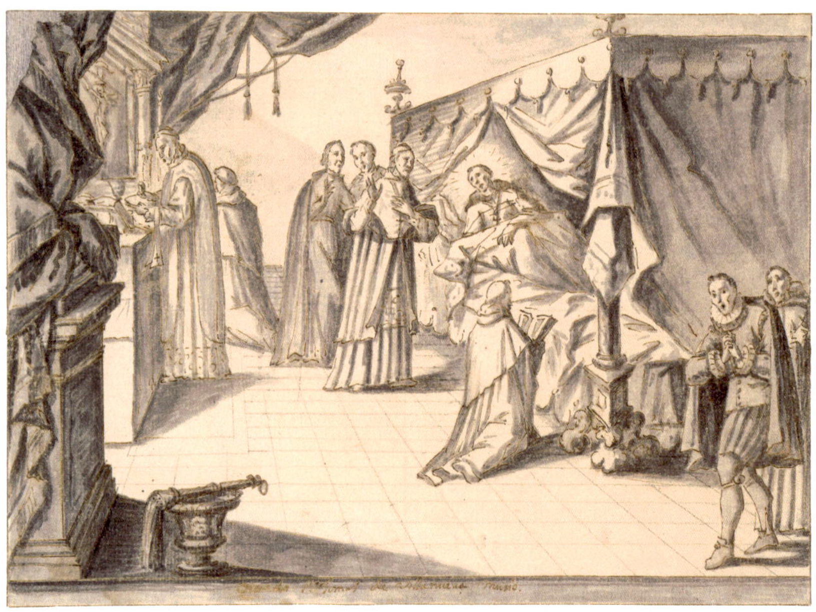

Fig. 19.1 Juan Antonio Conchillos y Falcó, Spanish, 1614–1711: *Saint Thomas of Villanueva on His Deathbed*. Museo de Bellas Artes, Valencia (4210 A.E.).

Señora del Socorro, where Saint Thomas of Villanueva was interred. Although nothing more is known of the paintings, this project supports the possibility of his authorship of the series of drawings of the saint's life.[17] LAB

1 Pérez Sánchez 1986, 312ff; and Espinós Díaz 1997, 210.
2 Palomino 1987, 377.
3 Angulo Íñiguez and Pérez Sánchez 1975–88, vol. 4, 21, nos. 18–19.
4 Espinós Díaz 1997, 210–11.
5 Palomino 1987, 379.
6 Ibid., 378.
7 Examples are in Museo de Bellas Artes, Valencia (catalogued by Adela Espinós Díaz); Real Academia de Bellas Artes de San Fernando, Madrid; the Stanford University Art Museum, Stanford; Musée du Louvre, Paris; and Biblioteca Nacional, Madrid.
8 Real Academia de Bellas Artes de San Fernando, no. 2186.
9 Palomino 1987, 279; and Angulo Íñiguez and Pérez Sánchez 1975–88, vol. 4, 21, no. 16.
10 Espinós Díaz 1997, 244–63, esp. 262, nos. 93–102.
11 Ibid., 248. Nothing further is known about the painting series for this now-destroyed convent.
12 Espinós Díaz discusses the different hands in the inscriptions on the Madrid drawings and their different provenance. The drawings at Valencia all came to the Museo de Bellas Artes from the Real Academia de Bellas Artes de San Carlos, without further details on provenance prior to their acquisition. She posits a source for the compositions in the *Libro de la santa vida y Milagros del…señor don Fr. Thomas de Villanueva, Arçobispo de Valencia*, by Miguel Salom, 1620, with a revised edition in 1652. As she points out, the drawings in the Prado are attributed to Conchillos in a later hand, and the Valencia group from this series does not have these attributions.
13 Espinós Díaz 1997, 262–63.
14 Ibid.
15 These small sketches occupy the top third of the verso of the drawing.
16 Museo de Bellas Artes Valencia, no. 36; discussed in Espinós Díaz 1997, 242–43, no. 92; Museo de Bellas Artes Valencia, no. 35 A.E; and discussed in Espinós Díaz 1997, 222–23, no. 84.
17 Espinós Díaz 1997, 262.

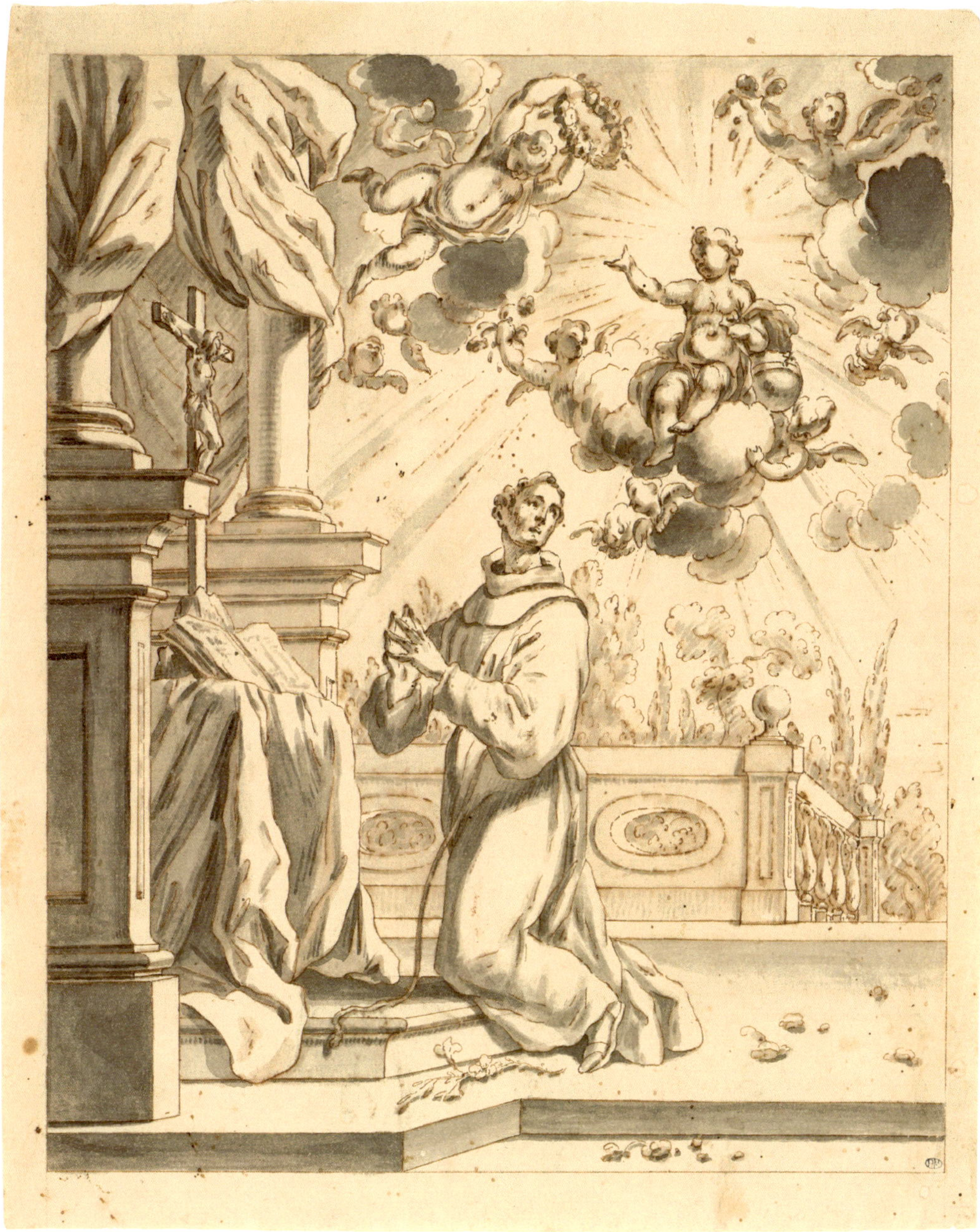

ALONSO MIGUEL DE TOVAR

Higuera de la Sierra, 1678–1752, Madrid

Alonso Miguel de Tovar was born near Aracena into a noble family distantly related to the Marqueses of Berlanga. He moved to Seville in 1690 to begin studying with Juan Antonio Fajardo (active 1666–1672) and received several important commissions in Seville before 1729, when he was called to Madrid by King Philip V, replacing Teodoro Ardemans (1664–1726) as *pintor de cámara.*[1] A facile copyist of Murillo's work, according to Ceán Bermúdez, Tovar is best known for the paintings he copied rather than for his own original work. He was one of a number of followers of Murillo in the next generation, and only a handful of drawings are attributed to him—even those without certainty.[2] Among his most important work is the signed painting *Divina Pastora (Mary as Holy Shepherd)* of 1748 in the church at Corelazor near Aracena, a portrait of Cardinal Molina, and several copies of paintings by Murillo, including genre scenes.[3]

Attributed to Alonso Miguel de Tovar

20. *Saint Margaret of Antioch*

Charcoal and black chalk with traces of white gouache, on gray laid paper

19.3 x 12.6 cm. (7$\frac{9}{16}$ x 4$\frac{15}{16}$ in.)

Inscribed verso, in graphite, upper center: *Tovar* and lower center (in different hand): *Tobar*

Provenance: Mathias Polakovits, Paris and New York, stamp (Lugt 3561) recto, lower right, in black

Reference: Princeton 2003, 123

Museum purchase, Laura P. Hall Memorial Fund and Fowler McCormick, Class of 1921, Fund 2002-101

In this drawing, Saint Margaret of Antioch tramples a dragon, his tail curling out from beneath her flowing robe at left. Traces of white gouache heighten the folds of her garment, especially on her shoulder, belly, and upper thigh. The saint, described in Jacobus de Voragine's *Golden Legend,* was said to be a virgin martyr who was the daughter of Theodosius, the patriarch and prince of Antioch. She was imprisoned after being beaten and tortured; subsequently, it was said, she was swallowed by Satan in the form of a dragon, from whose belly she emerged when her crucifix irritated him or she made the sign of the cross. Later, she was martyred by beheading. In Tovar's drawing she holds both the martyr's palm and the crucifix that helped her triumph over Satan. Although Saint Margaret of Antioch was deemed apocryphal by Pope Gelasius I in 494, she was associated with childbirth and was widely revered in Spain. In 1631, Zurbarán depicted Saint Margaret as a jaunty shepherdess, with the dragon curling behind her (The National Gallery, London).

The attribution of this drawing to Tovar is written on the verso in two places in two distinct hands, with different spellings. The attributions likely postdate the drawing itself, but there is no reason to doubt their veracity. Only a handful of drawings are attributed to Alonso Miguel de Tovar, and in most cases, including the sheet at Princeton, the attributions are traditional. The drawings are in pen and ink with wash; the two drawings attributed to Tovar at Hamburg, of *Young Saint John the Baptist* (fig. 20.1) and *Infant Christ in Glory,* demonstrate the artist's debt to Bartolomé Murillo. LAB

1 Ceán Bermúdez 1800, vol. 5, 48–50.
2 Brown 1976, 42–43.
3 Quiles García 2005, 18. Also see Luna 1980, 457 ill.

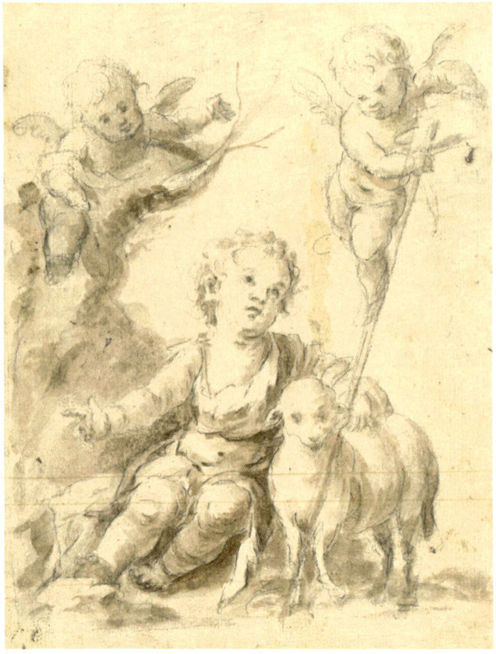

Fig. 20.1 Alonso Miguel de Tovar, Spanish, 1678–1752: *Young Saint John the Baptist.* Black chalk with brown wash, 24 x 18.5 cm. Hamburger Kunsthalle (38611).

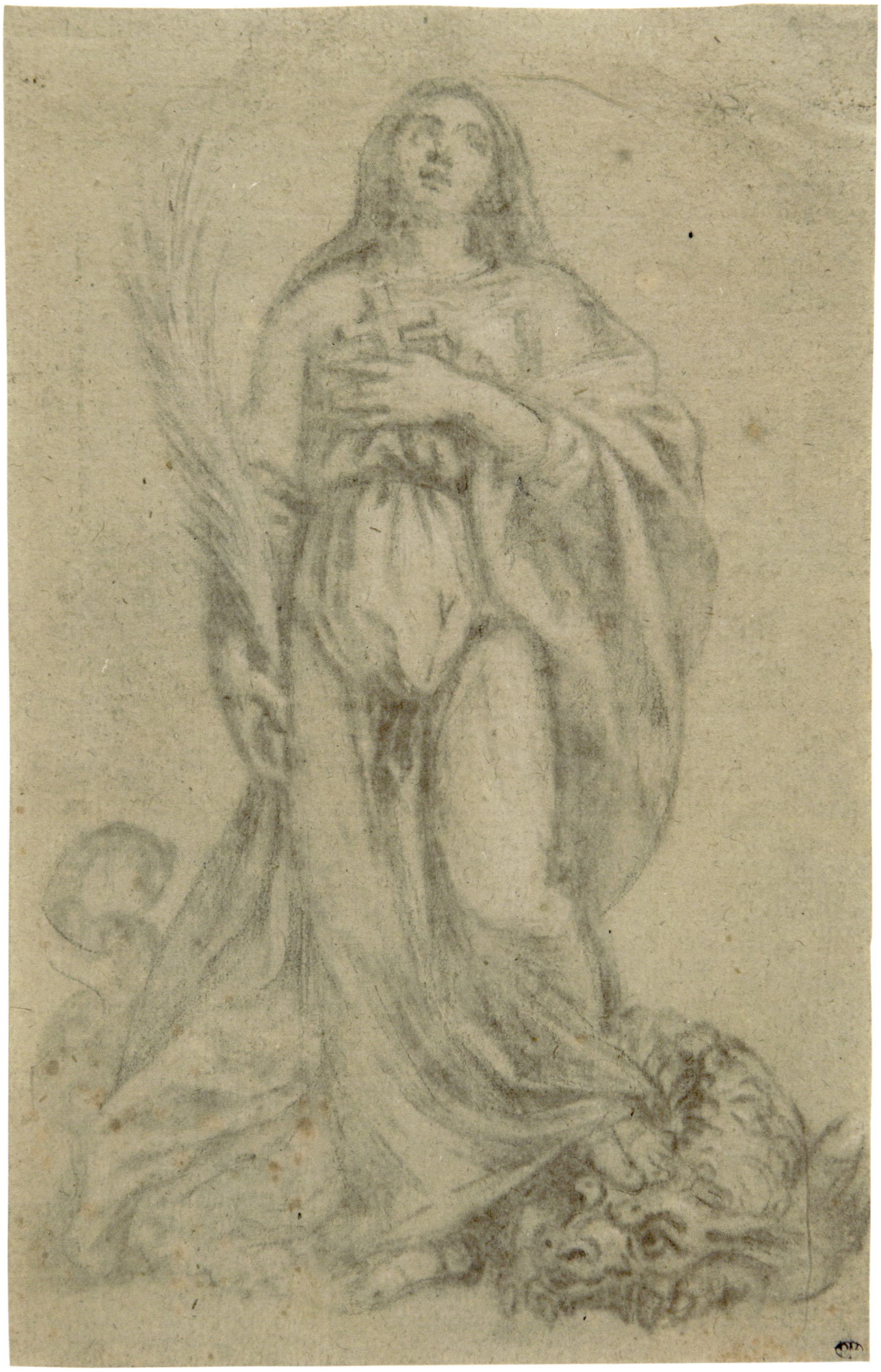

LUIS GONZÁLEZ VELÁZQUEZ

Madrid, 1715–Madrid, 1764

Luis González Velázquez was the eldest of the three sons of Pablo González Velázquez and spent his life in Madrid; his work has been the subject of less study than that of his brothers. He executed ephemeral decorations for the Buen Retiro palace and for the coronation of Ferdinand VI in 1746 and also assisted his brothers in their commissions for decorations in the royal palaces. Luis was a member of the Real Academia de San Fernando and worked closely with master printmakers at court, including Manuel Salvador Carmona. For example, he provided the portrait drawing of the musician José Herrando that was engraved by Manuel Salvador Carmona for the Duke of Arcos, departing from the more schematic works that he completed at the palace.

Attributed to Luis González Velázquez

21. *Apotheosis of Saint Margaret*

Pen and brown ink with brush and gray-brown wash over traces of black chalk, on beige laid paper, lined

27.7 x 14.0 cm. (10 15/16 x 5 1/2 in.)

Inscribed in pen and brown ink on mount, lower right: *Caraci*

Provenance: Richard Norton Collection (per note on the old mat); Frank Jewett Mather Jr.

Reference: Gibbons 1977, no. 898, ill., as "*The Apotheosis of Saint Margaret*, Region Unknown, Eighteenth century"

Exhibitions: New York 1930, no. 78; Iowa 1951, no. 64; Princeton 1995; Princeton 1997

Gift of Frank Jewett Mather Jr.
x1948-1792

In 1983, Jonathan Brown recognized this drawing as the work of Luis González Velázquez, although it had been published with Princeton's Italian drawings in 1977. The numerous changes to the attribution result from close stylistic affinities among the eighteenth-century Spanish pupils of Italian masters—many of whom worked and taught in Spain and whose style was also transmitted through Corrado Giaquinto (ca. 1694–1765), who painted for the king.

The subject of the drawing, the Apotheosis of Saint Margaret, or the Assumption of Saint Margaret, is typical for a Spanish royal patron. Several Habsburg queens were named Margaret, and the image of the virgin martyr treading on the dragon was conflated with an image of the Woman of the Apocalypse, described in the vision of St. John encountering a dragon (Rev. 12:1–8). Because of the identification of the Virgin Mary (Virgen Inmaculada) with the Woman of the Apocalypse, and Margaret's similarities with the Woman from Revelation, the story of Saint Margaret, although considered an apocryphal legend, was popular in Spain and elsewhere.[1]

Here Margaret rises on clouds, supported by an angel who indicates her ascension, toward a heaven where angels blow trumpets and putti play stringed instruments. Below,

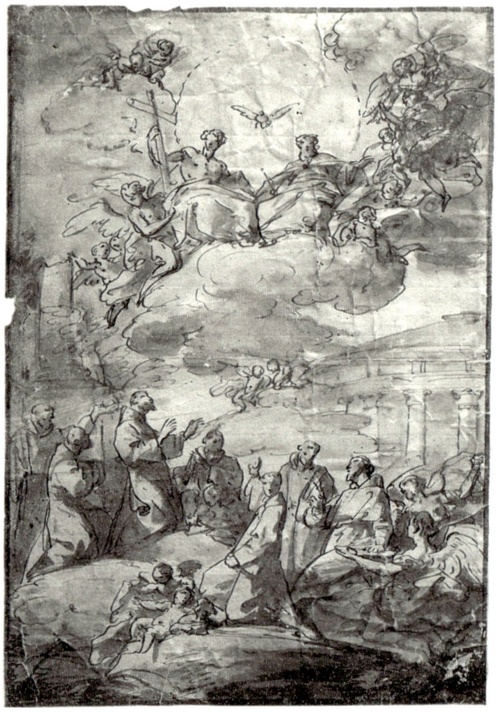

Fig. 21.1 Luis González Velázquez, Spanish, 1715–1764: *The Holy Trinity and Franciscan Saints.* Brown gouache and pen on paper, 39.6 x 26.3 cm. Museo Nacional del Prado, Madrid (D03803).

three male figures offer laurel wreaths as she rises from the belly of the dragon, which lies defeated and split open on the ground. The three figures might represent her father, the pagan priest Aedesius; the Roman provost Olybrius, who tried to seduce her and ordered

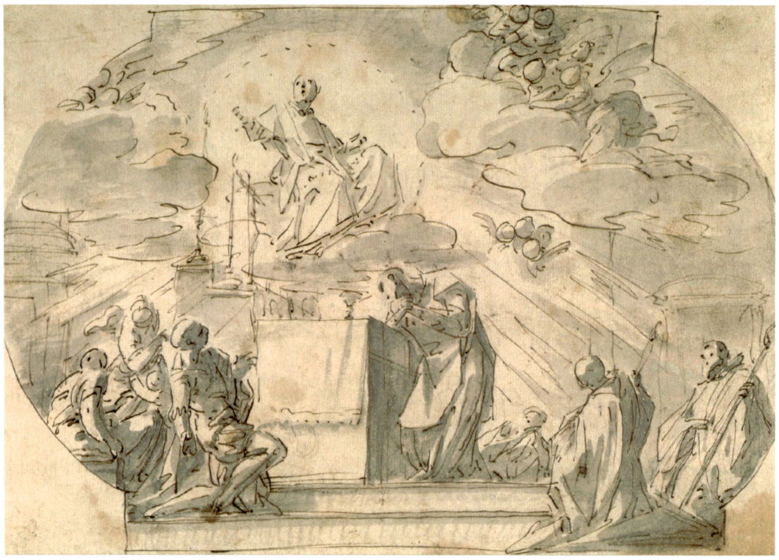

Fig. 21.2 Luis González Velázquez, Spanish, 1715–1764: *Apparition of Saint Francis of Sales to Saint Claudio Croeix.* Brown gouache and pen on paper, 18.2 x 26.5 cm. Museo Nacional del Prado, Madrid (D03459).

her martyrdom; and Diocletian, who persecuted Margaret and other early Christians. The saint's head is wreathed in stars, alluding to the Woman of the Apocalypse, who is often shown triumphing over evil—in the form of the dragon on the ground—and whose imagery is frequently conflated with that of the Virgin Immaculate.

Two drawings by Luis González Velázquez in the Museo del Prado have similar characteristics. *The Holy Trinity and Franciscan Saints* (fig. 21.1) resembles this drawing in several respects, especially the technique and the curving sweep of the composition in a vertical format. A second drawing by Luis González Velázquez, *Apparition of Saint Francis of Sales to Saint Claudio Croeix* (fig. 21.2), is executed with the same technique as the Princeton sheet: a layer of gray wash over black chalk and final drawing in pen and brown ink. A shaped framing line around the composition indicates that the painting was made on a shaped panel, perhaps as a frescoed wall or ceiling decoration. LAB

1 The drawing was previously attributed to Carracci on the old mount, and Ann Sutherland Harris suggested it was Neapolitan, n.d.

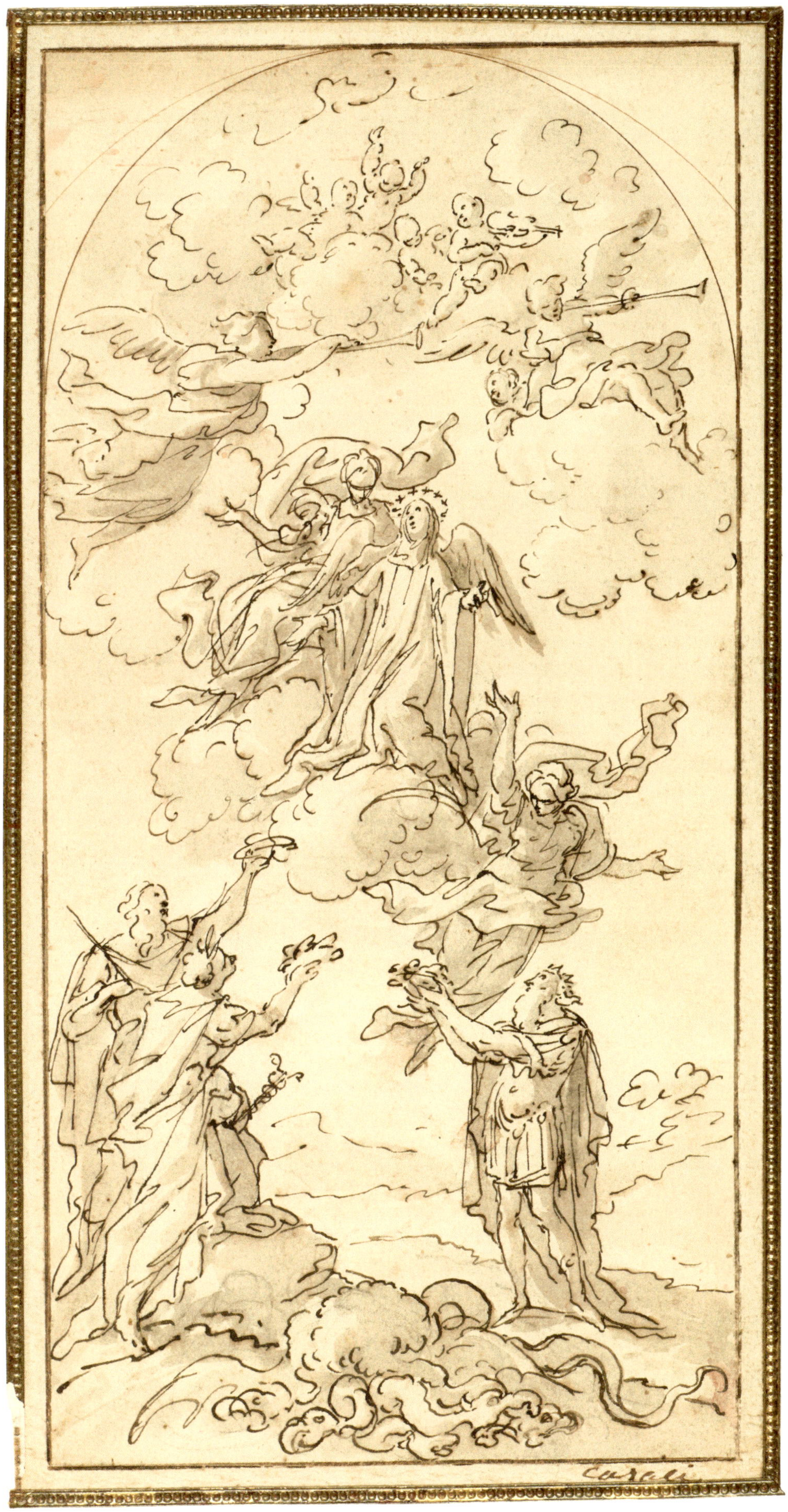

ANTONIO GONZÁLEZ VELÁZQUEZ

Madrid, 1723–1794, Madrid

One of a family of artists who worked at court, Antonio González Velázquez was the youngest of the three sons of sculptor Pablo González Velázquez (1664–1727) and brother to Luis (1715–1764) and Alejandro (1719–1772).[1] His children, Zacarías (1763–1834), Isidro (1765–1829), and Castor (1768–1822), continued the family tradition as painters and architects.

González Velázquez was sent to Rome on a royal pension and worked there with Corrado Giaquinto (1703–1765). He returned to Spain with *bocetos*, or sketches, and drawings for the newly completed basilica of El Pilar at Zaragoza. In 1753, after painting the chapel of Our Lady of El Pilar in the basilica, the artist returned to Madrid, where he began to work with Giaquinto in the newly rebuilt royal palace. He also painted the cupola and pendentives for the Convent of the Encarnación. Antonio's reception piece for the Real Academia de Bellas Artes de San Fernando, the *Anointment of King David*, also completed in that year, reflects the influence of Giaquinto's soft colors and swirling draperies.

One of the artist's first independent commissions was the main altarpiece featuring the *Assumption of the Virgin* at Cuenca, completed before 1774, when it was discussed by Antonio Ponz. González Velázquez was made director of the Real Academia de Bellas Artes de San Fernando by Charles III in 1765 and—with Giaquinto, Mariano Salvador Maella, and several others—painted allegories to decorate the private rooms of the king and queen in the palace. In the early 1770s, González Velázquez began working with Juan Antonio Salvador Carmona (1745–1805) on a project to illustrate a *Flos Sanctorum*, or calendar of saints' days, that was marketed through a Madrid bookseller. The project did not continue beyond illustrations for mid-February; only forty-one prints were completed.

ATTRIBUTED TO ANTONIO GONZÁLEZ VELÁZQUEZ

22. *Cardinal Saint Meeting Angel*, ca. 1770

Verso: *Sketch of Seated Figure*

Pen and brown ink with brush and brown wash over black chalk, on beige laid paper; verso: black chalk

18.2 x 14.3 cm. (7 3/16 x 5 5/8 in.)

Inscribed in graphite on verso, upper left: *Ec Espag?*; center right: *Ec Madrid* (. . .) *17:1*

PROVENANCE: Mathias Polakovits, Paris and New York, stamp (Lugt 3561) recto, lower right, in black

REFERENCE: Princeton 2003, 115, as "Spanish, Anonymous, 17th century"

Museum purchase, Laura P. Hall Memorial Fund and Fowler McCormick, Class of 1921, Fund 2002-107

In this drawing, an angel greets a saintly cardinal, whose head is surrounded by short strokes that emphasize the white of the paper around the most important figure in the composition. The striking use of this white—on the figure of the angel as well as on the sleeve, hand, and robe of the cardinal saint—indicates the places where light seems to emanate. Minimal strokes suggest a city in the background, and framing lines enclose the composition. With summary pen and ink lines indicating faces as well as the shape and folds of drapery, the subtly applied wash technique is typical of Antonio González Velázquez. Several similar drawings that he made as part of a series for a *Flos Sanctorum* include *Santa Casilda* (fig. 22.1) and *San Julián* (fig. 22.2).[2] The drawings are not of uniform size; Princeton's sheet is closer in size to *Santa Casilda.*

González Velázquez might have made Princeton's sketch as a preparatory idea that

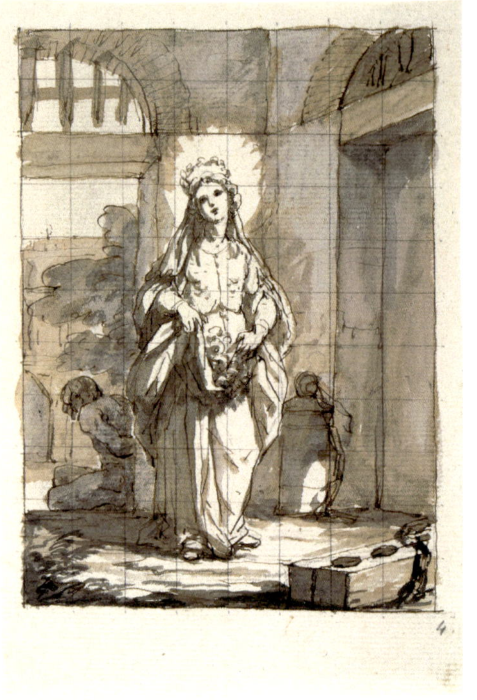

Fig. 22.1 Antonio González Velázquez, Spanish, 1723–1794: *Santa Casilda.* Brown gouache and pen on paper, 18.6 x 12.5 cm. Museo Nacional del Prado, Madrid (D03458).

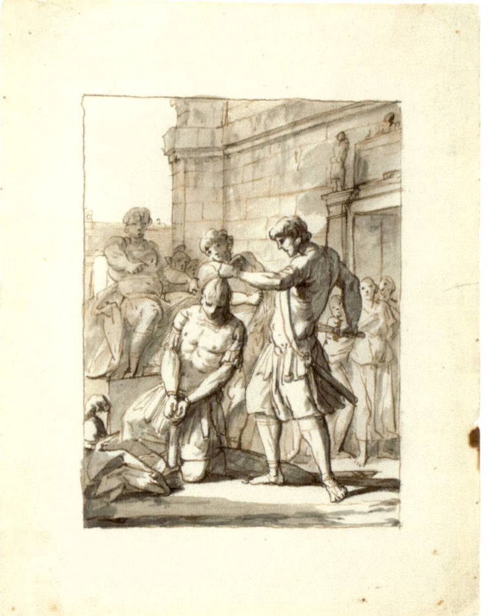

Fig. 22.2 Antonio González Velázquez, Spanish, 1723–1794: *San Julián,* 1773. Gray gouache, brown gouache, pen, prepared in pencil, brown ink on paper, 27.9 x 22.0 cm. Museo Nacional del Prado, Madrid (D07411).

was not executed as a print for an edition of the *Flos Sanctorum* that he prepared from 1770 to1773. Based on the 1761 edition published by Joaquín Ibarra, the *Flos Sanctorum* edition that González Velázquez used had slight differences from the original 1616 printing, and the survival of certain drawings and the prints after them confirm that he must have known the 1761 edition.[3]

Initially offered for sale in the Madrid bookshop of D. Antonio Baylo, the first forty-one drawings for the calendar of saints were engraved by Juan Antonio Salvador Carmona in a collaborative project that was only partially completed.[4] Two sets of the prints exist, in the Biblioteca Nacional in Madrid and in the Hispanic Society in New York. Additional *estampas sueltas,* or loose prints, survive in the collection of the Museo Municipal de Madrid.[5] Twenty-one drawings were known prior to the publication of Princeton's drawing, and some of the finished drawings were signed and dated by the artist. A few were kept together with the prints that were made from them in an album (referred to as the "Vicente Camarón album") until their sale on the Madrid art market.[6] In some cases, the drawings differed from the final prints, showing the collaborative nature of the project.

The cardinal represented here is Saint Bonaventure, sometimes called the "Seraphic Doctor," whose feast day is in mid-July, later than the date in mid-February for which González Velázquez and Salvador Carmona stopped making prints.[7] The total number of drawings that González Velázquez prepared and completed for the *Flos Sanctorum* is unknown.

LAB

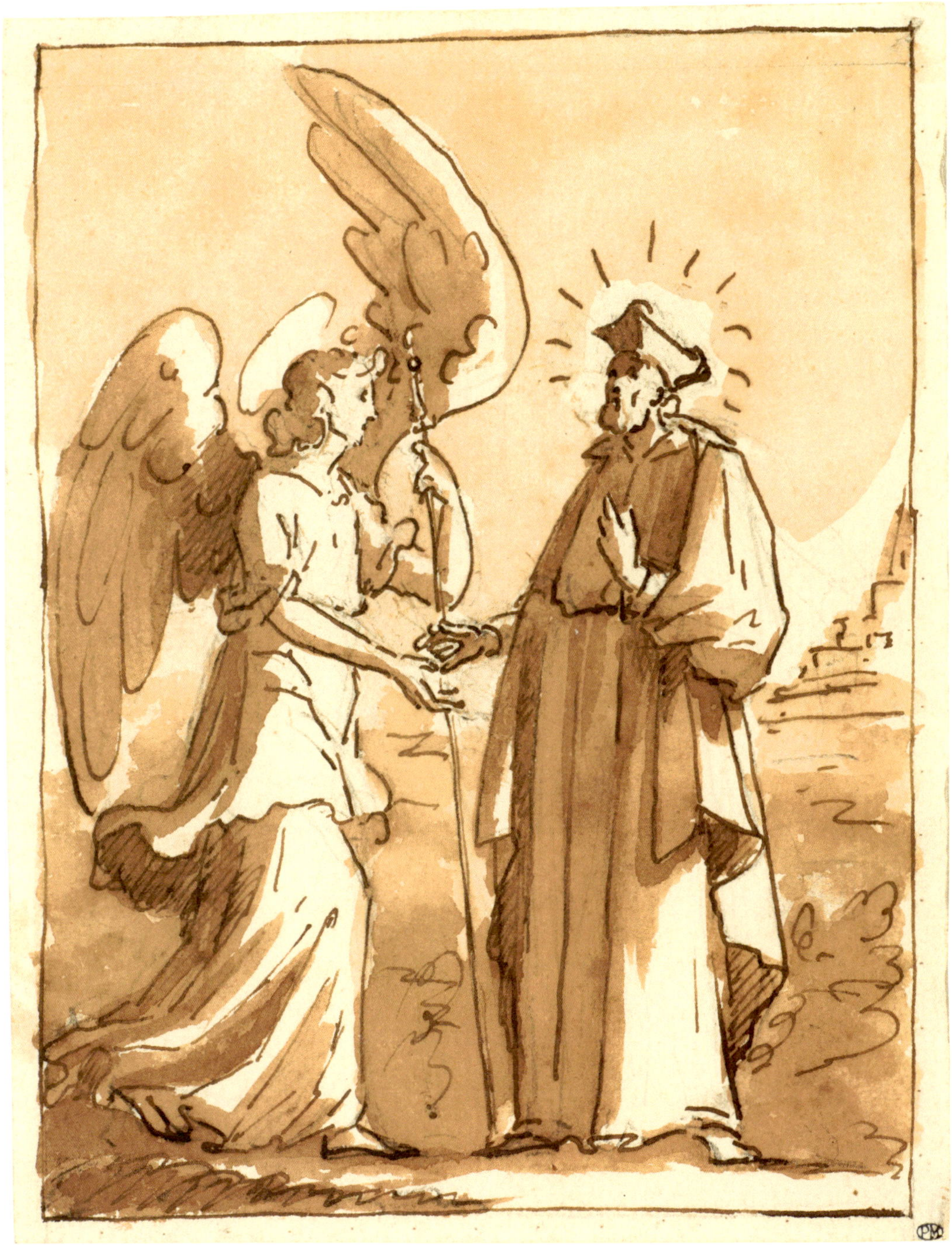

1 Ceán Bermúdez 1800, 221–25.

2 Arnáiz 1988. Also see, José Manuel Arnáiz, *Antonio González Velázquez, Pintor de Cámara de su Majestad, 1723–1794* (Madrid: Antiquaria, D.L., 1999), 127–34.

3 Arnáiz 1988.

4 Ibid. Rodríguez Moñino published Salvador Carmona's own description of the project in 1952. This information comes from the first print, for the first day of January, which bears the title "Circuncisión del Señor Antonio Velázquez inv.—Juan Ant. Salvador Carmona sculp"; see ibid.,181–89.

5 Ibid.,181.

6 "Subasta de Dibujos Antiguos hasta 1900," *Subastas Segre,* Tuesday, Dec. 18, 2007, lots 27–31.

7 Bonaventure wrote the life of Saint Francis; his own hagiography has been lost. A series of important paintings by Zurbarán, executed from 1626 to 1628, illustrates the important events in the life of the saint, including the moment when he accepted the call to be a cardinal. See *Saint Bonaventure and the Angel,* Gemäldegalerie Alte Meister, Staatliche Kunstsammlungen, Dresden.

DOMINGO DE AGUIRRE

Orán, ca. 1742–1805, Madrid

Domingo de Aguirre was primarily an army officer and an engineer at the court in Madrid, but his career as a draftsman—of architectural plans, topography, and views of palaces, cities, and monuments—is documented through his drawings and manuscripts. Aguirre made many watercolors and architectural renderings of important royal sites and cities.[1]

In 1770 he wrote a history of the Order of Saint John of Jerusalem, dedicated to Prince Gabriel Antonio de Borbón, the grand prior of that Order, and illustrated it with plans and drawings.[2] At the end of the manuscript, completed in 1772, Aguirre requested a benefice of the *alcaidía* of the castle of Consuegra, but this was denied and instead he was sent to prepare drawings of the royal site of Aranjuez.[3]

From 1772 to 1773, Aguirre completed a series of views of the palace of Aranjuez. Seven etchings after the drawings were made by Juan Barzelón (1739–1801), Josef Joaquín Fabregat (1748–1807), Jerónimo Antonio Gil (1732–1789), Joaquín Ballester (1740–1808), Manuel Salvador Carmona (1734–1820), Fernando Selma (1752–1810), and Juan Minguet (1737?–1804?); the project was one of several to document buildings and public works erected during the reigns of Bourbon kings Ferdinand VI and Charles III.[4] While Aguirre's drawings served as inspirations for the prints, in some cases they do not correspond directly to the final works. Aguirre's later watercolor series of views of the court and city of Madrid, dated 1780, is divided between the Museo Municipal of Madrid and the Biblioteca Nacional and demonstrates his simple, straightforward manner of architectural rendering and his naive treatment of figures.[5]

Aguirre's contributions also include series of watercolor plans documenting the state of the Alcázar of Toledo, with detailed descriptions prepared under the supervision of the Duque de Huéscar.[6] As a military engineer, Aguirre also made drawings of the Buen Retiro palace and other Madrid sites, now kept in the Biblioteca Nacional and the Museo Municipal, Madrid.

ATTRIBUTED TO DOMINGO DE AGUIRRE

23. *The Arrival of King Charles III at the Royal Palace of Aranjuez*, ca. 1773?

Brush and gray wash over graphite on light tan laid paper

31.9 x 50.5 cm. (12 9/16 x 19 7/8 in.)

Inscribed in pen and brown ink, at lower right corner of recto: *n329*; in pen and dark brown ink on verso, center, possibly in the same hand: *disegni d'alcune campagniole, e / Giardini*; inscribed in brush and gray wash at lower right corner of recto: *13*

Annotation in pen and dark brown ink at lower right corner of recto: *n 329*

WATERMARK: JHonig; cf. partial Heawood 3347 (London 1724–26) (see appendix)

PROVENANCE: Dr. Alfred Scharf, London?; Nathan Chaikin, Switzerland

EXHIBITIONS: Princeton 1995; Princeton 1997

Gift of Nathan Chaikin
x1970-27

This large gray wash drawing is here attributed to Domingo de Aguirre, whose series of watercolors of the royal palace of Aranjuez were completed in 1772–73 and later engraved by artists from the Real Academia in Madrid. The drawing was previously attributed to Pablo Minguet (active 1733–1770s) and later to Juan Minguet (Barcelona, 1737?–Madrid ca. 1804?). Pablo Minguet's treatises, including the 1761 *Demostración para saber grabar láminas de cobre y de madera*, demonstrate his skill with printing techniques. Juan Minguet was an engraver at the court and worked on a series of engravings from drawings made by Domingo de Aguirre and others. Neither Minguet is known for architectural drawings, however, whereas Aguirre completed a set of watercolors of the palace at Aranjuez, the subject of Princeton's sheet.

Beginning in 1772, Domingo de Aguirre was sent to prepare drawings of Aranjuez, including the topography, to complete a project begun by royal engineer Bernardo Fillera (active 1750s–1770s) in 1760.[7] Other surviving watercolor drawings by Aguirre's hand for this series, of similar horizontal format although slightly larger, are also executed in gray and black ink washes and demonstrate the same careful attention to perspective and a similarly naive treatment of figures, which are used to show the scale of the buildings. Prints made from the drawings vary in size.[8]

The general composition loosely resembles aspects of the print *Royal Palace of Aranjuez, seen from the Puente de Barcas* (fig. 23.1), based on a drawing by Aguirre, which shows the palace from a similar angle.[9] The orientation and proportions of the engraving roughly correspond to the proportions of this sheet.[10]

This large and ambitious wash drawing shows no evidence of having been used in the preparation of a print: there are no incised lines and the verso is not blackened for transfer. At lower right the artist painted the number "13" in the same brush and gray wash as the drawing itself. A later annotation, "n 329," was added by the hand that annotated the verso of the drawing in Italian, suggesting that the view might have been part of an album or a series of other landscape drawings or views of palaces with gardens.

In the lower right a large triple-masted barge flies a flag with the indication of a royal crown, on a field of fleurs-de-lis, suggesting that the vessel is carrying a member of the Bourbon family. A second boat, depicted on the right side of the sheet, carries a flag that is being lowered; a third follows it. Punts are visible behind and in front of the royal party's

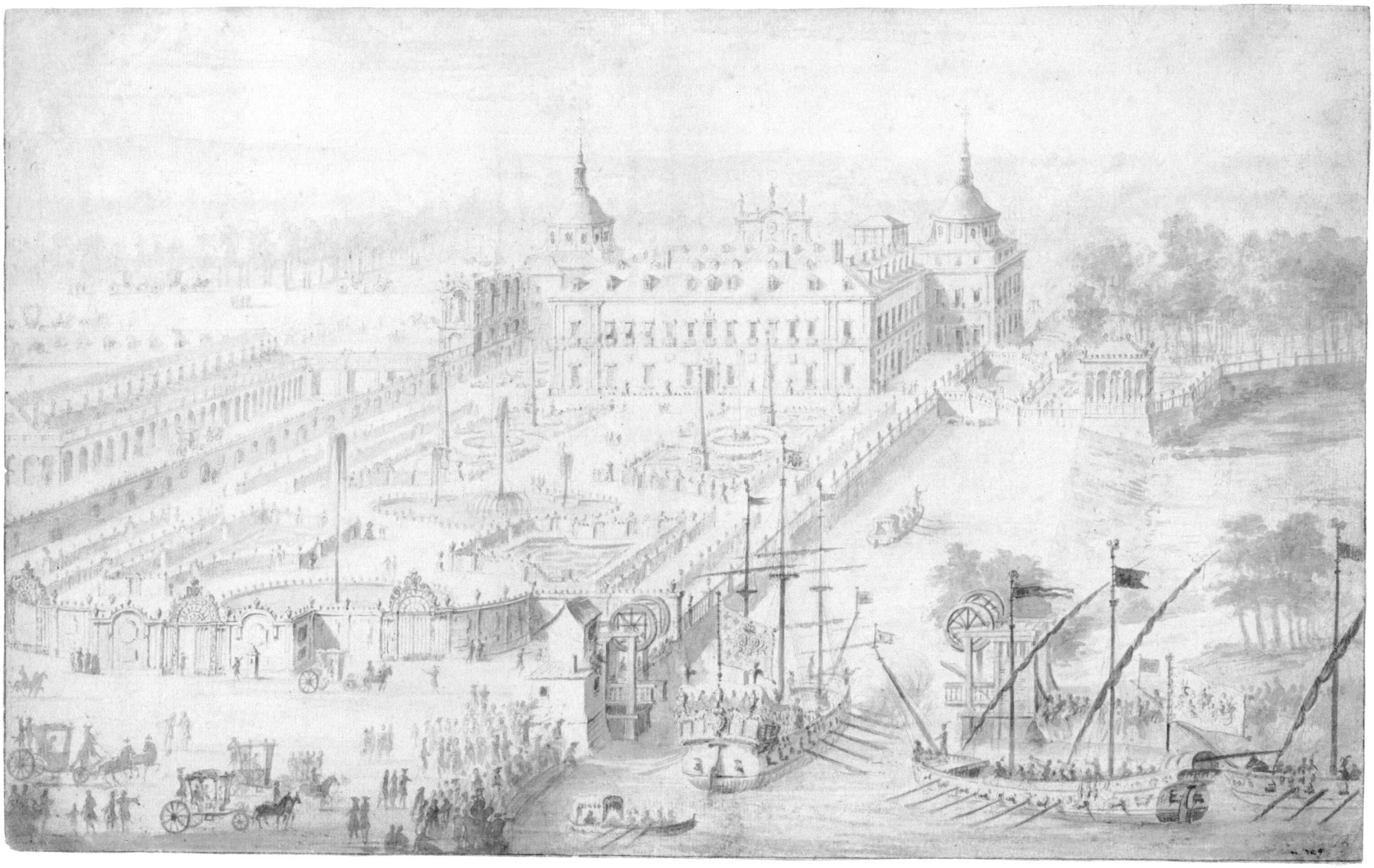

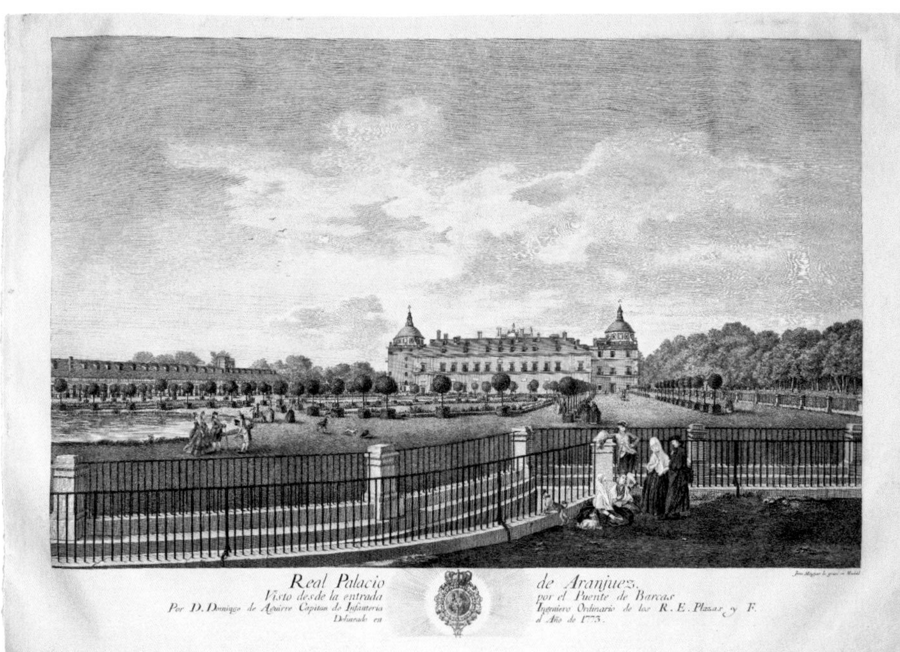

Fig. 23.1 Juan Minguet, Spanish, 1737–1804?: *Royal Palace of Aranjuez seen from the Puente de Barcas, drawn by Domingo Aguirre*, 1773. Engraving, 55.2 x 79.8 cm. Hispanic Society of America, New York (HSA Q2).

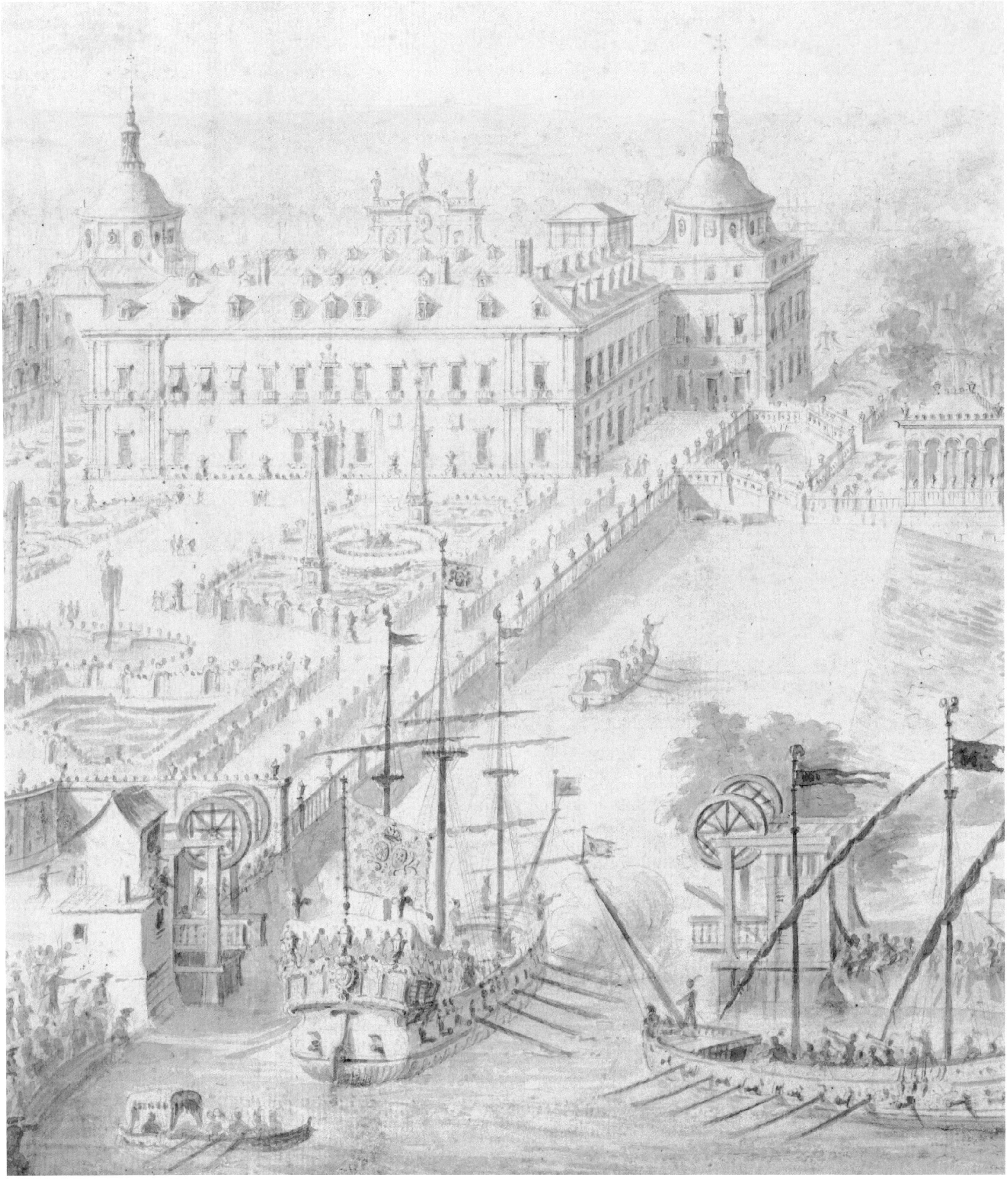

Detail, cat. 23

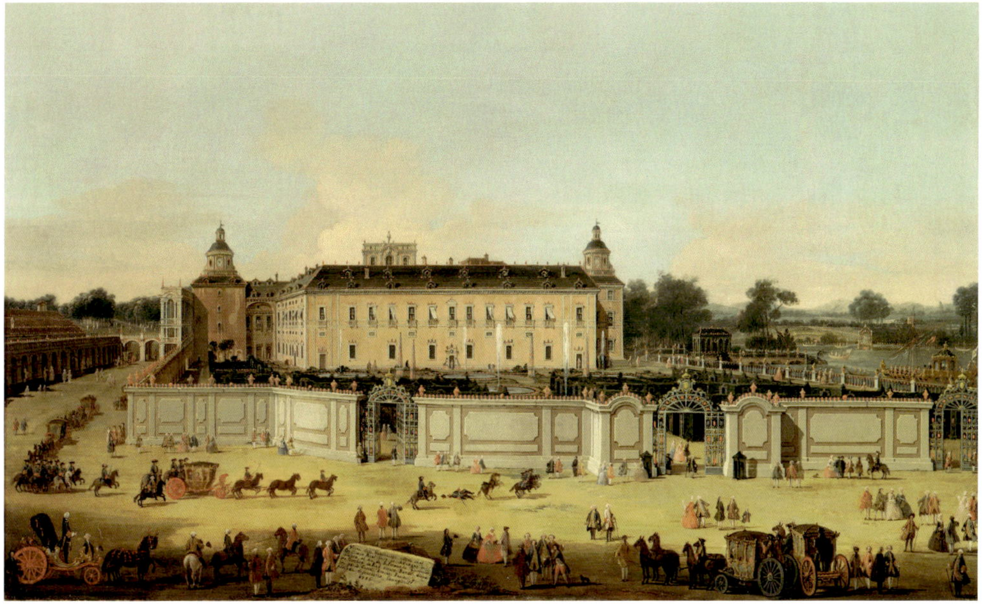

Fig. 23.3 Francesco Battaglioli, Italian, ca. 1725–1796: *The Guests Arriving at the Palace of Aranjuez for the St. Ferdinand's Day Celebration,* 1756. Oil on canvas, 68 x 112 cm. Museo Nacional del Prado, Madrid (P04180).

barge. The painterly use of wash and the delicate tonal qualities of the boats, buildings, people, carriages, and fountains suggest that the artist was attentive to the accuracy of his rendering of the palace and the gardens, perhaps recording a specific event and day. The watercolor serves mostly as a documentary record, rather than an interpretive landscape drawing, although it is animated by a certain charm and liveliness because of the depiction of the arrival of the royal party.

A letter from the Conde de Ricla to the Marqués de Grimaldi, dated May 5, 1772, documents Aguirre's arrival at Aranjuez, coinciding with the residence of the royal family at the palace, which usually extended from the beginning of April until the beginning of July.[11] Aguirre's responsibilities included contracting the engravings that would be based on his drawings. He completed the task in July 1773 and engaged Juan Antonio (1740–1805) and Manuel Salvador Carmona (1734–1820) to engrave the topographical prints as well as Jerónimo Antonio Gil, Francisco Muntaner, Francisco Selma, Juan Minguet, Juan Barcelón, José Joaquín Fabregat, and Joaquín Ballester to make engravings of the views and buildings; three hundred sets were made between 1773 and 1776.[12] While numerous views of the Palace of Aranjuez survive in engravings, often made by artists visiting the court, they feature the palace building itself rather than the approach from the water, shown in Princeton's drawing.[13]

The palace at Aranjuez, first begun under Philip II, was extended by Philip V in 1715 and continued to serve as a royal retreat and summer palace until 1748, when it was partially destroyed by a fire. Francesco Battaglioli (ca. 1725–ca. 1796) painted two works that record the appearance of the palace in 1756 after its rebuilding following the fire of 1748 (fig. 23.3). They record the festivities planned by Barbara de Braganza to surprise her husband, Ferdinand VI, and offer a similar view to Princeton's wash drawing.[14] LAB

1 Rodríguez Ruiz and García-Toraño Martínez 2009, 4–10, cat. 2–5 ill.
2 Two copies of the manuscript exist: one in the Biblioteca del Palacio Real and one at the Biblioteca Nacional, both in Madrid.
3 Rodríguez Ruiz and García-Toraño Martínez 2009, 14.
4 Minguet's activity at the Real Academia is discussed in Bédat 1989, 298.
5 Rodríguez Ruiz and García-Toraño Martínez 2009, 4–10, cat. 2–5 ill.
6 Ibid., 11–14, cat. 7–10 ill.
7 Ibid., 4–10 ill.
8 Páez Ríos 1982, 223, no. 7, ill. pl. 1402. Also see Carrete Parrondo, De Diego, and Vega 1985, 151–52, nn. 5–6.
9 The engraving by Juan Minguet of the *Real Palacio de Aranjuez visto desde la entrada por el Puente* (1773) is published in Páez Ríos 1982, 223, pl. 1402, no. 7.
10 Ibid.
11 Rodríguez Ruiz and García-Toraño Martínez 2009, 10, cat. 6.
12 Ibid.
13 Aguerri Martínez and Salas Vázquez 1989; see, for example, no. 71, *View of the Palace of Aranjuez*, or no. 104, *El Palacio de Aranjuez*.
14 Other views of the palace of Aranjuez depicting royal festivities were painted by Antonio Joli (1700–1777), who was called to Aranjuez in 1749 to replace Bolognese painter Giacomo Pavia (1655–1740). Joli stayed until 1754, painting set designs. Of the three autograph versions two are in private collections and one is in the collection of the Palazzo Reale, Naples.

PERE PAU MUNTANYA I PLACETA

Barcelona, 1749–1803, Barcelona

Pere Pau Muntanya i Placeta and his son Pau Muntanya Cantó (1775–1801) worked in Barcelona, although both had ties to court and to Madrid. Pere Pau Muntanya i Placeta is known for his sophisticated religious paintings and drawings, which were often based on old master prints. His heavy reliance on Dürer, in particular, is noticeable in a small number of surviving autograph drawings, which center around the Lives of Christ and the Virgin. Most of these works were created with the point of the brush and varied tones of gray wash over black chalk on fine laid paper, reflecting the influence of the court painter Mariano Salvador Maella (1739–1819).

24. *Flight into Egypt*

Brush and gray wash over black chalk, on cream laid paper, squared in black chalk, tipped onto blue-gray card

28.1 x 20.0 cm. (11 1/16 x 7 7/8 in.)

Inscribed in pen and brown ink (partially erased) on mount, lower right: [. . .] *Collon*; in pen and brown ink on verso of mount, lower right: *Coll comte d'Auffay / 1809–1861*

Provenance: Alfred-Laurent-Joseph Le Poultier, comte d'Auffay (1809–1861), stamp (Lugt 63) verso, upper left on mount, in black; Mathias Polakovits, Paris and New York, stamp (Lugt 3561) recto, lower right, in black

Reference: Princeton 2003, 118, as "Francisco Camilo"

Exhibitions: Princeton 1995; Princeton 1997; Princeton 2001

Museum purchase, Laura P. Hall Memorial Fund and Fowler McCormick, Class of 1921, Fund 2002-86

When this delicate wash drawing first entered Princeton's collection, it was attributed to Francisco Camilo (ca. 1615–1673), a seventeenth-century painter whose brush drawing *Rest on the Flight into Egypt* in red brown ink over red chalk is in the British Museum. The few drawings that have been securely attributed to Camilo, based on their relationships to known commissions, are generally complex drawings in chalk with pen and ink and white highlighting.[1] For Princeton's drawing, an attribution to Camilo is untenable based on technique and style; this sheet is instead by an eighteenth-century hand.

Recent work on the Catalan artists of the eighteenth century has changed the perception of the distinctive techniques of a group of sophisticated painters and draftsmen, including Manuel (1715–1791) and Francesc Tramulles (1717–1773) and their disciples, all followers of Antoni Viladomat i Manalt (1678–1755).[2] In the Princeton drawing, lightly applied gray wash and the leaning figures of Joseph and the Virgin are typical of the Catalan artist Pere Pau Muntanya i Placeta, another of Viladomat's pupils. Muntanya's drawings are found at the Museu Nacional d'Art de Catalunya, and most examples, including his *Doubting Thomas* and *Washing of Feet* from the Life of Christ series (fig. 24.1), demonstrate his dependence on engravings by Albrecht Dürer and other northern artists.[3]

Flight into Egypt was included frequently in altarpieces dedicated to the Life of the Virgin, a theme that proliferated in Spain during the second half of the seventeenth century and became increasingly popular in the eighteenth century. The composition features a date palm, the tree most frequently depicted in this scene, as the Holy Family was thought to have rested and taken nourishment under a date palm before continuing their journey. The vertical composition used here derived from woodcuts of *Flight into Egypt* like that created by Dürer (fig. 24.2), who included an elaborate landscape and a bridge. Dürer's print influenced the vertical presentation of the subject; however, in Princeton's drawing, Muntanya

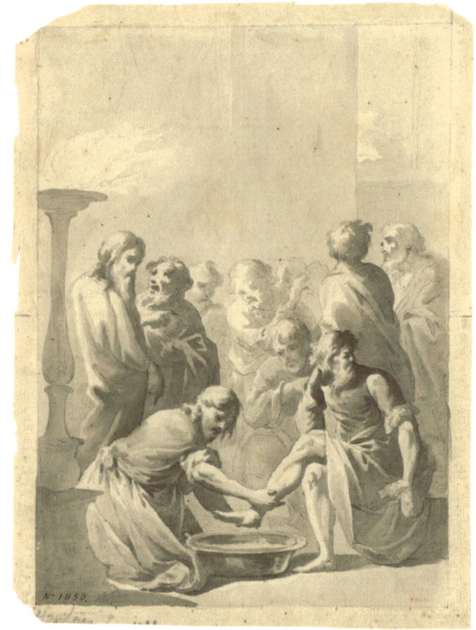

Fig. 24.1 Pere Pau Muntanya i Placeta, Spanish, 1749–1803: *Christ Washing the Feet of the Apostles.* Graphite pencil and watercolor wash, 18 x 24 cm. Museu Nacional d'Art de Catalunya, Barcelona (MNAC 027162-D).

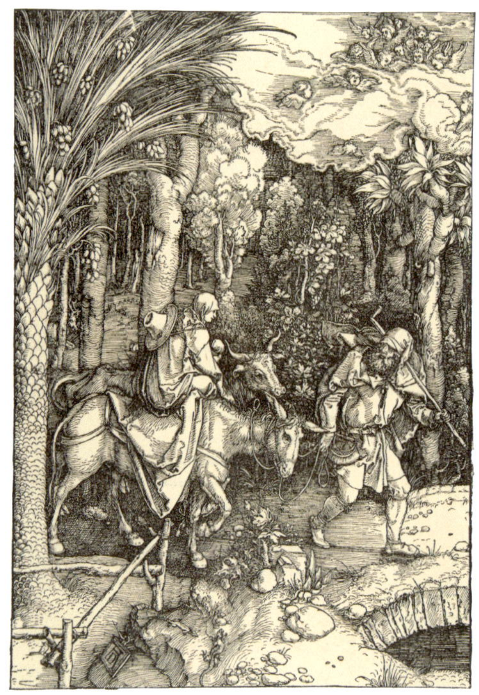

Fig. 24.2 Albrecht Dürer, German, 1471–1528: *The Flight into Egypt*, from *The Life of the Virgin*, 1511. Woodcut, 41.3 x 30.2 cm. (sheet), 29.8 x 20.6 cm. (block). The Metropolitan Museum of Art, The George Khuner Collection, Gift of Mrs. George Khuner, 1975 (1975.653.3).

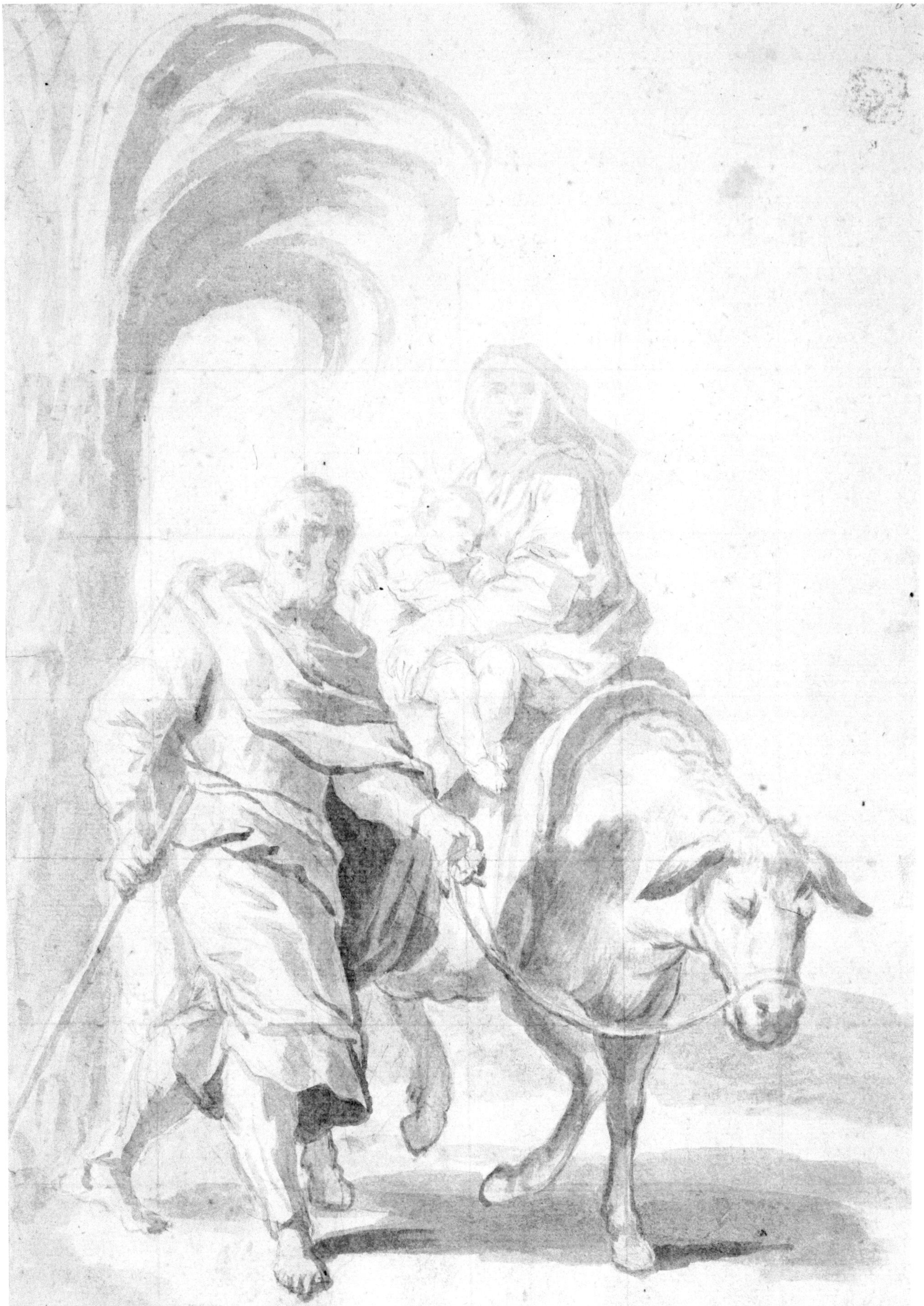

eliminated the background setting, including only the date palm at left, making the figures—rather than the landscape—the primary focus. With a low horizon, Muntanya pushes the figures to the foreground. Rather than turning inward toward the Virgin, Saint Joseph directly engages the viewer, while the Virgin looks out from her perch on the donkey's back and the baby nestles against her. As in his series of drawings of the Life of Christ, Muntanya's focus, in contrast to that of Dürer's print, is on the human action and interaction, rather than the setting.

The Princeton drawing is attached to a blue-gray card-stock mount. A reference to a previous collection, written in a neat slanting hand in pen and dark brown ink, has been vigorously erased. The erasure may have eliminated information about the provenance of this drawing prior to its attachment to the mount, although the stamp of Alfred-Laurent-Joseph Le Poultier, comte d'Auffay (1809–1861), on the verso suggests that he mounted the drawing in this way for display in the mid-nineteenth century.[4] LAB

1 One such work is in the Metropolitan Museum of Art: Francisco Camilo, *The Martyrdom of Saint Peter Martyr*, 1975.131.203.
2 *La Màscara Reial, Festa i allegoria a Barcelona l'any 1764*, Museu Nacional d'Art de Catalunya, 2001.
3 Barcelona 1993, 122–24.
4 The Comte d'Auffay's drawings are not listed in his library sale of April 13, 1863, Paris.

ZACARÍAS GONZÁLEZ VELÁZQUEZ

Madrid, 1763–1834, Madrid

Zacarías González Velázquez was born to a family of artists who had worked at the Spanish royal court. Although his father, Antonio González Velázquez (1723–1794), doubtless gave him his earliest lessons in drawing, Zacarías apprenticed with Mariano Salvador Maella (1739–1819) at the court, and in 1777, at the age of fourteen, he enrolled in the Real Academia de Bellas Artes San Fernando, where his father was director.[1] He finished his studies in 1782 and became a professor at the Academy in 1790. Princeton's collection includes drawings by three artists from this family: Zacarías González Velázquez; his father, Antonio González Velázquez; and his uncle Luis González Velázquez (1715–1763).

González Velázquez earned many fresco commissions; his most important was the series of the *Life of Saint Francis* painted for San Francisco el Grande in Madrid, commissioned around 1786. With three other artists, Antonio Carnicero (1748–1814), José Camarón Boronat (1731–1803), and Manuel de la Cruz (1750–1792), González Velázquez completed twelve of the series of thirty-three paintings for San Francisco el Grande and prepared the series with many drawings.

A slightly younger contemporary of Francisco Goya (1746–1828), González Velázquez did not adopt the more modern vision that Goya began to develop, and his drawing style remained true to the academic techniques that he learned under Maella and his father at the Academy, rooted in late eighteenth-century neoclassicism and colored with the luminous tones of Neapolitan Corrado Giaquinto's (1703–1765) palette.

25. *San Pascual Bailón, Kneeling, with a Sketch of His Head*, ca. 1767

Black chalk heightened with white chalk, on tan laid paper, prepared with gray ground

24.0 x 19.3 cm. (9 7/16 x 7 9/16 in.)

Inscribed in black chalk, upper left: *L [ ]*

Provenance: Mathias Polakovits, Paris and New York, stamp (Lugt 3561) recto, lower right, in black

Exhibitions: Princeton 1995; Princeton 1997

Museum purchase, Laura P. Hall Memorial Fund and Fowler McCormick, Class of 1921, Fund 2002-84

Although this drawing was previously attributed to Francisco Bayeu (1734–1795), it is instead a strong example of the work of Zacarías González Velázquez, whose oeuvre was not well studied previously. González Velázquez frequently worked out specific details of a head, or the pose of hands, at a corner of the sheet, adding interest to the final drawing but, from the artist's perspective, simply using the page to develop his ideas fully. These studies, often for larger paintings, offer a window into the artist's process, in which he presented the whole figure and then focused on the details.

This figure of the Franciscan saint San Pascual Bailón might have been influenced by the composition by Giovanni Battista Tiepolo (1696–1770), who painted the subject for the lower register of the main altarpiece of the Convent of San Pascual Bailón at Aranjuez (completed between 1767 and 1769 for Charles III), establishing a possible date *post quem* for this drawing. In González Velázquez's interpretation, the saint kneels and holds his arms across his chest, with his face raised to an invisible sight at the upper left. The painting for the altarpiece is now in the Prado, and the composition was cut so that the figure of San Pascual Bailón is isolated. A print after the altarpiece by Giovanni Domenico Tiepolo (1727–1804) was used to reconstruct the painting.

Developing a distinctive working method, González Velázquez prepared his paper with a gray wash, painted thickly onto tan laid paper. Several drawings in this technique are preparatory studies for the frescoes at San Francisco el Grande attributed to González Velázquez (Museu Nacional d'Art de Catalunya, Barcelona). Artists at the court frequently used black and white chalk in combination on a dark ground, a technique favored by Corrado Giaquinto and taught to his students, including González Velázquez's father. Princeton's drawing is executed in the same technique as a preparatory drawing of Saint Francis giving his cape to a poor person, which was used for two related paintings of the subject by González Velázquez: the sketch, or *boceto*, in the Lázaro Galdiano Museum, Madrid, and the large-scale painting on deposit at the church of San Francisco el Grande (Museo del Prado, Madrid).[2] LAB

1 De la Mano 2010a, 37–39.
2 Ibid.

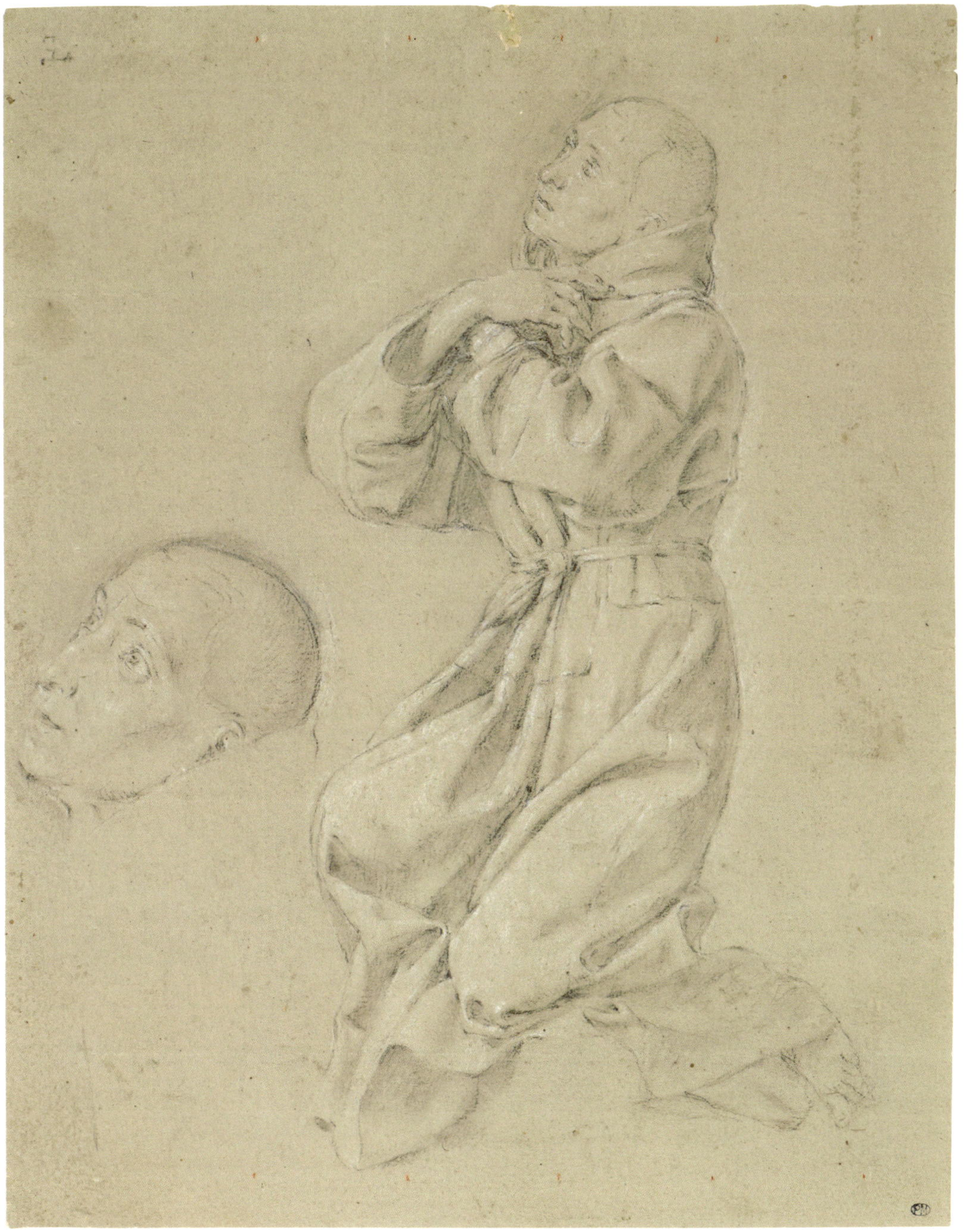

MARIANO SALVADOR MAELLA

Valencia, 1739–1819, Madrid

Mariano Salvador Maella studied drawing in Madrid with the sculptor Felipe de Castro (1711–1775). After 1752, he continued his training with Antonio González Velázquez at the recently created Real Academia de Bellas Artes de San Fernando in Madrid.[1] In 1758, after a failed attempt to travel to America, Maella went to Rome, where he was awarded an extraordinary pension to study with Francisco Preciado de la Vega (1712–1789), a principe of the Italian Academia de San Luca.[2] Like Pacheco and Carducho before him, Preciado de la Vega wrote an art treatise in Spanish, the *Arcadia Pictórica*, intended to instruct young painters. While few of Preciado's drawings survive, those that do are often executed in chalk with white highlights on dark paper, a technique that Maella learned and mastered in Rome and then brought back to Madrid.[3] During his career, Maella worked as a painter, engraver, and draftsman; multiple examples of his work survive in all media.

Upon Maella's return to Madrid in 1765, he was elected to the Academia de Bellas Artes de San Fernando, where he also taught, and began working closely with Anton Raphael Mengs (1728–1779) on royal commissions. The court favored Maella's classicism and light palette, influenced by Corrado Giaquinto (ca. 1694–1765), who had spent the years from 1753 to 1762 at the court of Madrid before returning to Naples. After the death of Giovanni Battista Tiepolo in 1770, Maella and Bayeu were asked to finish the work begun by him at the Real Colegiata de la Santísima Trinidad at the Palace of La Granja. Soon after, in 1774, Maella was made *pintor de cámara*. Maella's drawings were prized training tools for pupils at the Real Academia, and, as a professor, he approved drawings that were made during his classes. Thus, drawings from the Academia may have rubrics indicating a professor's approval or, at times, a scribbled name.[4]

After a series of honors and posts at the Real Academia de Bellas Artes de San Fernando, Maella became director in 1795. Four years later, in the same year as Goya, Maella was made Painter to the King. In 1814, Maella was relieved of his duties and relegated to a lesser role upon the restoration of Fernando VII to the throne, due to his service to José Bonaparte during the French occupation (1808–1814). He remained in obscurity thereafter until he died.[5]

Student of Mariano Salvador Maella

26. *Sketches of a Child's Head, copy after Agostino Cornacchini's sculpture "Grupo de niños"*

Verso: *Partial Sketch of Seated Nude*

Black chalk heightened with white chalk on brown laid paper

22.6 x 36.4 cm. (8 15/16 x 14 5/16 in.)

Inscribed in pen and brown ink on verso, lower right: *par Maella*

Watermark: Three lines of lettering: [top line unreadable] / *Dauphine / 1742*

Provenance: Mathias Polakovits, Paris and New York, stamp (Lugt 3561) recto, lower right, in black

Exhibitions: Princeton 1995; Princeton 1997

Museum purchase, Laura P. Hall Memorial Fund and Fowler McCormick, Class of 1921, Fund 2002-95

The eight charming studies on this sheet show the movement of a child's head from frontal to profile to three-quarter poses, drawn quickly in black chalk with some white highlights and reinforcing strokes of charcoal finishing the sheet. Numerous sheets of this sort, attributed to Mariano Maella, survive in the Biblioteca Nacional, the Prado, the Hamburger Kunsthalle, and other collections.

Maella made several sheets like this one, a group of sketches or studies of a baby or child's head, which might explain why the drawing was initially attributed to him on the verso. Maella's role as a teacher and active court artist contributes to the survival of numerous sheets by him and to the confusion of many of his students' hands with his own; recent scholarship suggests that further study of Maella's role as a teacher and the use of his drawings in teaching other artists is needed. José Manuel de la Mano, author of the recent catalogue raisonné of Maella's drawings, does not believe this sheet to be by Maella's own hand and instead suggests that the artist is likely to be an eighteenth-century pupil of Maella who might have copied his drawings—thus the annotation on the verso, implying that the drawing is by Maella.[6] The technique of using black and white chalk on a dark paper was often imitated by Maella's followers and students at the Academy; at present, about two hundred drawings by Maella's hand have been identified.

Maella's stylized studies of babies or putti are quite different from the more naturalistic way in which the heads on the Princeton sheet are drawn. The cherub heads, with blunt noses, rosebud mouths, broad and smooth foreheads, and deep-set eyes, are much closer to the forms made in marble sculpture by Agostino Cornacchini (1686–1754) (fig. 26.1). Cornacchini's sculpture, captured on the frigate Thetis in 1783, was part of the royal collection before it entered the Museo del Prado.[7] The eight heads on this sheet echo the static putti of Cornacchini's sculpture, in both number and gesture, and the close connection between that sculpture and this sketch suggests that they were copied from the marble. Highlights along the eyes, foreheads, and cheeks also suggest that the artist was observing how light fell on marble surfaces. A study of two sculpture casts in the Fundación Lázaro Galdiano, "Dos niños sobre pedestales," executed in black chalk on a prepared paper, might be by the same hand and related to this study. LAB

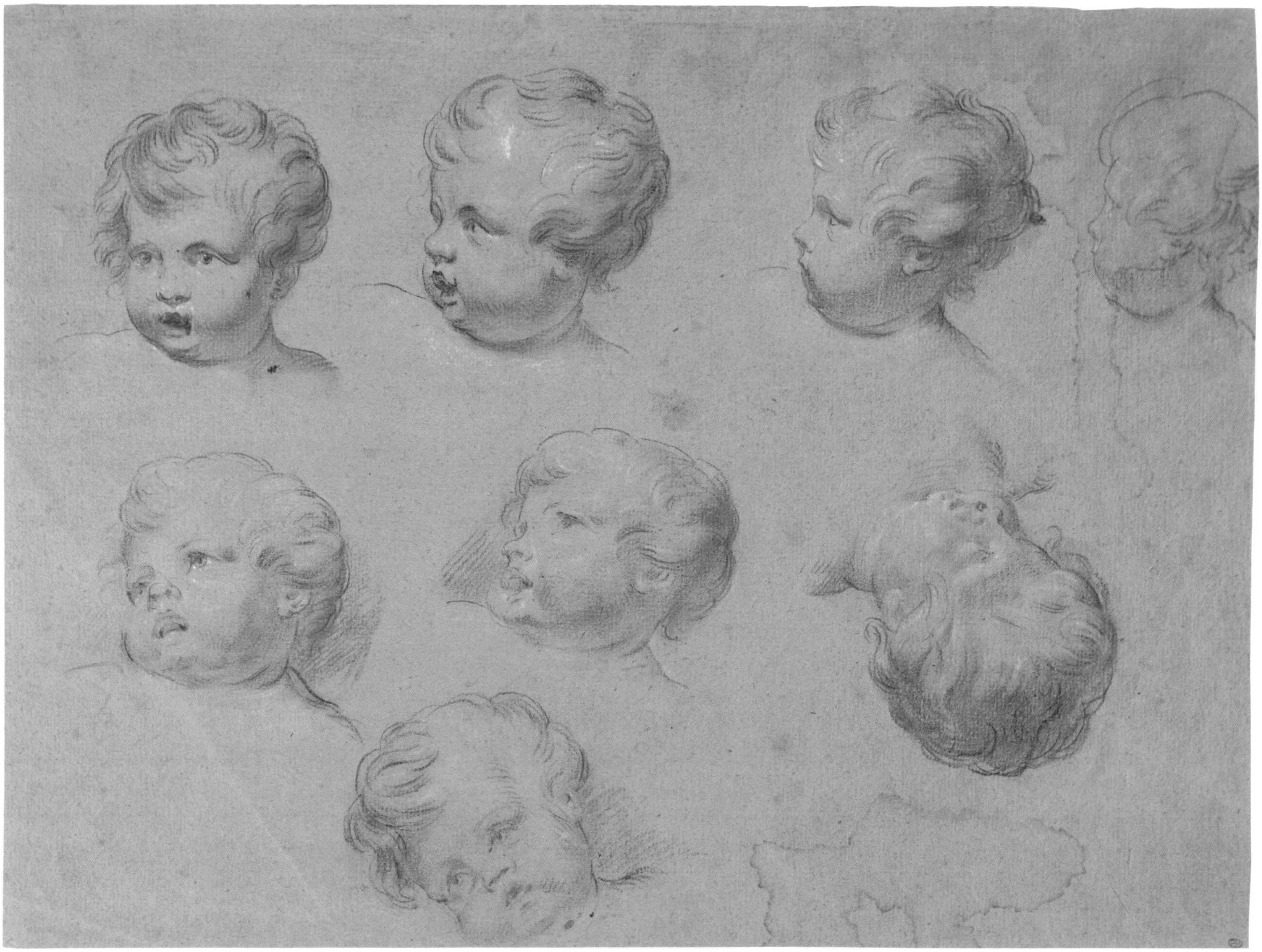

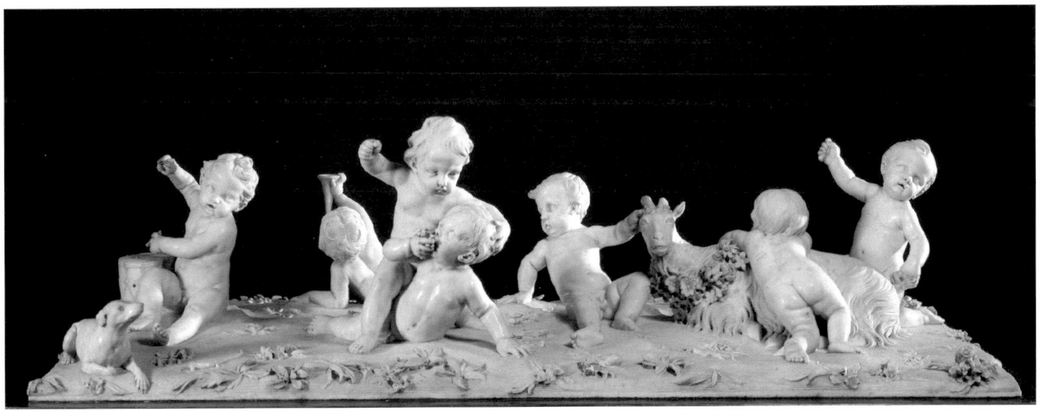

Fig. 26.1 Agostino Cornacchini, 1686–1754, *Group of Children*. Marble, 49 x 180 x 98 cm. Museo Nacional del Prado, Madrid (E00276).

1 *Enciclopedia* 2006, 1455–58; De la Mano 2002, 7ff.; New York 2010–11, 110–13. De la Mano 2011.

2 De la Mano 2002, 7ff. Also see de la Mano 2006, 20–41; and Morales y Marín 1996. Preciado de la Vega 1789. See Cornudella i Carré 1997, 97–122.

3 Pérez Sánchez 1986, 350–51. Mollinedo 1973, 145–57.

4 My thanks to Ascensión Ciruelos, Real Academia de Bellas Artes de San Fernando.

5 José Bonaparte was styled *José Napoleon Io, Rey de España y de las Indias* on a print at the Biblioteca Nacional, Madrid (IH/4619/3 Colección Carderera, 1808, Imprenta Real 1810). *Enciclopedia* 2006, 1457.

6 Conversation with the author, November 19, 2010. It is also José de la Mano's observation that the annotation reflects a later attribution rather than a signature. For the catalogue raisonné, see de la Mano 2011.

7 *Enciclopedia*, III, 847–48.

BONAVENTURA SALESA

Borja, 1756–1819, Zaragoza

Bonaventura Salesa's early career was spent at the Escuela de Bellas Artes de San Luis de Zaragoza. In the "Concurso para los Premios de Pintura" held in 1772 at the Real Academia de Bellas Artes de San Fernando, Madrid, Salesa, known as "Ventura," won second prize—and a pension from the king—for his drawing after the Farnese Hercules, a plaster cast of which was in the Real Academia.[1] Later, his pension continued under the guise of his work as director of painting at the Academia de San Luis de Zaragoza.[2]

Salesa studied at the Spanish Academy in Rome on a pension from Charles III and made copies after Raphael that he sent back to Madrid.[3] Later he returned to Spain, primarily to provide drawings to engravers for the Imprenta Real, under the patronage of Don José Nicolás de Azara, Marqués de Nibbiano (1730–1804), the Spanish king's representative in Rome from 1765 to 1798 (hereafter Azara). Salesa studied with Anton Raphael Mengs (1728–1779) in Rome after 1777 and later was a pensioner at the Spanish Academy under the direction of Francisco Preciado de la Vega (1712–1789), alongside other Spanish students who were pensioned by Charles III.[4]

Salesa's most notable achievement as a painter was a portrait of Mengs commissioned by Azara.[5] He drew several copies of works by Mengs that were engraved for books, including the *Portrait of Winckelmann* (Metropolitan Museum of Art, 1948.141) completed in 1755–56. Azara hired Salesa to draw a copy after the portrait in his possession by 1787, which was later engraved by Jacques Louis Copia (1764–1799) for the frontispiece of Winckelmann's *Histoire de l'Art chez les anciens*, published in 1794.[6]

After demonstrating the mastery of copying antique sculptures, Salesa was commissioned by Azara to complete many copies after the antique, some of which were later engraved. For example, he copied *Head of Caesar Augustus* from an antique marble found at Palma de Mallorca, in the collection of Cardinal Despuig; he also drew *Head of Jupiter Aegiacus*, a copy after a cameo in the collection of the Venetian Senator Giuliani. Several of Salesa's drawings were engraved by Raphael Morghen, who worked for the Grand Duke of Tuscany, Ferdinand III.[7]

Favored with Azara's patronage, Salesa contributed drawings that were later engraved for other translations by the Marqués, including José Goya y Muniain's *Los Comentarios* of Julius Caesar (Madrid, Imprenta Real, 1790), with a frontispiece to the first volume designed by Antonio Carnicero and engravings by Fernando Selma.[8] Azara also gave Salesa commissions for many drawings of Italian archaeological monuments and discoveries from 1794 to 1798.[9]

27. *Male Nude Posing as Christ Crowned with Thorns*, 1777–84

Black crayon heightened with white crayon on cream laid paper, prepared with gray gouache ground, lined

53.0 x 37.5 cm. (20⅞ x 14¾ in.)

PROVENANCE: Sale, Christie's, London, April 1, 1987, lot 171; Joseph F. McCrindle, Princeton and New York

Gift of the Joseph F. McCrindle Foundation 2009-58

Salesa's academic study of a model posing as Christ Crowned with Thorns was likely executed by the young artist while he lived in Rome, and the clean lines and classic simplicity of his forms demonstrate the influence of Mengs. The artist signed his name "Bonaventura Salesa Espagnol," continuing the tradition of Spanish artists working in Italy who noted their heritage as a way of distinguishing themselves.

Based on the facts of Salesa's life and the academic quality of the study, the drawing most likely dates from the artist's time at the Spanish Academy in Rome, prior to 1784. Salesa's drawings are rather rare, although two are kept at the Real Academia de Bellas Artes de San Fernando (inv. 1573/P. *Hércules Farnesio* and inv. 1575/P. *Apolino*). Prints after his drawings can be found in numerous collections worldwide, including the Metropolitan Museum of Art and the Smithsonian Institution. LAB

1 Azcárate Luxán 1994, 128–30, figs. 106–107.
2 Ibid., 130.
3 Bédat 1989, 263.
4 These artists include Manuel Nápoli (1758–1831), Carlos Espinosa y Moya (1758–after 1818), Francesc Agustín i Grande (1753–1801), and Francisco Javier Ramos y Albertos (1744–1817).
5 Azara was also an important figure in the artistic life of Spanish students sent to study in Rome. Azara edited Mengs's collected writings in 1780 and included a list of the works in Spanish royal collections. José Nicolás Azara, ed., *Obras de D. Antonio Rafael Mengs, Primer Pintor de Cámara del Rey* (Madrid: Imprenta Real de la Gazeta, 1780). Mengs, who worked in Madrid from 1761 to 1768 and 1773 to 1777, was a pivotal figure in introducing neoclassicism into Spanish painting at court. As Salesa's most important patron, Azara commissioned the artist to draw fifty-four illustrations for the four volumes of Conyers Middleton's *Historia de la Vida de Marco Tulio Cicerón*, translated by Azara and published by the Imprenta Real in Madrid in 1790. *Summa Artis* 1987–88, 546–547, 565. Although Manuel Salvador Carmona also contributed fourteen plates to the first volume, Salesa was awarded the majority of the work. *Summa Artis* 1987–88, 546.
6 The Metropolitan Museum of Art curatorial files.
7 Frederic Robert Halsey, *Raphael Morghen's Engraved Works* (New York: G. P. Putnam's Sons, The Knickerbocker Press, 1885), 16, 66, 147. Also see Michael Bryan, *Dictionary of Painters and Engravers: Biographical and Critical*, vol. 2 (London: George Bell and Sons, 1889), 174. Azara commissioned several other engravings from Morghen and also from Giovanni Volpato, including Mengs's *Descent from the Cross*, engraved in 1791 after Salesa's drawing. *Summa Artis* 1987–88, 564–65.
8 *Summa Artis* 1987–88, 547.
9 Ibid.

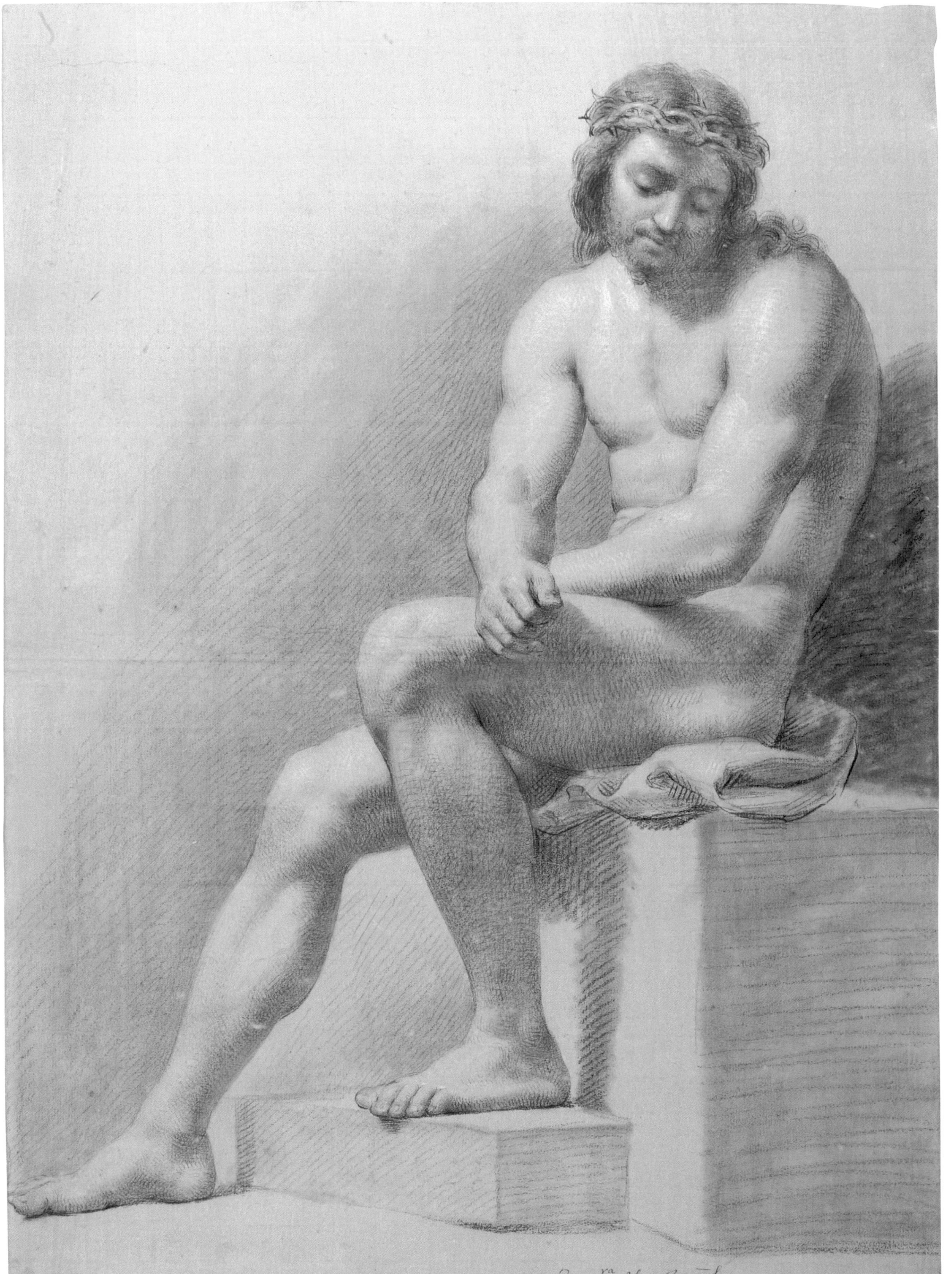
Bonav.ra Salesa Español

LUIS ANTONIO PLANES

Valencia, 1742–1821, Valencia

Luis Antonio Planes was the son of Tomás Planes (1703–1783?), a Valencian engraver. At an early age he entered the Academia de San Carlos, where he studied with Juan Collado and José Camarón, and he was later sent to the Real Academia de Bellas Artes de San Fernando, Madrid. In 1758, Planes failed to win a scholarship to study in Rome, but won the first prize for painting in the Concurso General in 1763. A solid though unremarkable draftsman whose works are in the collection of the Museo de Bellas Artes, Valencia, Planes employed a retardataire style that was influenced by his study of paintings by Vicente Carducho at El Paular, executed more than one hundred years earlier.[1] Planes's drawings are primarily in Valencian collections and are frequently executed in black chalk with light washes.

Attributed to Luis Antonio Planes

28. *The Origin of Painting*

Pen and brown ink with brush and brown wash over black chalk, on off-white laid paper, edge mounted on heavy cream Bristol paper; verso: very faint sketches in black chalk

15.4 x 21.4 cm (6 1/16 x 8 7/16 in.)

Inscribed on verso, in pen and brown ink, upper left: *6*

Provenance: Private collection, Valencia; Private collection, Paris; Galerie Jean-Marie le Fell, Paris, 2004, no. 15

Reference: Le Fell 2004, 21, no. 15, as "Rafael Ximeno y Planes"

Exhibition: Le Fell 2004, 21, no. 15, as "Rafael Ximeno y Planes"

Museum purchase, Laura P. Hall Memorial Fund and Fowler McCormick, Class of 1921, Fund 2005-59

Although originally attributed to Rafael Ximeno y Planes (1759–1825), this drawing is much more likely the work of his uncle Luis Antonio Planes. Here, Planes depicts the origin of painting, a neoclassical subject favored by academic artists in the eighteenth century. The young woman at the right of the sheet draws her lover's profile by tracing the shadow of his face on a canvas held by Time, who also carries an hourglass. The drawing depicts a story related by Pliny on the origins of painting, recounted by several Spanish treatise writers.[2] Love's presence is indicated by the small winged cupid hovering behind the lover at the upper left.

The portfolio in which this sheet was discovered remained in Valencia until recently, suggesting that an artist who spent his career in Valencia, as Luis Antonio Planes did, was the more likely author than Rafael Ximeno y Planes (who left the majority of his late work, and most of his drawings, in Mexico).[3] Other sheets in the album, by artists within Planes's circle at the Real Academia de San Carlos, also date from the late eighteenth century, a fact supported by datable watermarks found in the papers of several of the other sheets.[4]

There is a faint sketch in black chalk on the verso of the drawing, suggesting an arch, as well as a vine with some leaves and an outlined "P" at the lower edge. The P might stand for "Planes," although it is unclear whether he monogrammed other drawings in this way. Faintly visible—but more defined when the sheet is viewed under ultraviolet light—are the figures of two old women standing in front of a crenellated architectural setting at the bottom of the verso. The woman at right holds rosary beads. These figures might have been transferred to the verso of the sheet due to pressure when the album was still bound, although there is no other drawing in the Le Fell catalogue that includes these figures. At the upper left corner of the verso, the number "6" is visible in pen and gray ink, implying that the sheet was once part of a notebook or album. As discussed when the drawing was first published in 2004, this group of drawings was kept loose in an old folder, which might have contained other sheets that now are dispersed. For example, several sheets by Mariano Salvador Maella were also part of the original group. This sheet by Planes was among drawings by several eighteenth-century Valencian masters, including Vicente López y Portaña (1772–1850), José Camarón y Boronat (1731–1803), and José Camarón y Meliá (1760–1819). Other sheets attributed to Planes's nephew, Rafael Ximeno y Planes were acquired by the Hispanic Society of America, New York.[5]

Luis Antonio Planes's loose manner of using wash over figures drawn with quick pen lines over black chalk closely resembles that in his drawings of *Saint Peter in Prison*, for example, and the preparatory drawing for the *Last Supper*, both at the Museo de Bellas Artes in Valencia.[6] LAB

1 Pérez Sánchez 1986, 435–37.
2 Robert Rosenblum, "The Origin of Painting: A Problem in the Iconography of Romantic Classicism," *Art Bulletin* 39, no. 4 (December 1957): 279–90.
3 Madrid 2006–7a; and Turner and Bray 2004.
4 Turner and Bray 2004, 21, no. 15; and Madrid 2006–7a, 287–88.
5 Ibid.
6 Espinós Díaz 1994, 138–39, illustrated pl. 346, pl. 347. See discussion of the drawing for the Last Supper, which was attributed to Vicente López until it was recently restored to Luis Antonio Planes. Valencia 1999, 662–63.

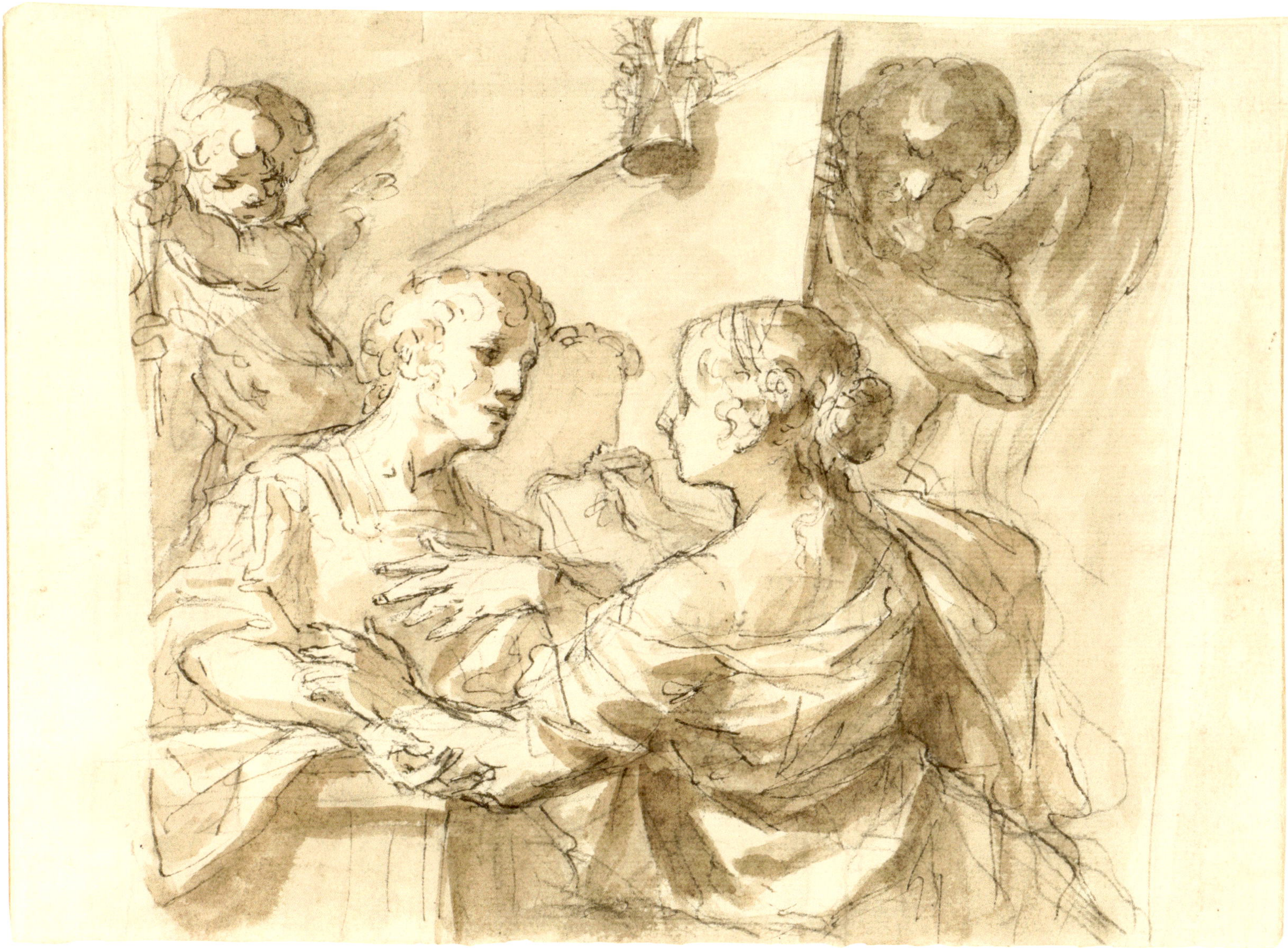

FRANCISCO JOSÉ DE GOYA Y LUCIENTES

Fuendetodos, 1746–1828, Bordeaux

Francisco José de Goya y Lucientes is widely regarded as the most important Spanish artist of the late eighteenth and early nineteenth centuries, one whose evolution over the course of a long career—from his beginnings as a court artist to the haunting and disturbing images in his late paintings—marks him as one of the first truly "modern" artists. Goya was a painter and printmaker as well as a draftsman, and his work is grounded in two traditions: the dark tonalities of such artists as Ribera and Velázquez and the fluid and delicate brushstrokes and drawing of Francisco Bayeu (1734–1795) and Giovanni Battista Tiepolo (1696–1770). His witness to the events and horrors of his time and his stylistic and compositional innovations have given his work durable power.

Goya first studied drawing in Zaragoza with José Luzán Martínez (1710–1785) and continued the practice throughout his life.[1] After a sojourn in Rome (1770–71), where he filled at least one sketchbook with drawings and studies after sculpture and paintings, as well as with classical and biblical themes (Museo del Prado, Madrid), Goya returned to Zaragoza, where he undertook his first important commission (1771–72), for frescoes at the Basilica of El Pilar. At El Pilar he worked alongside Francisco Bayeu, who became his brother-in-law when Goya married Josefa Bayeu.

Goya was introduced to the Spanish royal workshops in 1774, when the German painter Anton Raphael Mengs (1728–1779) asked him to work on tapestry cartoons, or preliminary paintings, for the Royal Tapestry Factory at Santa Bárbara. Goya painted sixty-three cartoons for two royal palaces, which included nine hunting scenes for the dining room at San Lorenzo del Escorial and ten cartoons for tapestries destined for the dining room at El Pardo. The tapestry scenes depict leisure activities of people from all walks of life, in a style comparable to that of Tiepolo.

Goya worked for many years at court, painting portraits and religious scenes, but he also soon began to copy the Velázquez paintings in the royal collection at Mengs's suggestion, in preparation for etchings (1778). His paintings of members of the royal family and of the nobility are marked by fluidity and an interest in surfaces on which broad brushstrokes capture the brilliance of fine clothing and adornment. In 1780 he was named to the Real Academia de Bellas Artes de San Fernando, becoming deputy director of painting in 1785. The following year he was named painter to the king and completed several portraits, including Charles III as a hunter (1787) and several members of his family. After Charles III died in 1788, Goya portrayed his son *Charles IV in Red* (1789).[2] Charles IV appointed him first painter to the king in 1789. Goya's subsequent paintings of the new royal family combined politic representation of a regal family with a naturalism that was surprising for the era.

In 1792 he sent a strongly worded report to the Real Academia de Bellas Artes de San Fernando about the quality of teaching. The following year, Goya became ill with a fever that left him deaf. He went to Cádiz in Andalusia, where he convalesced at the home of Sebastián Martínez, a wealthy businessman and art collector, and then returned to Madrid the following year. In 1796, Goya accompanied the Duchess of Alba on a trip to Andalusia. During this time he began to create the drawings that fill the first of at least eight known albums (A–H).

In 1799, Goya was named first court painter, and in the same year he published works of political and social satire, the *Caprichos*, a suite of eighty allegorical etchings representing a fantasy world of witches, ghosts, and fantastical creatures that invade the mind, a nightmarish vision of a world asleep and without reason. Following Napoleon's invasion of Spain in 1808, Goya created the eighty-five prints of the *Disasters of War* (ca. 1810–15, published in 1863), depicting the atrocities committed during Spain's struggle for independence from France. Ultimately, with the addition of the *Tauromaquia* (1816) and the *Disparates* (ca. 1815–20, left unfinished at his death and ultimately published in 1864 as *Los Proverbios*),[3] Goya created four series of prints of enduring power, each of which was prepared with numerous drawings.

Following the restoration of the Bourbon monarchy with Napoleon's fall in 1814, Goya proved his loyalty to the restored monarchy through such paintings as *The Second of May 1808* (Museo del Prado, Madrid). In 1819, Goya bought a two-story home on the outskirts of Madrid, known as the "Quinta del Sordo," or house of the deaf man, after a previous owner. He began a series of private paintings in fresco there, known as the Black Paintings, which revealed his dark and extraordinary imagination.[4] He left Spain in 1824, definitively, under the guise of seeking medical care. Goya regarded himself as a political exile and went to France, where he died in Bordeaux, home to a community of Spanish exiles, in 1828. At his death, Goya left more than 550 drawings, many of which remained in the hands of his son, Javier. Javier later bequeathed them to Goya's grandson, Mariano, who sold them in 1854.

Fascination with Goya's art has continued during the nearly two centuries since his death and has extended to films, music, and heated academic debate.[5] In these discussions, Goya's drawings are frequently used as proof of his modern sensibility as well as his propensity for artistic exploration through varied media, using subtle and innovative techniques. Drawings are also among the earliest documented work by Goya: his Roman sketchbook (*Cuaderno italiano*) dates from 1770–71 (Museo del Prado, Madrid) and a *Head of an Angel* dates from 1771–72, the time of his first commission at Zaragoza (Musée du Louvre, Paris). Drawings are also Goya's final works, including those from the two Bordeaux albums and intimate ivories that are works of profound imagination and innovative technique.[6] Princeton has both a drawing and an ivory by Goya, capturing both the lyrical early and the late dark sides of this extraordinary artist.

29. *Two Majas Embracing*, ca. 1796–97 (Album B.13/B.14)

Verso: *Maja Parading before Three Others*, ca. 1796–97

Brush and black and gray wash on cream laid paper inlaid into tan wove paper

23.6 x 14.7 cm. (9 5/16 x 5 13/16 in.)

Inscribed in pen and black ink, upper right corner: *13*; inscribed on verso in pen and black ink, upper left corner: *14*

Provenance: Felix Wildenstein (1883–1952), New York; his sale, Parke-Bernet Galleries, New York, Nov. 8, 1952, lot 247, p. 47 ill., as "Dancers: Double-sided drawing"

References: Princeton 1953, 39; López-Rey 1953, vol. 1, 29, 174, and vol. 2, figs. 15–16; Gassier and Wilson 1971, nos. 383–84; Gassier 1973, 124, B.13 and B.14; Paris 1979, nos. 158–59, figs. 152–53; Princeton 2007, 278

Exhibitions: "A Loan Exhibition of Goya, for the benefit of the Institute of Fine Arts, New York University," Wildenstein & Co., New York, Nov. 9–Dec. 16, 1950, no. 52; "The Carl Otto von Kienbusch, Jr. Memorial Collection," The Art Museum, Princeton University, June 1956, no. 71; Lawrence 1958, no. 62; Paris 1979, nos. 158–59, figs. 152–53; Princeton 1995; Princeton 1997

Gift of Carl Otto von Kienbusch, Class of 1906, for the Carl Otto von Kienbusch Jr. Memorial Collection
x1952-83

Goya's double-sided sheet from Album B, known as the Madrid Album, was likely begun during a trip with the Duchess of Alba to Sanlúcar de Barrameda (one of the Andalusian country seats of the House of Medina-Sidonia, near Cádiz) during the years 1796–97.[7] Pierre Gassier has argued that Goya may have begun the album at Cádiz and then completed some of the drawings from imagination upon his return to Madrid.[8]

Doña María del Pilar Teresa Cayetana de Silva-Álvarez de Toledo y Silva, thirteenth Duchess of Alba de Tormes and Grandee of Spain, was a Spanish aristocrat whose marriage to José María Álvarez de Toledo y Gonzaga, fifteenth Duke of Medina-Sidonia, made her and her husband the wealthiest couple in Spain. Goya executed several well-known portraits of the Duchess of Alba, most of them during his stay at Sanlúcar de Barrameda, shortly after the death of her husband. The nature of these portraits has long aroused speculation that Goya and the duchess were lovers, but this has never been confirmed.

Goya's obvious interest in female sexuality was expressed in a number of his drawings, which often depict nudes and intimate scenes. His focused study of women began in Album A and continues through the beginning of Album B. As noted by Gassier, the theme of parading women like those in the Princeton drawing occurs in a drawing from Album A, known as A.g (Museo del Prado, Madrid), and then again in drawings from Album B (B.5, B.6, B.20, B.28, and B.38).

On the recto of Princeton's sheet two women greet each other in a tight embrace; they are fashionably dressed as *majas*, women originally from the lower classes of Spanish society, especially in Madrid, who distinguished themselves by their elaborate style in dress and manner, as well as by their irreverent behavior. On the verso, one *maja*—dressed in a sheer lace mantilla and tight-fitting dress with a low décolleté—struts in front of a group of three other women, drawn with point of brush and light wash in the background. The contrast between the dark shadow behind the *maja* in front and the pale shadow of the group at back emphasizes their distance from her both physically and psychologically. The question of whether Goya observed the scenes he depicted in this album, or whether they were drawn from imagination, remains an open one. The woman in the foreground stands with arms outstretched and raised, as if in a dance pose. Her weight is balanced on the forward foot. Her hand holds a tightly closed fan. The women in the background are brushed in the palest shades of gray wash, but their intent gaze is focused on the woman in front, as if they are watching or waiting. The dancing woman in the front has been identified with the Duchess of Alba, opening the meaning of the drawing to further speculation.

Eleanor Sayre noted in her 1958 essay, "An Old Man Writing: A Study of Goya's Albums," that it was Valentín Carderera who first suggested that the woman in the mantilla in these drawings was the Duchess of Alba in Albums A (known as the Sanlúcar Album) and B, and she adhered to that notion, but this idea has not been accepted universally.[9] LAB

1 Madrid 2006–7a, 246–47.
2 London 2001, 14.
3 Ibid., 11.
4 Madrid 2006–7a, 246–47; and Muller 1984.
5 Debate about the Black paintings is only one of the intellectual explorations that have occurred in the last ten years. More has been written of late about attribution of some paintings that may be by followers or workshops.
6 New York 2006. The exhibition *Goya's Last Works* combined late drawings from the G and H albums, ivories, and paintings from the last years of Goya's life.
7 Gassier discusses Goya's travels around Andalusia, from the Duchess of Alba's estate to Cádiz and then to Madrid. Gassier 1973.
8 Ibid., 124.
9 Sayre's 1958 essay was translated and reprinted in the 1979 Paris exhibition catalogue (Paris 1979), raising the question of the Duchess's presence. Goya's intention is unstated but fuels endless speculation. See also Gassier 1973, 124; Album B.13[28], p. 55, who observes that "there is no reason to suppose or even suggest that the Duchess of Alba is shown here."

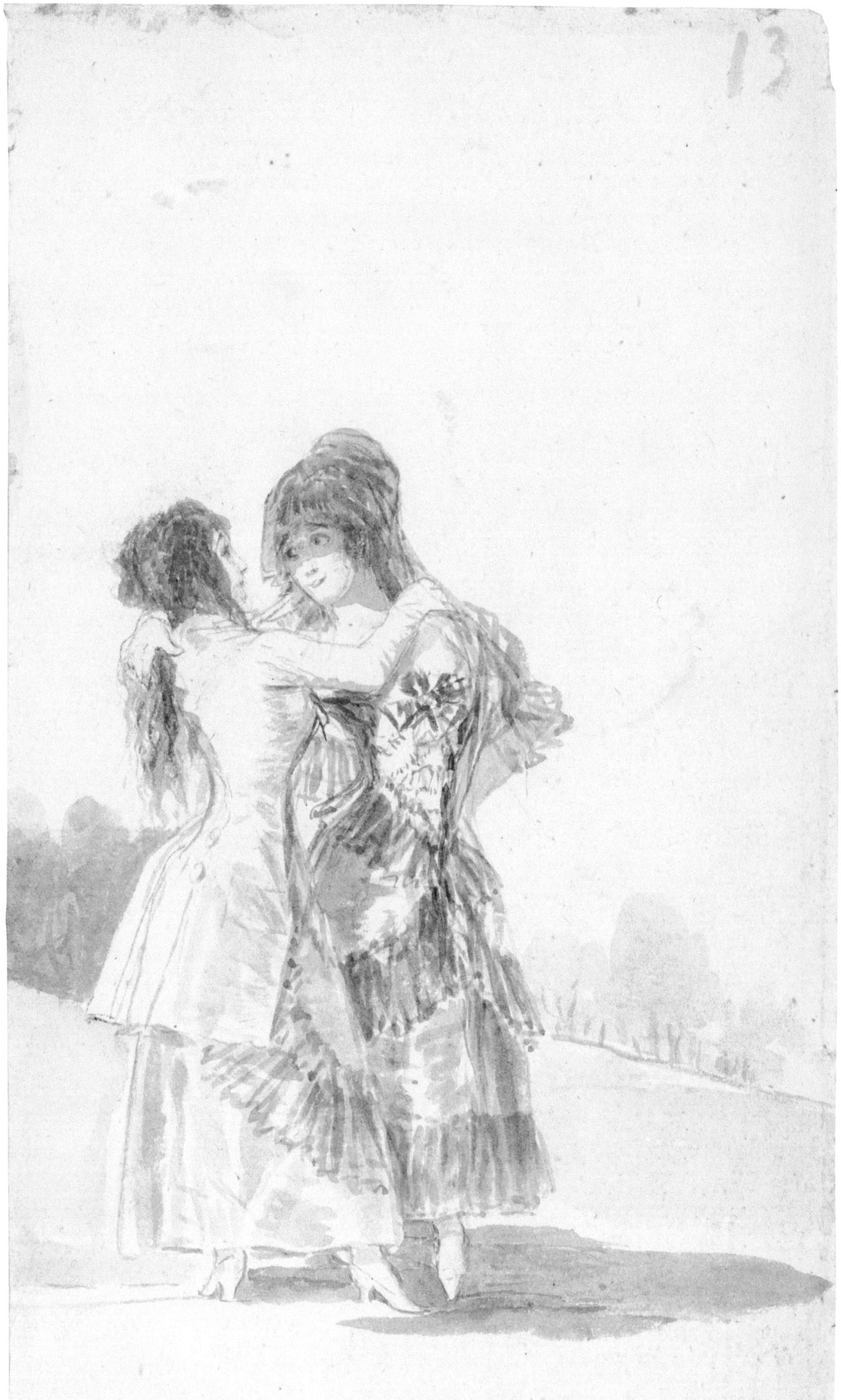

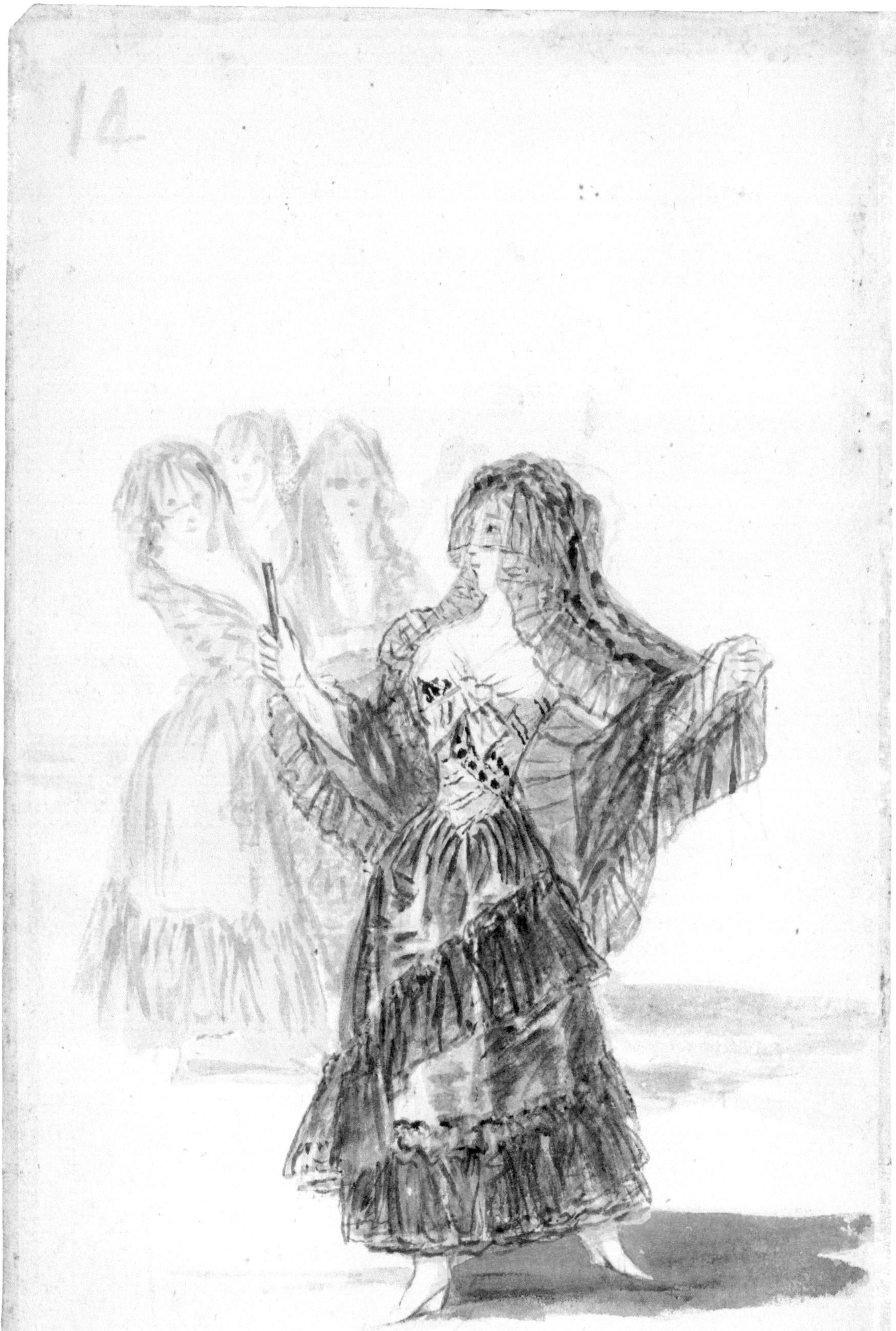

Verso, cat. 29

EUGENIO LUCAS VELÁZQUEZ

Alcalá de Henares, 1817–1870, Madrid

Several recent studies of Eugenio Lucas's work have clarified the artistic personality of the artist, whose drawings have been confused not infrequently with those by Goya—a common scenario for artists who were heavily influenced by the master's work.[1] Part of this confusion stems from the persistent copying of Goya's work by those who wished to learn his techniques. Lucas's free handling of material and his success at imitating certain aspects of Goya's invention led others to imitate his work, as well, muddying the question of attributions to Lucas.

Eugenio Lucas Velázquez was an autodidact, and his lack of academic training might in part explain the often experimental quality of his work; his frequent—if sometimes awkward—copies after Velázquez and Goya; and the loose quality of his handling of paint and pen and ink. Lucas began to paint and exhibit his work in the 1840s. In 1849, recognized by the queen's consort, Francisco de Asís, he began to benefit from more public recognition; in 1850, he decorated the vault of the Teatro Real in Madrid, and in 1851 he was made painter to the queen, or *pintor de cámara.* In 1853 he received the Order of Charles III. In 1855, Lucas participated in the Exposition Universelle de Paris, and his work was praised by Théophile Gautier.[2]

Although there are many reasons why Lucas began to experiment with "*dibujos de manchas*" or "stain drawings," the coincidence of other artists working in the same technique merits discussion. Victor Hugo (1802–1885), who had been in Spain during the Napoleonic occupation, returned to the country in 1843 and in 1859 exhibited some of his own wash drawings made with ink and brush in a similar, abstracted way.[3] Both Hugo and Lucas seem to have been familiar with a book by English painter Alexander Cozens (1717–1786), *A New Method of Assisting the Invention in Drawing Original Compositions of Landscape* (first published in London in 1785) and absorbed some of Cozens's lessons about ink and brush technique.[4] The modern sensibility achieved by Lucas in the *mancha* drawings and his prolific output provided a body of work that deserves further study.

A group of thirty-two Lucas ink stain drawings were lost in the fire at the Instituto Jovellanos de Gijón in 1936. They had been a gift from Acisclo Fernández Vellín, but because they were not catalogued in a detailed fashion and had not been published by José Moreno Villa in the 1926 *Dibujos del Instituto Jovellanos de Gijón, Catálogo,* there are no known extant photographs or further records on this group of drawings.[5] This lack of documentation prevents any further association of newly discovered sheets to the group that originally belonged to Acisclo Fernández Vellín. All that remains is the suggestion of their prior provenance.

Attributed to Eugenio Lucas Velázquez

30. *La Maja Vestida (after Goya),* ca. 1850

Brush and brown watercolor wash on cream laid paper

17.0 x 28.7 cm. (6 11/16 x 11 5/16 in.)

Watermark: A double-headed eagle, with a shield on its chest, cf. Archivo del Reino de Galicia: Real Independencia de Galicia: C.37/142 [not in Bofarull y Sans, 1910 - ?] (see appendix)

Provenance: Scott and Fowles Gallery, 1928; Collection of Esther Slater Kerrigan (1928–1942); her sale, Parke-Bernet Galleries, April 1942, lot 241, as "Francisco José de Goya"; Frank Jewett Mather Jr.

Reference: Princeton 1948, as "Goya"

Gift of Frank Jewett Mather Jr.
x1948-1818

When it was sold in 1942, this drawing was attributed to Francisco Goya, perhaps because of the pose of the half-nude model, whose reclining figure was inspired by Goya's paired paintings *Clothed Maja* (1800–1803, Museo Nacional del Prado, Madrid) and *Nude Maja* (1795, Museo Nacional del Prado, Madrid).[6] Like the figure painted by Goya, the woman lies on a bed with her head at right, her arms behind her head, and a shadow flowing across the pillow. In the sale description, a note reads: "apparently a sketch for the famous painting of *The Maja* (clothed) from the Prado, Madrid."

Instead, this ink and wash drawing was drawn after that famous painting, likely by Eugenio Lucas, who used an inkblot technique after about 1850. Lucas's first experiments with more abstracted forms and new techniques of drawing and painting were fluid and loose. Although departing from *Clothed Maja,* the artist who made this drawing depicted the figure as a sensual abstraction rather than a woman of flesh and blood, somewhat diminishing her appeal.

Lucas emulated both *Clothed Maja* and *Nude Maja.* The artist's *La Maja Dormida* depicts a woman with a nude bust reclining on a sofa, similar in pose to Princeton's drawing.[7] However, the experimental technique in Princeton's drawing, in contrast to the more traditional handling of the subject in *La Maja Dormida,* suggests that this sheet might be an independent, unrelated study of the subject. The pretty face on the subject here, similar to that in Lucas's *Coloquio Galante* (Fuendetodos 16, former María Cristina de Borbón collection) and *Tertulia o Salón* (Fuendetodos 32) of about 1850, helps to establish a date and context for this drawing.

Sheets by Lucas copying Goya's drawings in the loose ink-wash "*mancha*" technique were once in the María Luisa de Borbón collection.[8] The 2009 exhibition at Fuendetodos focused on the variety and success of Goya's imitators, exploring their techniques and

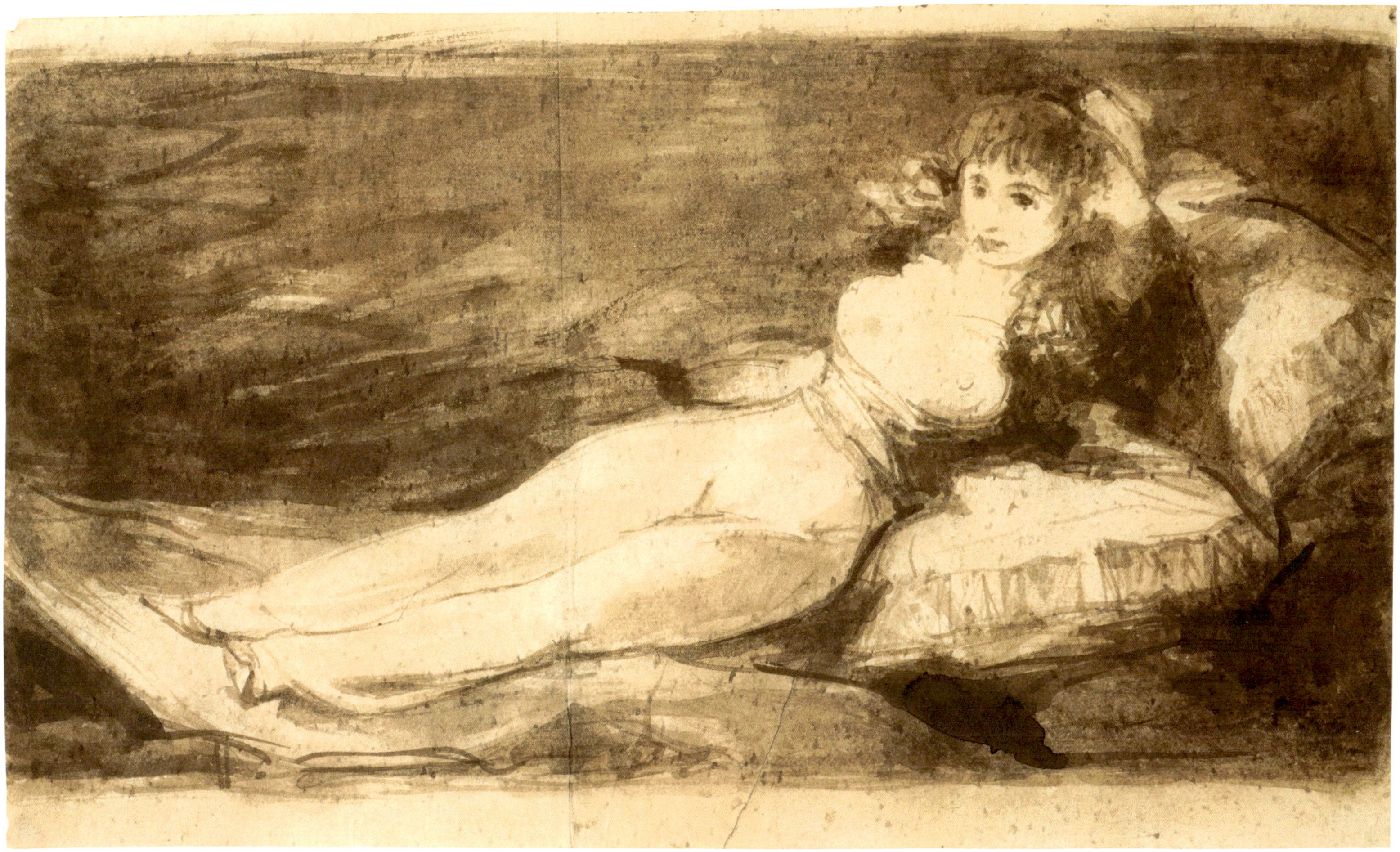

demonstrating their accomplishments. Many of the works were free copies of known paintings or drawings by Goya, clearly by Lucas's hand. The artist's well-known association with Goya's son and grandson, and his appraisal of the Quinta del Sordo in 1855 after the death of Javier Goya, are evidence of the relationship of trust that he had with Goya's family.[9] Perhaps Lucas's copies after the album drawings were made in order to have a record prior to the dispersal of the more than 450 drawings that were in the estate at Goya's death.[10]

Not all of the sheets from the María Cristina de Borbón collection were illustrated in the Fuendetodos catalogue, but several by Lucas's contemporaries and imitators also had watermarks, including no. 42, which has a sketch of a nude woman on the verso.[11] The watermark in the paper of Princeton's drawing is similar to that found on a document dated 1742 from Valencia and deposited in the Archivo del Reino de Galicia: Real Independencia de Galicia: C.37/142.[12] This suggests that the artist might have used an end sheet from an old book, perhaps for the effect of a fine laid paper, for the color it imparted to his drawing, or simply because it was at hand when he conceived the drawing. Such use of an eighteenth-century paper suggests that the artist was looking for a fine paper in order to make a drawing, perhaps for an important client. LAB

1 The exhibition *L'imaginari d'Eugenio Lucas: La influència de Goya a la poètica romàntica* at the Museu Nacional d'Art de Catalunya placed Lucas's drawings in the context of modernism, demonstrating a progression from the modernist impulse of Goya to the nascent abstraction of Lucas's late work.

2 Fuendetodos 2009.

3 Barcelona 2002, 36.

4 Ibid., 5. Also see Arnáiz 1981.

5 Barcelona 2002, 5–7.

6 Moreno Villa 1926. Alfonso E. Pérez Sánchez, *Catálogo de la Colección de Dibujos del Instituto Jovellanos de Gijón* (Madrid: Blass, 1969), p. 82. While all the drawings in the Instituto Jovellanos are thought to have perished completely in the fire, the suggestion has been made on more than one occasion that random sheets might have survived the devastation. Pérez Sánchez and Lafuente Ferrari 2003.

7 When the work first was acquired by the Museum, Xavier Salas wrote on the mat, "Not Goya; could be Lucas," November 7, 1956. As Janis Tomlinson has pointed out in her 1996 article about the perception of authentic works by Goya, "verbal, rather than visual, conceptions of Goya—often based on preconceptions of what Spanish painting was about—provided the criteria for judging authenticity." See Tomlinson 1996, 189–202. However, in the case of this drawing, the artist has made use of a technique that echoes Lucas's determined imitation of Goya's subject matter, in his own free and brushy technique with ink washes. Lucas created a new and different way of working; it appears to have inspired many copyists.

8 Arnáiz 1981, 500, no. 383.

9 Fuendetodos 2009, front cover, back cover, no. 32, 51, 55. My thanks to José Manuel Matilla and to Francesc Quílez.

10 Ibid., 12–13.

11 Ibid. Ansón Navarro proposes that Lucas received the copper plates of Goya's *Disparates* in payment or consideration for the service that he performed for the family in appraising the Quinta del Sordo and the Black Paintings.

12 The watermarks are not described. I am grateful to Carmen Hidalgo, Jefe de Servicio de Libros y documentos, Instituto del Patrimonio Cultural de España, and to Isabel García-Toraño Martínez, Sección de Bellas Artes, Biblioteca Nacional, Madrid, for their help on this matter.

Many followers of Goya imitated his *Caprichos,* a widely circulated group of prints made in 1796–97. The followers, however, did not have Goya's genius for invention, nor did they produce drawings with quite the same level of effortless accomplishment that the master could. Among those who were facile draftsmen—and whose ties to Goya were fairly well established, meaning that they had access to the original works or to a set of prints—a few are noteworthy. Leonardo Alenza, Eugenio Lucas, José Zapata, and Mariano Fortuny are among those who closely copied, and then departed from, Goya's work.

During his brief life and artistic career, Leonardo Alenza y Nieto (1807–1845) developed a reputation for following in Goya's footsteps, echoing the *Caprichos* and mastering a fluid and rapid pen stroke that seemed to some to be close to Goya's own. Alenza left a large oeuvre that explored some of the same motifs as Goya's: the picaresque themes of daily life and satirical views of certain characters in society. Although he emulated his idol in many regards, Alenza did not intend to be confused with him or to have his work taken for Goya's own, usually monogramming his work with a strong, flourished "A." Most of Alenza's *Capricho* drawings were made in groups for his friends; the album in the Metropolitan Museum of Art is one of these groups that remains intact—as it was originally intended and prepared by the artist—outside of Spain. The largest concentration of Alenza's work on paper remains in Madrid, with 465 drawings in albums at the Biblioteca Nacional and additional sheets at the Real Academia de Bellas Artes de San Fernando and the Museo Lázaro Galdiano, Madrid. The groups of albums at the Biblioteca Nacional are similarly maintained in their original albums, although they are more sketches or random ideas than a single, concerted effort to create a coherent album of related drawings.

Perhaps the clearest artistic statement Alenza made of his relationship to Goya was the reception piece that he submitted to the Real Academia de Bellas Artes de San Fernando, a painting of *David and Goliath* that he prepared first with a small pen and ink sketch (fig. 31.1). Alenza's David does not simply conquer Goliath; he seems to wrestle with him. Alenza studied under Juan Antonio Ribera y Fernández de Velasco (1779–1860) and José de Madrazo (1781–1859) and became a member of the Academy only in 1842, three years before his death. The artist's conscious emulation of Goya has created challenges in identifying works by Alenza, in assessing his artistic identity, and in studying the hundreds of drawings he left. However, in mirroring Goya's work, Alenza incorporated his own ideas, using simple line drawings in pen and dark brown ink to capture scenes of daily life and figures observed on the street. His line drawings appeared in contemporary periodicals published in the *Semanario Pintoresco,* for example, until his death in 1845.

In 1877 the printer Rosell engraved nineteen of Alenza's *Caprichos,* which won a third-place medal at the Exposición de Bellas Artes in Madrid in 1878.[1] Alenza had been dead for more than thirty years when those prints were made. Subsequently, Rosell and his colleague Cristóbal Férriz selected an additional sixty-six of Alenza's *Caprichos* to engrave as a set, adding captions to the engravings.

Some of the confusion between Alenza's work and Goya's occurred after the latter's death because of such posthumous printing of engravings after his drawings. The exceptionally modern character of Goya's prints and the freedom of his lines, reinterpreted by Alenza with his own free handling of drawing media, seemed "too good" to be by a less-known artist. Alenza's work has not been widely imitated, however, nor is it well represented outside of Spain, as the majority of the artist's drawings remain in his native country. Only thirty-six of Alenza's drawings are in New York museum collections: thirty *Caprichos* in an album at the Metropolitan Museum of Art and six loose sheets at the Hispanic Society of America.[2] A corresponding set of *Caprichos,* engraved after Alenza's album at the Metropolitan, is at the Hispanic Society.[3]

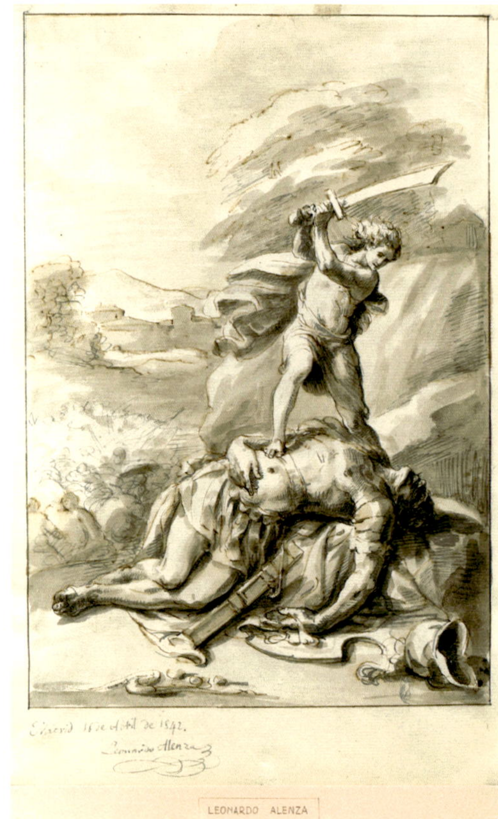

Fig. 31.1 Leonardo Alenza: *David and Goliath.* Real Academia de Bellas Artes de San Fernando.

Drawings after Goya by Eugenio Lucas, another follower, hewed close to the originals, as Lucas was given privileged access to Goya's paintings and his private albums of drawings by his grandson. This access inspired Lucas to try an adventurous new tack, and he began to work on his *mancha* drawings, wildly abstracted visions departing from Goya's compositions. Starting with a *Capricho,* Lucas would transform the original figures into abstracted blotches of ink and white reserved paper. His imitations of Goya, commissioned by private patrons, usually acknowledge Goya's authorship as the original "inventor" of the idea, yet in tone, palette, and the addition of color to works on paper, Lucas popularized Goya's original stark gray conceptions.

Mariano Fortuny freely wrote private letters about the copies he was making after Goya's drawings. He gained access to these through his marriage to Cecilia de Madrazo and through the group of artists and collectors with whom he exchanged ideas in Paris and Rome; Raimundo de Madrazo would send Fortuny watercolor papers on which to work. Fortuny made copies of no fewer than three Goya drawings of prisoners, at least one of which was in the Baron Davillier collection. Most likely, Fortuny made these for his own private purposes, but he died young and unexpectedly. After his death, some works entered the Fortuny studio sale; others remained with his family and were sold slowly over subsequent years.

Drawings formerly attributed to Leonardo Alenza, now Anonymous Follower of Goya, 19th century

Because of the many problems of attribution that plague the followers of Goya—particularly those who copied Goya's work firsthand, including Lucas, Alenza, and Fortuny—the drawings at Princeton must be seen within the larger context of the debate. Fifteen drawings at Princeton previously have been attributed to Alenza; they are in two different formats, as if from two separate albums.

Traces of adhesive material at the corners of the versos indicate that the drawings likely were once mounted onto secondary supports and pasted into albums, as were so many groups of drawings collected in Spain during the nineteenth century. In the 1950s, Xavier de Salas made notations on the mats of the entire set, stating that in his opinion these drawings were not by Alenza—despite the artist's relative obscurity to American collectors and the repeated attributions of these two sets of drawings to him. In the June 1944 *Bulletin of the Department of Art and Archaeology*, Frank Jewett Mather acknowledged the extraordinary gift to the Art Museum that had been made by Dan Fellows Platt's widow in the previous year: more than 2,500 sheets. Mather noted that Platt had given "in the Spanish school . . . a group of some fifteen Alenzas. . . . a really able follower and imitator of Goya's diabolism, in the *Caprichos*, a powerful designer in his own right with whom the Goya collector must reckon seriously."[4]

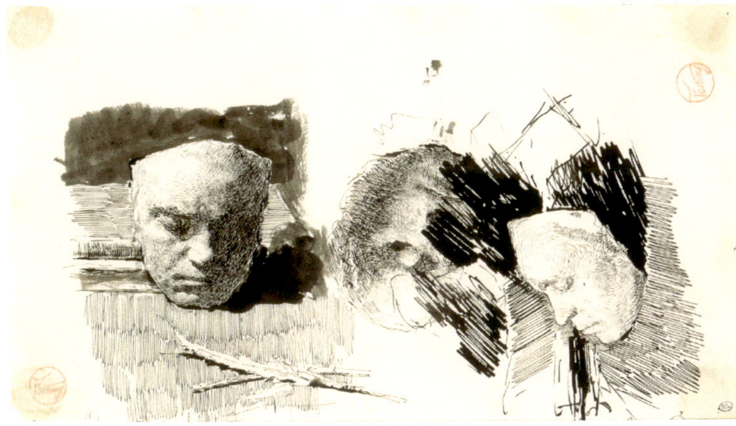

Fig. 31.2 Mariano Fortuny i Marsal, Spanish, 1838–1874: *The Mask of Beethoven on a Table in Front of Books.* Black ink, brown ink, pen (drawing), wash with black, 18.7 x 27.3 cm. Musée du Louvre, Paris, France (29821, 29822).

Contrary to Mather's opinion, Salas believed these sheets to be by a late nineteenth-century artist whose style closely copied Goya's *Caprichos*, combining the figures into new compositions. Both the 1948 group and the 1949 group have their own internal cohesion in terms of size, format, and paper types. They do not have a narrative and are not random sketches (as for a sketchbook) and thus can be considered two distinct groups of *Caprichos*. Additional drawings that remain in private collections relate to these works.[5]

Perhaps Salas had seen the one drawing that corresponds to the size of this group that was separated or held back. It was sold prior to 1998, and its current location is unknown. This drawing, more strikingly caricature-like than the rest of the group at Princeton, is modern in sentiment and technique, in contrast to drawings by Alenza that closely mimic Goya's *Caprichos* and yet remain romantic interpretations of quotidian themes.

Although we have learned a great deal about Alenza and the other followers of Goya in the last twenty-five years, the fifteen drawings at Princeton formerly attributed to Alenza can now only be attributed to an anonymous follower of Goya. Some clues as to their authorship are present in the drawings themselves, however, and a sketchbook by Fortuny with several hundred leaves might allow a new hypothesis to emerge.

In a sketchbook now at the Louvre, Fortuny copied some of the very Goya drawings that were acquired by the Metropolitan Museum of Art in 1935, a year before Ferargil Galleries sold the drawings at Princeton. In particular, Fortuny made a loose but faithful copy of at least one of the drawings now at the Metropolitan (Goya, *Two Prisoners in Irons, F.80,* Metropolitan Museum of Art, 35.103.44). The artist discusses some of these copies in his letters published by Baron Charles Davillier in 1875.[6] Further, some of Goya's prisoner drawings in wash were owned by Charles Yriarte, a close friend of Fortuny who wrote the artist's biography, and Fortuny made several loose but exact copies of Goya's prisoners in the late 1860s.[7] These belonged to the collection of Valentín Carderera, in whose home Fortuny copied the originals in 1868.[8]

Other loose sketches, pen drawings, and a notebook were bequeathed to the Louvre by Fortuny's relative, Henriette Fortuny, at her death in 1950. Some of the pen drawings bear an uncanny resemblance to the pen handling of these two suites of "*Caprichos.*" In particular, two pen and ink studies of Beethoven's death mask and a loose sheet with a man's face at the right side (see fig. 31.2) demonstrate Fortuny's pen handling, with frenetic short strokes and rapid layering of lines to create volume and shadow. The same sort of strokes, created in imitation of engraved lines, appear in Princeton's drawing formerly attributed to

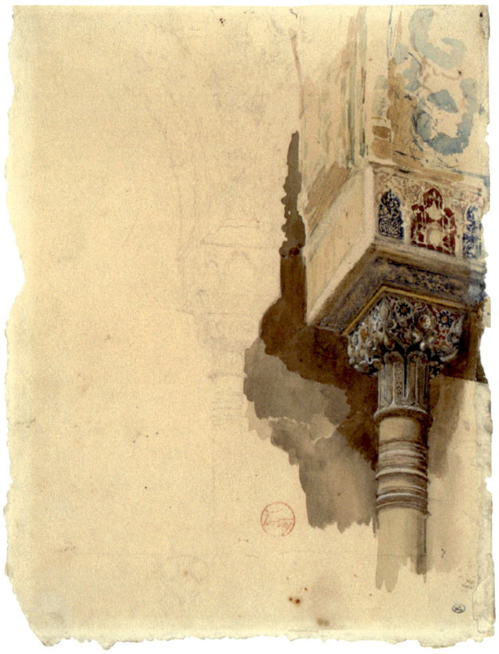

Fig. 31.3 Mariano Fortuny i Marsal, Spanish, 1838–1874: *Study after an Arab Tent at the Alhambra in Granada*. Black ink, black lead, 28 x 22.2 cm. Musée du Louvre, Paris, France (RC 29782).

Alenza, *Man in Plumed Hat with Other Figures* (see cat. 37). The face from the right center panel on the Louvre's sheet of sketches is the same as that in the Princeton sheet, copied from Goya's *Capricho*, 24, *No hubo remedio* (Nothing Could Be Done about It). The delicate pilaster at the right of Princeton's sheet, transparently brushed in wash, echoes the pilasters of the Alhambra, of which Fortuny made hundreds of drawings (fig. 31.3).

When an artist copies from an engraved print or an etching, the use of short parallel lines becomes a default shading method because it repeats the strokes of the burin on the engraving plate or the mottled effect of acid on an etching plate. This characteristic is seen in all of the drawings formerly attributed to Alenza at Princeton. Fortuny's exquisite pen handling and mastery of wash made his mimicry of Goya's etchings an artistic game, to which he alluded in letters to Davillier and other friends and artists. In several of the drawings here, the artist used figures repeatedly, creating new "*Capricho*" drawings that are certainly not by Goya but are difficult to attribute with confidence to the artist who made them. They were exercises meant to convey meaning and also to explore visual conceits. None of Princeton's drawings have captions to explain them, however, and many of Alenza's drawings, including sketchbook sheets and *Capricho* series have both captions and an "A" to identify his authorship.

Platt bought the drawings from Ferargil Galleries, although there is a handwritten note on each stating that they came from the "Marqués de Socorro" (sic) collection. José Solano y Eulate (1844–1912) was the fourth Marqués del Socorro, descended from a distinguished Spanish patriot. His ancestor, Francisco Solano Ortiz de Rozas (1768–1808), had been an important general who attempted to resist the Napoleonic invasion of Spain. Examination of the Ferargil Galleries records has yielded no further information on the provenance of this group of drawings.[9] The timing of their appearance, however—at the start of the Spanish Civil War in 1936, at a gallery closely linked with Platt—makes one wonder about the unusual provenance. The drawings were sold to Platt in 1936, but "Socorro" is written differently on each of the drawings. Only one drawing, a strikingly modern group of head studies, remained apart (location unknown).

Among the numerous followers of Goya, whose styles incorporate pastiches of his themes, Alenza transformed Goya's motifs into new tableaus, although his work generally is less inventive and bold than these drawings.[10] It may seem capricious to believe that these drawings could not be by Alenza, as at the time they were acquired there was no reason to doubt their attribution. Salas, however, doubted that the extreme modernity of the strokes and compositions could reflect Alenza's graphic work. Mariano Fortuny owned some Goya prints and had access to the drawings and prints through the Madrazo family. A reexamination of Fortuny's eclectic style, fine pen work, and intimate connection with the Madrazo family demands closer scrutiny with regard to these drawings. His exploration of Goya's work through his own meticulous copies is known but has not been as well studied as his own graphic oeuvre.

31. *San Isidro Labrador*

Pen and black ink with brush and gray wash on tan wove paper

22.9 x 19.4 cm. (9 x 7⅝ in.)

Inscribed in graphite on verso, lower edge: *H-80* (with red pencil *X* above) *L Alenza / Ferargil Gal. 1936 / Ex Marqués de Socorro* [sic]

Provenance: Marqués del Socorro collection, until 1912; Ferargil Galleries, New York, until 1936; Dan Fellows Platt

Bequest of Dan Fellows Platt, Class of 1895
x1949-90

This drawing is a variation on a theme that both Goya and Alenza took up frequently: San Isidro Labrador, patron saint of Madrid, on his knees at his conversion. Although initially copied after Goya's print composition of the same subject [H2],[11] *San Isidro Labrador* is a subject that Alenza drew many times, developing his own relationship to the saint of Madrid—and likely inspiring the former attribution. Goya's many variations on the themes of San Isidro and the penitent figure absorbed the long history of such representations by Spanish draftsmen. He powerfully represented penitents in pen and brown ink, for example, in *Repentance* (Gassier, 1973, Album F.c), placing a cross in front of the humbled man.[12]

In this sheet, San Isidro kneels in front of a cross with his arms open and face turned heavenward, illuminated in a triangle of light. Drawings by Alenza of San Isidro can be found in the Biblioteca Nacional, Madrid, and the Museo Lázaro Galdiano, Madrid.

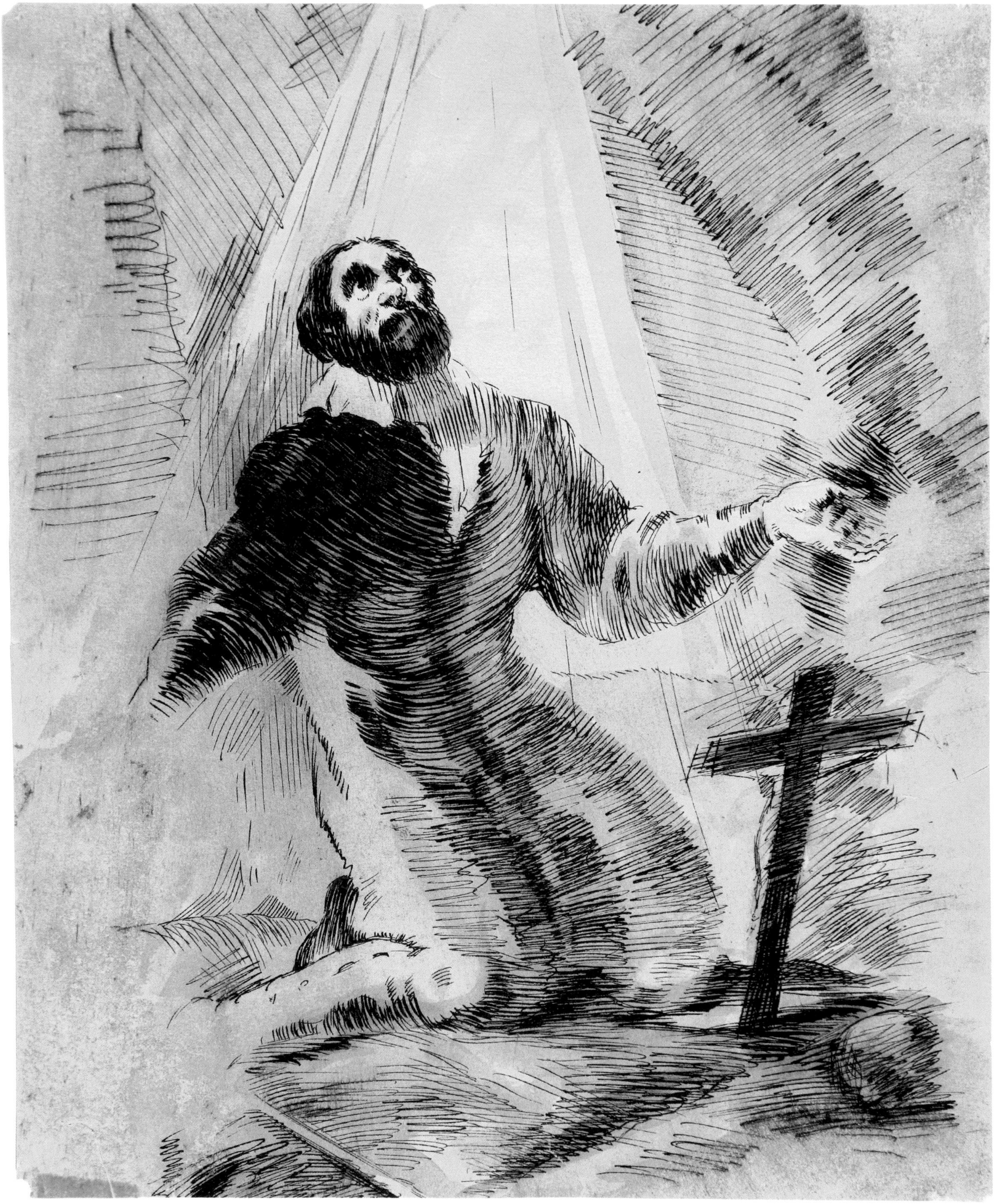

32. *Woman and Man*

Pen and black ink with brush and gray wash on tan wove paper

23.3 x 18.5 cm. (9 3/16 x 7 5/16 in.)

Inscribed in graphite on verso, lower edge: *H-84* (with red pencil *X* above) *L. Alenza / Ferargil Gals. 1936 / Ex Marqués de Socorro* [sic]

PROVENANCE: Marqués del Socorro, until 1912; Ferargil Galleries, New York, until 1936; Dan Fellows Platt

Bequest of Dan Fellows Platt, Class of 1895
x1949-91

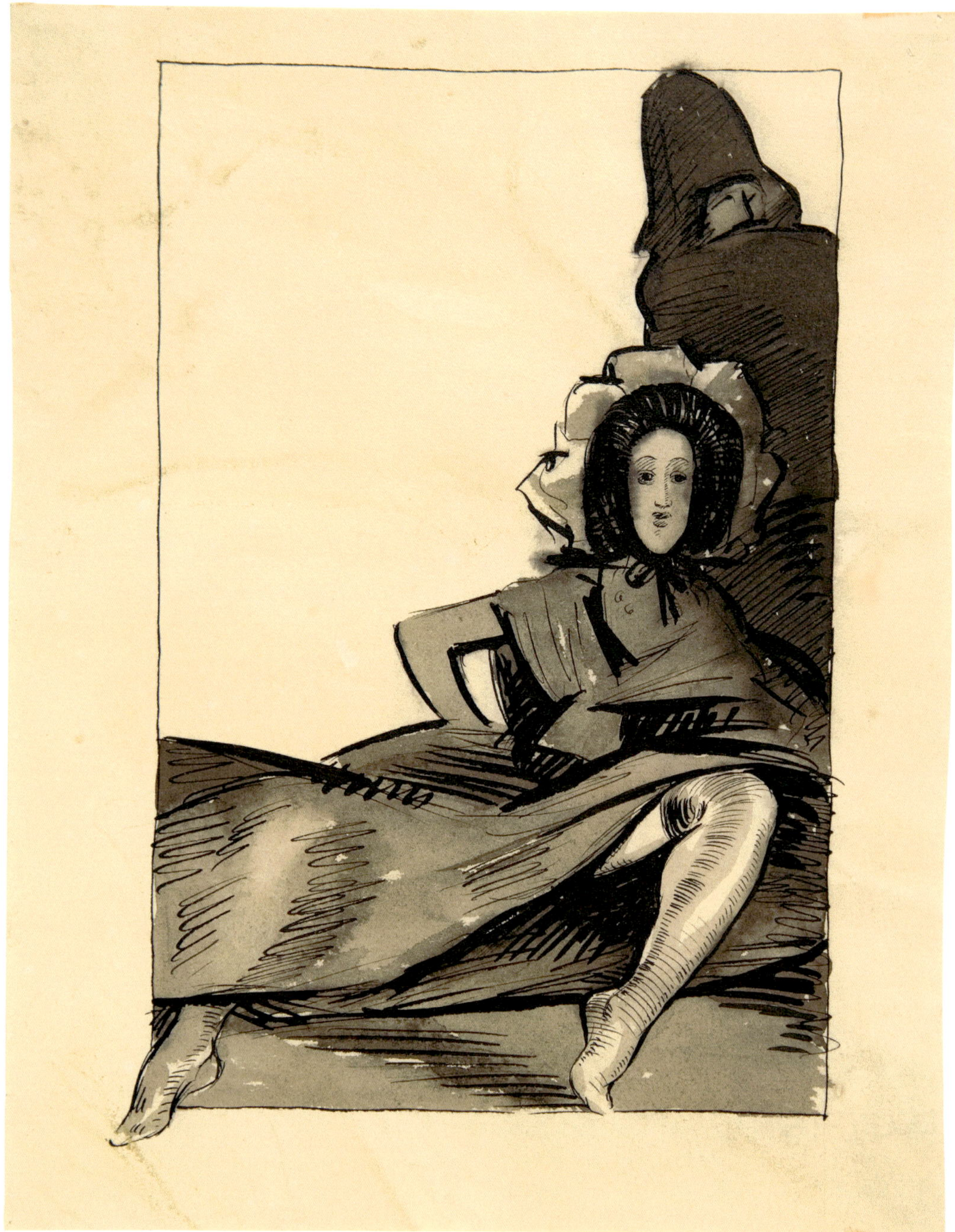

The woman's foot breaks the boundary of a framing line drawn around this composition, protruding out of the image space and into the border around it in a very modern conception of space. This drawing adapts the mask-like face peering between the lovers in Goya's *Capricho* 7, *Ni así la distingue* (Even Thus He Cannot Make Her Out) [H 42] [D 44]. The cloaked figure in the background also resembles the cloaked figure in *Capricho* 79, *Nadie nos ha visto* (No One Has Seen Us) [H 114] [D 116], but this menacing figure appears in many of Goya's prints.

33. *Bust of Bald Man*

Pen and black ink with brush and gray wash on tan wove paper

26.9 x 20.4 cm. (10 9/16 x 8 1/16 in.)

Inscribed in graphite on verso, lower edge: *H.7* (with red pencil *X* above) - *L. Alenza / Ferargil Gals 1936 / Ex Marqués de Socorro* [sic]

PROVENANCE: Marqués del Socorro collection, until 1912; Ferargil Galleries, New York, until 1936; Dan Fellows Platt

Bequest of Dan Fellows Platt, Class of 1895
x1949-92

The bust-length head of a bald man, with eyes closed or shut in blindness, is similar to the tilted head seen in *Man and Goat* (cat. 36). A play on Goya's *Que Pico de Oro!* (What a Golden Beak!) [H 88] [D 90] (fig. 33.1), the figure at the extreme left is manipulated to fill the sheet.

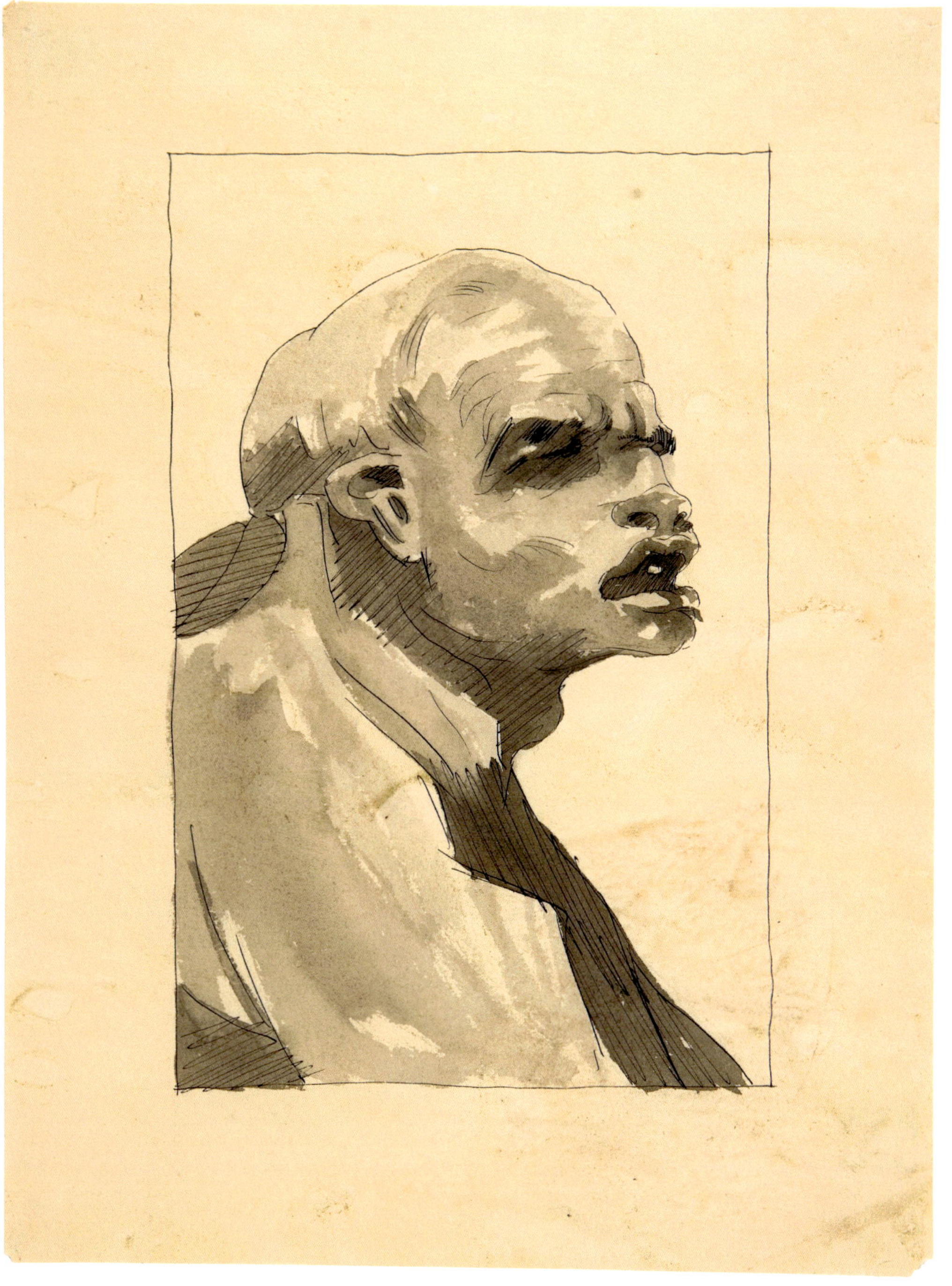

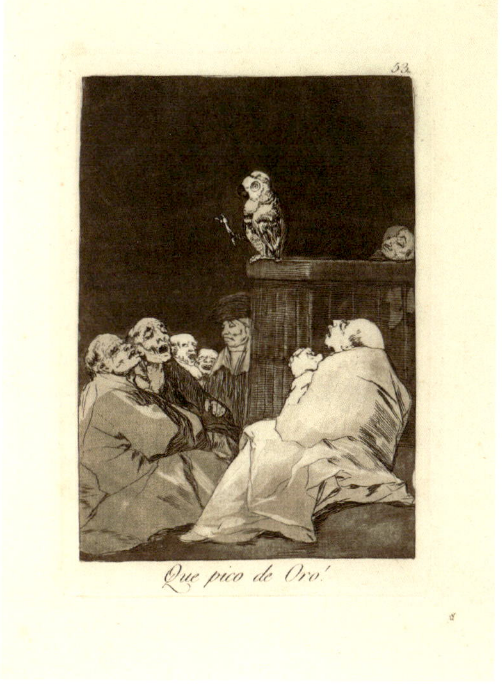

Fig. 33.1 Francisco José de Goya y Lucientes, Spanish, 1746–1828: *Que pico de Oro!* (What a Golden Beak!), from *Caprichos*, 1799. Etching and aquatint, 22 x 32 cm. Princeton University Art Museum, Laura P. Hall Memorial Collection (1946-246).

34. *Cloaked Figure, with Others Wearing Pointed Hats*

Pen and black ink with brush and black and gray washes on brown wove paper

26.0 x 22.4 cm. (10¼ x 8 13/16 in.)

Inscribed in graphite on verso, lower edge: *H-82* (with red pencil *X* above) *L. Alenza / Ferargil Gals 1936 / (Ex Marqués de Socorro)* [sic]

PROVENANCE: Marqués del Socorro, until 1912; Ferargil Galleries, New York, until 1936; Dan Fellows Platt

Bequest of Dan Fellows Platt, Class of 1895
x1949-93

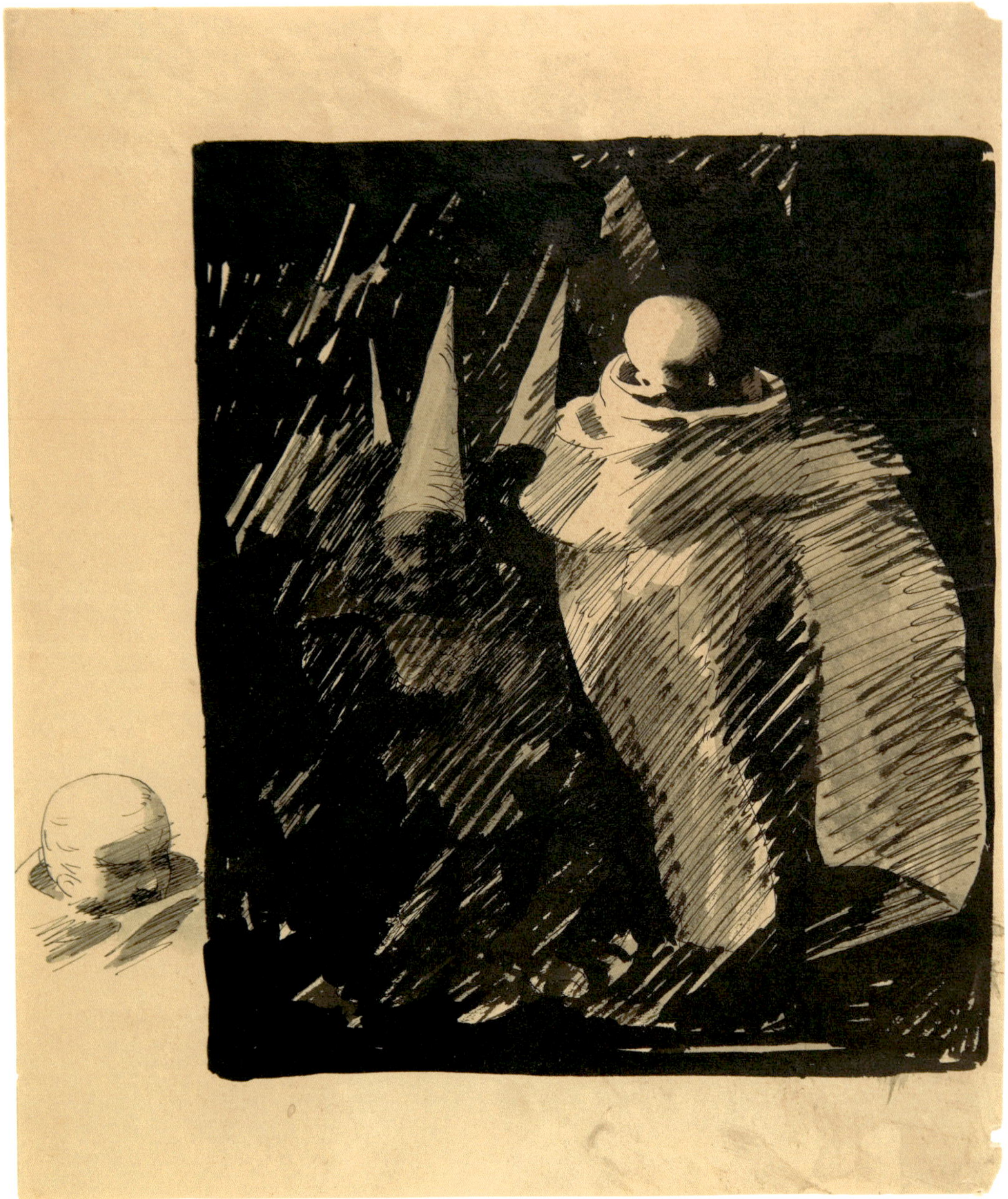

This dark study, almost entirely covered in slashing lines and saturated black ink wash, reveals some figures on the reserved white paper. The pointed hats, taken from the penitents standing before the Inquisition, can be seen in several of Goya's *Caprichos*; the subject also was adopted by Lucas, Alenza, and other early nineteenth-century followers of Goya. *Capricho* 23, *Aquellos polbos* (Those Specks of Dust) [H 58] [D 60], with the condemned man seated and his head bowed, possibly served as the model for the bald man at the right of Princeton's drawing. In this drawing the conical hat is repeated on several figures that appear behind him, like haunting reminders of lost souls. Just outside the border of the composition the artist studied the head in a small sketch, enlarging and adding detail to the facial features.

35. *Three Figures*

Pen and black ink with brush and gray wash, over traces of graphite, on tan wove paper

26.6 x 21.9 cm. (10 7/16 x 8 9/16 in.)

Inscribed in graphite on verso, lower edge: *H81* (with red pencil *X* above) – *L. Alenza / Ferargil Gals - 1936 / ex Marqués de Socorro* [sic]

PROVENANCE: Marqués del Socorro, until 1912; Ferargil Galleries, New York, until 1936; Dan Fellows Platt

Bequest of Dan Fellows Platt, Class of 1895
x1949-94

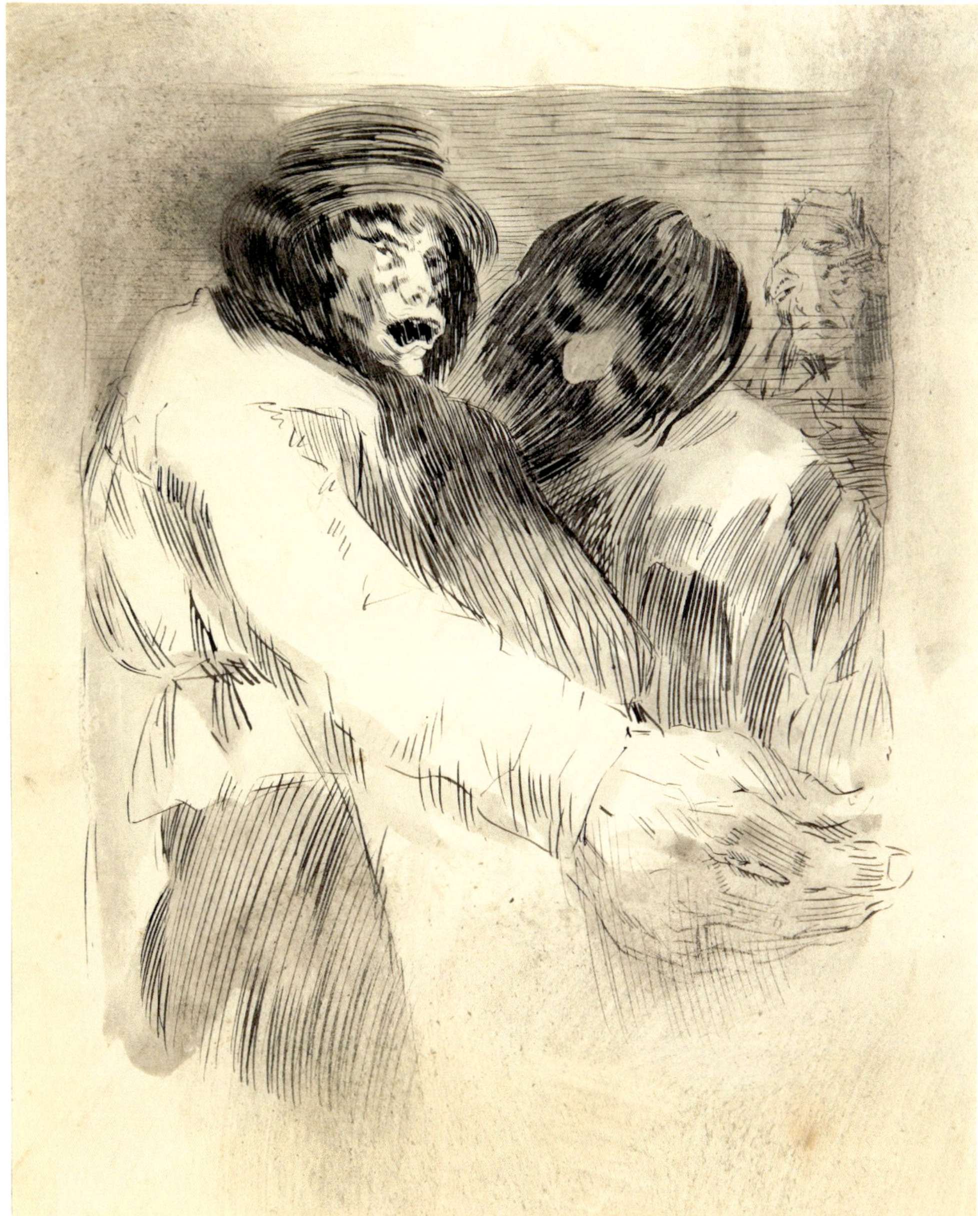

This drawing takes elements from several of Goya's *Caprichos* and combines them. The gross exaggeration of the faces and features on the men in Goya's *Caprichos* 30 and 46, *Porque esconderlos* (Why Hide Them?) [H 65] [D 67] and *Corrección* (Correction) [H 81] [D 83] are deployed here to create a new and more menacing group of only three faces. The large, central figure in the foreground is based on the figure at the extreme left of *Capricho* 30; his features are a conflation of the standing, laughing figure and the seated, toothless figure of Goya's etching. In Princeton's drawing the outstretched hand is grossly exaggerated, extended toward the lower right.

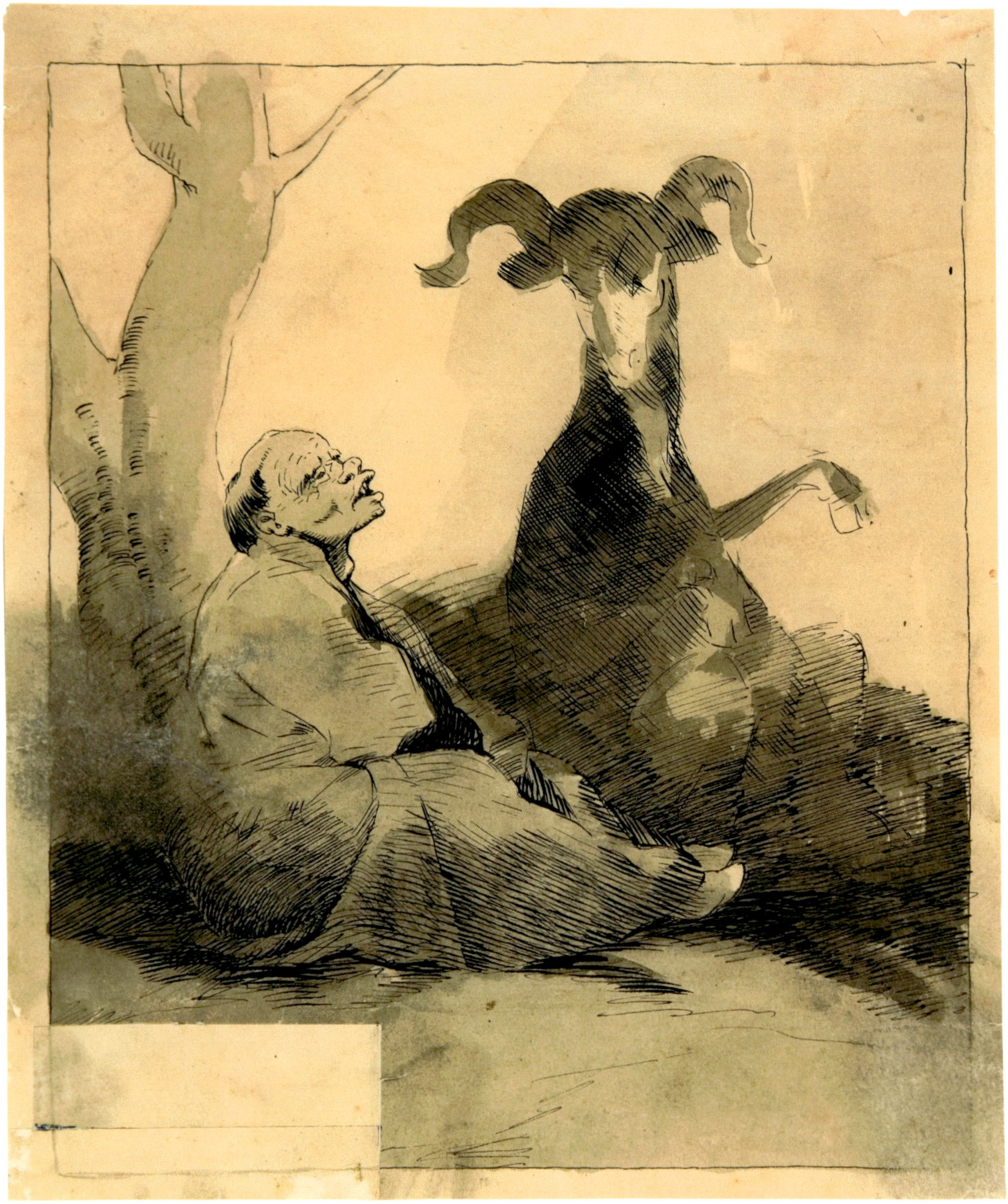

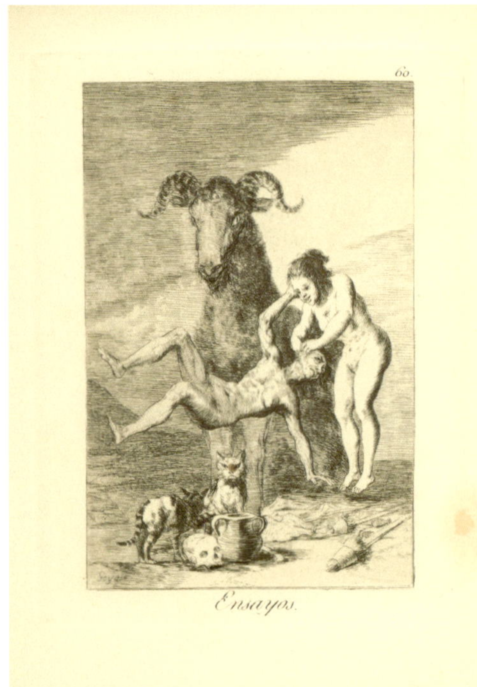

Fig. 36.1 Francisco José de Goya y Lucientes, Spanish, 1746–1828: *Ensayos* (Trials), from *Caprichos*, 1799, fifth edition, 1881–86. Etching, 21.5 x 15 cm. Princeton University Art Museum, Gift of Alan Weinstein, Class of 1961, and Nina Weinstein in honor of their children Rachel Weinstein-Abrams, Anna Weinstein, Daniel Weinstein, and Adam Weinstein (2004-377.60).

36. *Man and Goat*

Pen and black ink with brush and gray wash on tan wove paper prepared with light brown wash

25.2 x 21.6 cm. ($9\frac{15}{16}$ x $8\frac{1}{2}$ in.)

Inscribed in graphite on verso, lower edge: *H 86* (with red pencil *X* above) *L. Alenza / Ferargil Gals 1936 / Ex Marqués de Socorro* [sic]

Provenance: Marqués del Socorro, until 1912; Ferargil Galleries, New York, until 1936; Dan Fellows Platt

Bequest of Dan Fellows Platt, Class of 1895
x1949-95

The goat appears to be a free adaptation of the goat in the background of *Capricho* 60, *Ensayos* (Trials) [H 95] [D 97] (fig. 36.1), combined with the seated man at left from *Caprichos* 53, *Que pico de Oro!* (What a Golden Beak!) [H88] [D 90] (see fig. 33.1), who appears in several of these drawings.

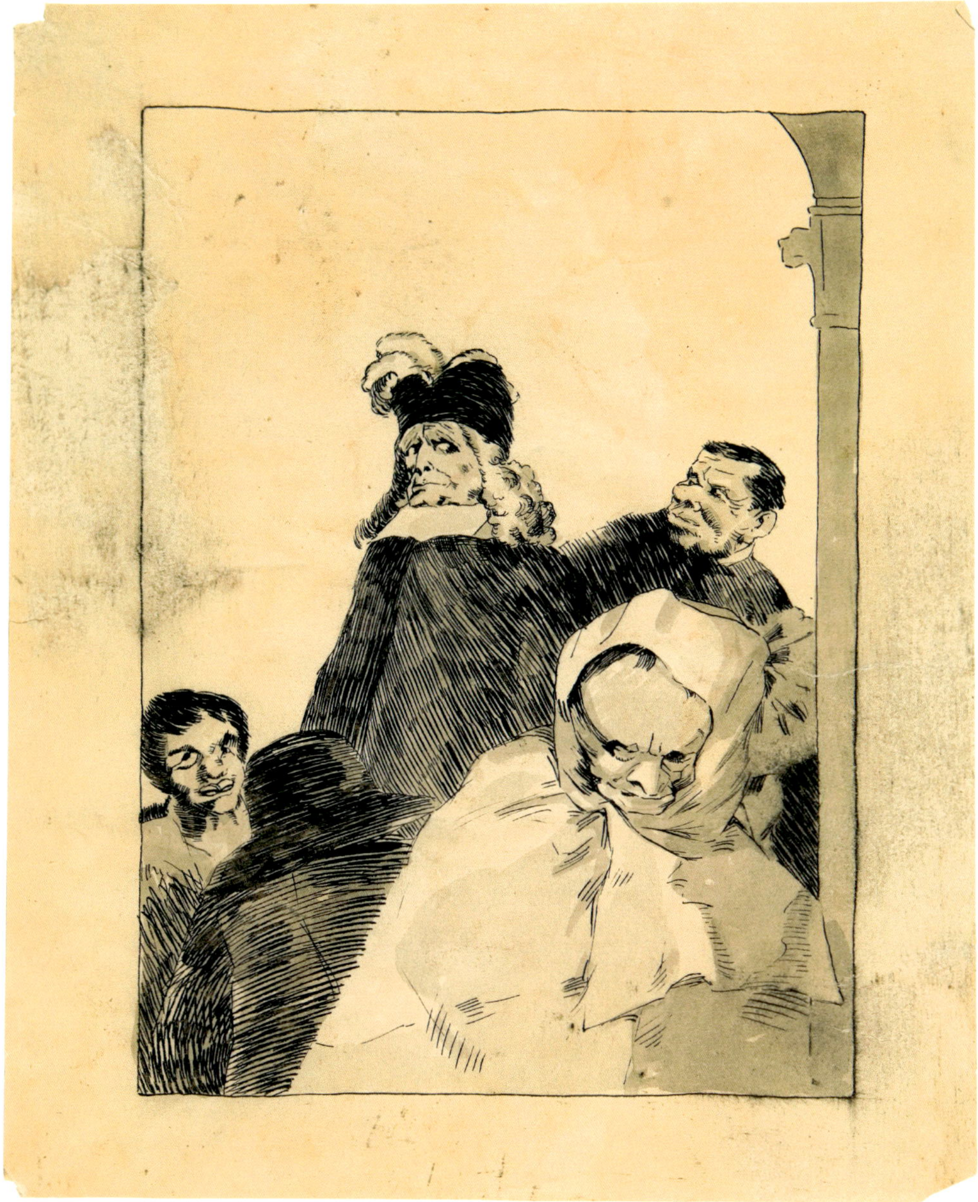

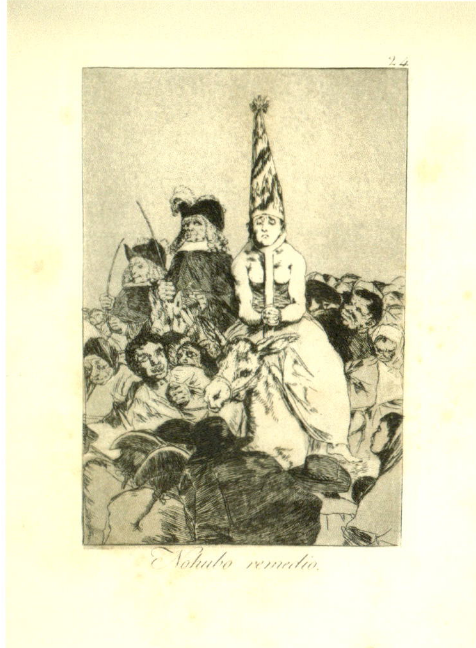

Fig. 37.1 Francisco José de Goya y Lucientes, Spanish, 1746–1828: *No hubo remedio* (Nothing Could be Done about It), from *Caprichos*, 1799, fifth edition, 1881–86. Etching, 21.5 x 15 cm. Princeton University Art Museum, Gift of Alan Weinstein, Class of 1961, and Nina Weinstein in honor of their children Rachel Weinstein-Abrams, Anna Weinstein, Daniel Weinstein, and Adam Weinstein (2004-377.24).

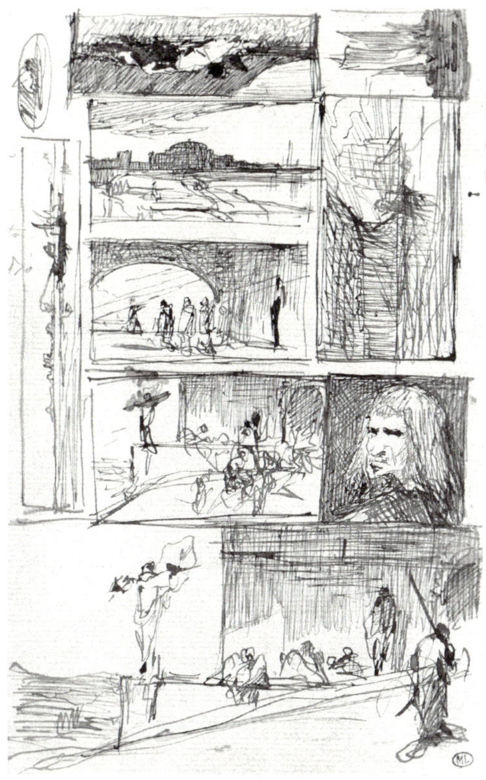

Fig. 37.2 Mariano Fortuny i Marsal, Spanish, 1838–1874: *Ten sketches, a portrait and landscape.* Pen and ink on paper, 20 x 13 cm. Musée du Louvre, Paris, France.

37. *Man in Plumed Hat with Other Figures*

Pen and black ink with brush and gray wash on tan wove paper

26.5 x 21.9 cm. ($10\frac{7}{16}$ x $8\frac{9}{16}$ in.)

Inscribed in graphite on verso, lower edge: *H66* (with red pencil *X* above) *Leonardo Alenza / cf 283-19 / Ferargil Galls. 1936 – ex / Marqués de Socorro* [sic] *- cf Goya*

Provenance: Marqués del Socorro, until 1912; Ferargil Galleries, New York, until 1936; Dan Fellows Platt

Bequest of Dan Fellows Platt, Class of 1895
x1949-96

The striking figure in the background of Princeton's drawing is based on Goya's *Capricho* 24, *No hubo remedio* (Nothing Could be Done about It) [H 59] [D 61] (fig. 37.1). In *Capricho* 24 the figure wears a plumed hat, and his white collar draws attention. A strikingly similar bust-length figure appears in Fortuny's sketchbook (fig. 37.2), executed in pen and ink with similar slashing hatchmarks.

38. *Standing Man*

Pen and black ink with brush and gray wash on tan wove paper

26.3 x 21.3 cm. (10 5/16 x 8 3/8 in.)

Inscribed in graphite on verso, lower edge: *H-77* (with red pencil *X* above) *L Alenza / Ferargil Gals – 1936 / Ex Marqués de Socorro* [sic]

PROVENANCE: Marqués del Socorro collection, until 1912; Ferargil Galleries, New York, until 1936; Dan Fellows Platt

Bequest of Dan Fellows Platt, Class of 1895
x1949-97

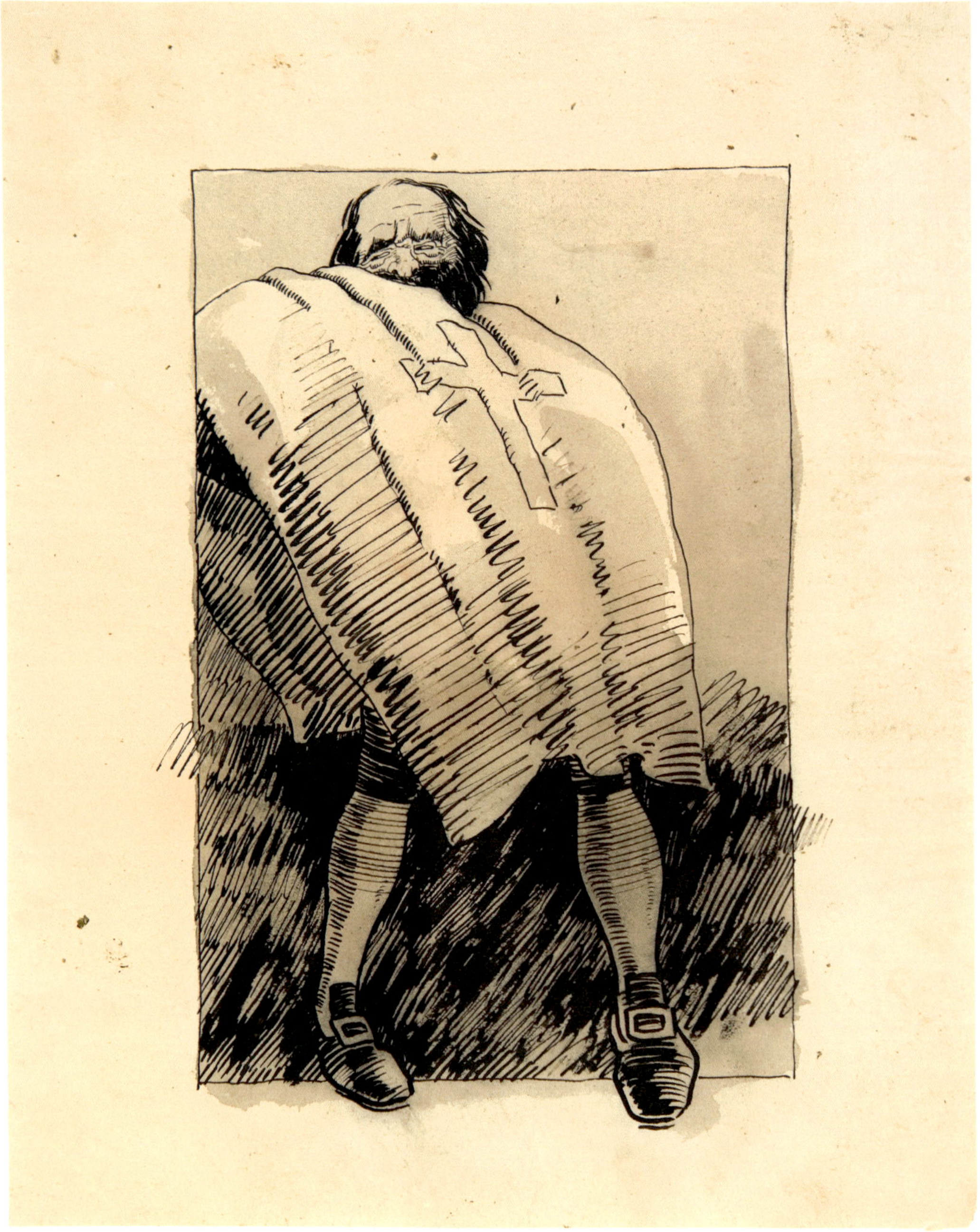

Goya's *Capricho* 18, *Y se le quema la casa* (And His House Is on Fire) [H 53] [D 55], inspired the figure here, cloaked in a flag with a cross. As in several other anonymous *Caprichos* at Princeton, the figure's feet break the framing line, creating a modern conception of the boundary of the frame and the agency of the figure within it. The buckled shoes recall the exaggerated costumes of paintings made à la mode, parodying society and ridiculing those whose pretensions are obvious by their dress.

39. *Caricature of a Man*

Pen and black ink with brush and gray wash on tan wove paper

22.9 x 18.0 cm. (9 x 7 1/16 in.)

Inscribed in graphite on verso, lower edge: *H.83 L. Alenza* (with red pencil *X* above) / *Ferargil Gals – 1936* / *Ex Marqués de Socorro* [sic]

PROVENANCE: Marqués del Socorro collection, until 1912; Ferargil Galleries, New York, until 1936; Dan Fellows Platt

Bequest of Dan Fellows Platt, Class of 1895
x1948-950

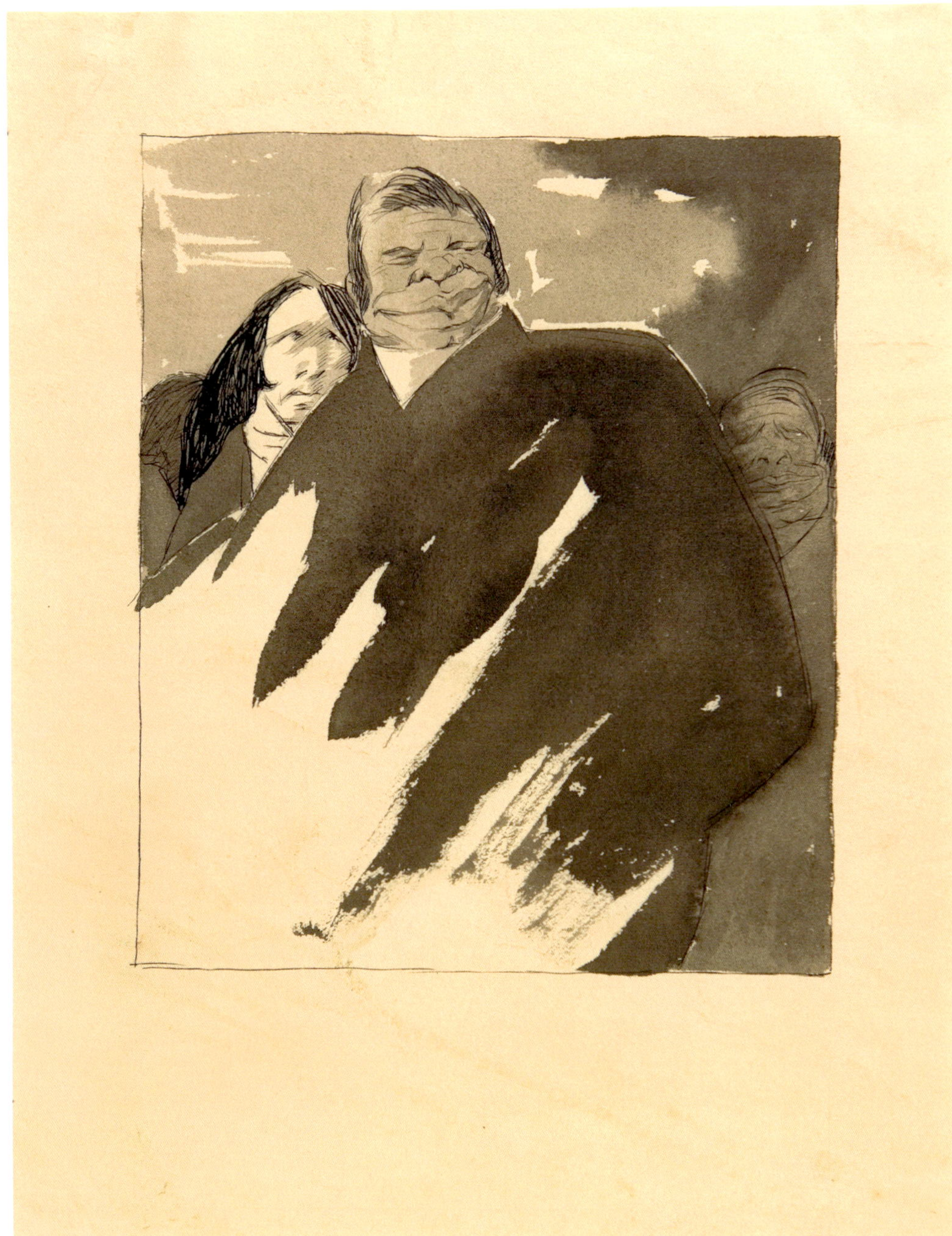

The pose of the fatuous large man in front almost completely obscures the two figures in the background. One peers at him from over his proper right shoulder; the other is almost hidden behind his proper left elbow, covered in wash and darkness. The artist's use of wash in this drawing, leaving large areas of the reserved paper untouched, adds a modern dash of bravura to the image. The wet on wet technique used to apply wash at the upper right corner, where the dark gray leeches into a paler shade applied below, is typical of Fortuny, whose marvelous ability with wash and watercolor gave him a ready stream of commissions.

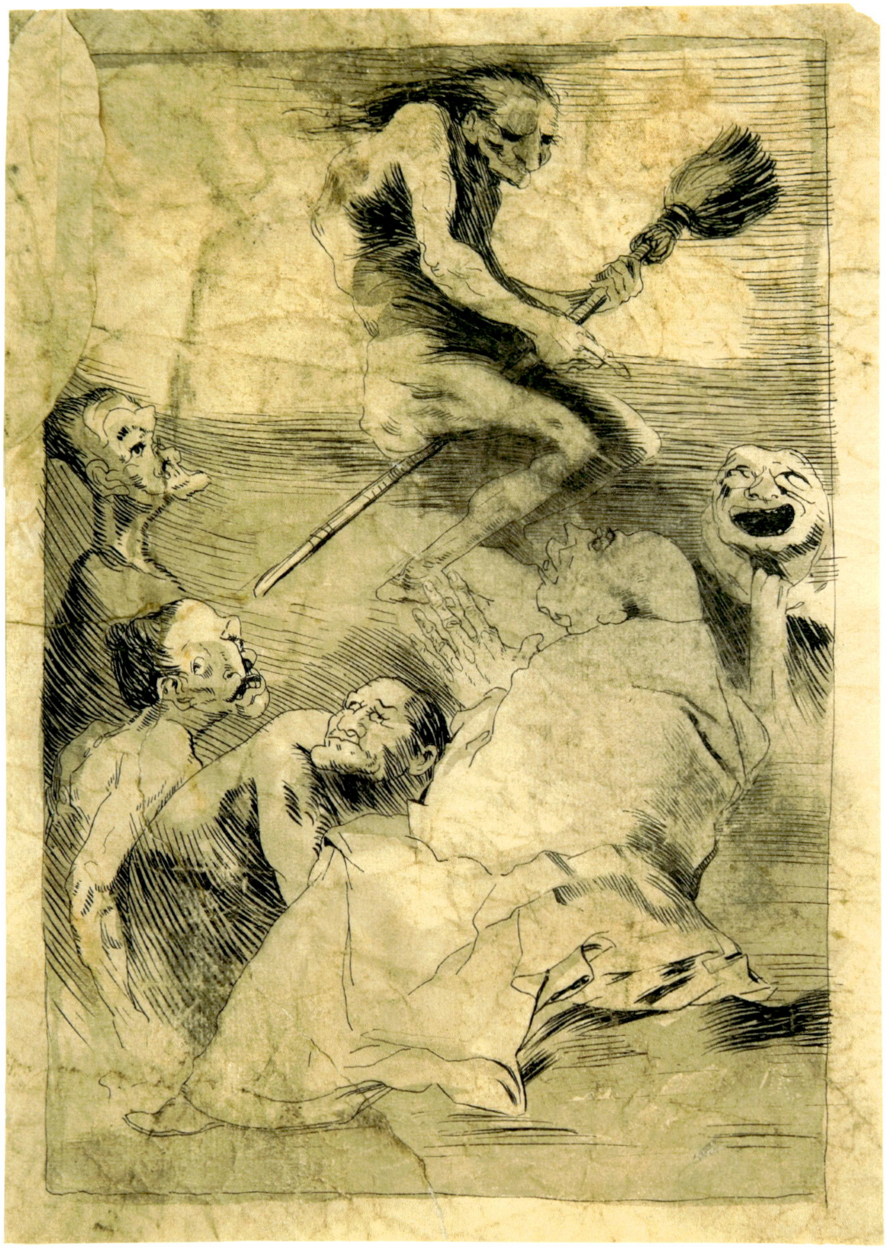

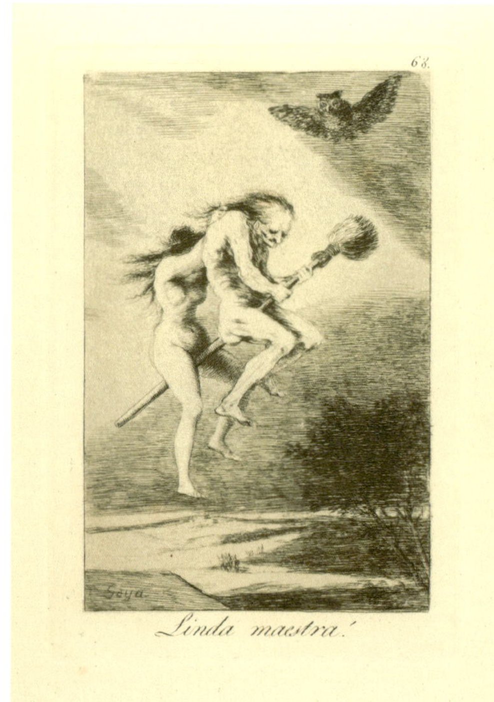

Fig. 40.1 Francisco José de Goya y Lucientes, Spanish, 1746–1828: *Linda maestra!* (Pretty Teacher!), from *Caprichos*, 1799, fifth edition, 1881–86. Etching, 21.5 x 15 cm. Princeton University Art Museum, Gift of Alan Weinstein, Class of 1961, and Nina Weinstein in honor of their children Rachel Weinstein-Abrams, Anna Weinstein, Daniel Weinstein, and Adam Weinstein (2004-377.68).

40. *Hag Riding Broomstick*

Pen and black ink with brush and gray wash on tan laid paper

26.8 x 19.5 cm. (10 9/16 x 7 11/16 in.)

Inscribed in graphite on piece of tape adhered to verso, lower edge: *H-70* (with red pencil *X* above) *L. Alenza - / Ferargil 1936 cf. 156-124 / 283-42*

Provenance: Marqués del Socorro collection, until 1912; Ferargil Galleries, New York, until 1936; Dan Fellows Platt

Bequest of Dan Fellows Platt, Class of 1895 x1948-951

The figure of the witch on a broomstick derives from Goya's *Capricho* 68, *Linda maestra!* (Pretty Teacher!) [H 103] [D 105] (fig. 40.1) although the artist here has not copied the second figure on the broomstick that appears in Goya's print. The artist added several other grotesque figures below, a group that replicates certain aspects of other of Goya's prints without copying them in their entirety. The monk at lower right, adapted from *Capricho* 53, *Que Pico de Oro!* (What a Golden Beak!) [H 88] [D 90] (see fig. 33.1), also appears in two of the other drawings at Princeton (cats. 41, 44), but here his eyes are open in surprise and his bony fingers are unclasped and extended toward the flying hag above.

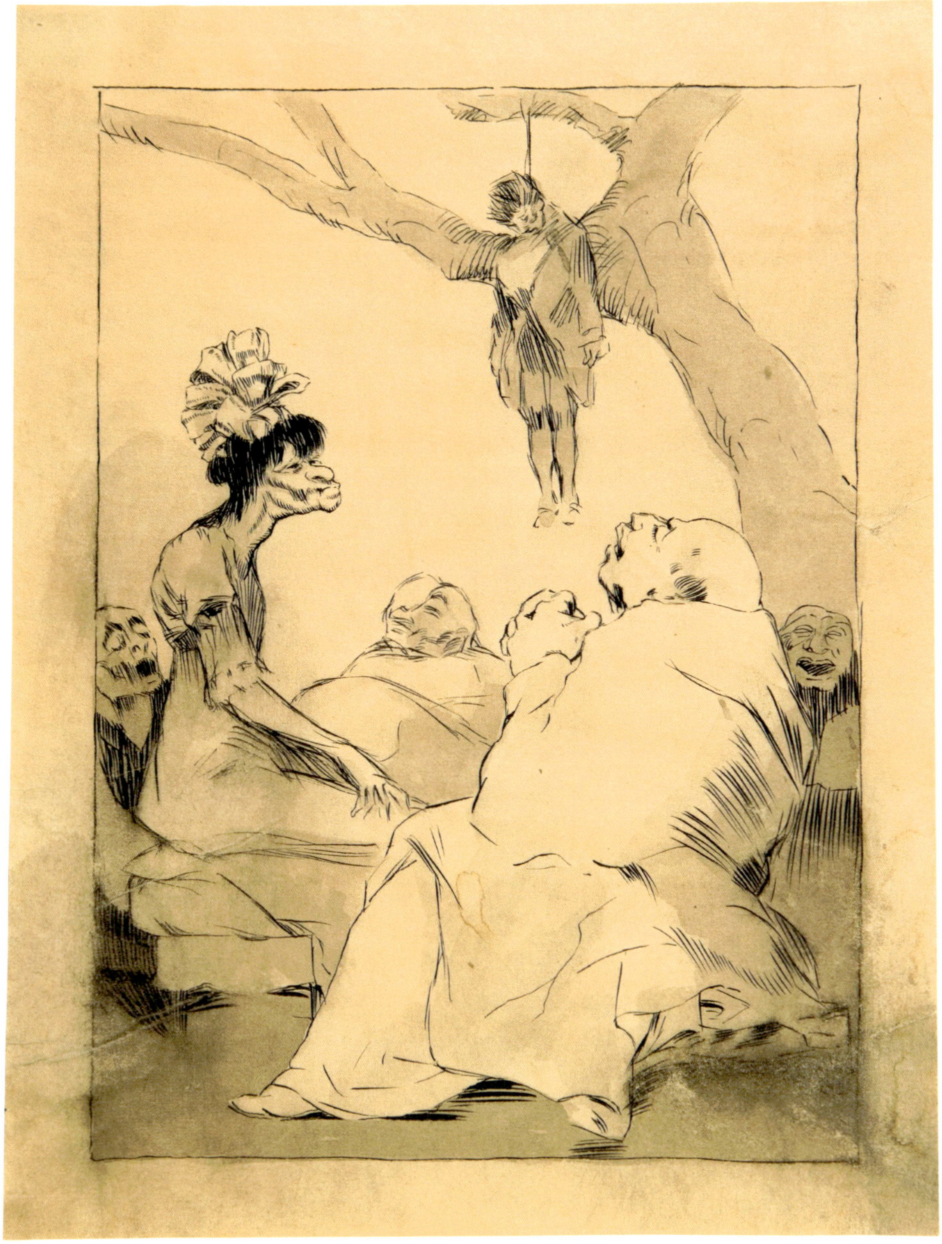

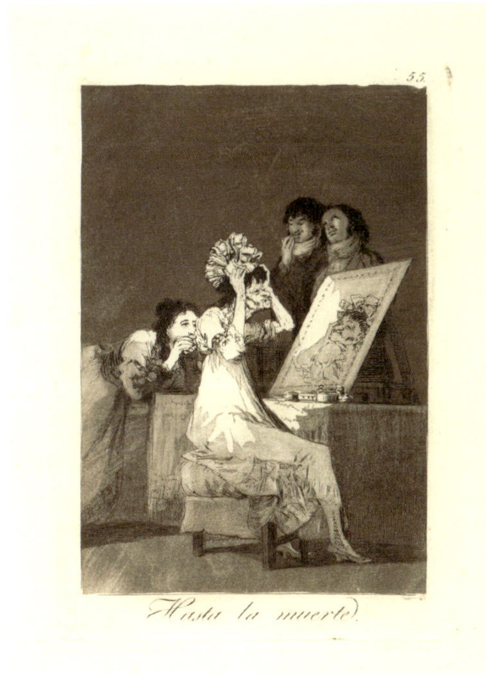

Fig. 41.1 Francisco José de Goya y Lucientes, Spanish, 1746–1828: *Hasta la muerte* (Until Death), from *Caprichos*. Etching, burnished aquatint, and drypoint, 22.3 x 31.7 cm. Princeton University Art Museum, Laura P. Hall Memorial Collection (x1946-247).

41. *Figures Seated Beneath Hanged Man*

Pen and black ink with brush and gray wash on brown wove paper

25.0 x 19.3 cm. (9$\frac{13}{16}$ x 7$\frac{9}{16}$ in.)

Inscribed in graphite on verso, lower edge: *H-71* (with red pencil *X* above) *L. Alenza / Ferargil 1936 / cf. 156-123 / 283-35*

PROVENANCE: Marqués del Socorro collection, until 1912; Ferargil Galleries, New York, until 1936; Dan Fellows Platt

Bequest of Dan Fellows Platt, Class of 1895
x1948-952

The figure of the monk at right, who reappears in several of these drawings, is taken from *Capricho* 53, *Que pico de oro!* (What a Golden Beak!) [H 88] [D 90] (see fig. 33.1); the figure at the extreme left, behind the woman's back, is copied from the same print, as is the figure at the extreme right. Although Platt erroneously associated this drawing with *Capricho* 36, *Mala Noche* (A Bad Night) [H 71] [D 73], instead it is a marriage of imagery from at least two other prints among Goya's *Caprichos*. The hanging figure of a man is a reduced copy of the principal figure in *Capricho* 12, *A caza de dientes* (Out Hunting for Teeth) [H 47] [D 49]. The old woman is an adaptation of the old woman in front of a mirror in *Capricho* 55, *Hasta la muerte* (Until Death) [H 90] [D 92] (fig. 41.1).

42. *Grotesque*

Pen and black ink with brush and gray wash on brown wove paper

24.7 x 19.4 cm. (9 11/16 x 7 5/8 in.)

Inscribed in graphite on verso, lower edge: *H 74* (with red pencil *X* above) – *L Alenza / Ferargil Gal. 1936 / "Ex Marqués de Socorro"* [sic]

Provenance: Marqués del Socorro collection, until 1912; Ferargil Galleries, New York, until 1936; Dan Fellows Platt

Bequest of Dan Fellows Platt, Class of 1895
x1948-953

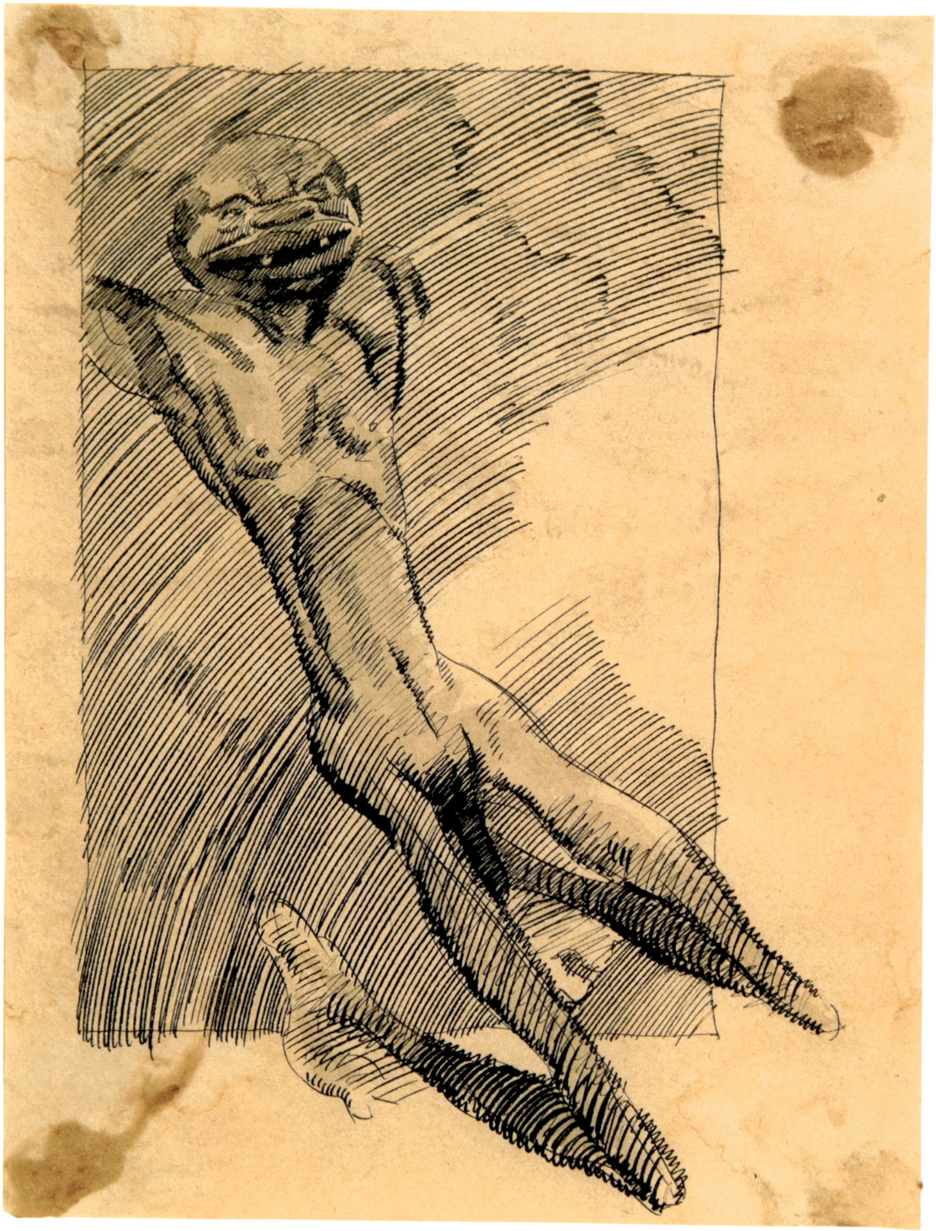

This strange figure, with elongated torso and phallus but no arms, grins at the viewer from inside a series of short and rounded shading lines. The figure is an enlarged version of the tiny armless doll presented to the Master in *Capricho* 47, *Obsequio al maestro* (A Gift for the Master) [H 82] [D 84] and perhaps also alludes to the small figure being used as a bellows in *Capricho* 56, *Subir y Bajar* (To Rise and To Fall) [H 91] [D 93]. The strong curving strokes in the background form waves with tide lines; the motion of the artist's wrist and confident, close parallel lines come from rapid sweeping movement. Although at times such strokes are seen in Alenza's work, they relate closely to a drawing of caricature heads formerly with the Shepherd Gallery (location unknown).

43. *Caricature of a Monk*

Pen and black ink with brush and gray wash on brown wove paper

25.9 x 19.8 cm. (10$^{3}/_{16}$ x 7$^{13}/_{16}$ in.)

Inscribed in graphite on verso, lower edge: *C-67. Leonardo Alenza / Ex Marqués de Socorro* [sic] / *Ferargil Gal 1936 - / cf 156-123 / cf 283-32 (Goya)*

Provenance: Marqués del Socorro collection, until 1912; Ferargil Galleries, New York, until 1936; Dan Fellows Platt

Bequest of Dan Fellows Platt, Class of 1895
x1948-954

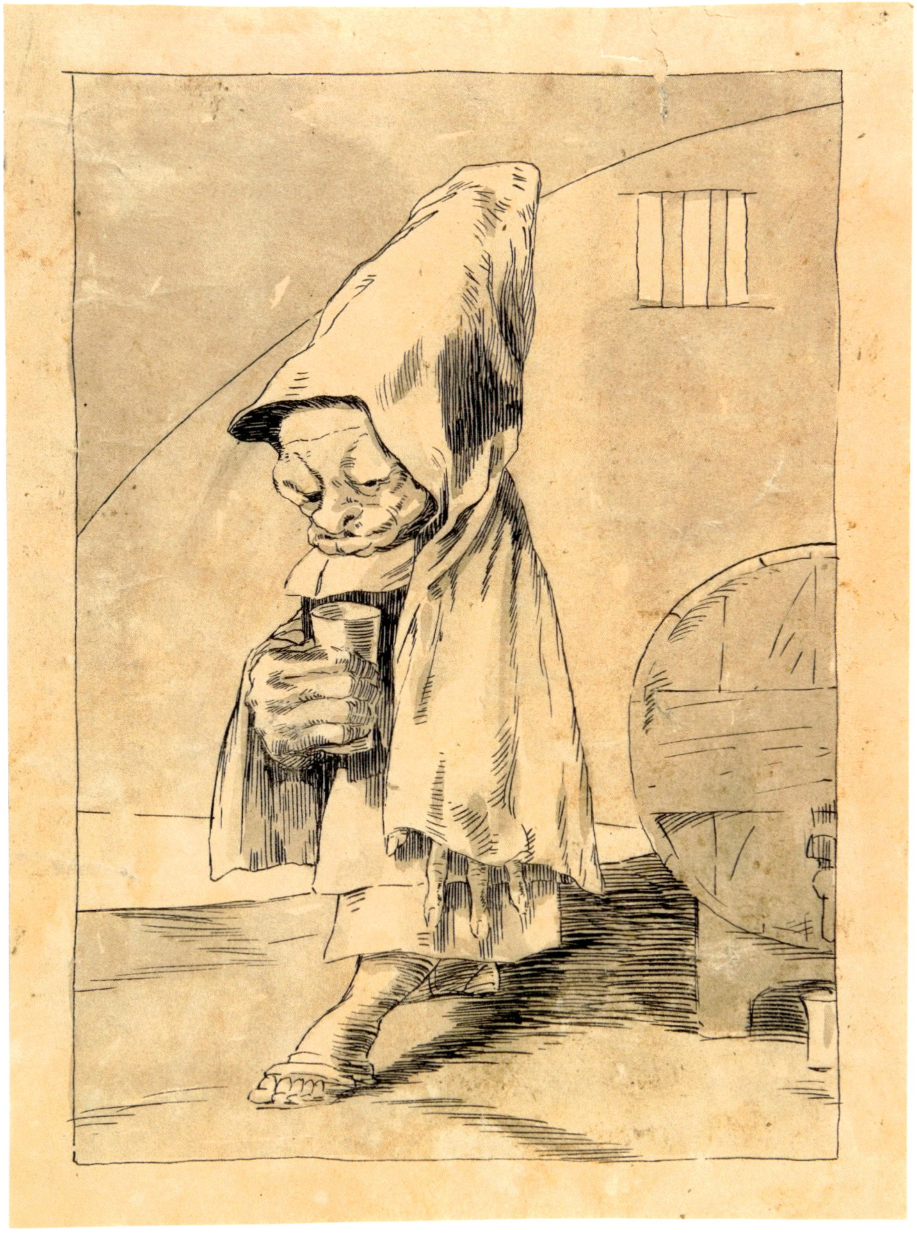

This drawing extracts a figure from *Capricho* 49, *Duendecitos* (Hobgoblins) [H 84] [D 86] and, in a free copy, transforms him into a hooded figure whose enormous hand clutches a glass while a barrel of wine sits on the floor behind him. The barrel and the face of the goblin are taken from *Capricho* 79, *Nadie nos ha visto* (No One Has Seen Us) [H 114] [D 116] . The prison window seen in *Capricho* 49 has been reduced to only two bars, decreasing the amount of light. The other two figures in the print have been eliminated to focus on the solitary nature of the hobgoblin's problem and his private incarceration.

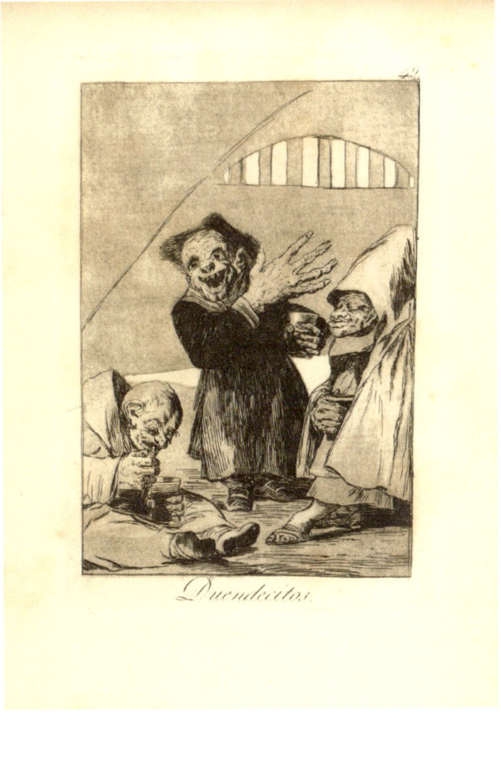

Fig. 43.1 Francisco José de Goya y Lucientes, Spanish, 1746–1828: *Duendecitos* (Hobgoblins), from *Caprichos*, 1799, fifth edition, 1881–86. Etching, 21.5 x 15 cm. Princeton University Art Museum, Gift of Alan Weinstein, Class of 1961, and Nina Weinstein in honor of their children Rachel Weinstein-Abrams, Anna Weinstein, Daniel Weinstein, and Adam Weinstein (2004-377.49).

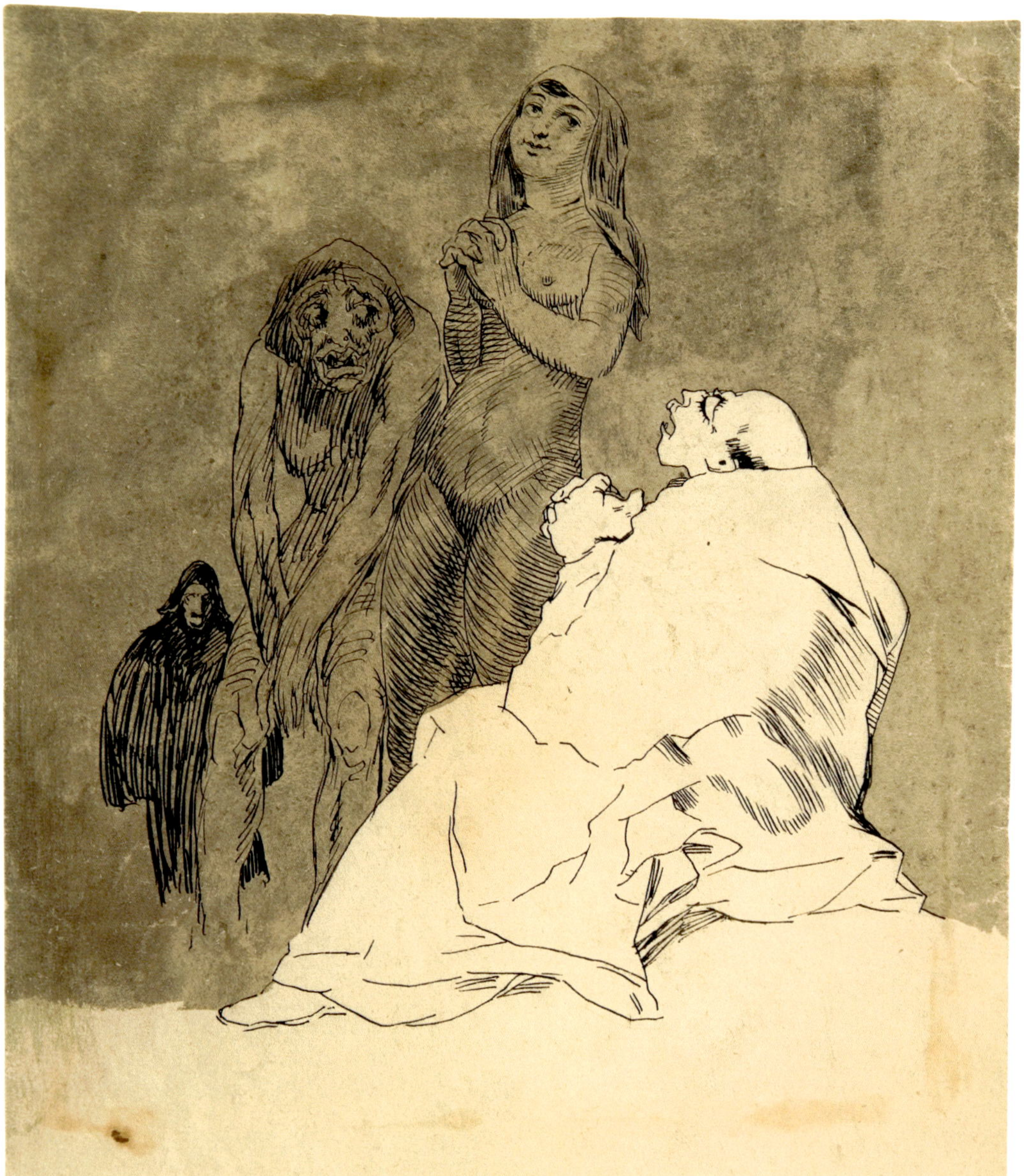

44. *Seated Monk before Nudes*

Pen and black ink with brush and gray wash on light tan wove paper

23.4 x 20.7 cm. (9³⁄₁₆ x 8³⁄₁₆ in.)

Inscribed in graphite on verso, lower edge: *H 69* (with red pencil *X* above) *L. Alenza / Ferargil Galls 1936 /* [*Ex Marqués del Socorro*]

PROVENANCE: Marqués del Socorro collection, until 1912; Ferargil Galleries, New York, until 1936; Dan Fellows Platt

Bequest of Dan Fellows Platt, Class of 1895
x1948-955

The artist adapted the monk in this drawing, who sits clasping his hands in front of a parrot, from *Capricho* 53, *Que pico de oro!* (What a Golden Beak!) [H 88] [D 90] (see fig. 33.1). Here the artist depicts the monk closing his eyes in front of two nudes, while the shadowy figure of a cloaked man approaches from behind. The two women are adapted from Goya's *Caprichos*, especially the figures of the Celestina and the young woman in *Capricho* 73, *Mejor es holgar* (It Is Better To Be Lazy) [H 108] [D 110], yet they appear naked.

45. *Man and Woman Embracing*

Pen and black ink with brush and gray wash over traces of graphite on tan wove paper

28.8 x 23.3 cm. (11⁵⁄₁₆ x 9³⁄₁₆ in.)

Inscribed in graphite on verso, lower edge: *H-76* (with red pencil *X* above) *L Alenza / Ferargil Gals 1936 / Ex Marqués de Socorro* [sic] / *cf: 56-131 (Goya) 283-10*

PROVENANCE: Marqués del Socorro collection, until 1912; Ferargil Galleries, New York, until 1936; Dan Fellows Platt

Bequest of Dan Fellows Platt, Class of 1895
x1948-956

Goya entitled his *Capricho* 10, from which this drawing was copied, *El Amor y la Muerte* (Love and Death) [H45] [D 47] (fig. 45.1). The composition depicts a couple embracing after the man has been mortally wounded in a duel; the woman supports his body as his legs slip out from under him. A sword lies on the ground in both Goya's preparatory drawing for *Love and Death* and his *Capricho*. In Princeton's drawing, the artist has copied the print but has eliminated the sword—or perhaps reinterpreted the composition and its ironic double entendre, leaving the two lovers apparently singing to one another in a strange, deathly embrace. The man's wilting weight is supported by the woman, but the Princeton drawing lacks the full mortal pathos of Goya's depiction.

1 Palencia Tubau 192–?, 9.
2 Alenza's *Caprichos* at the Metropolitan Museum of Art were described in 1895 in the catalogue by Bernard Quaritch, bookseller in London, as *Caprichos* in the style of Goya. Prior to that, the drawings were included in the November 11 sale of Sotheby, Wilkinson & Hodge, London, lot 77, p. 5. Described as "30 very clever original drawings in the style of Goya, mounted on tinted paper. . . ," that set of *Caprichos* was also discussed in Palencia Tubau 192–?, 9. Also see Bernard Quaritch, *Biblioteca Hispana* (London, 1895), no. 2280. The album, now at the Metropolitan Museum of Art, was first owned by the bookseller Mariano Murillo. It contains drawings with captions written below, in the manner of Goya's *Caprichos*.
3 The Hispanic Society curatorial files and archives, Priscilla Muller correspondence, concerning the

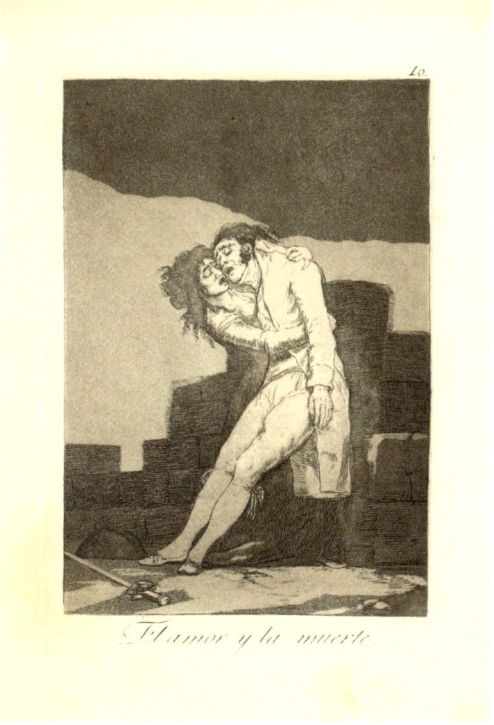

45.1 Francisco José de Goya y Lucientes, Spanish, 1746–1828: *El Amor y la Muerte* (Love and Death), from *Caprichos*, 1799, fifth edition, 1881–86. Etching, 21.5 x 15 cm. Princeton University Art Museum, Gift of Alan Weinstein, Class of 1961, and Nina Weinstein in honor of their children Rachel Weinstein-Abrams, Anna Weinstein, Daniel Weinstein, and Adam Weinstein (2004-377.10).

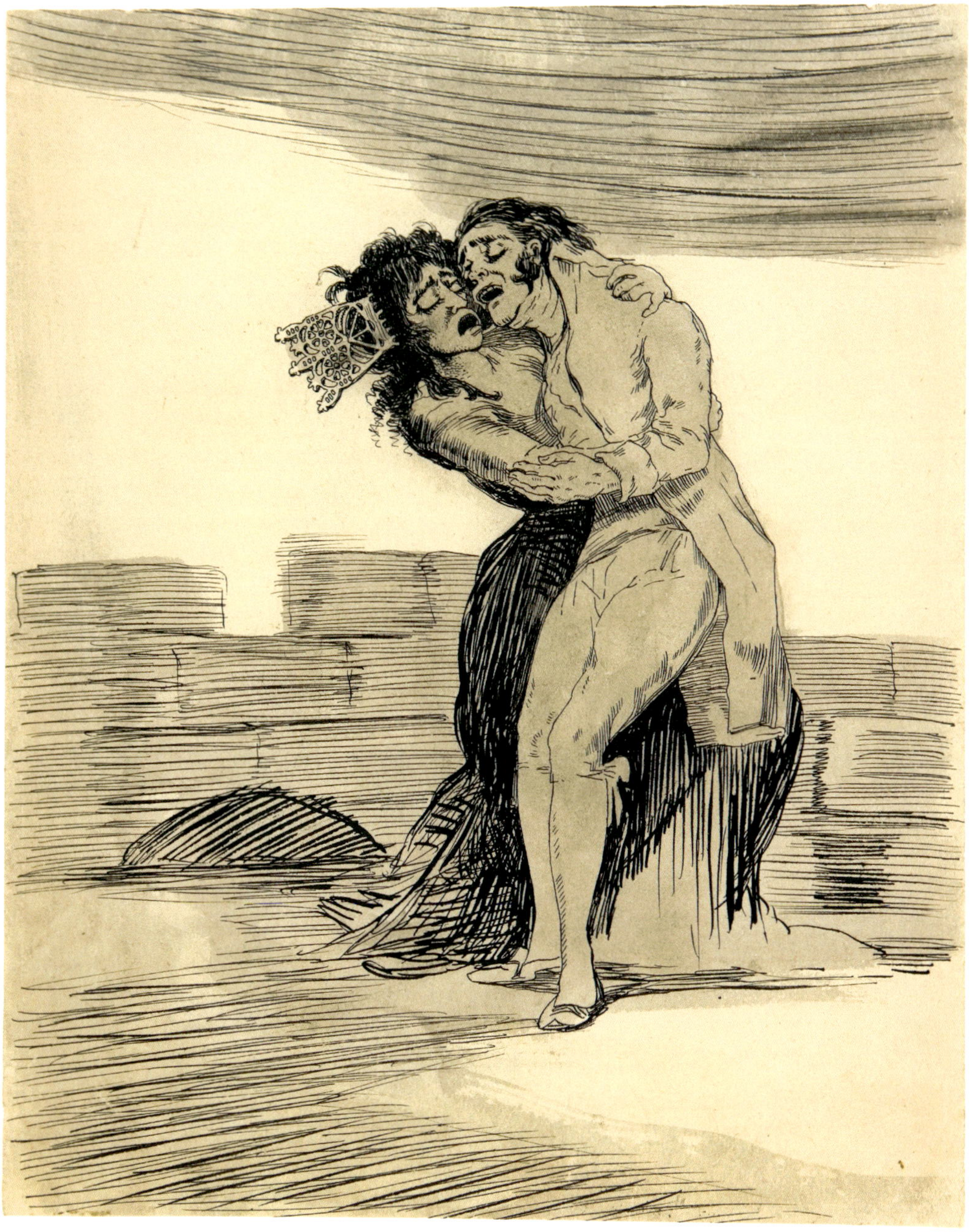

Alenza prints at the Hispanic Society of America.

4 Frank Jewett Mather Jr., "The Platt Collection of Drawings," *Bulletin of the Department of Art and Archaeology, Princeton University* (June 1944): 5.

5 One such drawing belonged to a New York private collector. See Frick Art Reference Library, photo archives.

6 Davillier 1875.

7 Charles Yriarte sale, Succession Charles Yriarte, no. 108, Goya, *Le Prisonnier*, December 26–28, 1898; *Prisoner*, copy after Goya, MNAC, Barcelona, 1868, Barcelona 2003–4, 420–21.

8 Francesc Quílez i Corella, in Barcelona 2003–4, 419–31.

9 The Ferargil Gallery correspondence archive is part of the Archives of American Art, Smithsonian Institution.

10 Recent examinations of the many followers of Goya and the contemporaries of Lucas and Alenza have provided some clarity.

11 The print by Goya is a unique proof now in the Biblioteca Nacional, Madrid. See Harris 1964, cat. 2; Gassier and Wilson 1971, cat. 53; and Santiago Páez 1997, cat. 2. The two references most frequently cited for Goya's prints are Tomás Harris, *Goya: Engravings and Lithographs* (Oxford: B. Cassirer, 1964), and Loys Delteil, *Le Peintre–Graveur Illustré: XIXè et XXè siècle. Francisco Goya*, volumes XIV and XV (Paris: 1922; New York: Da Capo Press, 1969). The Harris [H] and Delteil [D] numbers included here refer to the catalogue entries in those texts.

12 The drawing is in a New York private collection. See New York 2010–11, 148, cat. 40.

13 Quílez i Corella, in Barcelona 2003–4, 420–21.

MARIANO FORTUNY I MARSAL

Reus, 1838–1874, Rome

Born in Reus, in Tarragona, Fortuny moved to Barcelona in 1852 and began drawing classes with Claudi Lorenzale (1816–1889).[1] In 1860, the Diputación de Barcelona sent him to Morocco as a journalist-draftsman recording the events of the Spanish-Moroccan War (1859–60); the resulting paintings were completed in Rome from the sketches that he made on that trip. The extraordinary *Battle of Tetuan* (1862–64, Museu Nacional d'Art de Catalunya, Barcelona) and the *Battle of Wad-ras* (1862, Museo del Prado, Madrid) are among the large-scale masterpieces that Fortuny completed to record the battles he witnessed. He made a second trip to Morocco in 1862, and the resulting drawings, including many sketches and watercolors of robed figures, beggars, and colorful Moroccan street life, are among Fortuny's most frequently reproduced works.

In 1865 the pension from the Barcelona Diputación ended. Fortuny's style changed direction that year, when he received a pension from the Duke of Riansares, second husband of the widowed queen María Cristina, and began to paint an increasing number of society portraits (e.g., *Portrait of Señora Gaye*, Metropolitan Museum of Art). Two years later, Fortuny married Cecilia de Madrazo, the daughter of artist Federico de Madrazo (1815–1894), and began to copy paintings in the Prado to sell to tourists as souvenirs. In 1868, Fortuny went to Seville with his brother-in-law Raimundo de Madrazo (1841–1920) and traveled to Rome and other parts of Italy with his wife. This trip led to a transformation in both his subject matter and his style. He spent several months in Paris, from the end of 1869 to the late spring of 1870. Working to suit his dealers was difficult for Fortuny, however, and he retreated in 1870 to Andalusia, to recapture a less commercial aspect. He traveled with other artists, including Martín Rico (1833–1908), and spent time in Seville and later Granada, which made a dramatic impression on him. Fortuny spent two years in Granada, absorbing and incorporating the influence of Islamo-Hispanic culture into his art and developing the extraordinary sense of color that made him famous. In 1872 he returned to Italy, where he created watercolors and paintings for the commercial market as well as more intimate works for himself and his family. Only two years later the artist died in Rome.

A number of Fortuny's drawings were reproduced during his lifetime, including *The Anchorite* (Museum of Fine Arts, Boston), prepared with a preliminary drawing sold to the Hispanic Society, New York, by Fortuny's widow's family. The rough, brittle lines are close to those of the final print, demonstrating the artist's understanding of the printmaker's technique and his ability to translate his work from one medium to another.

46. *Seated Man Reading a Book*

Graphite and pen and black ink on beige wove paper

35.5 x 28.0 cm. (13 15/16 x 11 1/16 in.)

Inscribed in pen and black ink, lower right: *Fortuny / 1869*

Provenance: M. Secretan Collection, Paris, 1886; Frank Jewett Mather Jr.

References: Charles Yriarte, *Fortuny* (Paris, 1886), 35 ill.; Lucien Solvay, *L'art espagnol* (Paris, J. Rouam, 1887), 277; González López and Martí Ayxelá 1989, vol. 2, 174, EP-0.04.69

Gift of Frank Jewett Mather Jr.
x1941-115

Fortuny signed and dated this energetic pen and ink drawing in 1869, during the few months that the artist was in Paris and when he was experimenting with new pen and ink drawing techniques. In 1886, when it was reproduced in Charles Yriarte's book *Fortuny* (Paris, 1886, 35), the drawing was in the collection of Monsieur Secretan; its subsequent locations are unknown until it was acquired by Frank Jewett Mather Jr.

The illustration in Yriarte's book was made with heliogravure, a modern technique of reproduction that uses light to transfer the image onto a copper printing plate.[2] Joseph Niepce first used the process in 1826–27 and it was in almost continuous use for about a century. The technique's particular advantage is that images are not reproduced in reverse, transforming the reproduction of drawings. Like Vierge, Fortuny was probably introduced to this early photographic reproduction technique through his work as a war correspondent.

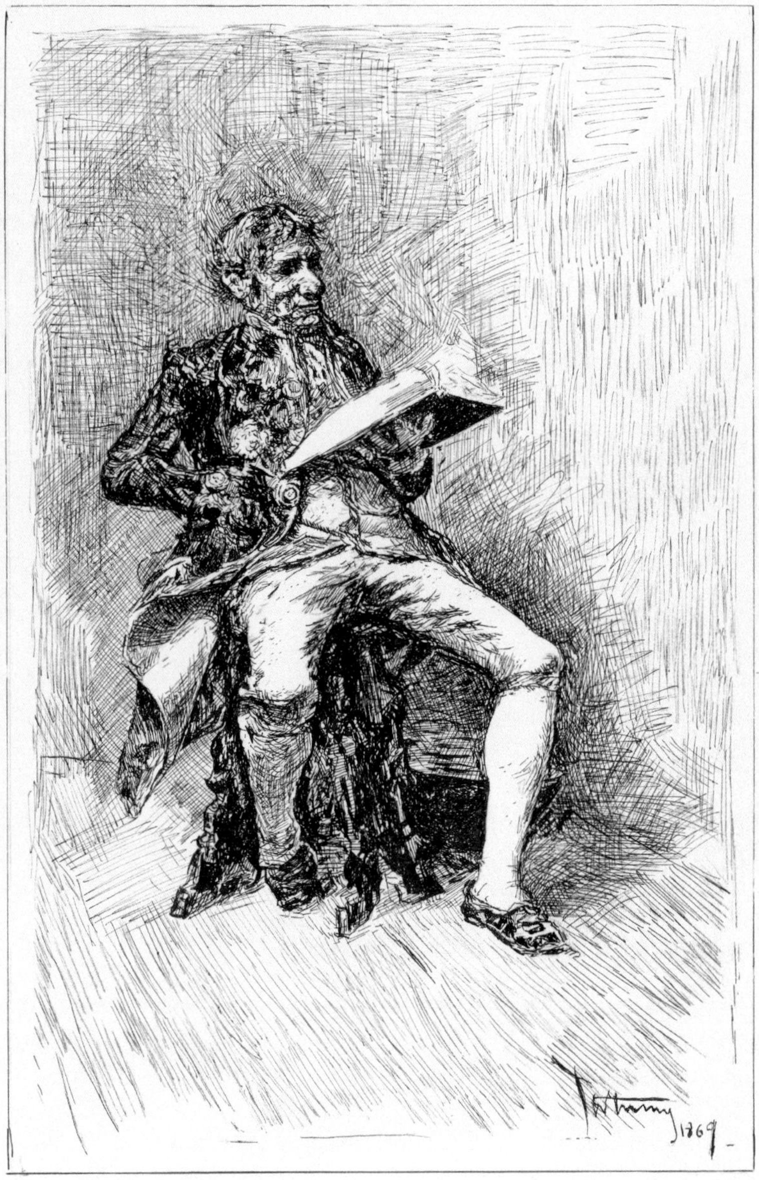

47. *Señora Agrasot Sewing*, 1874

Pen and brown ink on beige paper

16.7 x 11.0 cm. (6 9/16 x 4 5/16 in.)

Inscribed in pen and brown ink, lower left: *Croquis que hizo Mariano Fortuny / en Portici—año 1874 / "La Sra de Agrasot que está bordando";* lower right: *a Dn Matías Errázuriz / dedica este dibujo original / de Mariano Fortuny. / Su amigo / Ricardo de Madrazo* / Madrid [2 de De] 1907; inscribed in graphite on verso, along left edge (partially erased): *Bfor 24-28* (. . .) [Vives reads the date as "Madrid 28(. . .) 1907"]

Provenance: Mr. and Mrs. Stuart P. Feld, Class of 1957, New York

References: Princeton 1973, 21; González López and Martí Ayxelá 1989, vol. 2, 138, RT-1.30.74; *Mariano Fortuny* (Madrid: Biblioteca Nacional, 1994), 276 n. 155

Gift of Stuart P. Feld, Class of 1957, and Mrs. Feld x1972-38

The inscription on this intimate sketch provides insight into the relationship between Mariano Fortuny and his brother-in-law Ricardo de Madrazo. After Fortuny's death, the Madrazo family retained the artist's estate, including drawings and paintings. Ricardo de Madrazo gave this drawing to Don Matías Errázuriz in Madrid in 1907; he inscribed the work, annotating the details.[3]

The drawing depicts a favorite subject for Fortuny: Señora Agrasot, wife of Joaquín Agrasot (1836–1919), a painter, friend, and contemporary of Fortuny who trained at the Real Academia de Bellas Artes de San Fernando in Madrid and was pensioned by the Diputación of Alicante. In 1873, Agrasot married Emma Zaragoza, the daughter of the businessman who was sent to deliver the news of his pension.[4] Shortly after their marriage the couple moved to Rome, where they met Fortuny. In the summer of 1874 they shared the Villa Arata in Portici with Fortuny and his family, and Fortuny frequently depicted Emma engaged in domestic tasks such as sewing or embroidery. In a watercolor portrait of her from the same year, Señora Agrasot sits with a large fan in front of her, potted plants at one side, and an impressionistic Japanese screen with flying cranes behind her (Collection Klein Andreu, Barcelona).

This intimate observation in pen and ink is related to other studies that Fortuny made of Emma, completed around the same time, including a drawing at the Biblioteca Nacional from the same year. Other pen sketches reflect the same quiet mood and intimacy, such as that reproduced in Barcelona 1974, no. 1620 (Museu Nacional d'Art de Catalunya, Barcelona, inv. 35.755) or in the sheet of studies (MNAC, inv. 35.765).

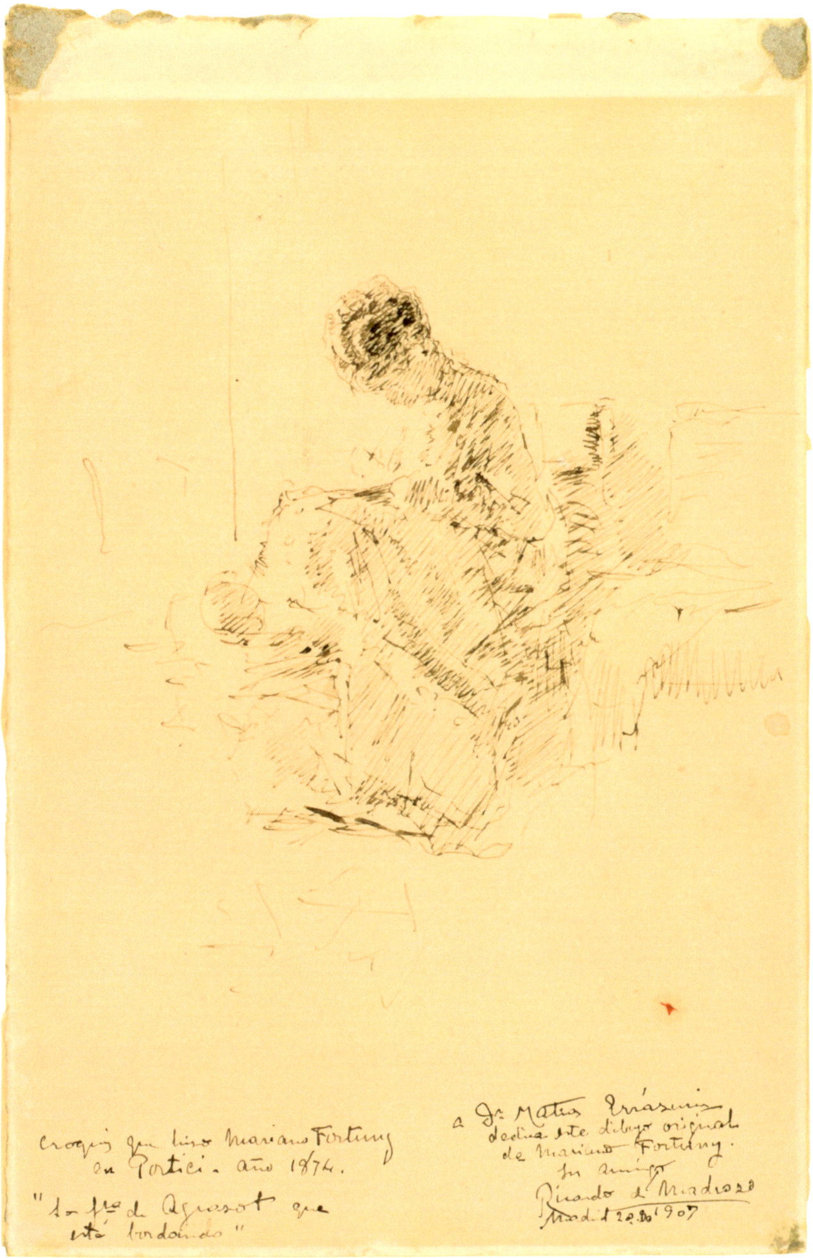

48. *Mandolin Player*

Verso: *Sketch of Horse*

Watercolor over graphite on light tan wove paper

47.8 x 35.7 cm. (18 13/16 x 14 1/16 in.)

Provenance: Frank Jewett Mather Jr. (?)

Reference: González López and Martí Ayxelá 1989, vol. 2, 71, EP=2.01.64/65.

Gift of Frank Jewett Mather Jr. (?)
x1940-106

The provenance of this sheet is unknown, although it is thought to have entered the collection as a gift from Frank Jewett Mather in 1940. The unusual use of watercolor characterizes Fortuny's watercolors and impressionistic paintings from around 1868 and resulted in the attribution to him. A watercolor entitled *The Calabrian* (fig. 48.1), dated 1868, exhibits the same masterful application of saturated watercolor brushed onto paper, without pencil underdrawing. The contrast between the man's dignity and his begging hand is the sort of social commentary that Fortuny mastered in his brief career.

The jovial tone of the laughing figure in the *Mandolin Player* and the half-finished donkey on the verso suggest that this sheet contains two preparatory studies for larger, probably unrelated, compositions. The figure of the harlequin was a frequent subject for Fortuny, who inverted the serious self-absorption depicted in *The Little Count* (fig. 48.2), a watercolor of a serious dandy from 1861, and transformed it into the laughing man holding a mandolin.

Many of Fortuny's close followers used watercolor in a similar way, brushing blocks of watercolor with a very saturated brush. Among those who perfected the technique are Francisco Pradilla Ortiz (1848–1921), José Tapiró y Baró (1836–1913), José Villegas Cordero (1844–1921), and Antonio Fabrés y Costa (1854–1936). LAB

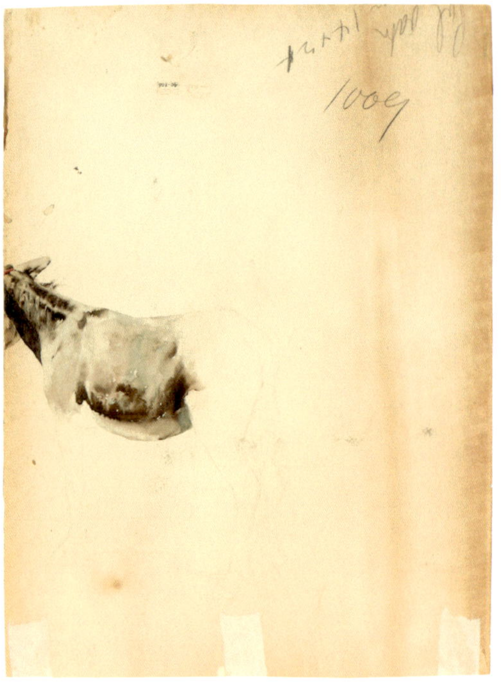

Verso, cat. 48

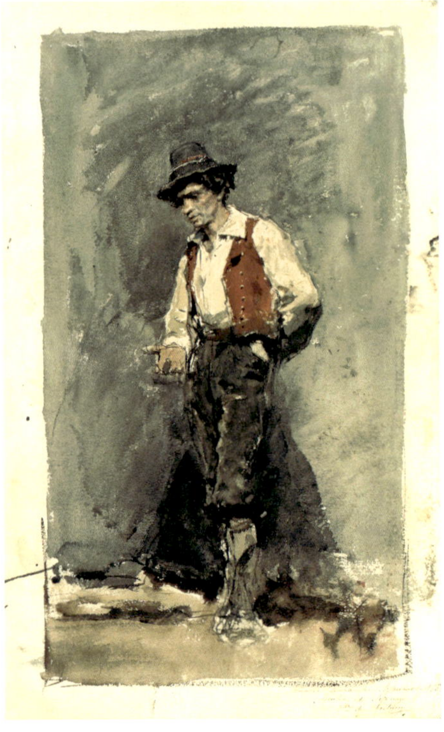

Fig. 48.1 Mariano Fortuny i Marsal, Spanish, 1838–1874: *The Calabrian*, 1868. Watercolor on paper. Museu Nacional d'Art de Catalunya, Barcelona (010697-DOA).

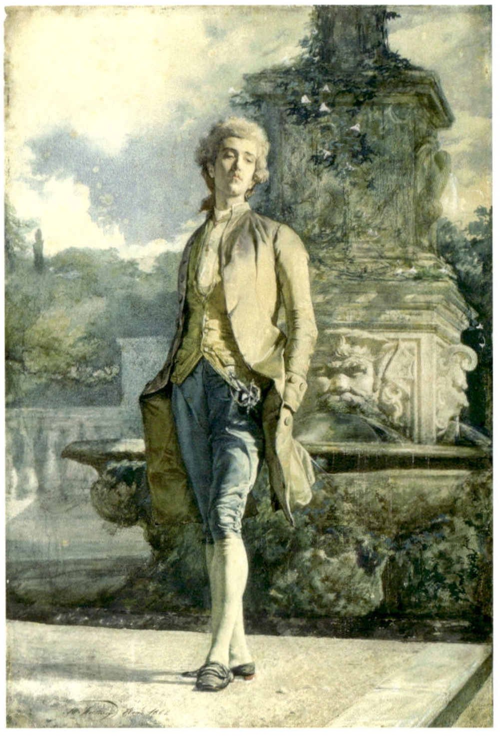

Fig. 48.2 Mariano Fortuny i Marsal, Spanish, 1838–1874: *The Little Count*, 1861. Watercolor on paper. Museu Nacional d'Art de Catalunya, Barcelona (010692-D).

1 Barcelona 1993, 342.

2 Rosa Vives i Piqué, *Fortuny, Gravador, Estudi Crític i Catàleg Raonat* (Reus, 1991), 222; the author records three engravings, here nos. 2 and 9 (two examples), two drawings, and a heliogravure of *Child in a Japanese Salon*. The author must have overlooked one of the three drawings, all of which are published elsewhere.

3 Errázuriz is a fairly common Basque name. It is also the name of a political family influential in Chile, descended from a Basque immigrant.

4 González López and Martí Ayxelá 1989. Santiago Alcolea, "Fortuny," *Archivo Español de Arte* 63, no. 249 (1990): n. 252. *Mariano Fortuny* (Madrid: Biblioteca Nacional, 1994), 276.

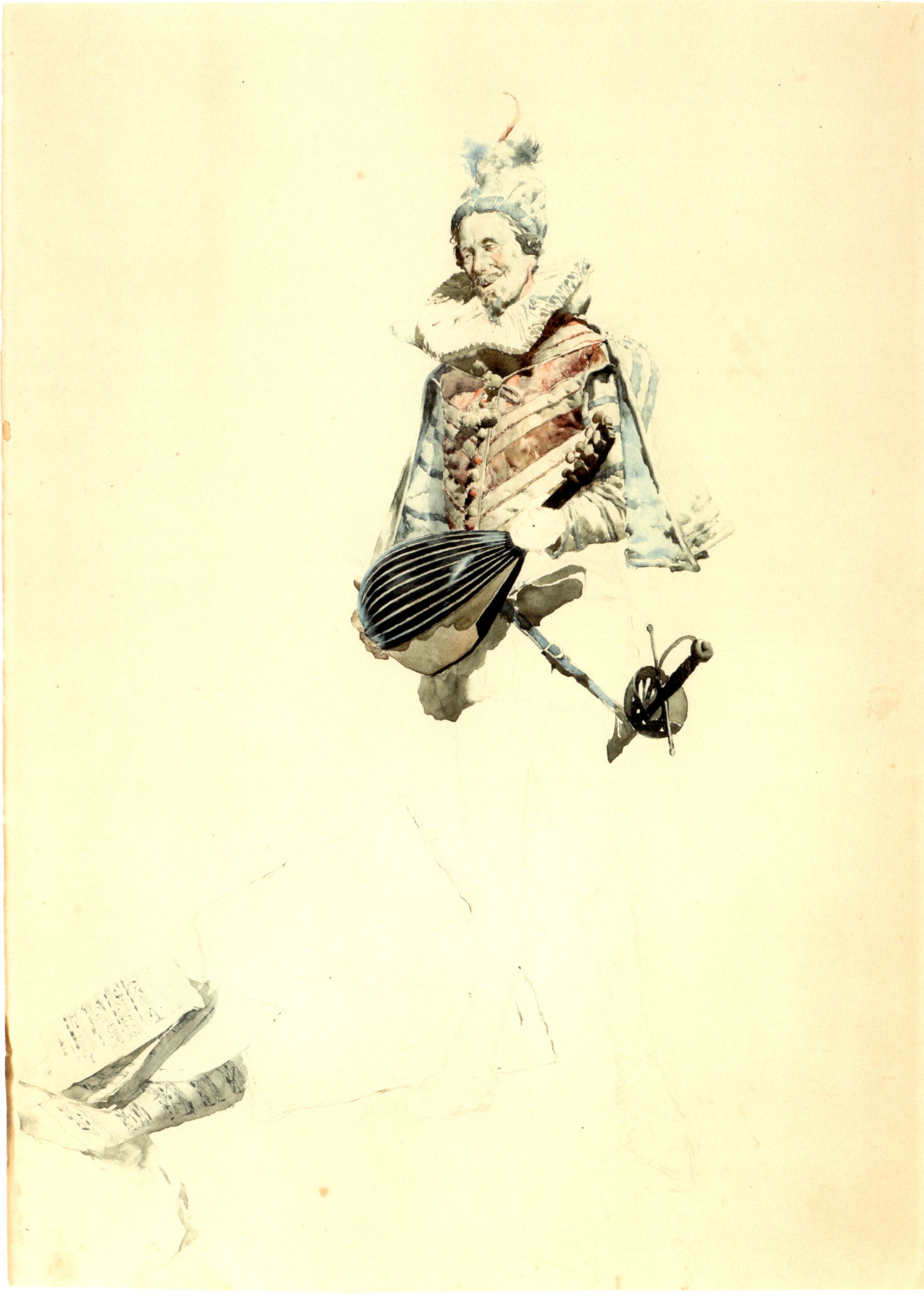

DANIEL URRABIETA VIERGE

Madrid, 1851–1904, Boulogne-sur-Seine

Daniel Urrabieta Vierge was the son of another Spanish book illustrator, Vicente Urrabieta Ortiz (1800–1879), and signed some of his work with his mother's last name, Vierge, to distinguish himself from his father.[1] Thus, he is known in Spain as Daniel Urrabieta Vierge and to the rest of the world as Daniel Vierge, as he signed most of his mature work.[2]

Vierge moved to Paris after completing his studies at the Academia de San Fernando with Federico de Madrazo (1815–1894), Carlos Luis de Ribera (1815–1891), and Carlos de Haes (1826–1898). In February 1870 he published his first drawing in *Le Monde Illustré* and after July 1870 began sending illustrations of the Franco-Prussian War to this periodical from the front. The serious subject matter of these drawings added to his renown, and Vierge was soon a major contributor of illustrations to such French magazines as *La Vie Moderne*, *L'Illustration*, *Le Monde Illustré*, *Gil Blas Illustré*, and others; he also began sending his work to English and American publications, including *The Century Magazine*, *Illustrated London News*, *Harper's*, and *Scribner's*.[3] Although magazine work was his primary source of income, Vierge's book illustrations were clearly where his talents flourished. He illustrated *La Maison de Nazareth* by Aimé Giron (1874), *Histoire de Gil Blas de Santillane* by Alain René Lesage (1875), *Bosnie et Herzegovine* by Charles Yriarte (1876), *Histoire de France* by J. Michelet (1876–78), and *Voyage au pays de milliards: Les Prussiens en Allemagne/Voyage au pays annexés* by Victor Tissot (1878). From about 1877, possibly in response to his study of Japanese prints, Vierge developed a distinctly recognizable style using focal points of black ink.[4]

From June to October 1880, Vierge traveled in Spain with Martín Rico y Ortega (1833–1908), drawing en plein air. Upon his return to Paris, however, Vierge had a stroke that paralyzed his right side, losing the use of his right hand and his speech. This illness occurred at the peak of his career, when the edition of Francisco de Quevedo's *Histoire de Pablo de Segovie* (*El gran Tacaño*) (1882) was about to be published with 110 of his illustrations. In the same year, Vierge received the Order of Isabel la Católica, recognizing his contributions to Spanish art. Vierge taught himself to draw with his left hand and developed an incredible facility with his less dominant side. The subsequent 1892 English edition of *Pablo de Segovia* contains numerous drawings that Vierge made with his left hand.

49. "Pablo Returning Home, After Having Fallen in the Sewer," Illustration for Chapter Two, Francisco de Quevedo's *Pablo de Segovia*, French edition, Paris, 1882

Pen and black ink, with scraping corrections, on light tan machine-made heavy card; Bristol board

37.2 x 25.6 cm. (14⅝ x 10$^{1}/_{16}$ in.)

Signed in black ink, lower left: *VIERGE*

PROVENANCE: with León Bonhoure, Paris, 1882; London, Hall of Barnard's Inn, Holborn, 1892; Frank Jewett Mather Jr.

REFERENCES: Quevedo 1882, 26 ill.; Joseph Pennell, "Original Drawings by Daniel Vierge for Pablo de Segovia & a Selection of his Other Work" (London: Hall of Barnard's Inn, Holborn, 1892), "Drawings from *Pablo de Segovia*," 24, no. 9 (15). The number (15) represents the folio in the 1892 volume on which the drawing appears.

EXHIBITION: Joseph Pennell, "Original Drawings by Daniel Vierge for Pablo de Segovia & a Selection of his Other Work" (London: Hall of Barnard's Inn, Holborn, 1892), no. 9

Gift of Frank Jewett Mather Jr.
x1941-129

This ink drawing—from the series of illustrations that the artist completed for the French edition of Francisco de Quevedo's *Histoire de Pablo de Segovie* (*El gran Tacaño*), published in Paris in 1882—exemplifies the technique that the artist used until 1882.[5] The Princeton drawing illustrates a scene from the second chapter of the picaresque novel: Pablo de Segovia has fallen into a sewer and passersby are clearly affronted by the stench.[6] The artist frequently used a machine-made paperboard, called Bristol board, and his book illustrations usually were executed in black ink.[7] The use of a strong black shape on the figure of Pablo de Segovia is indicative of the impact of Japanese woodblock prints on the artist's oeuvre, in which a strong single-color shape often is used to focus attention.

Some of the drawings that Vierge made for the 1892 English edition of *Pablo de Segovia* are now in the collection of the Hispanic Society of America (A803–A814); in these drawings, the artist's technique of using a strong black form to focus the composition is evident. Other Pablo de Segovia drawings belong to the Musée du Luxembourg, Paris.[8] Although the drawing at Princeton seems to be one of the few that was used in both the 1882 and 1892 editions, the drawings from the 1892 edition at the Hispanic Society share a common provenance from the Old Barnard Inn, Holborn, London, in 1894.[9] This group was also exhibited at and acquired from the Galeries Georges Petit, Paris, in 1901.[10] Although it is not known from where Frank Jewett Mather Jr. purchased the Princeton drawing, the same provenance is possible. A 1912 exhibition of Vierge's work at the Palais du Louvre, Pavilion de Marsan, included at least twenty pen and ink drawings for *Pablo de Segovia*, borrowed from a variety of private collectors and lenders, including Vierge's widow.[11]

The drawing at Princeton was exhibited in London in 1892 to promote the English version of *Pablo de Segovia*, published with additional illustrations by Vierge and a

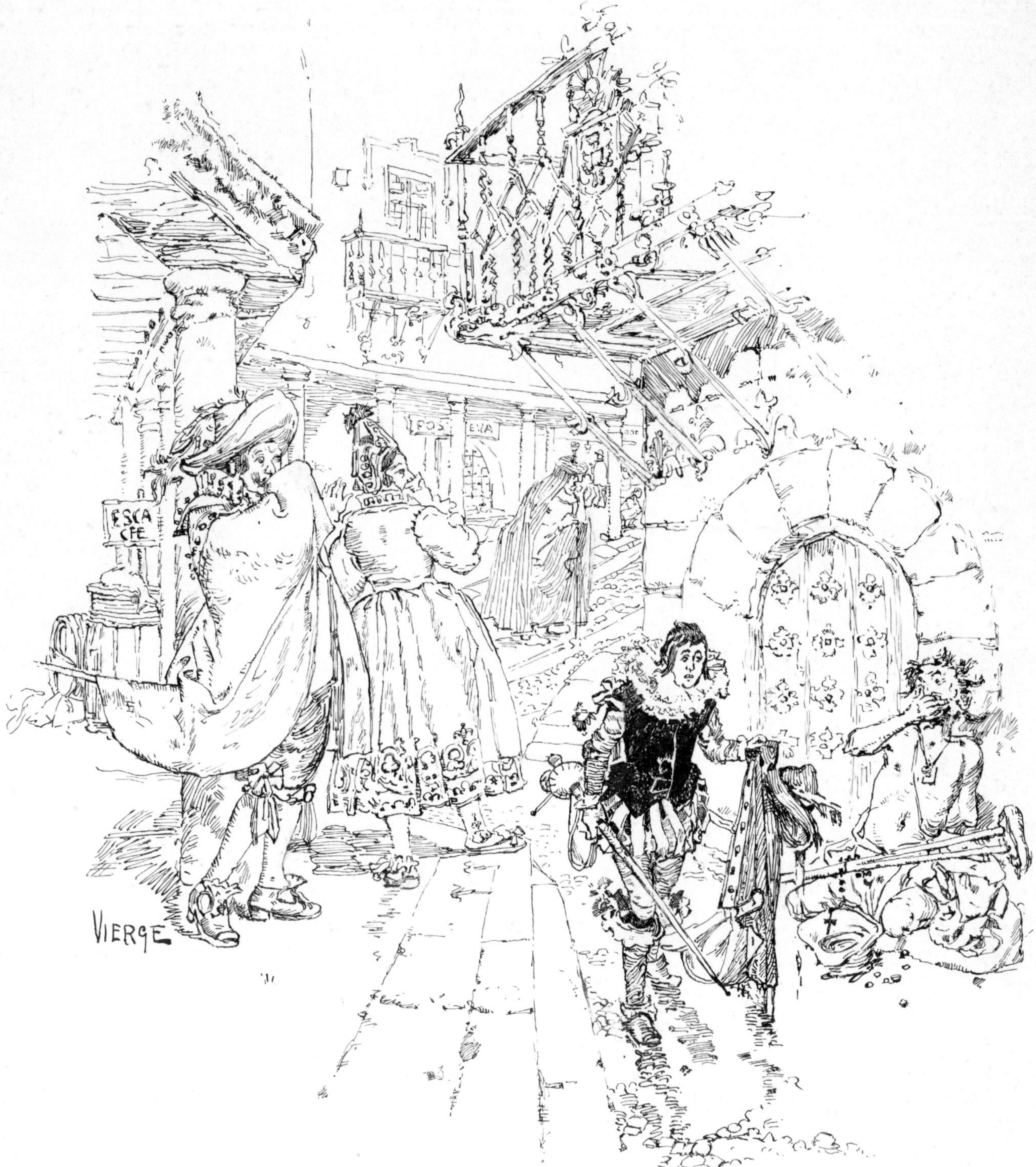
VIERGE

laudatory introductory essay by Joseph Pennell.[12] Although a 1902 edition of *Pablo de Segovia* was issued in which many illustrations from the 1892 edition were re-used, the Princeton drawing does not appear to have been used a third time. As described in Pennell's essay, Charles Gillot reduced Vierge's drawings in size to fit the pages: "by means of photography and handwork, [Gillot] produced in a metal block a reproduction of the original drawing."[13] Vierge's use of Bristol board, a stiff support, facilitated the reproduction of the drawings in heliogravure, a reproductive printing technique dependent on light exposure.[14] As Pennell described:

> *When it came to reproduction, most of the drawings had to be much reduced. This was beautifully done by Gillot (and it is interesting to compare the latter's work of ten years ago with that in this volume done by him to-day), while the printing of Lahure was most careful and satisfactory; but the appearance of Vierge's work in many cases was entirely changed, though he himself knew how it would be changed. Vierge, as anyone can see from these new reproductions drew openly, freely, boldly, but most carefully. The reproductions in Bonhoure's edition gave one the impression of exquisite delicacy, a refinement of line which did not altogether exist in the original drawings, but was produced because the artist knew exactly what he wanted, and . . . the engraver was able to obtain it.*[15]

Pennell also remarked on Vierge's remarkable finesse of line, resulting from the use of a glass pen and liquid black ink: "the drawings were made upon white paper—Bristol board or drawing paper—with a pen and liquid Indian ink. Vierge uses now a glass pen like an old stylus."[16] Unfortunately, the white paper that Pennell described has changed with age, due to the inherent vice of a high-acid-content paper, to appear more beige. This change has not, however, affected the strong, delicate lines of Vierge's humorous drawing for this classic Spanish picaresque novel. LAB

1 Patrick Lenaghan, "El arte y las ilustraciones de Daniel Vierge," in Madrid 2005–6, 77.
2 Casado Cimiano 2006. The Hispanic Society of America maintains the Spanish convention, and his work is accessioned as "Urrabieta Vierge."
3 "Exposition Daniel Vierge," exh. cat., Musée des arts décoratifs, Paris (Jan. 11–Feb. 12, 1912), 14.
4 Javier Krahe, "Daniel Urrabieta Vierge. Su vida y su época," in Madrid 2005–6, 13–75.
5 Quevedo 1882, 26. According to the colophon, there were 105 luxury copies of the book printed on special papers. My thanks to Edwin Rolón and Patrick Lenaghan.
6 Ibid., chap. 2.
7 The Bristol boards were usually embossed with the logo of the company at the upper left corner.
8 "Exposition Daniel Vierge," 36.
9 This is noted in the curatorial records for the drawings. My thanks to Marcus Burke.
10 Curatorial files, the Hispanic Society of America.
11 At least twenty, because some drawings were listed as "*dessin*" with no further description. There were also pen and ink studies for Pablo de Segovia that were not used in the publications. See "Exposition Daniel Vierge."
12 Patrick Lenaghan, "El arte y las ilustraciones de Daniel Vierge," in Madrid 2005–6, 103.
13 Pennell essay, in Quevedo 1892, ix.
14 The process is also called photogravure and is a photomechanical process that produced high-quality reproductions, especially of works of art. Heliogravure, or photogravure was in use through the 1940s for making reproductions of works of art in books. See for example, John Petrina, *Art work, how produced, how reproduced: the making and the reproduction of drawings, watercolors, oil paintings, monotypes, block prints, lithographs, etchings, etc.* (New York: Pitman Publishing Co., 1934). As Lenaghan noted, technological advances ensured that the reproductions were incredibly faithful to Vierge's original drawings. Patrick Lenaghan, "El Arte y las ilustraciones de Daniel Vierge," in Madrid 2005–6a, 77.
15 Pennell essay, in Quevedo 1892, viii–ix.
16 Ibid., ix.

PAU ROIG I CISA

Premiá de Mar, 1879–1955, Barcelona

Pau Roig i Cisa studied with the painter Francisco Torrescasana (1845–1918) in the Escuela de Bellas Artes in Barcelona and participated in his first competition in 1896, with the oil painting *Una Flor.*[1] He was best known as an illustrator and won many awards for his magazine covers, including the 1898 prize for the covers of *La Esquella de la Torratxa*, a Catalan almanac.

Although Roig never gained the fame of Santiago Rusiñol (1861–1931), Ramón Casas (1866–1932), or Carlos Verger (1872–1929) as an illustrator and draftsman, he found some success as a Catalan *modernista.*[2] In one instance, *Pèl & Ploma*, a Barcelona magazine, offered a prize for the best poster announcing a carnival; Picasso made an impressive poster, but Roig, who had moved to Paris in 1899, was named the winner.[3] The first prize was officially declared vacant, however, and the award of one hundred *pesetas* was divided among six claimants, including Roig, Carles Casagemas (1880–1901), and Picasso. The judges for the competition were Joaquín Mir, Manolo Hugué, and Joan Planella.[4]

The following year, Roig showed in the Salon National (1901) and the Salon des Indépendants (1902).[5] From 1906 to 1932, while living in Paris, he worked extensively in print media, creating posters, engravings, and illustrations for magazines and other periodicals. He published drawings in the magazines *Iris* and *Hispania*; completed a series of circus lithographs, published as *La Suite del Circ* (1906); and worked in an art nouveau style on marquetry design for the *modernista* furniture workshop of Gaspar Homar, often drawing figures for mosaics that feature the same flowing lines and simplicity of his drawings.[6]

Roig's drawings are reminiscent of those by Théophile-Alexandre Steinlen (1859–1923), the Swiss-born printmaker and painter, and Henri de Toulouse-Lautrec (1864–1901), whose work he emulated in studies like the *Woman Turned to the Left* (1903, Harvard University Art Museum) and *Woman* (1902,

Harvard University Art Museum). In Paris, Roig filled sketchbooks with figures drawn in rapid strokes with pastels and grease crayons, smudging the strong outlines of his figure studies. He chose subjects similar to those captured by Toulouse-Lautrec—performers and circus figures, women emerging from the bath or braiding their hair—and colored them with charged blue, orange, and purple pastels. Among his most accomplished pastel drawings are portraits made in charcoal and pastels.

Roig returned from Paris to Premià de Mar in 1933 and around 1943 moved to Barcelona, where he had several solo exhibitions.[7] He exhibited in Barcelona at the Saló d'Art Modern, Exposició de Primavera, in 1935 and 1936.[8] Roig also began to exhibit in Brussels, represented by the Belgian dealer L. H. Devillez.[9] In 1944 he exhibited late paintings that were reminiscent of Bonnard or Matisse at Argos in Barcelona.[10] Roig continued to exhibit new work until his death, participating in the Exposición Municipal de Otoño de Barcelona 1951 and in 1952 showing new drawings, paintings, prints, and watercolors at the Galería de San Jorge, Barcelona.[11]

Signed and dated drawings by Roig are in the collections of the Harvard University Art Museums; the Musée Goya-Jaurès, Castres; the Biblioteca de Catalunya, Barcelona; the Museu Nacional d'Art de Catalunya, Barcelona; and private collections. This group of six drawings was given to the Princeton University Art Museum in 1948 by the widow of Dan Fellows Platt, indicated by the estate stamp on the verso of each (Lugt 750a). Dan Fellows Platt died in 1938, and Ethel Platt later gave more than 2,000 drawings from his collection to Princeton.[12]

On the verso of each of these drawings, in graphite, is an inscription in Dan Fellows Platt's handwriting indicating the artist's name, the gallery, and the year of purchase. This systematic notation corresponds to notes in Platt's handwritten travel diaries, where he recorded the purchase of drawings in Paris in 1925, 1926, and 1927.[13] On a page at the back of the notebook, likely referring to the purchase of these drawings, he wrote: "Paris: Drawings," and then lists "Le Garrée, 39 bis, Rue Chateaud[. . .] 9th arr. Only modern."

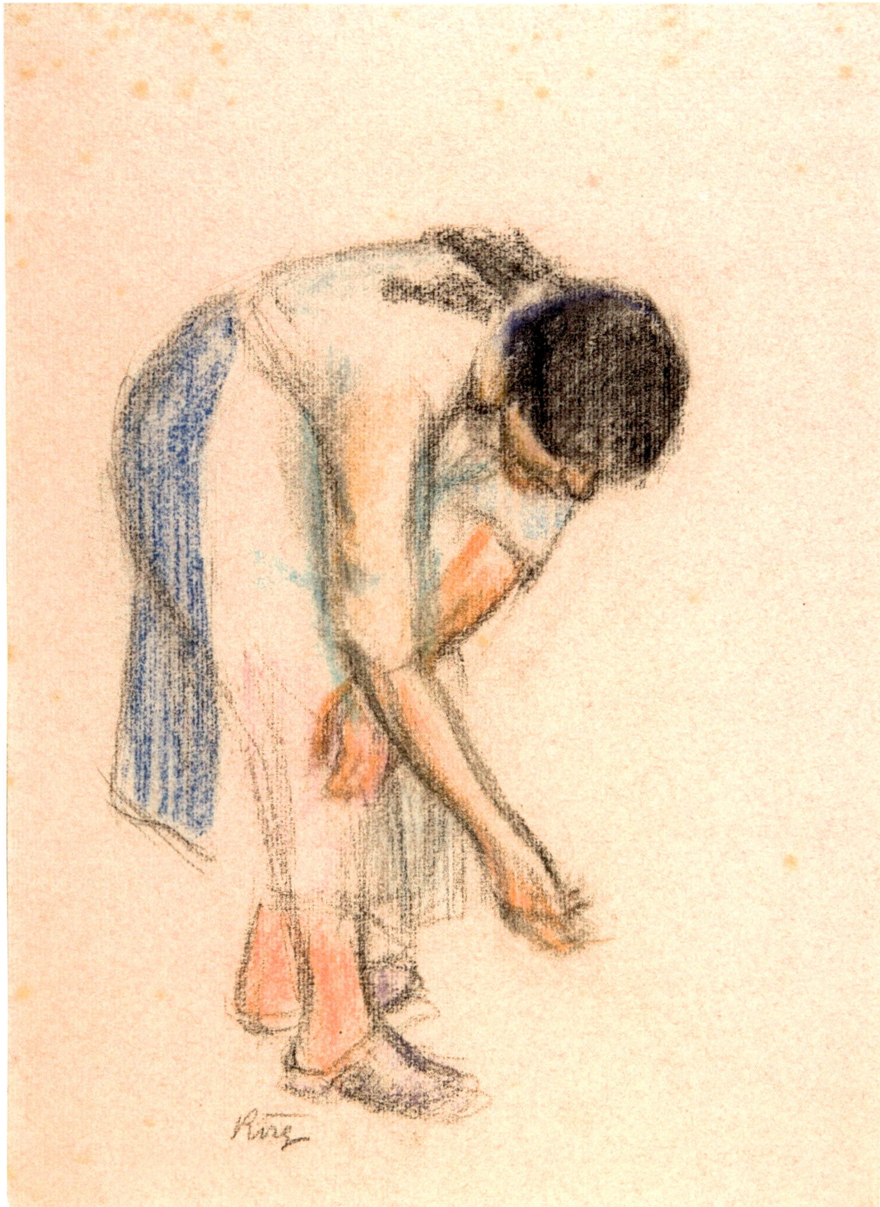

50. *Bending Woman*, ca. 1902–8

Pastel on pink laid paper

30.5 x 23.2 cm (12 x 9⅛ in.)

Signed in black pastel, lower left: *Roig*; inscribed on verso in graphite, lower edge: *Etude de jeune fille / Donnant a manger aux poules / E195 Roig Le Garrée 1927*

WATERMARK: Double oval with initials *AL*, heart and strap (Catalan machine-made paper, Guarro Casas papermaker [see Madrid 1993, 327, no. 190]) (see appendix)

PROVENANCE: Gallery Le Garrée, Paris, purchased in 1927; Dan Fellows Platt, stamped with his posthumous estate stamp (Lugt 750a); with his widow, Ethel Platt, until 1948

Bequest of Dan Fellows Platt, Class of 1895 x1948-957

This drawing on colored paper demonstrates Roig's strong use of black chalk outlines in figure studies. The free handling of the pastel and the use of purple and blue can be compared to a signed and dated drawing of a woman in a headscarf by Roig in the Museu Nacional d'Art de Catalunya, dated 1908. Princeton's sheet was acquired by Dan Fellows Platt in Paris in 1927.

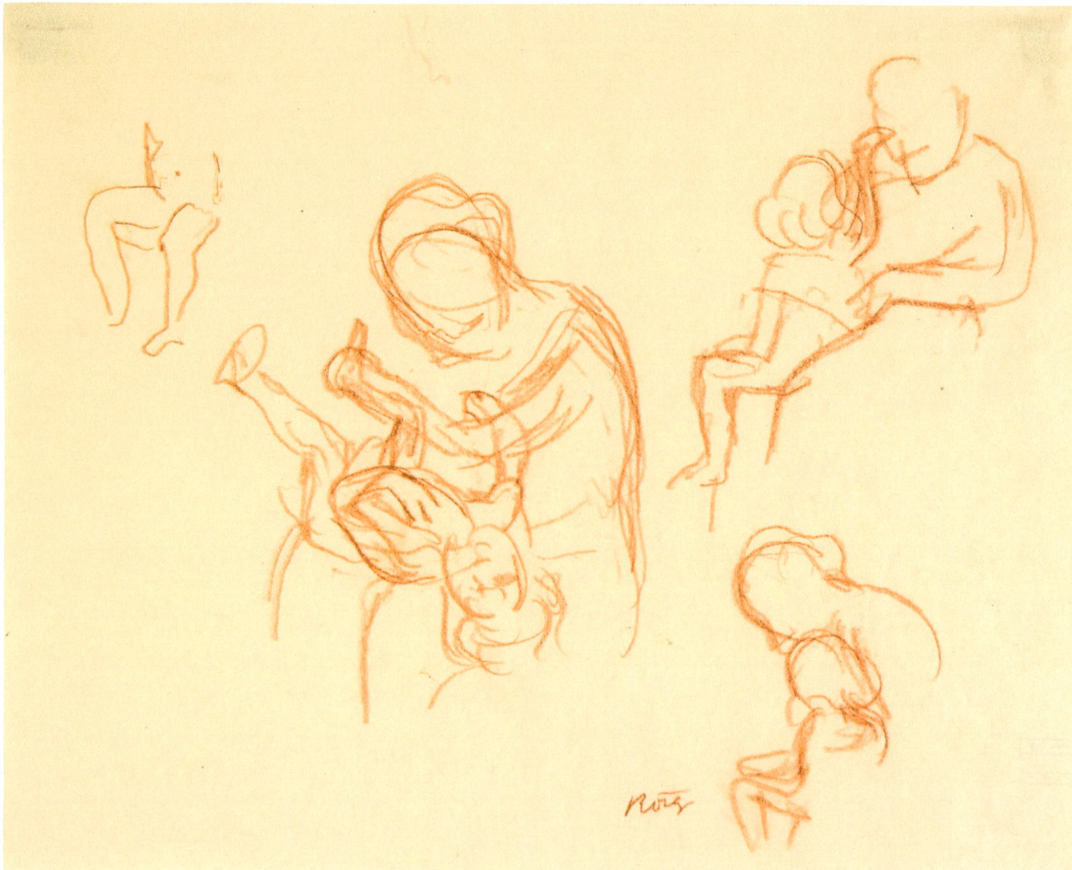

51. *Sketches of Woman and Child*, ca. 1902–8

Sanguine pencil on light tan wove paper

24.9 x 31.6 cm. (9 13/16 x 12 7/16 in.)

Signed in sanguine pencil, lower center: *Roig*; inscribed on verso in graphite, on left edge: *E-201—Roig—Le Garrée – 1927* with red pencil *X* above *201*

Provenance: Gallery Le Garrée, Paris, purchased in 1927; Dan Fellows Platt Collection, stamped with his posthumous estate stamp (Lugt 750a); with his widow, Ethel Platt, until 1948

Bequest of Dan Fellows Platt, Class of 1895
x1948-959

This sheet and the related folded sheet of smaller sketches (cat. 55) depict a woman holding a small child in poses of maternal intimacy. They relate closely to sheets now in Barcelona of seated and standing women who hold small children. As with the rest of the sheets in this group, this one seems to have come from a sketchbook of such scenes that has been separated and signed by the artist.

52. *Sketches of Seated Woman*, ca. 1902–8

Pastel on light tan laid paper

31.3 x 24.4 cm. (12 5/16 x 9 9/16 in.)

Signed in graphite, lower right corner: *Roig*; inscribed on verso in graphite, lower edge: *E 197 Roig—Le Garrée 1926*

Provenance: Gallery Le Garrée, Paris, purchased in 1926; Dan Fellows Platt Collection, stamped with his posthumous estate stamp (Lugt 750a)

Bequest of Dan Fellows Platt, Class of 1895
x1948-958

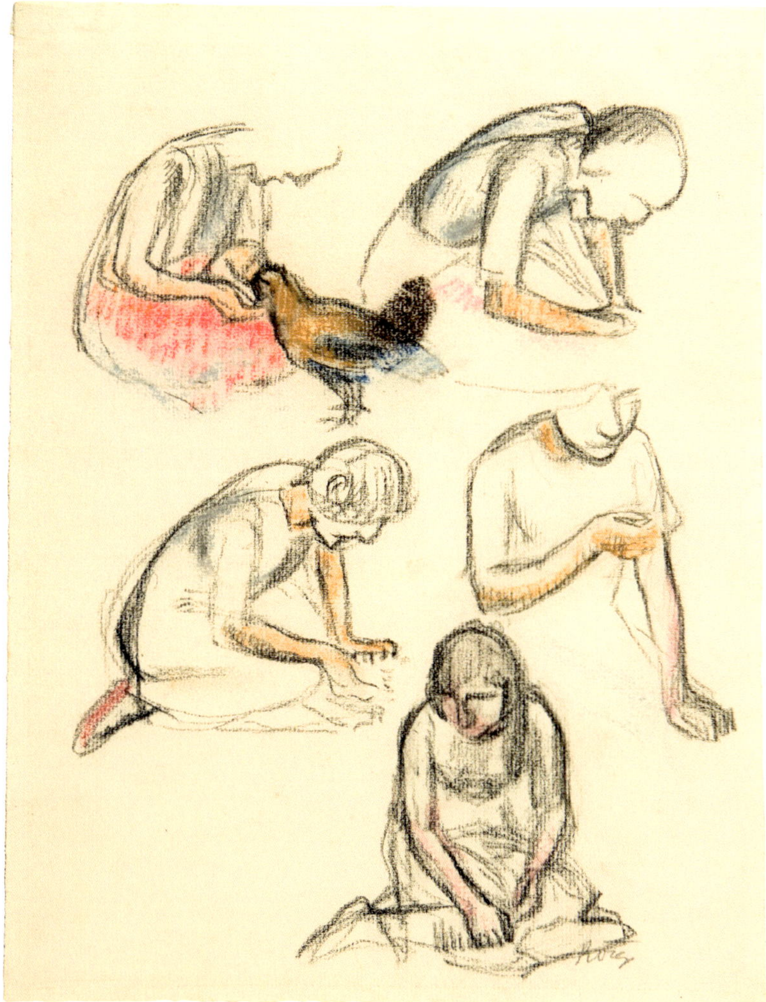

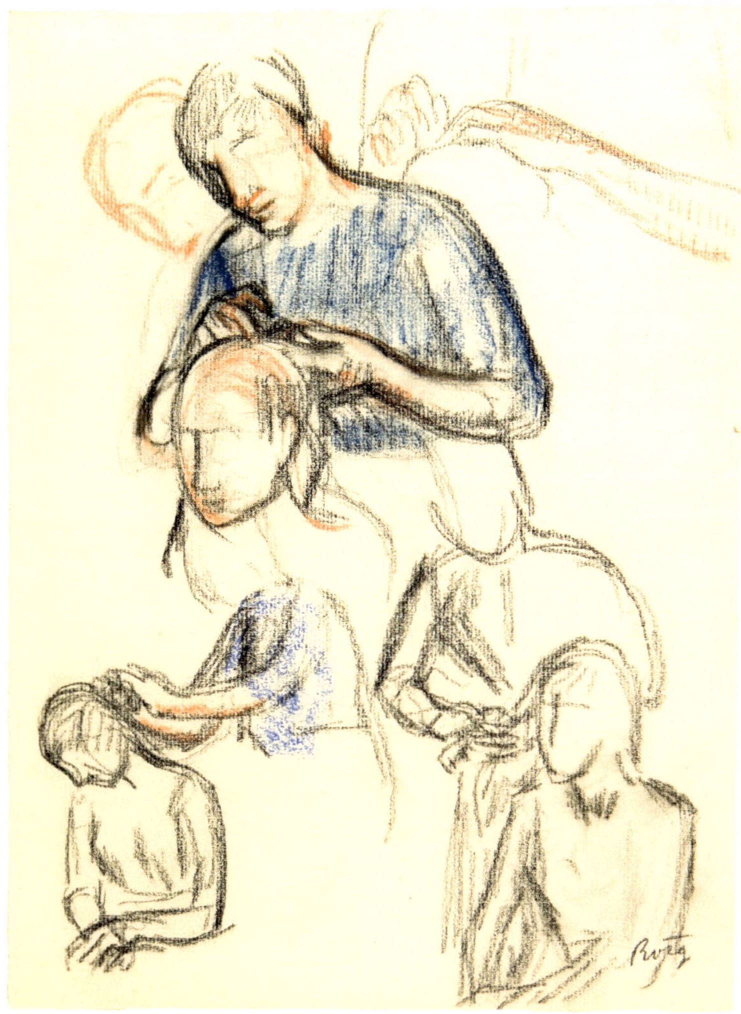

This group of intimate sketches of a woman seated on the ground feeding a chicken was acquired by Dan Fellows Platt in 1926 in Paris. The vertical composition relates closely to *Bending Woman* (cat. 50), who also seems engaged in a domestic task. The sinuous curve of the woman's back and her bent arms seem to have fascinated Roig, who repeatedly drew compositions in pastel and black chalk that focused on a woman's torso and arms in gestures of bending. This sheet of sketches can be compared with a larger study of a kneeling woman with a basket (Museu Nacional d'Art de Catalunya).

53. *La Coiffure, Three Sketches,* ca. 1902–8

Pastel on light tan wove paper

31.7 x 24.0 cm. ($12\frac{7}{16}$ x $9\frac{7}{16}$ in.)

Signed in black pastel, lower right corner: *Roig*; inscribed on verso in graphite, on lower edge: *la coiffure E198—Roig / Le Garrée 1927*

Provenance: Gallery Le Garrée, Paris, purchased in 1927; Dan Fellows Platt Collection, stamped with his posthumous estate stamp (Lugt 750a); with his widow, Ethel Platt, until 1948

Bequest of Dan Fellows Platt, Class of 1895
x1948-960

Roig's interest in the female form, with bent arms braiding hair, here seems closest to a drawing in Barcelona also executed in sanguine, or red chalk with black pastel, as well as another dated sketch from 1905 of a squatting female figure.

54. *Two Sketches of a Woman*, ca. 1902–8

Charcoal pencil and sanguine pencil on beige wove paper

20.0 x 29.5 cm. (7⅞ x 11⅝ in.)

Signed in charcoal pencil, lower right: *Roig*; inscribed on verso in graphite, left edge: *E202 - Roig – Le Garrée 1927*— with red pencil *X* above *202*

PROVENANCE: Gallery Le Garrée, Paris, purchased in 1927; Dan Fellows Platt Collection, stamped with his posthumous estate stamp (Lugt 750a); with his widow, Ethel Platt, until 1948

Bequest of Dan Fellows Platt, Class of 1895
x1948-961

This forceful sketch relates closely to sheets in Barcelona of a Degas-like squatting figure drying herself after a bath or a woman with a long black braid, seated and in profile. Roig used the dark red sanguine pencil to highlight and animate the figures of two women braiding their hair, their arms bending in smooth, unbroken lines, in a manner similar to the figure of the woman crouching, whose long back and bended knees are drawn with similar flowing strokes.

55. *Sketches of Woman and Child*, ca. 1902–8

Charcoal pencil, pastel, and blue color pencils on beige laid paper

24.6 x 30.9 cm. (9¹¹⁄₁₆ x 12³⁄₁₆ in.)

Signed in charcoal pencil, lower center: *Roig*; inscribed on verso in graphite, lower left: *Roig* with red pencil *X* above / *E-200 Le Garrée 1925*

WATERMARK: *INGRES* (Catalan machine-made paper, Guarro Casas papermaker [see Madrid 1993, 327, no. 190]) (see appendix)

PROVENANCE: Gallery Le Garrée, Paris, purchased in 1925; Dan Fellows Platt Collection, stamped with his posthumous estate stamp (Lugt 750a); with his widow, Ethel Platt, until 1948

Bequest of Dan Fellows Platt, Class of 1895
x1948-962

Roig's use of blue pastel to draw the figures of mother and child can be compared to other sketchbook sheets in Barcelona: of a squatting nude figure, executed in black pastel and in blue pastel. Using the same technique as in the Barcelona drawings, here Roig stumped and smudged the pastels along the black outlines, softening the contours and heightening the intimacy of the sketch of the mother and child. LAB

1 Arnáiz, López Jiménez, and Merchán Díaz 1992, 240.
2 See Francesc M. Quílez i Corella, "The Art of the Poster," in Cleveland/New York 2006-7, 69–71.
3 Richardson 1991, 127; Cirici Pellicer 1951, 419.
4 Ocaña 1995, 298.
5 Arnáiz, López Jiménez, and Merchán Díaz 1992, 240.
6 Cirici Pellicer 1951, 228, 258.
7 Arnáiz, López Jiménez, and Merchán Díaz 1992, 240.
8 Fontbona et al. 2002, 256, 262–63.
9 Ibid.
10 Cirici Pellicer 1951, 419.
11 Arnáiz, López Jiménez, and Merchán Díaz 1992, 240.
12 Ross 1996, 135–54.
13 Dan Fellows Platt Papers, Firestone Library, Princeton University, C0860, IX. *Journals and Diaries, 1888–1934*, Box 5. Manuscript Travel Diary 1924–1931. The note appears in a meticulous account of the money Platt spent on an extended trip in France and Spain.

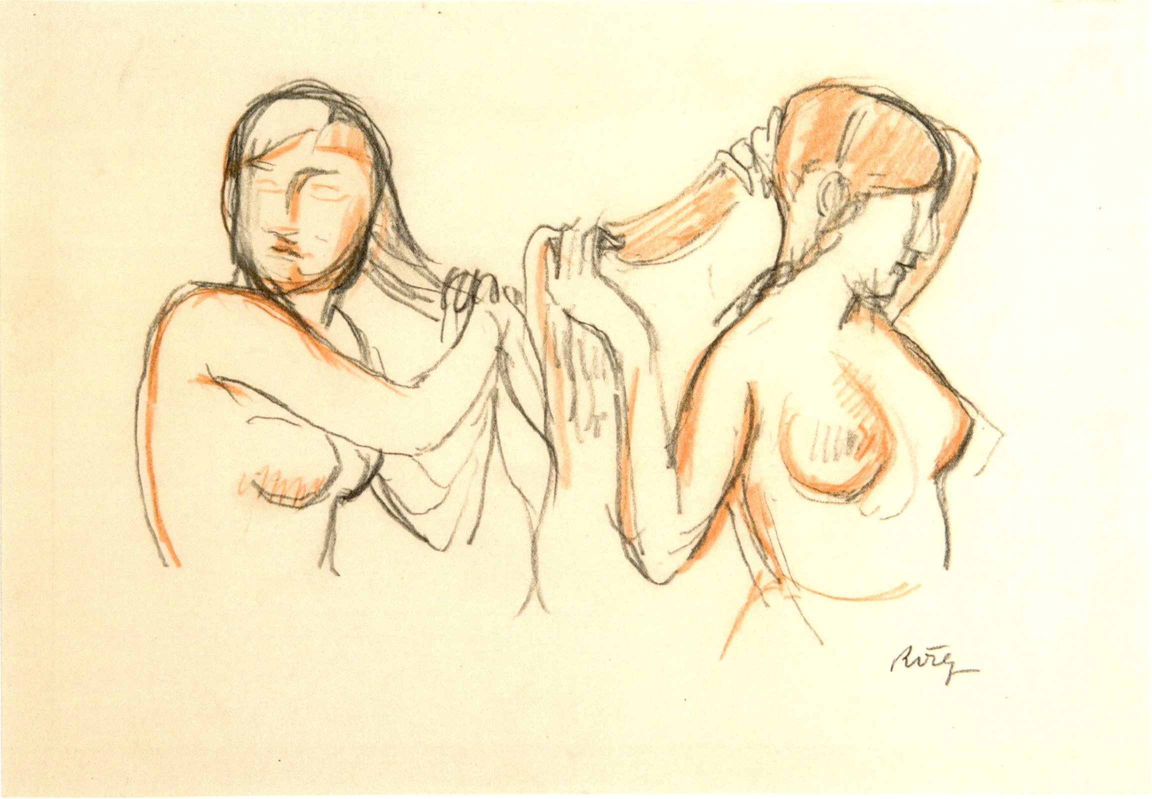

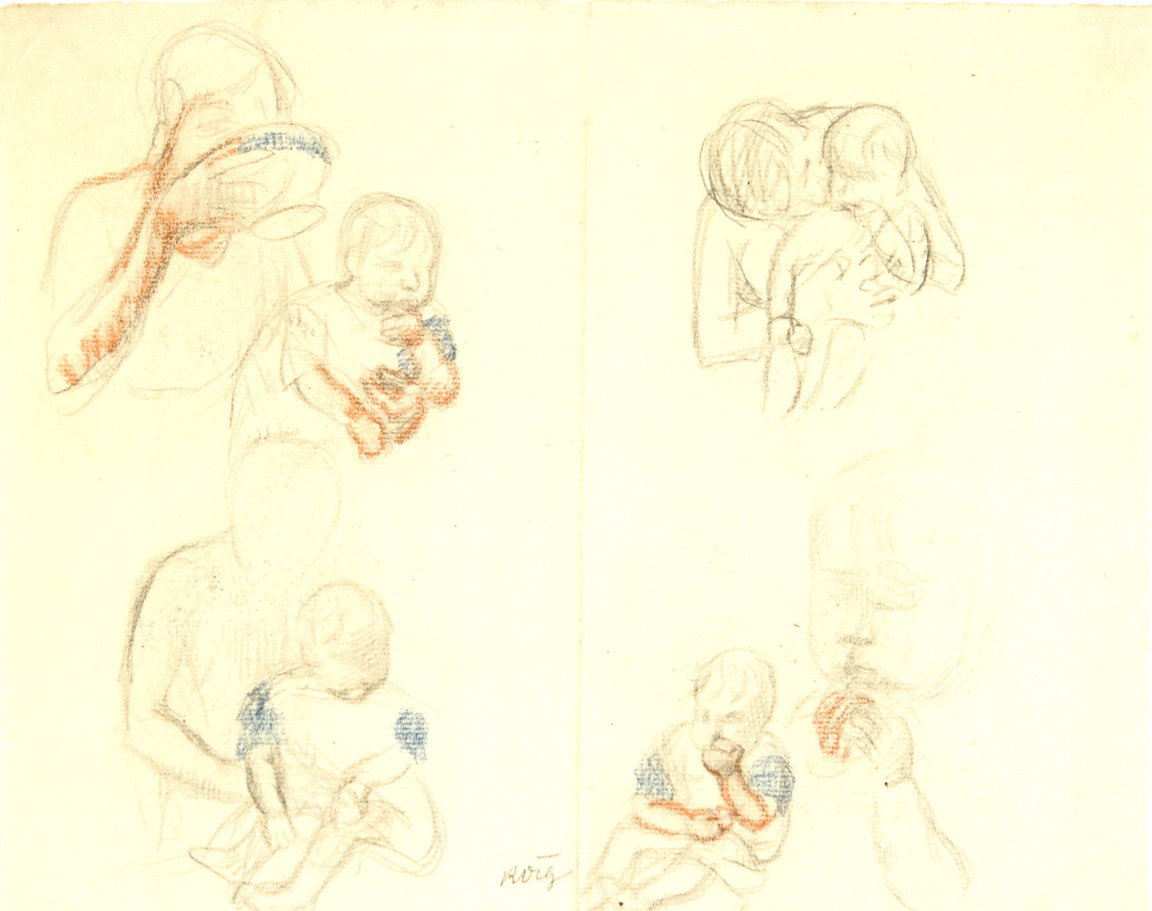

PABLO PICASSO

Málaga, 1881–1973, Mougins, France

One can hardly think of a modern artist for whom drawing was a more central practice than Pablo Picasso. Between 1894 and 1967 the Spanish master produced some 175 sketchbooks containing independent drawings, notes, caricatures, preparatory studies for paintings and sculptures, aide-mémoire of works already completed, and sketches that are related to extant works both directly and indirectly.[1] For *Les Demoiselles d'Avignon*—Picasso's culminating work of 1907—alone, the artist filled forty-one sketchbooks, attesting to the importance that drawing held for him. Over the next seven decades Picasso continued to sketch avidly, working with a wide variety of media and material supports, from fine artists' papers to cardboard and even paper napkins from restaurants.

Pablo Ruiz Picasso was born in Málaga, Spain, on October 25, 1881. The youngest child of José Ruiz Blasco (1838–1913), an academic painter who specialized in compositions featuring pigeons, and María Picasso López, the young Pablo demonstrated his precocious talent from an early age. After a four-year stint in La Coruña, during which time José Ruiz was employed as a professor at the School of Fine Arts, the family relocated to Barcelona in 1895. In 1897, at the age of sixteen, Picasso was sent to Madrid's Real Academia de Bellas Artes de San Fernando, but he was more interested in the local nightlife and in studying Old Master works at the Prado than in attending classes. Upon his return to Barcelona, Picasso found his niche among the city's bohemian avant-garde, celebrating his first one-man show in February 1900 at the famous Quatre Gats tavern, where he exhibited portrait drawings of local friends and acquaintances.

That same year, Picasso traveled to Paris to visit the Exposition Universelle and to secure a dealer. Over the next several years he returned to the French capital four times, settling permanently in Montmartre in the spring of 1904. Soon thereafter he befriended André Salmon (1881–1969), Guillaume Apollinaire (1880–1918), and Max Jacob (1876–1944), who would remain loyal friends for years to come. In 1905, the twenty-four-year-old artist also met the American expatriate author Gertrude Stein (1874–1946), who became his patron and introduced Picasso to Henri Matisse (1869–1954), his friend and artistic rival throughout his life.

From late 1908 until the beginning of World War I, Picasso worked closely with Georges Braque (1882–1963) in the joint enterprise that would be called Cubism. Once again drawing was central to Picasso's approach. Not only did the Spanish artist execute a number of important drawings of nudes in 1910—in which he explored the relation between the body and the grid as a structural scaffold—he also rehearsed and reconfigured the descriptive functions of line as shading, contour, and sign through his work in papier collé of 1912–13 (see fig. 56.1).[2]

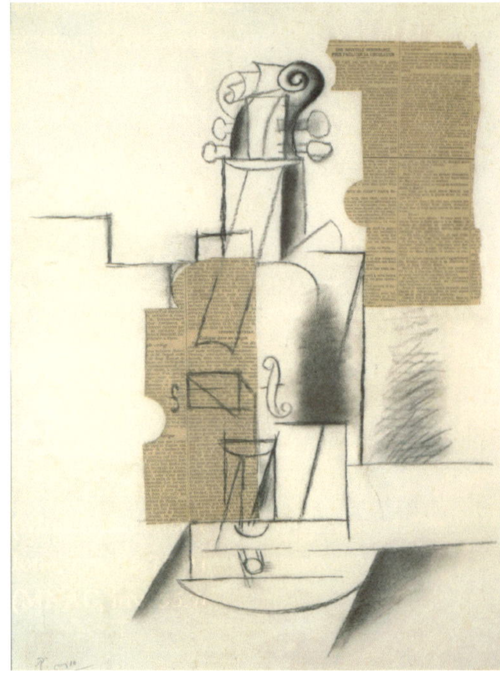

Fig. 56.1 Pablo Picasso, Spanish, 1881–1973: *Violin*, December 3, 1912, or later. Cut-and-pasted newspaper and charcoal on paper, 62 x 47 cm. Musée National d'Art Moderne, Centre Georges Pompidou.

With the outbreak of World War I in August 1914, Picasso and Braque parted ways. A new mood of classicism—the so-called "retour-à-l'ordre"— swept over French art and culture, and Picasso, like so many of his contemporaries, was not immune to wartime restraint and conservatism. Under the dual influence of Cézanne (1839–1906) and Ingres (1780–1867) he reconceived his drawing practice, working in both Cubist and more traditional representational modes. Over the next decade Picasso became the much sought-after darling of Right Bank society, courted by wealthy French and international patrons. In the summer of 1918 he married Olga Khokhlova, a dancer with Sergei Diaghilev's Ballets Russes (Picasso had designed the sets and costumes for the company's ballet *Parade* a year earlier), and three years later his first and only legitimate child, Paulo, was born. More theatrical collaborations followed *Parade*, including designs for Manuel de Falla's *Three-Cornered Hat* (1919), Igor Stravinsky's *Pulcinella* (1920), and the ballet *Mercure* (1924), for which Erik Satie composed the music, just as he had for *Parade*.

In the 1920s, the nascent Surrealist movement captured Picasso's attention. Despite André Breton's (1896–1966) best efforts, however, Picasso was never an official member of the group. Nevertheless, his penchant for surprising juxtapositions—the yoking of disparate ideas and materials that was essential to the practice of collage—brought Picasso close to the Surrealists, who viewed him as an artistic progenitor of sorts. Erotic subjects, often of a violent nature, found a new place in Picasso's work, and the idea of metamorphosis became a basic operational procedure. In 1927 the seventeen-year-old Marie-Thérèse Walter entered Picasso's life and art, and his relationship with Olga deteriorated. On September 5, 1935, Marie-Thérèse gave birth to Maya Picasso, the artist's second child. Throughout the 1930s, sculpture occupied Picasso's attention to an increasing degree, just as his graphic production resulted in such exquisite masterpieces as his illustrations for Ovid's *Metamorphoses*, the famous *Vollard Suite*, and the biting political indictment *Dream and Lie of Franco*. Picasso's anti-fascist position was well known, and he welcomed the opportunity to contribute a major work to the Spanish Republican Pavilion of the 1937 Paris World's Fair, the famous mural-sized painting *Guernica*, for which the artist executed numerous drawings and studies.

During World War II, Picasso remained in occupied France while many of his friends and colleagues immigrated to the United States. His new lover, the photographer Dora Maar, became his model of choice, but generally Picasso's work of these years is austere and somber: interiors with skulls and makeshift still lifes are ciphers of privation and loss. With the Salon de la Libération in 1944, Picasso was again in the limelight. His decision to join the Communist Party immediately rehabilitated him as the leading artistic figure of the French Left. In 1943 he had met the young painter Françoise Gilot, with whom he would have two more children: Claude, born in 1947, and Paloma, born in 1949.

Picasso's output continued unabated in his last decades. In addition to his work as a draftsman, painter, sculptor, and printmaker, he also produced a copious oeuvre in ceramics, working with local artisans in the French village of Vallauris. In 1953, Gilot left Picasso, taking Claude and Paloma with her. A year earlier the artist had met Jacqueline Roque, who, in 1961, would become his second wife. Jacqueline was Picasso's constant companion and model, and her countenance appears in numerous paintings and drawings of Picasso's late years.

In the final two decades of his life, with his reputation as modernism's Old Master secured, Picasso began a long series of meditations on the history of art. Poussin and David metaphorically entered his studio, as did Delacroix, Courbet, and Manet in Picasso's series of variations on Old Master paintings. Drawing, too, occupied a privileged position in Picasso's late work, which includes many depictions of musketeers, arcadian themes, reclining nudes, and the artist and his model, works executed in crayon, pencil, and ink in a loose and gestural late style.[3] On April 8, 1973, Picasso died in Mougins, France, six months shy of his ninety-first birthday. The twentieth century belonged to Picasso, whose contributions forever changed the procedures and practices of modern art.

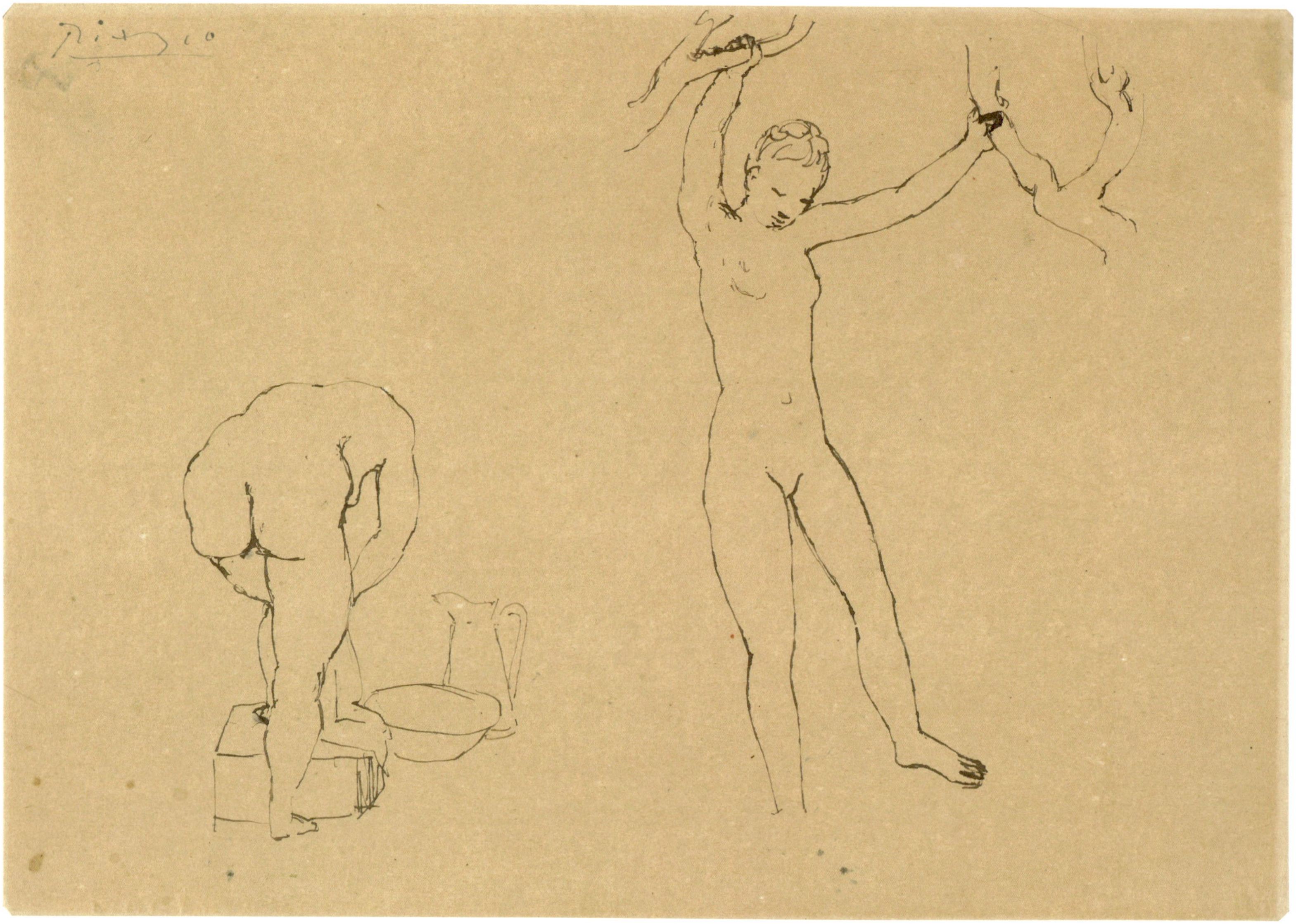

56. *Two Studies of Female Nudes* ("Le Bain"), 1905–6

Pen and black ink on light brown wove paper mounted to cardboard

28 x 40.5 cm. (11 1/16 x 15 15/16 in.)

INSCRIPTION: Signed in pen and blue-black ink, upper left: *Picasso*; stamped on verso of mount, French customs mark, in black

PROVENANCE: Gertrude Stein; given to her brother, Leo Stein; Curt Valentin (?); Kleeman Galleries, New York

REFERENCES: DeWald 1948, 10, ill.; Zervos 1954, no. 740, ill.; San Francisco/Paris/New York 2010–11, 440, no. 319, ill.

EXHIBITIONS: Princeton 1949, no. 6, ill.; Lawrence 1958, no. 63; New York 1970, 167; Princeton 1972, 68–69, ill.; Bielefeld 2011–12.

Museum purchase, Laura P. Hall Memorial Fund
x1948-1808

This delicate drawing is a single sheet containing two sketches: a bathing woman viewed from the back, with her foot on a plinth before a water bowl and jug, and another female figure, whose outstretched arms grasp the limbs of a tree. Using summary details and approaching his composition with great visual economy, Picasso engages in a kind of linear shorthand in this masterful study of contour and gesture. Although the artist's line is not continuous it demonstrates considerable control, as Picasso adjusts the stylus of his pen to emphasize the curve of a thigh or pubis, the fold of the buttocks, or the cryptic features of the face. His friend, the poet and critic Guillaume Apollinaire, described Picasso's use of contour line in the costumes of the artist's saltimbanques from this period in terms that might well be applied to the Princeton drawing: "The harlequins live in faded finery where the painting brings its colors together, warms or whitens them, to express strength and the durability of passion, where lines following the shape of the costume curve, cross or leap upwards."[4]

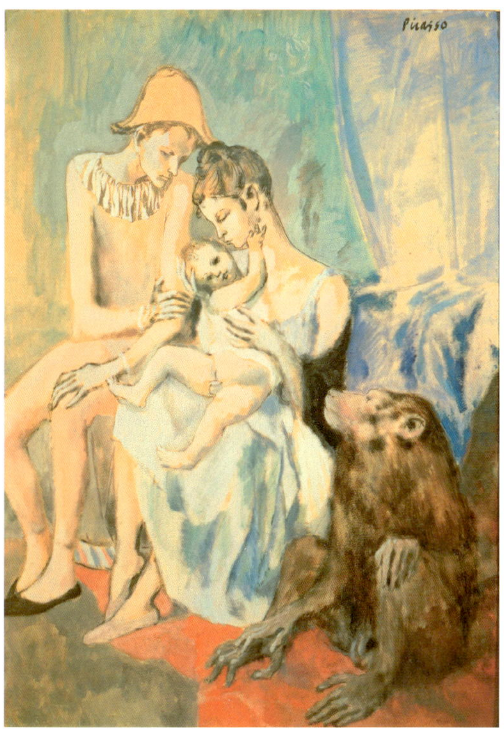

Fig. 56.2 Pablo Picasso, Spanish, 1881–1973: *The Acrobat Family*, 1905. Watercolor, gouache, and ink on paper, 104 x 75 cm. Gothenburg Museum of Art, Sweden.

Apollinaire made these remarks in a review of Picasso's exhibition at the Galeries Serrurier, Paris, which ran from February 25 to March 6, 1905.[5] Although the Princeton drawing does not relate directly to the artist's images of circus performers from the "Rose" period (particularly the figure of the acrobat, who entered Picasso's work in late 1904), it can be grouped among the many domestic scenes of adolescent children and women at the toilette that the artist produced over the course of 1905 and 1906. In Picasso's universe there is considerable crossover between these types, as many of his scenes of circus performers at rest or engaged in various activities offstage are also vignettes of family life and quiet domesticity. When the sheet was shown in a loan exhibition of Picasso's drawings in 1949 a related study of "Three Nudes," dated 1905 in the catalogue, accompanied it. Given the subject and style of the Princeton drawing, however, a date of spring or summer 1906 seems more likely for both sketches. The theme of the woman at her toilette relates to a series of drawings and paintings that Picasso executed just prior to and during his stay in the remote village of Gósol that summer, and the nude with outstretched arms grasping the branches of a tree implies a pastoral setting that might reflect the artist's sojourn in the village.

Additional anecdotal evidence points to a spring/summer 1906 date. The first owners of the drawing were Gertrude and Leo Stein. Picasso met Leo in the spring of 1905, after the collector had visited his exhibition at the Galeries Serrurier.[6] By November 1905 the Steins had acquired their first works by the artist, *The Acrobat Family* (fig. 56.2) and *Girl with a Basket of Flowers*, the former a drawing rendered in watercolor, gouache, and ink on paper and the latter a painting executed in oil on canvas, both from 1905.[7] By 1906, as Picasso's friendship and professional relationship with the Stein family intensified, he executed portraits of Gertrude, Leo, and their nephew, Allan. Between 1905 and 1913–14, when their collection was divided, Gertrude and Leo jointly acquired nearly sixty paintings and works on paper by Picasso dating to the years 1905–6. RSL

57. *Harlequin*, 1917

Graphite on brown wove paper

26.8 x 19.5 cm. (10 9/16 x 7 11/16 in.)

Signed in pen and black ink, bottom right: *Picasso*

WATERMARK: three-pronged anchor (see appendix)

PROVENANCE: Interart, S.A., Lucerne, Switzerland

REFERENCE: Princeton 1953, 39

Museum purchase, John Maclean Magie, Class of 1892, and Gertrude Magie Fund
x1952-145

This masterful depiction of Harlequin, one of the most colorful characters of the Italian commedia dell'arte, is characteristic of Picasso's cubist work in 1917. Emphasizing precise geometries, the artist structured his composition around a series of crisscrossing orthogonal lines that define broad, flattened

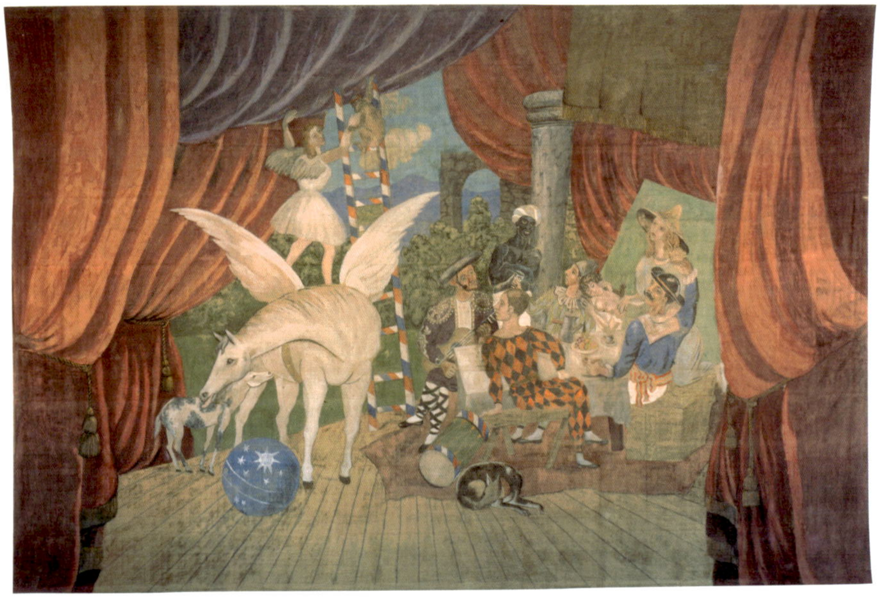

Fig. 57.1 Pablo Picasso, Spanish, 1881–1973: Curtain design for the ballet *Parade*, 1917. 105 x 164 cm. Musée National d'Art Moderne, Centre Georges Pompidou.

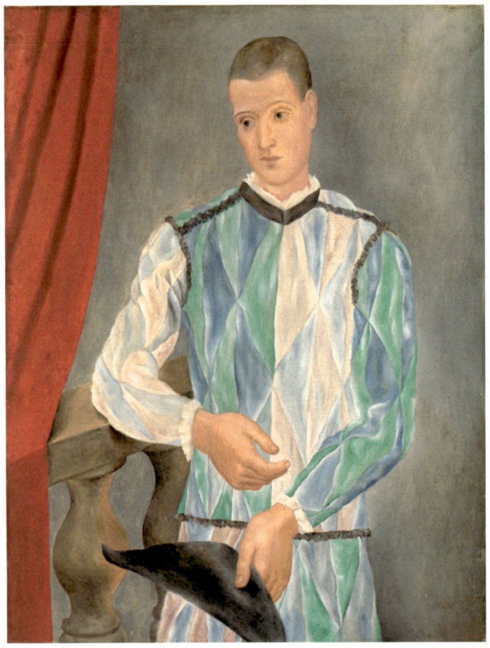

Fig. 57.2 Pablo Picasso, Spanish, 1881–1973: *Harlequin* (Portrait of Léonide Massine), 1917. Oil on canvas, 117 x 89.5 cm. Museu Picasso, Barcelona, Document Collection, donated by the artist, 1919 (MPB 10.941).

planes. Surface detail is applied judiciously to the figure's costume, including his ruffled collar, which repeats the organizing lines of the composition as a whole. Set within a shallow space and seemingly locked into place by the wainscoting that extends from both sides of his hips, the figure has a monumental and imposing stature. Picasso's line is crisp and immaculate, holding in check the complex game of formal alliteration and visual rhymes in which he clearly delights.

The Harlequin theme was topical for Picasso in 1917. On February 19 the artist arrived in Rome with Jean Cocteau to work with Sergei Diaghilev and Léonide Massine on the sets and costumes for the ballet *Parade*, for which Erik Satie had written the score.[8] Harlequin makes an appearance on the overture curtain of the ballet, alongside other Commedia dell'Arte figures (fig. 57.1), and Picasso would also paint a magnificent portrait of Massine dressed as Harlequin during the troupe's sojourn in Barcelona later that year (fig. 57.2). Although circus performers had been a staple of Picasso's work during the Rose Period of 1904–5, the figure of Harlequin had a special resonance for Picasso, who seems to have adopted the character as his alter ego.[9] Harlequin dates to the Italian visual record of the sixteenth century, and he was a stock figure in French passion plays. His attributes are a motley costume composed of diamond-shaped lozenges, a mask covering his eyes that is secured by a chinstrap, thick eyebrows, a wiry mustache, and a cornered hat; he generally appears carrying a saber or a wooden baton. Decidedly lustful, Harlequin was also known for his hearty appetite. Dim-witted and capricious, yet sympathetic, by the eighteenth century the figure of Harlequin had been transformed from his early associations with death into a romantic hero, a social critic who commented upon and inverted the established order of things—an association Picasso cannot but have appreciated.[10]

The Princeton drawing should be located within a trilogy of related images. In his pursuit of geometric rigor and compositional balance Picasso produced a nearly identical second version of this drawing, in which the design of the costume and the articulation of the figure's left hand are simplified.[11] The artist also executed a copper plate etching based on this composition, reversed in printing, in which the figure's arms are rendered more organically, with a quasi-naturalistic treatment of the musculature. The geometric armature that encloses the figure in the print invites interesting comparisons with the costumes that Picasso had designed for the French and American Managers in *Parade*. The etching illustrated Max Jacob's *Cornet à Dés*, a compilation of prose poems the author published in 1917.[12] RSL

1 Glimcher and Glimcher 1986.
2 For an extended discussion of Picasso's analysis of the tools of Western pictorial representation in relation to his work in the medium of *papier collé*, see Poggi 1992; New York 2011; and Karmel 2003.
3 Gert Schiff, *Picasso, The Last Years, 1963–73* (New York: The Solomon R. Guggenheim Museum and The Grey Art Gallery, 1983).
4 Guillaume Apollinaire, "Young Artists: Picasso the Painter," *La Plume* (Paris) (May 25, 1905); in Breunig 1988, 14–16.
5 The exhibition included twenty-eight paintings and drawings, prints, and a sketchbook, including a group of large-scale drawings for saltimbanques. For a discussion, see Marilyn McCully, "Early Critical Responses to Picasso's Drawings," in New York/Washington, D.C. 2011–12, 37–38.
6 On Leo Stein's introduction to Picasso, see Kate Mendillo's chronology in San Francisco/Paris/New York 2011–12, 315–16. Gertrude would meet Picasso shortly thereafter.
7 For a discussion of these acquisitions, see Robert McD. Parker's "Catalogue of the Stein Collections," in ibid., nos. 232 and 291.
8 For a complete account of Picasso's life in Rome, see Richardson 2007.
9 Reff 1971.
10 Barcelona 2006–7, 56–64.
11 The drawing appears in Christian Zervos' s catalogue raisonné of Picasso, vol. 29, no. 210.
12 Max Jacob, *Cornet à Dés ("Recueil de Poèmes en Prose, 1904–1914")* (Paris, 1917). In a letter to Picasso dated March 7, 1917, while the artist was in Rome working on the sets and costumes for *Parade*, Jacob asked his friend for an etching to accompany his forthcoming book. For a discussion, see Quimper/Paris 1994, 143–44.

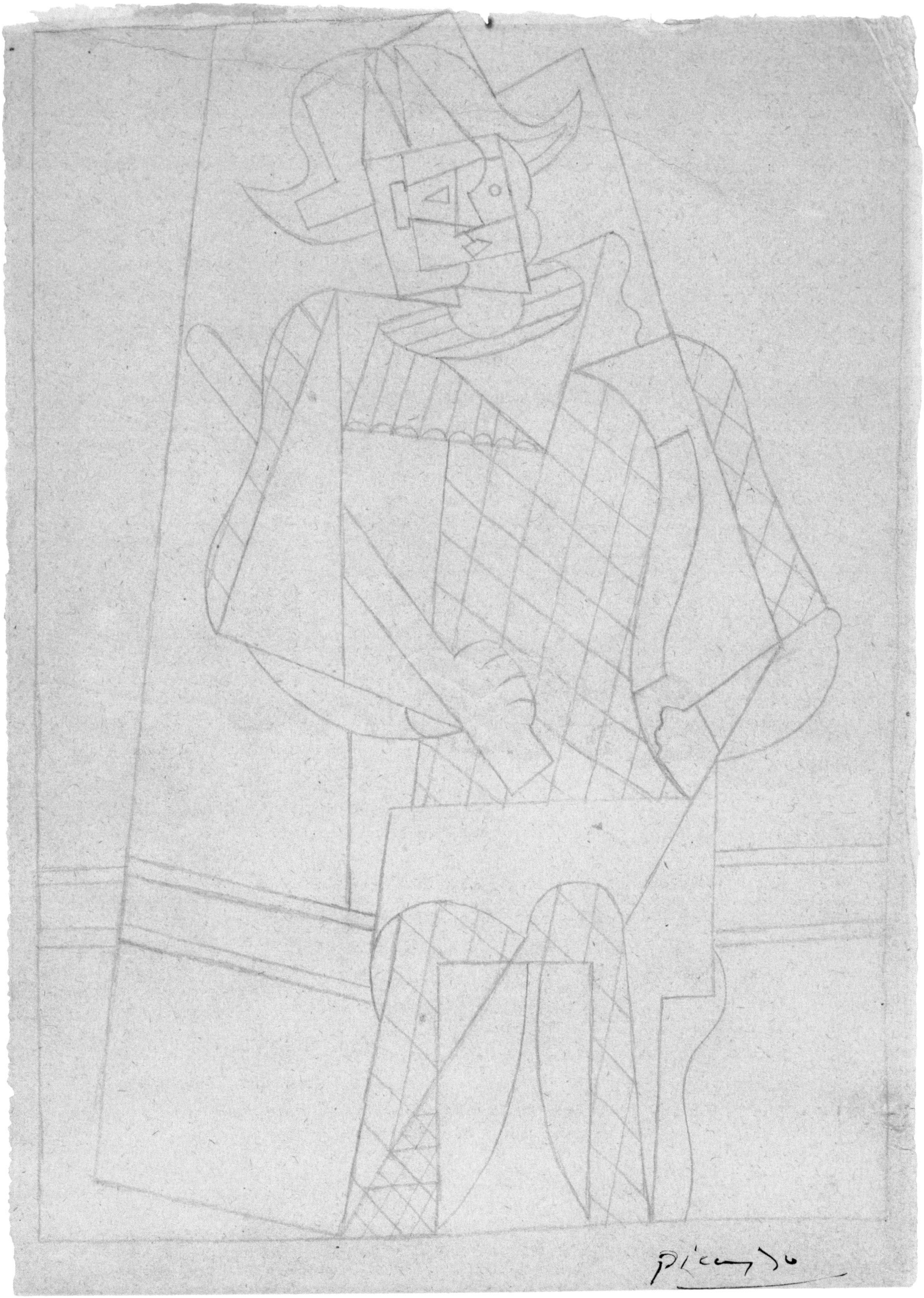

JUAN GRIS

Madrid, 1887–1927, Boulogne-sur-Seine

José Victoriano Carmelo Carlos González Pérez, commonly known by his professional name Juan Gris, was born in Madrid on March 23, 1887. After studying mechanical drawing at the Escuela de Artes e Industrias in Madrid from 1902 to 1904, and then painting under the academic artist José Moreno Carbonero (1860–1942), Gris pursued a successful career as an illustrator, publishing drawings in the popular Spanish journal *Blanco y Negro* and illustrating *Alma América–Poemas Indo-Españoles* by José Santos Chocano. In 1906, Gris immigrated to Paris, where he would spend the rest of his life as an expatriate artist. Shortly after his arrival in the French capital he befriended the young Pablo Picasso (1881–1973) and soon entered into a circle of painters, critics, and poets that included Georges Braque (1882–1963), Fernand Léger (1881–1955), Guillaume Apollinaire (1880–1918), Maurice Raynal (1884–1954), and Max Jacob (1876–1944). During his early years in Paris, Gris continued to earn a living as an illustrator, publishing humorous drawings in *L'Assiette au beurre*, *Le Charivari*, *Le Cri de Paris*, *Le Témoin*, and *L'Indiscret!* It was not until 1910 that Gris seriously turned his attention to painting, emerging by 1912 as a core member of the nascent cubist group alongside Picasso, Braque, and Léger.

Christian Derouet has noted the different types and functions of drawing in Gris's oeuvre: "notes, sketches, sketchbooks, outlines, signed drawings, drawings with inscriptions, watercolors, gouaches and a more specific category of illustration commissions."[1] With the exception of some large-scale studies and preliminary drawings for cubist paintings of 1912–13, the majority of Gris's drawings were conceived as independent exercises. As Paloma Esteban Leal has observed, "it is usually more accurate to speak about drawings that are related to specific paintings than about sketches or preparatory drawings in their strict sense."[2] Often, Gris would work out formal problems in different mediums, using drawing as a way to control his line and to strip a composition down to its bare essentials.

In 1912 the artist confirmed his cubist credentials by submitting his "reception piece," *Homage to Picasso*, to that year's Salon des Indépendants. From that point Gris emerged in the eyes of critics as a "demon of logic,"[3] organizing his paintings according to precise geometric formulas and exhibiting with the Salon de la Section d'Or that autumn. The same year, Gris showed paintings in the Exposició d'Art Cubista in Barcelona, at Herwarth Walden's Der Sturm gallery in Berlin, and at the Société Normande de Peinture Moderne in Rouen. In 1913 he signed a contract with the celebrated dealer of cubism, Daniel-Henry Kahnweiler (1884–1979).

With the outbreak of World War I in August 1914 and Kahnweiler's self-imposed exile in Switzerland, Gris fell upon hard times. Despite economic hardship, it was during the war that the artist consolidated his mature style. In 1916 he entered into a contractual agreement with the dealer Léonce Rosenberg (1877–1947), who promoted a cubist group style. It was at Rosenberg's gallery that Gris celebrated his first one-man exhibition in April 1919 with fifty works dating from 1916–18, including drawings. In his review of the exhibition at Rosenberg's Galerie de L'Effort Moderne, the artist André Lhote (1885–1962) described Gris's drawings as "happy exceptions to the cubist rule. It is thanks to such 'weaknesses' that one can immediately recognize those cubists who fortunately allow themselves to be ruled by their heart rather than simply by their head."[4] In November 1919, Gris showed ten works at Rosenberg's gallery in a group show dedicated to drawings by the gallery's artists. Although it is difficult to identify specific drawings from these shows, Rosenberg's aesthetic predilections suggest that Gris exhibited cubist works.

Cubism, however, was only one of a number of aesthetic directions that Gris pursued in the period between 1916 and 1919. In 1916 the artist began a series of drawings and paintings after Modern and Old Master works, ranging from *Madonna Tempi* of 1507–8 by Raphael to Corot's *Woman with a Mandolin* of 1860–65, and Cézanne's *Three Bathers* of 1879–82 and *Harlequin* of 1888–90. At the same time, Gris executed a number of carefully controlled drawings of common household objects—cups, bowls, fruit bowls, plates, knives, teapots, coffee grinders, pitchers, glasses, wine bottles, flasks—in a Cézannist vein, in which he indulged his talent for more naturalistic representation (see fig. 58.1). The critic Roland Chavenon enthusiastically reported that Gris "produces drawings in which there is nothing frightful, but in which we cannot help but admire the modeling, the use of light and shade, painterly in its gradation, the remarkably powerful realism, and the portrayal of volume. I have just seen a series of drawings which show

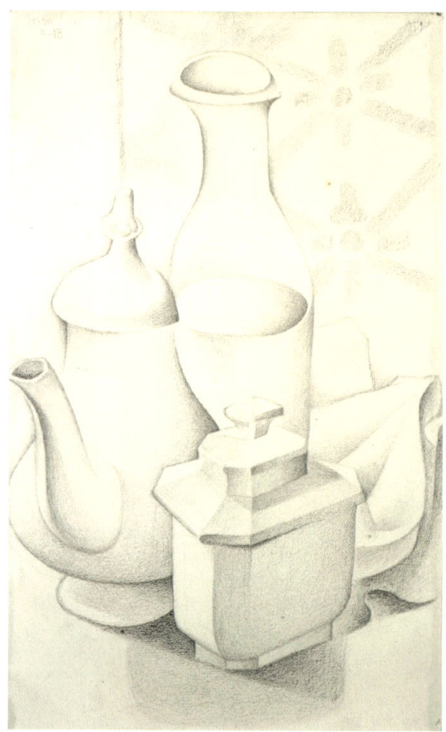

Fig. 58.1 Juan Gris, Spanish, 1887–1927: *Still Life*, 1918. Pencil on paper, 46 x 29.5 cm. Kröller-Müller Museum, Otterlo, The Netherlands.

that the path beaten impulsively by Cézanne did not end in a dead end."[5]

Gris continued to practice drawing until his death at the age of forty on May 11, 1927. In his later years the artist also published numerous writings, including his "Notes on My Painting" (1923)—which followed his second major one-man exhibition, at Kahnweiler's new Galerie Simon—and "Des possibilités de la peinture," a lecture he delivered at the Sorbonne on May 15, 1924. Gris had also contributed a statement about his aesthetic credo to the avant-garde journal *L'Esprit Nouveau* in February 1921 and collaborated with Sergei Diaghilev's Ballet Russes between 1922 and 1924, following in the footsteps of his compatriot Picasso. On May 13, 1927, Gris was laid to rest in the cemetery of Boulogne-sur-Seine in the presence of his son Georges and his loyal friends Kahnweiler, Jacques Lipchitz (1891–1973), Maurice Raynal, and Picasso.

58. *Tumbler, Knife, and Plate of Fruit,* 1918

Graphite on light tan wove paper

25.8 x 33.4 cm. (10³⁄₁₆ x 13³⁄₁₆ in.)

Inscribed in graphite on verso of mount, upper right: *73* in circle; and upper left: *5934*

PROVENANCE: Galerie Louise Leiris, Paris; Saidenberg Gallery, New York; Clinton Wilder

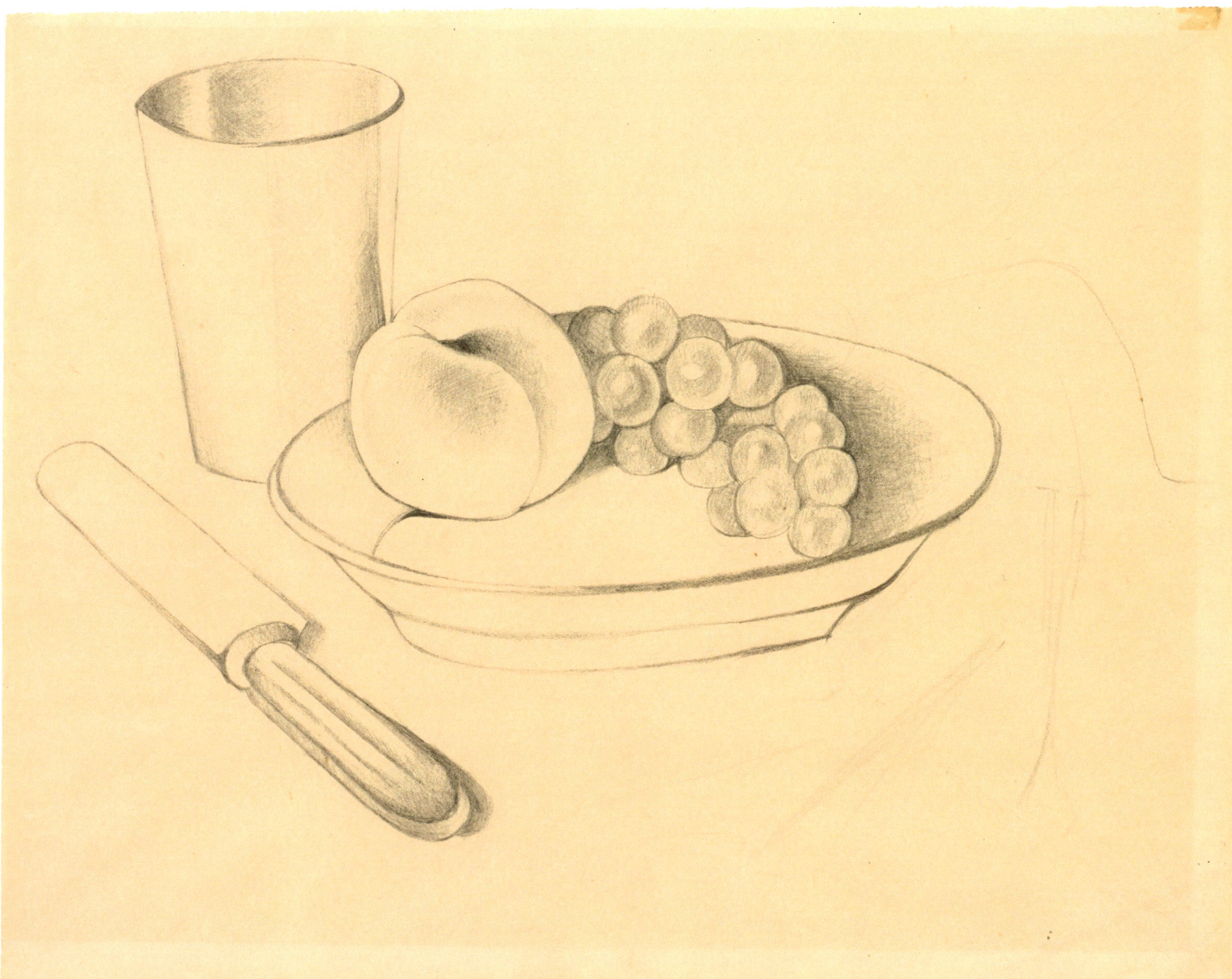

Reference: Princeton 1987, 24, 26 ill.

Exhibition: "Juan Gris: Dessins et Gouaches, 1910–1927," Galerie Louise Leiris, Paris, June 17–July 17, 1965 (exh. cat., 40, no. 38 ill)

Bequest of Clinton Wilder, Class of 1943
x1986-91

Although Gris conceived of his work as a draftsman separately from his production in painting, drawing was an integral part of his practice from his earliest days as a professional artist. In a letter to the Belgian poet and critic Paul Dermée from the village of Beaulieu-près-Loches, where Gris spent part of the war,[6] the artist wrote: "Work goes ahead and I paint for eight or nine hours each day, except for two hours which I spend drawing from nature."[7] As art historian Christopher Green has cautioned, "This is not . . . to say that his (or any artist's) drawings could ever be a simple record of retinal sensations, and thus unmediated . . . This is obviously so when he extracts . . . hints of a flattened geometry from what he depicts . . . The crisp, controlled line, the carefully modulated shading, the slightly or grossly distorted details, all make it so . . . Gris plainly extracts forms in rhyming relationships."[8]

Gris attentively studied the compositional strategies of modern and old master artists at this time, including Velázquez, Corot, and Cézanne. He would carefully map a series of organizing lines onto reproductions of paintings that he found interesting, in an effort to reveal their underlying pictorial structures. Even when he worked directly from nature, the lessons he had learned from these exercises informed his practice as a draftsman. With a clear nod to Cézanne, specifically the Provençal artist's *Nature morte au compotier* of 1879–80, a postcard reproduction of which Gris owned, *Tumbler, Knife, and Plate of Fruit* is a tour de force of combined stasis and dynamic equilibrium. Gris is careful to maintain a series of visual rhymes throughout: the ellipse that defines the top of the glass mirrors the shape of the bowl, which in turn acts as literal and figurative container for the modeled circular forms of the grapes and peach. The knife in the lower right lends the composition ballast and establishes a clear orthogonal that pushes the composition into depth and unifies it visually. In a related drawing of the same composition, Gris uses more summary modeling, establishing a more planar effect as the still life elements appear to float on the page, grounded only by the summary lines of the tablecloth on the far right.

The organizing lines that Gris drew on the postcard reproduction reveal his profound understanding of Cézanne's underlying geometries. Discussing the artist's copies after Cézanne—a category that extends to his independently conceived drawings—Christian Derouet explains that Gris "would take hold of the Aix master's compositions, explore them with his pencil, take the lay-outs, alter them by removing all superfluous detail to achieve a greater intensity. This practice of producing variations was more than just a way of unwinding at the end of a day spent painting: it was a reflection of the restlessness which was taking hold of artists tired of production line Cubism and of the attraction of 'Cézannism,' with its secure and rising value, as a way forward."[9] As Gris described his deductive method of composition in 1921, "I believe that the architectural side of painting is mathematics, the abstract side. I want to humanize it: Cézanne makes a bottle into a cylinder; I, in contrast, start with this cylinder to create an individual specimen of a special archetype; I make a cylinder into a bottle, a specific bottle. Cézanne moves toward architecture; I start from there."[10] RSL

1 Christian Derouet, "Experimentation with a Return to Representation in Gris's Drawings," in Madrid 2005, 115.
2 Paloma Esteban Leal, "A Contained Passion," in ibid., 20.
3 Green 1992. See especially chap. 2, in which Green challenges the widely held view of Gris as a dispassionate painter lacking intuition.
4 André Lhote, review of Gris's drawings at the Galerie de l'Effort Moderne, *La Nouvelle Revue française* 70 (July 1, 1919): 313; cited by Derouet, "Experimentation with a Return to Representation," in Madrid 2005, 125.
5 Roland Chavenon, "L'art, les dessins de Juan Gris," *L'information* (1918). The undated clipping, found among papers at the Bibliothèque Jacques Doucet, is cited by Derouet, "Experimentation with a Return to Representation," in Madrid 2005, 125.
6 Gris made two sojourns to Beaulieu, where he lived from September to October 1916 and again from April to December 1918. At various times he was joined there by the sculptor Jacques Lipchitz (1891–1973), the painters Jean Metzinger (1883–1956) and María Blanchard (1881–1932), and the Chilean poet Vicente Huidobro (1893–1948).
7 Juan Gris to Paul Dermée, letter dated May 1918; cited by Green 1992, 76.
8 Ibid., 76.
9 Derouet, "Experimentation with a Return to Representation in Gris's Drawings," in Madrid 2005, 123.
10 Juan Gris, "Système esthétique," *L'Esprit Nouveau* (Paris) 5 (Feb. 1921): 533–34; see Paloma Esteban Leal, "A Contained Passion," in Madrid 2005, 17–64.

LUIS QUINTANILLA

Santander, 1893–1978, Madrid

Luis Quintanilla was born in Santander and moved with his family to Madrid in 1905, where he briefly studied architecture. He embarked on a series of travels that brought him to Paris in 1912; there, he met Juan Gris (see cat. 58). Returning to Spain in 1915, Quintanilla had an exhibition of his paintings in Santander. By 1920 he was back in Paris, meeting Amedeo Modigliani (1884–1920), Maurice de Vlaminck (1876–1958), and Ramiro de Maeztu y Whitney (1875–1936) as well as the American writer Ernest Hemingway (1899–1961).[1]

In 1924, Quintanilla received a stipend to study fresco painting in Italy, returning to Madrid in 1926 to begin his career in earnest.[2] As both an artist and a political activist, Quintanilla received attention in Madrid; he was arrested on October 5, 1934, for his political activities.[3] While imprisoned he executed drawings, one per day, which were published the next year as *La Carcel por Dentro*. He was released to begin work on a memorial to Pablo Iglesias, a work that was later destroyed in the Civil War.[4]

In 1933 the artist again met Hemingway, who would become his great advocate and patron. On September 1, 1934, Hemingway wrote a six-page letter to Alfred Barr, a 1922 graduate of Princeton University, from the Hotel de Ambos Mundos, Havana, describing his excitement about Quintanilla's work and asking Barr to consider exhibiting forty-one etchings by the artist at the Museum of Modern Art.[5] When Quintanilla was arrested in Madrid, Hemingway, acting as patron, arranged for the artist's work to be shown at the Pierre Matisse Gallery from November 20 to December 4, 1934, and encouraged a group to picket in front of the Spanish Consulate in New York to protest the artist's imprisonment.[6] The highly political nature of the work and of the artist's circumstances as a commentator on the events in Spain would later become an issue.

Both Hemingway and the American novelist John Dos Passos wrote about Quintantilla's work in exhibition catalogues from 1934 to 1939.[7] The artist's drawings and related etchings were observations recorded from life during a turbulent era, inspiring comparisons with Goya, a firsthand observer of war and a satirical commentator.[8] In the Pierre Matisse Gallery leaflet, Dos Passos compared Quintanilla's work to that of Georg Grosz (1893–1959) in Germany: "The political moment too is similar, a time of defeat of everything that gives men hope."[9]

In 1937, Quintanilla was made a member of the Junta de Incautación y Protección del Tesoro Artístico.[10] He toured war-torn areas of Spain, using a sketchbook to document what he saw. The drawings at Princeton were made in this year and served both as a record and a protest of the war. In some cases, Quintanilla used the drawings to prepare etchings, making selected images available to a wider audience. In 1938, convinced by Hemingway and working closely with Jay Allen, Alfred Barr agreed to show Quintanilla's drawings at the Museum of Modern Art, with the condition that there be no propaganda of any kind. Barr wrote to Allen on March 16, 1938, expressing concern that once the exhibition opened and newspaper coverage had appeared, "there should be no propaganda since our Museum is a public and nonpartisan institution." This concern came to the fore repeatedly, and a terse exchange of letters between Barr and Allen discusses the circumstances and the resolution.[11] With the controversy surrounding Diego Rivera's (1886–1957) charged political murals only a few years in the past, Barr was also considering the potential response of his major patrons, the Rockefeller family.

Though Barr was cautious and diplomatic in his approach to the sensitive matter of exhibiting work with a definitive political slant, once convinced he took up the cause of showing Quintanilla's drawings. A checklist from the exhibition, which also traveled to the Philadelphia Art Alliance, Brown University, Middlebury College, and Dartmouth College, was annotated with the names of several of the New York collectors who purchased works from the exhibition.[12]

In January 1939, together with the Catalan painter Joaquim Sunyer (1874–1956) and the sculptor Joan Rebull (1899–1981), Quintanilla was sent to the United States to paint a mural for the Spanish Pavilion at the World's Fair, entitled *Love Peace and Hate War*.[13] The mural was not shown at the fair, however, as the government in Spain changed and the mural was thought to have been lost for many years thereafter.[14] The mural panels were recently rediscovered by Esther López Sobrado and taken to Spain, where they were exhibited.[15] Quintanilla remained in New York as a political exile, joining a community of about 25,000 other Spaniards.[16] After eighteen years in New York, he returned to Paris.

Quintanilla's work is dominated by political ideology. On the other end of the political spectrum, Franco commissioned artists to evoke his vision of heroic deeds during the Spanish Civil War; many of these works depict similar scenes: old women huddled with children, men with eyes and arms raised, dead bodies, men with weapons, images of upheaval and destruction—images, like Quintanilla's, that are powerful reminders of the destruction and chaos of war.[17]

The drawings given to Princeton by Frank Jewett Mather Jr., in 1948 were made between July and December 1937. They are among a group that was shown at the Ritz Hotel in Barcelona in December 1937, then at the Museum of Modern Art from March 16 to April 18, 1938; part of the exhibition subsequently traveled to other venues.[18] The numbers on the versos of the sheets at Princeton, written in graphite, are references to Alfred Barr's exhibition list. All three of the drawings also appear on a list that was prepared for the exhibition.[19] After the 1938 exhibition, two of the Princeton drawings were included in *All the Brave*, a collaboration among Hemingway, Jay Allen, and Elliott Paul, with drawings and illustrations by Quintanilla.

Quintanilla's work has been shown in New York at the Pierre Matisse Gallery (1934), the Museum of Modern Art (1938), Knoedler Gallery (1944), and Wildenstein Gallery (1957), in addition to the Boyer Galleries in Philadelphia (1934), the Art Alliance in Philadelphia (1938); at the museums of Brown University (1938), Middlebury College (1938), and Dartmouth College (1939); in galleries in Paris; at the Museo Municipal de Bellas Artes, Santander (1978), Museo Español de Arte Contemporáneo, Madrid (1978), Godwin-Ternback Museum, Queens College, New York (1999), the University of Cantabria, Santander (2005), and, most recently, Museo del Barrio, New York (2010).

59. *Soldiers Gathering Orphans*, 1937

Pen and black ink on cream wove paper

41.4 x 32.0 cm. (16 5/16 x 12 9/16 in.)

Signed and dated in graphite, lower right: *Luis Quintanilla / 1937*; inscribed in graphite, lower left: *13*; inscribed on verso in graphite, lower right: 38.192; inscribed in graphite on recto of former mount, lower left: *Santa María de la Cabeza;* on the verso of the secondary support: *Sierra Morena, Soldiers gathering orphans*

Provenance: Frank Jewett Mather Jr.

References: Barcelona 1937; Exhibition checklist, 1938-1939, The Museum of Modern Art Archives, New York, CE II.1.117.7, series II, Sierra Morena, no. 13; Princeton 1948

Exhibitions: Barcelona 1937; New York 1938; Quintanilla 1938–39, series II, Sierra Morena, 13

Gift of Frank Jewett Mather Jr.
x1948-1819

This drawing's former mount bears the name Santa María de la Cabeza, a monastery in a village in the Sierra Morena, part of the Cordillera mountain range, which runs along the border of the central plateau in Spain. Santa María de la Cabeza was the site of a yearlong siege, during which about two hundred civil guards and their families remained inside a ruined monastery.[20] The obstinacy of both sides was legendary. On May 1, 1937, the guards surrendered to Republican forces.[21] The wounded and sick inside the church were sent to hospitals in Andújar, near Jaén, and the civil guards were taken prisoner and sent to San Miguel de los Reyes (Valencia). Women and children were evacuated to Viso del Marqués (Ciudad Real); this is the scene represented in Quintanilla's drawing.[22] LAB

60. *Death from the Air*, 1937

Pen and black ink on light tan wove paper

43.0 x 29.0 cm. (16 15/16 x 11 7/16 in.)

Signed and dated in graphite, lower right corner: *Luis Quintanilla / 1937*; inscribed in graphite on verso, lower right corner: *inscribed on old mount / Death from the Air/ 38.178*

Provenance: Frank Jewett Mather Jr.

References: Barcelona 1937; Exhibition checklists, The Museum of Modern Art Archives, New York, CE II.1.117.7 and REG. 74, 1938 exhibition, Andalusia, no. 3; Quintanilla 1938–39, series III, no. 2. Specific discussion in correspondence between the Museum of Modern Art and Dorothy Kohl, The Philadelphia Art Alliance, April–May 1938. The Museum of Modern Art Archives, New York, CE II.1.117.7, and REG. 74; Quintanilla 1939, 39; Princeton 1948.

Exhibitions: Barcelona 1937; New York 1938; Quintanilla 1938–39

Gift of Frank Jewett Mather Jr.
x1948-1820

In the section "Andalusia" of *All the Brave*, Elliott Paul and Jay Allen describe the people in this drawing as victims of war:

> *Is it any wonder that they were surprised and confused when Italian airplanes began swooping down at intervals and killing them? A man loads his mule-cart with vegetables, drives to the nearest market. His children, a daughter and a son, ask to go and he takes them along. On the long road home, when he is half asleep and the boy and girl, dressed for town, are watching the dozing mule, they are all aroused by the zoom of a motor and the rat-tat-tat of a machine gun. One of their neighbors a few yards ahead falls from his cart, the mules balk and wheel. The aviator passes over, and a rain of bullets stirs the dust. The man is alive, but bewildered, the boy white and trembling, the girl begins to scream.*[23]

This drawing, like the others illustrated in *All the Brave*, was made between July and December 1937, as Quintanilla traveled along the front lines of the war. The resulting works were exhibited in Barcelona in December 1937 and at the Museum of Modern Art in 1938. The latter exhibition, which traveled to several East Coast colleges, included 105 drawings, all representations of the war in Spain.[24] Although the artist stated that he wished the drawings "to be considered as objective works of art, not as partisan documents," in Elliot Paul's commentary their political nature was less disguised:

> *The art may approach surgery at times, but that is not Quintanilla's fault. In the early days of the Spanish Republic, he painted Castilian landscapes, portraits of men and women in the fullness of life, allegorical frescoes expressive of the struggle for a better society and of hopes for the future. All these were destroyed by bombs, shells, vandals and machine guns. So he stood his ground and made drawings of the war.*[25]

LAB

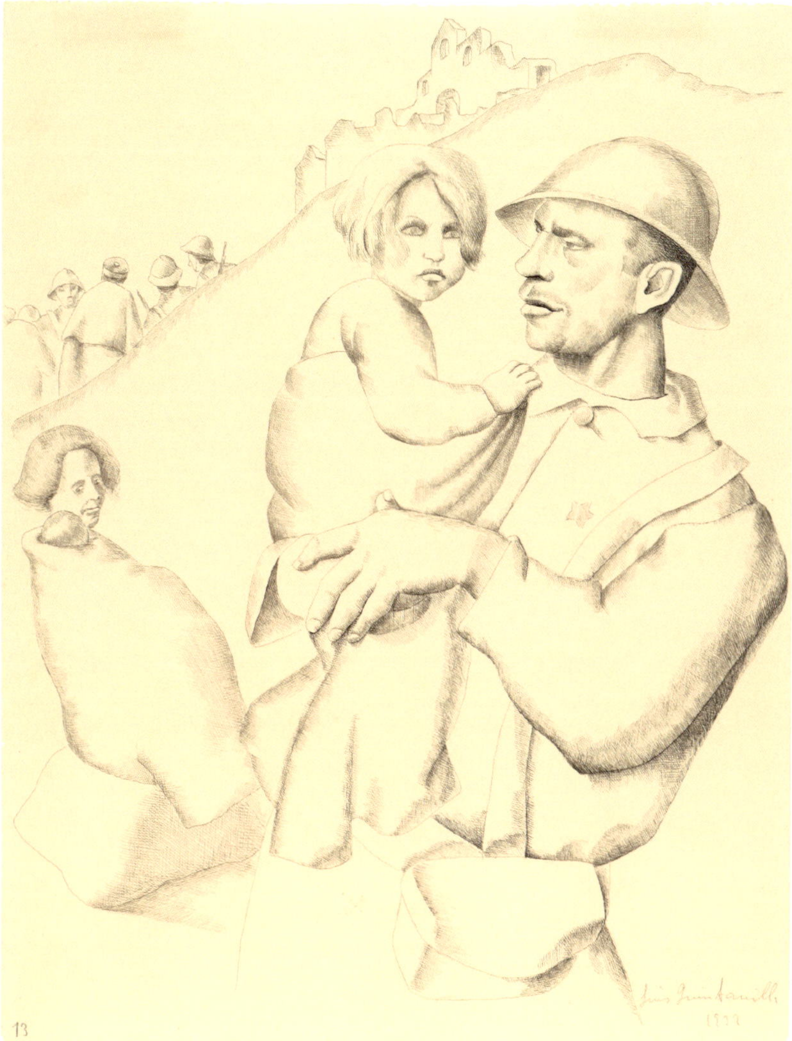

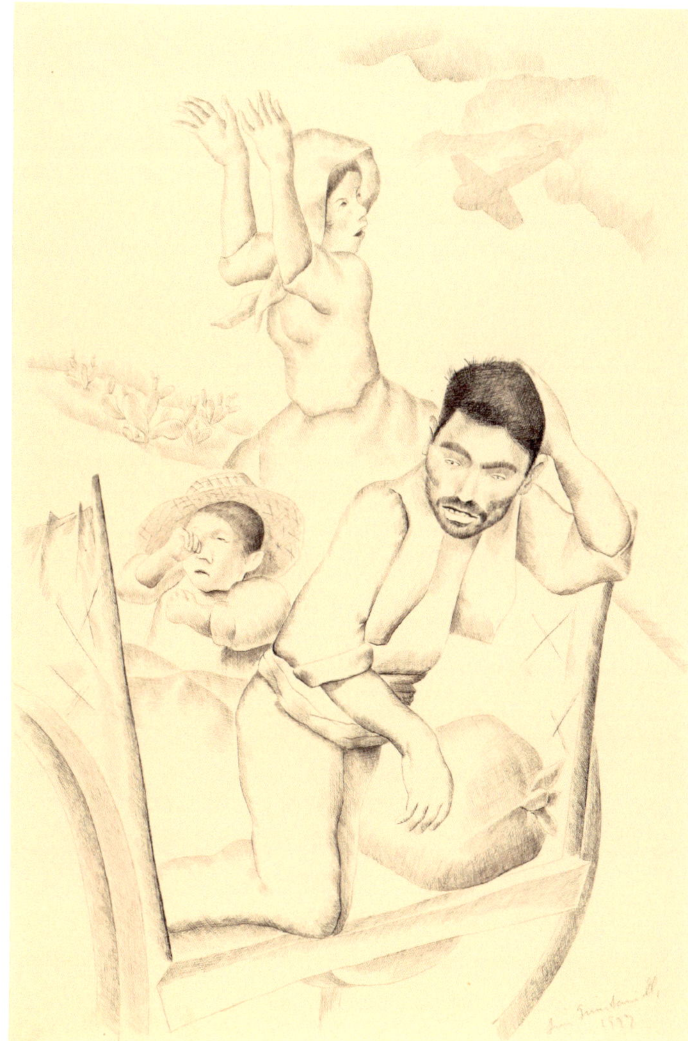

61. *Madrid, Plaza de la Cebada*, 1937

Pen and black ink on tan wove paper

50.0 x 39.3 cm. (19 11/16 x 15 7/16 in.)

Signed and dated in graphite, lower left corner: *Luis Quintanilla / 1937-*; inscribed in red pencil on verso, upper center: *Madrid—Plaza de la Cebada--*; lower right center: *Madrid: In line at the market./ A boy is reading to amuse the crowd / 38.248*

Provenance: Frank Jewett Mather Jr.

References: Barcelona 1937; New York 1938 Exhibition checklists, The Museum of Modern Art Archives, New York, CE II.1.117.7 and REG. 74, 1938 exhibition, Andalusia, no. 3; Quintanilla 1938–39, Madrid section, no. 23; Quintanilla 1938–39, series IV, no. 23; Quintanilla 1939, 55; Princeton 1948

Exhibitions: Barcelona 1937; New York 1938; Quintanilla 1938–39

Gift of Frank Jewett Mather Jr.
x1948-1821

The realities of rationing and shortages during war are conveyed in this drawing of women listening to a boy read the newspaper while they wait in a market line in the Plaza de la Cebada, Madrid. A portrayal of daily life continuing despite wartime hardships, the scene was exhibited in Barcelona and New York, then reproduced in *All the Brave* (1939). Ernest Hemingway wrote the introduction to the catalogue for the Museum of Modern Art exhibition in his reductive and essential manner:

> *Because great painters are scarcer than good soldiers, the Spanish Government ordered Quintanilla out of the army after the fascists were stopped outside Madrid. He worked on various diplomatic missions, and then returned to the front to make these drawings. The drawings are of war. They are to be looked at; not written about in an introduction. There is much to say about Quintanilla, but the drawings say all they need to say themselves.*[26]

Hemingway's preface served again to summarize the importance and impact of Quintanilla's drawings in *All the Brave.*[27] The author had written an introduction for the book on April 18, 1938, the closing date of the exhibition at the Museum of Modern Art. *Madrid, Plaza de la Cebada* is described in *All the Brave* by Elliott Paul and Jay Allen:

> *The food supply of Madrid was brought, for the most part, through Valencia, under the auspices of the labor unions. Milk was scarce and the housewives had to stand in line, sometimes for hours. Quintanilla's drawing of the food line, with a young boy reading aloud to keep up the spirits of the crowd, is filled with comradeship. There is a vast difference between fanatical devotion to a so-called state, impersonated by a dictator, and a simple love of one's neighbors and of mankind.*[28]

The drawings are technically brilliant, clearly made for easy reproduction with thin hatching and clean portrayals. The technique of all three drawings resembles the thin lines created by the artist when using an etching needle and conveys a sense of technical finesse and control that stands in contrast to the blunt observation of his subjects, with their simplified linear forms.[29]

Of the three drawings, this example most closely relates to the series of prints brought to Pierre Matisse's gallery in 1934, while Quintanilla was imprisoned.[30] It brings to the fore the urgency of Hemingway's first letter to Alfred Barr, written in September 1934 from Havana, as the author captured Quintanilla's importance as an observer of the war:

> *You who read the catalogue are all right, you know. You must not feel badly. Do not let it disturb you. Madrid is a long way away and you never heard of this man before. What did he get in trouble for anyway? Sure. That is the way to look at it. But look at the etchings. Take a good look at the etchings.*[31]

The same is true for Luis Quintanilla's spare, strong drawings. LAB

1 Arnáiz, López Jiménez, and Merchán Díaz 1992, 367–71.
2 Ibid., 367.
3 Quintanilla 2003. Also see New York 1934. Quintanilla was jailed for allowing the Comité Revolucionario de la Huelga to meet in his house; he was a friend of one of the committee members.
4 Quintanilla 1939, 19.
5 The Museum of Modern Art Archives, New York, CE II.1.117.7, and Registrar Exhibition Files, #74.
6 Santander 2005, 31. My thanks to Paul Quintanilla and to Esther López Sobrado for providing additional information about the artist.
7 As Quintanilla wrote in his autobiography, *Pasatiempo*, "mejores introductores en Norteamérica no podía tener," Quintanilla 2004, 322. The words written by John Dos Passos about Quintanilla's etchings in 1934, for the Pierre Matisse Gallery exhibition catalogue, can apply equally to his drawings, summarizing their importance: "The hardest thing to take, and the best quality in them, is their terrible sanity and clear balance. . . The clear expression of a clean eye and an uncluttered grown-up mind is something much more dangerous and explosive. These etchings . . . are the statement of a grown-up man facing a bitter world in the sun at noon."
8 Ernest Hemingway, introduction to Quintanilla 1939, 8.
9 New York 1934. Valeriano Bozal also commented on the realism of the drawings and the influence of Georg Grosz. See Valeriano Bozal Fernández, *El Realismo plástico en España, de 1900 a 1936* (Madrid: Ediciones Península, 1967), 163. Also see Santander 2005, 31.
10 Sarró 2005, 113.
11 This fascinating correspondence follows a *New York Times* article on Quintanilla, published on February 18, 1938, and continues for several weeks. Alfred Barr mused over the meaning of propaganda on March 16, 1938. The Museum of Modern Art Archives, New York, CE II.1.117.7, and REG. 74.
12 The Museum of Modern Art Archives, New York, CE II.1.117.7, and REG. 74. Although the Museum of Modern Art maintained a checklist, there does not seem to have been a printed catalogue for these exhibitions, as there was some discussion of the removal of several drawings and the printing preparations. The payment arrangements were made through Jay Allen and his wife. Correspondence on this subject and with the New York buyers of the drawings is in the Museum of Modern Art Archives, New York, CE II.1.117.7 and REG. 74.
13 Santander 2005, 37. Joaquim Sunyer (1874–1956) and Joan Rebull (1899–1981) were both Catalan artists.
14 Paul 1939.
15 López Sobrado 1992, 511–20. López Sobrado describes the discovery of the frescoes that Quintanilla painted for the World's Fair pavilion in 1939. In 1999, Professor Jerald Green entered into negotiations with the landlord of the building where the frescoes were found in 1990. They were entitled *Pain, Hunger, Destruction, Flight*, and *Soldiers*. In his last important fresco commission, ordered by Clarence Decker, Quintanilla completed six panels on the theme of Don Quixote and Sancho Panza in Kansas City, in 1940–41. The last panel depicts Don Quixote in the Real World, surrounded by horrors, including the figures of Mussolini, Franco, and Hitler. See Santander 2005, 41–43.
16 Carroll and Fernández 2007, 88. Esther López Sobrado is responsible for the return of these frescoes to Spain. See Julián Luzán, "Los otros 'Guernicas,'" *El País*, March 18, 2007. Also see López Sobrado

1992, 511–20. Also see University of Cantabria, "Presentando los frescos de Luis Quintanilla," March 6, 2007, regarding the installation of those murals at the University of Cantabria; and Santander 2005.

17 Arnáiz, López Jiménez, and Merchán Díaz, 1992, 367. An unusual exhibition showing many of the Franco-commissioned drawings was held in Madrid in 2010: *Dos Miradas, Una Visión: Los dibujos de Guerra de Carlos Sáenz de Tejada y Joaquín Valverde*, Galería José de la Mano, Madrid, May 26–July 2, 2010.

18 Esther López Sobrado, introduction to Quintanilla 2004, 16.

19 The Museum of Modern Art, New York, CE II.1.117.7 and REG. 74.

20 Sixteen drawings from this series were exhibited at the Museum of Modern Art in 1938 (back page of catalogue). Note that these drawings were brought to New York less than a year after the events took place, giving them historical poignancy.

21 The artist describes the scene and the making of the drawings in his autobiography: Quintanilla 2004, 430; there is a photograph of him with his sketchbook on pp. 383 and 436.

22 The artist happened to be there and wrote of the extraordinary scene in his memoirs; he was both participant and artist-observer. Quintanilla 2004, 430–31.

23 Quintanilla 1939, 34; "Andalusia" commentary by Elliot Paul.

24 Esther López Sobrado, introduction to Quintanilla 2004, 16. The artist reported that Alfred Barr allowed him 140 drawings, and that he built a special exhibition room for them at the museum; ibid., 450. However, the exhibition checklist and the subsequent correspondence report 105 drawings—or 104, if the handwritten note about Madrid, #24, *War in Madrid*, "not here" is taken seriously. See the checklist in REG. 74, and the letter from Alice Jayson, Secretary to Mr. Jay Allen, February 8, 1938, New York, to Alfred Barr, The Museum of Modern Art Archives, New York, REG. 74.

25 New York 1938, Alfred H. Barr Jr. note. Hemingway owned a drawing entitled *Why Kill Us* that was confused with this one; two drawings on the checklist bear the title *Death from the Air*, this one and 38.155. The Museum of Modern Art Archives, New York, CE II.1.117.7 and REG. 74. Quintanilla 1939, 34.

26 New York 1938.

27 Quintanilla 1939, 7.

28 Ibid., 54.

29 Concentrations of Quintanilla's prints can be found in the Biblioteca Nacional, Madrid, and at the Museo Nacional Centro de Arte Reina Sofía, Madrid.

30 Mather also gave the Princeton University Art Museum a drypoint etching by Quintanilla entitled *A Village Theater* (x1948-1822). It is signed in graphite at lower right and numbered at left in graphite below the plate mark: "no. 7." On the verso at top left the number twelve is inscribed in graphite. An etching with a similar title, *Teatro*, was exhibited as number eleven at Pierre Matisse Gallery from November 20 to December 4, 1934; whether this etching was included in the Pierre Matisse Gallery pamphlet is unclear.

31 New York 1934.

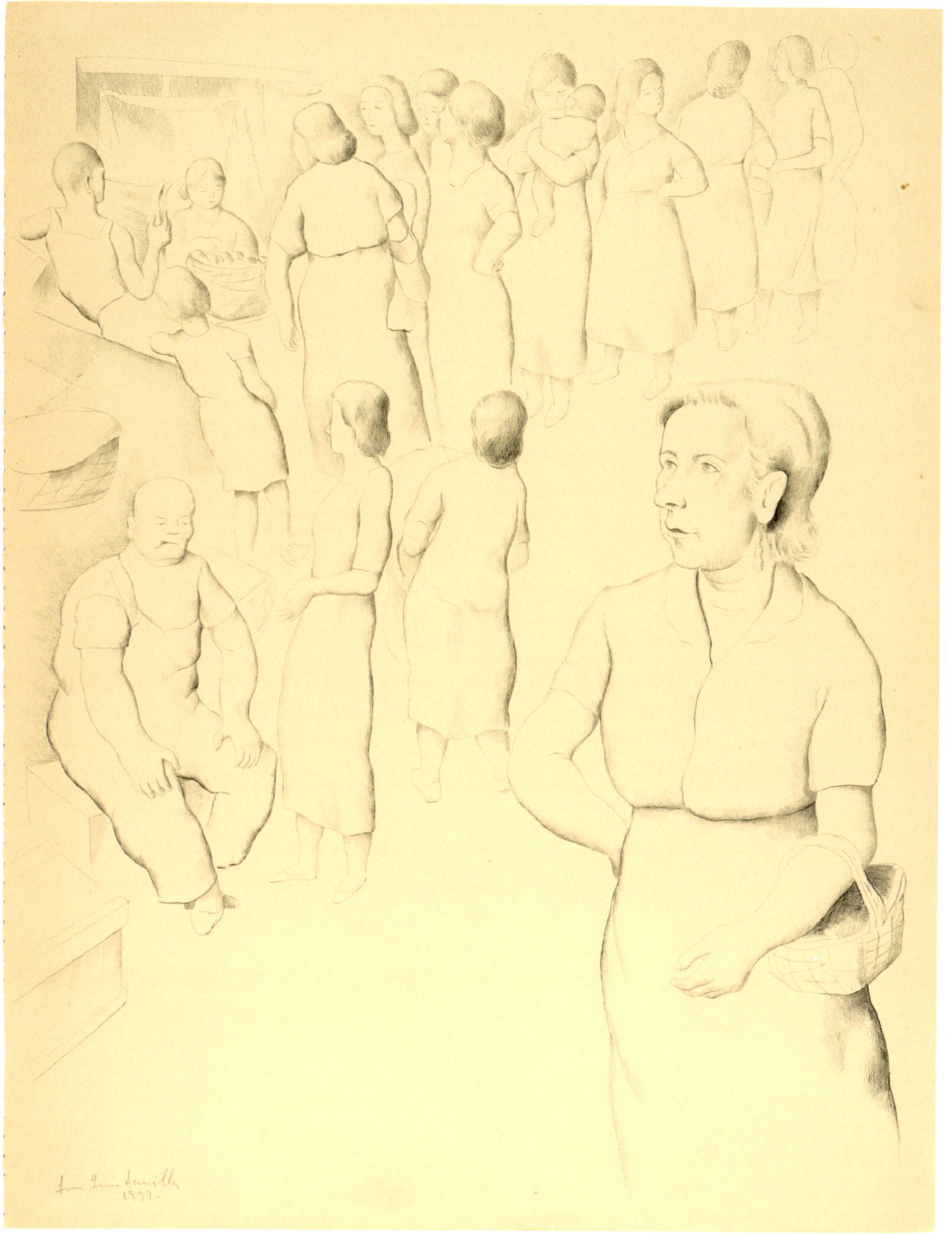

JOAN MIRÓ

Barcelona, 1893–1983, Palma de Mallorca

Joan Miró i Ferrà was born in Barcelona on April 20, 1893. After a period of study with the landscape painter Modest Urgell (1839–1919) and the decorative artist Josep Pasco (1855–1910) at Barcelona's Escuela Superior de Artes Industriales y Bellas Artes (La Lonja), Miró came under the tutelage of Francesc d'Assis Galí (1880–1965), who taught the young artist to draw from the sense of touch. From that point on, drawing played a key role in Miró's practice. An assiduous visitor to the Galeries Dalmau, which showcased the work of local and foreign avant-garde artists, Miró exhibited sixty-four paintings and drawings at the establishment on the occasion of his first one-man show (February 16–March 3, 1918). A commercial and critical failure, Miró was embittered by the provincial atmosphere of his native city, vowing to continue his studies in Paris.

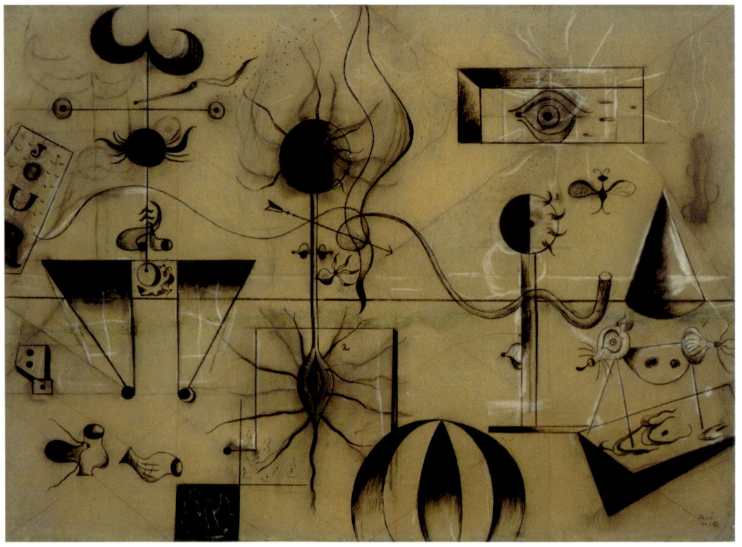

Fig. 62.1 Joan Miró, Spanish, 1893–1983: *The Family*, May 16, 1924. Charcoal, chalk, and conté crayon on flocked paper, 74.1 x 104.0 cm. Museum of Modern Art, gift of Mr. and Mrs. Jan Mitchell (395.1961).

Miró arrived in the French capital for the first time late in February 1920.[1] He attended a number of contemporary art exhibitions, visited Picasso's studio, and laid the groundwork for his first Paris exhibition, which Dalmau organized for him at the Galerie La Licorne in 1921 (April 29–May 14). Committed to his stated goal of becoming an "international Catalan,"[2] Miró now began to move freely between Barcelona, his family's farm in Montroig (his spiritual home), and the French capital.

In the spring of 1922, Miró rented a studio at 45 Rue Blomet in Paris, where his neighbors were André Masson (1896–1987) and the writer Roland Tual. Through Masson he met the ethnographer and writer Michel Leiris as well as the poets Robert Desnos, Paul Eluard, and Raymond Queneau, who soon would become important voices in the nascent Surrealist movement. In dialogue with his friends, by 1924 Miró achieved a major breakthrough in his work, reducing words and objects in his drawings and paintings to cryptic signs that float freely across the picture plane in an open, constellated structure (see fig. 62.1). The self-appointed "pope of Surrealism," André Breton (1896–1966) immediately recognized Miró as a kindred spirit, purchasing two paintings by the young artist in 1925 and encouraging him to participate in Surrealist activities. Although Breton championed Miró's creative spontaneity, the artist made preparatory sketches for almost all of his known paintings.

Throughout the 1920s, Miró adhered closely to Surrealist principles but was never a "card-carrying" member of the movement. He supported most of the group's initiatives but maintained a certain distance from Breton's attempts to align Surrealism with the French Communist Party. Instead, Miró used his art as a tool to critique bourgeois values and social complacency. In 1927 his much-quoted desire to "assassinate painting" became a battle cry for the Surrealists, as Miró and his colleagues systematically challenged the bourgeois tradition of *belle peinture* through collage and other means.

The 1930s saw the consolidation of Miró's mature style. He produced set designs and costumes for Sergei Diaghilev's *Jeux d'enfants* in 1932, collaborated with artistic organizations in Barcelona, and began exhibiting regularly at Pierre Matisse's gallery in New York. He continued to make notations and preliminary sketches for paintings in his notebooks, often returning to these drawings years later for reference or as points of departure for new works. Miró was deeply disturbed by right-wing violence in Paris in

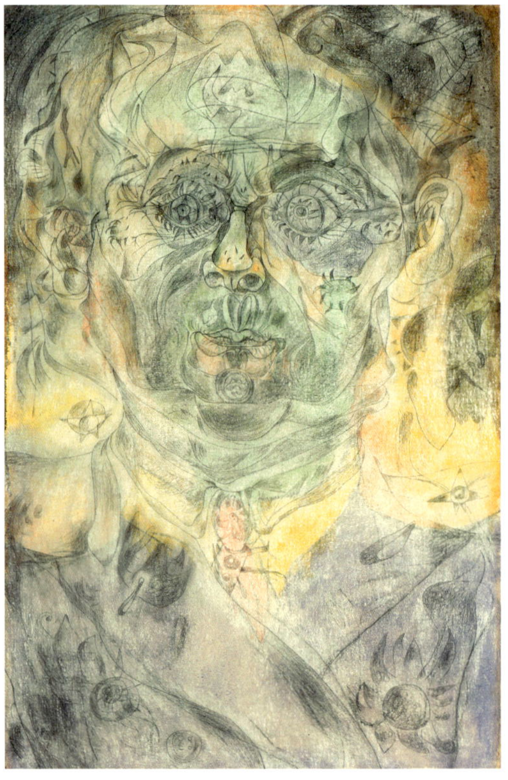

Fig. 62.2 Joan Miró, Spanish, 1893–1983: *Self-Portrait I*, October 1937–March 1938. Pencil, crayon and oil on canvas, 146.1 x 97.2 cm. Museum of Modern Art, James Thrall Soby Bequest (1238.1979).

1934 and the brutal repression by the military of an uprising by miners in Asturias the same year, and his work began to assume an increasingly dark and tragic character. Forced into exile in Paris with the outbreak of the Spanish Civil War in July 1936, Miró graphically expressed his sense of psychic turmoil in an important self-portrait rendered in pencil, crayon, and oil on canvas, executed between October 1937 and March 1938 (fig. 62.2). With the outbreak of World War II and the German occupation of Paris, Miró, his wife Pilar, and their daughter María Dolors relocated to the relative safety of Varengeville, Normandy, where Miró began his series of *Constellations*, small works executed in gouache, water, and ink on paper that are among the artist's finest achievements as a draftsman.

Throughout the 1940s and 1950s, Miró reaped the benefits of international acclaim. In 1958 he moved into a large studio and living compound outside of Palma de Mallorca, where he would realize projects in painting, drawing, ceramics, and the graphic arts. Over the next two decades, Miró's graphic production increased exponentially. Sculpture—ceramic, painted and cast bronze—also occupied Miró during these decades. In 1964 he installed the Labyrinth, a large sculpture garden at the Fondation Maeght in Saint-Paul-de-Vence. With additional work for the theater, monumental public art, and tapestry weavings, Miró continued to push the boundaries of his art until his death at the age of ninety on December 25, 1983.

62. *Human Figure, Animal, Three Stars*, 1959

Pen and black ink with watercolor on cream wove paper (letterpress document)

37.2 x 29.6 cm. (14 5/8 x 11 11/16 in.)

Signed in graphite, left center: *Miró*; inscribed in graphite on verso, along upper edge: *241=5-7-10-11* and *Juny 1959*

Reference: Princeton 1980, 54

Gift of Dr. Herbert Schorr, Graduate School Class of 1963
x1979-94

Executed on a subscription form for the Círculo Artístico de Sant Lluc, an artist's collective in Barcelona, *Human Figure, Animal, Three Stars* is a lyrical ink and wash drawing that is characteristic of Miró's mature style. With a retrospective glance back at his great *Constellation* series of 1940–41 (fig. 62.3), a facsimile edition of which Miró's New York dealer Pierre Matisse (1900–1989) had recently published,[3] the drawing comprises an open structure of free-floating signs accented only by a few summary washes of red, blue, yellow, and turquoise/green pigment. Freely applied, color exceeds the boundaries of contour and functions like a halo or aureole generated by the forms. Throughout, Miró's calligraphy is strong and his line emphatic and self-assured. The signs spread out across the page as if pulled by magnetic forces beyond their control, articulating the empty space of the subscription form in a complex dialogue with the inscription below.[4] In the lower right, the insignia of the Círculo (Saint Luke drawing, surrounded by a floral wreath) completes the figuration, as Miró conceives his drawing in relation to the whole page.

The Cercle Artístic de Sant Lluc, as its name is written in Catalan, was formed in 1893 by a faction within Barcelona's Círculo Artístico who protested the licentious behav-

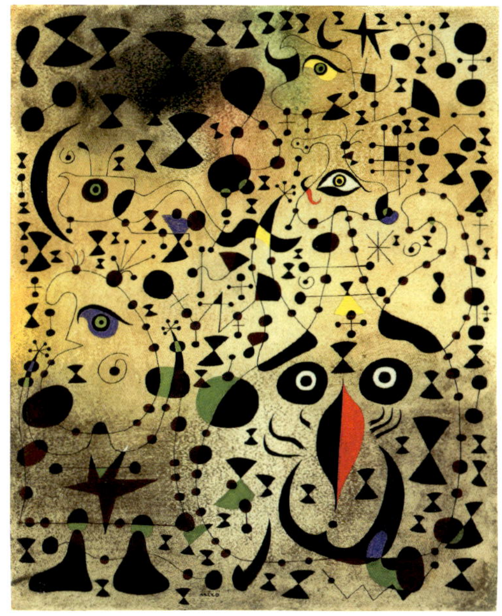

Fig. 62.3 Joan Miró, Spanish, 1893–1983: *The Beautiful Bird Revealing the Unknown to a Pair of Lovers*, from the *Constellation* series, July 23, 1941. Gouache, oil wash, and charcoal on paper, 45.7 x 38.1 cm. Museum of Modern Art, acquired through the Lillie P. Bliss Bequest (7.1945).

ior, capriciousness, and lack of commitment to the cause of Catalanism of the group's other members. The new organization maintained a decidedly Catalanista and confessional orientation under the patriarchal guidance of Bishop Josep Torras i Bages of Vic (1846–1916), whose writings on the social and moral functions of the arts emphasized what one critic has called a "Christian naturalism."[5] The confessional tone of the organization was present from the start. Modeled on the Accademia di San Luca in Rome, the group constituted itself "in the name of the Holy Trinity . . . and under the patronage of the evangelist Saint Luke and consecrated to the Sacred Heart of Jesus."[6]

Miró joined the Cercle on October 15, 1913, at the age of twenty, and participated in the group's eighth exhibition, held that year.[7] The Cercle boasted among its membership most of the key artists of Miró's generation, from his older colleagues Ramón Casas (1866–1932), Santiago Rusiñol (1861–1931), and

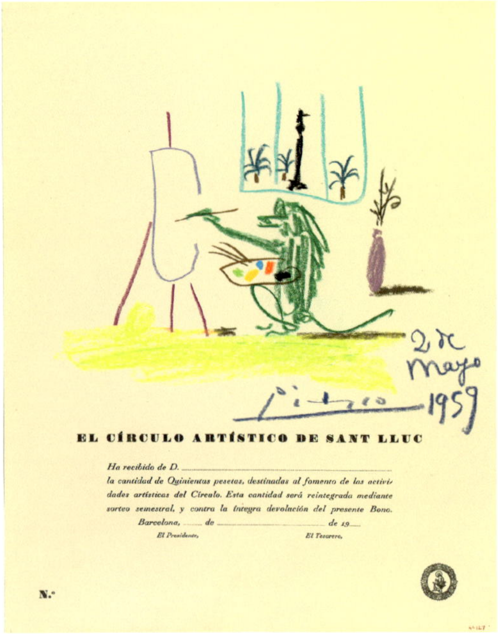

Fig. 62.4 Pablo Picasso, Spanish, 1881–1973: *The Monkey Painter*, 1959. Colored grease pencils on printed paper, 37 x 29.5 cm. Museu Picasso, Barcelona (MPB 66.127).

Antoni Gaudí (1852–1926) to Pau (Pablo) Gargallo (1881–1934), Joaquín Torres-García (1874–1949), and Miró's great friend—and later collaborator—the ceramist Josep Llorens Artigas (1892–1980). After twice changing locations, the Cercle found a permanent home in the Casa Martí, the site of the Quatre Gats tavern where Picasso had celebrated his first one-man exhibition in February 1900. Although nominally religious, the Cercle was also more liberal than other academies in Spain. Drawing from the live model was welcomed, and the organization contained meeting rooms and an excellent modern art library, which was largely destroyed by bombs during the Civil War. In 1953, the Cercle moved to its current location on the Carrer del Pi, No. 16, Barcelona.

During the years of Franco's dictatorship, the Cercle maintained a quiet profile. In 1956, with a rise in subscriptions and membership, a new initiative was begun: members of the Cercle were asked to submit drawings that would later be auctioned to support the group's activities. Miró and two hundred other artists, including Picasso and Dalí, participated in the initiative. Miró's entry, *Human Figure, Animal, Three Stars*, celebrates the Cercle's founding charter as his signs literally reach toward the stars in a gesture of freedom and spiritual ascendency. RSL

1 See Anne Umland's chronology in Carolyn Lanchner, *Joan Miró* (New York: The Museum of Modern Art, 1993), p. 321.

2 Miró to Ricart, letter dated Nov. 18, 1920; see Margit Rowell, *Joan Miró: Selected Writings and Interviews*, 1st ed. (London: Thames and Hudson, 1987), 73.

3 In conjunction with the publication of the facsimile edition, Miró exhibited some of the original gouaches for the series at the Galerie Berggruen, Paris (Jan. 20–Mar., 1959) and subsequently at the Pierre Matisse Gallery (Mar. 17–Apr. 11, 1959). A day after the Matisse opening, Miró celebrated his second retrospective at the Museum of Modern Art in New York (Mar. 18–May 10, 1959). On May 18 of the same year, Miró traveled to Washington, D.C., to receive the 1958 Guggenheim International Award from President Eisenhower.

4 Given the repression of the Catalan language under Franco's regime, the subscription notice is published in Castilian, although the name "Sant Lluc" is written in Catalan. The accompanying text reads: "The Artistic Circle of Saint Luke has received from (name of subscriber) the sum of 500 pesetas for the purpose of promoting the Circle's artistic activities. This amount will be disbursed each semester by raffle upon presentation of this ticket."

5 Enric Jardí, "L'ala dreta del modernisme i quelcom més," in Barcelona 1993, 25.

6 Ibid., 15.

7 Miró was undoubtedly encouraged to join the organization by his teacher, Francesc d'Assis Galí, who had been a member since October 1899. For a discussion, see Robert S. Lubar, "Miró before *The Farm*, 1915–1923: Catalan Nationalism and the Avant-Garde" (Ph.D. diss., New York University, 1988), 28 n. 46; and Jardí 1976, 83–84.

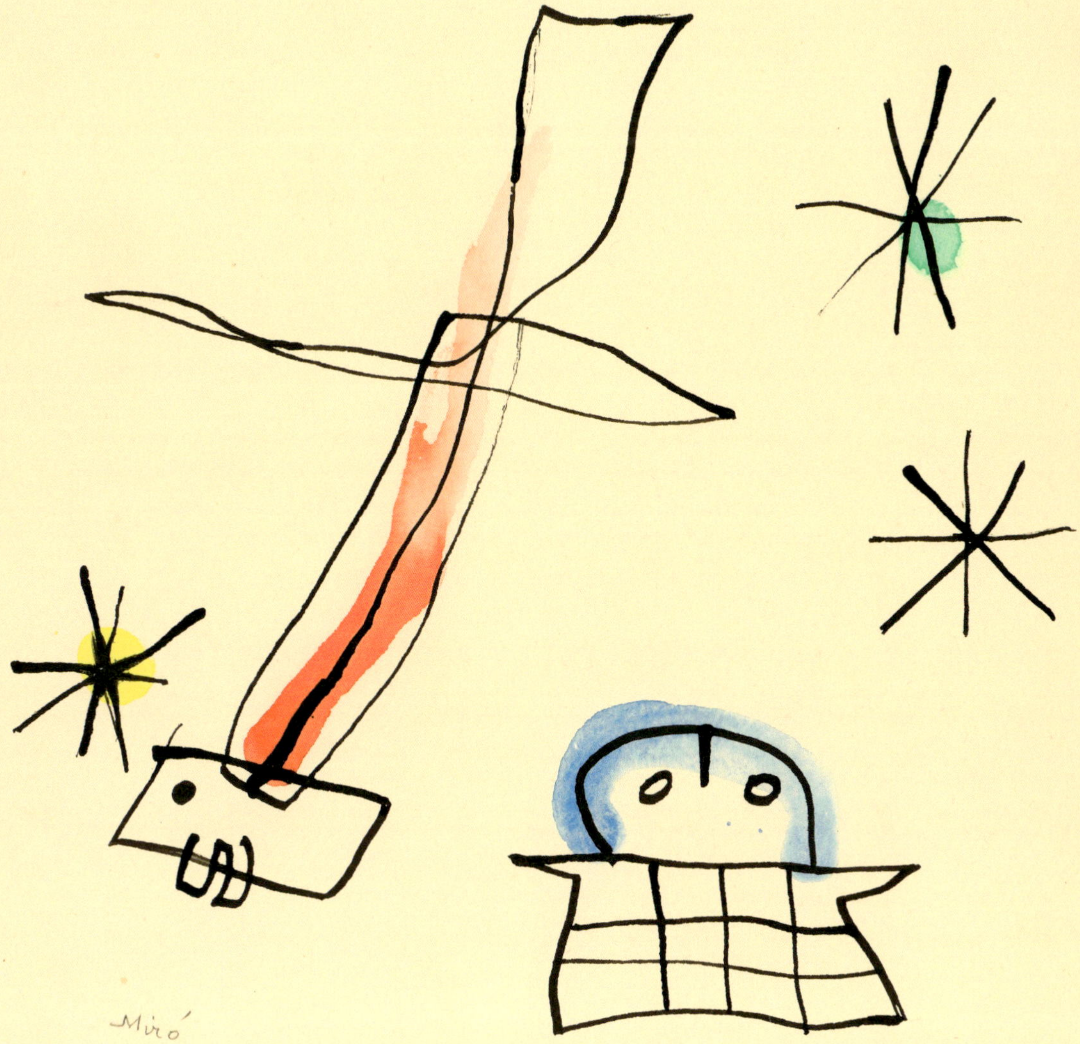

EL CÍRCULO ARTÍSTICO DE SANT LLUC

Ha recibido de D. ....

la cantidad de Quinientas pesetas, destinadas al fomento de las actividades artísticas del Círculo. Esta cantidad será reintegrada mediante sorteo semestral, y contra la íntegra devolución del presente Bono.

Barcelona, ... *de* .... *de 195*...

El Presidente, *El Tesorero,*

N.º 0002

SALVADOR DALÍ

Figueres, 1904–1989, Figueres

Salvador Felip Jacint Dalí Domènech was born in Figueres, Spain, on May 11, 1904.[1] His primary and secondary education took place at "Els Fossos," a Christian Brothers academy, at the Escola Municipal de Dibuix, and at the Figueres Institut. In 1922, at the age of eighteen, Dalí passed the entrance exam to the Real Academia de Bellas Artes de San Fernando in Madrid and moved into the Residencia de Estudiantes, a student dormitory where he befriended the poet Federico García Lorca and the filmmaker Luis Buñuel. Three years later, Dalí celebrated his first one-man show in Barcelona at the Galeries Dalmau (November 14–27, 1925), exhibiting seventeen paintings and five drawings.[2] The catalogue included quotes from *Pensées* by Jean-Auguste-Dominique Ingres, one of which read "drawing is the probity of art," attesting to Dalí's commitment to classical drawing. Indeed, in August 1927 the artist explicitly described the importance that precise draftsmanship held for all aspects of his artistic practice:

> *There always existed two kinds of painters: those who went beyond the line, and those who, patiently and with respectfulness, knew how to just reach their limit. The first, because of their impatience, were qualified as being impassioned and inspired. The second, because of their humble patience, were qualified as being cold and solely good craftsmen.*
>
> *If it is true, nevertheless, that going beyond the line is a form of impetuosity signifying always the beginning of intoxication, confusion and weakness, it is true as well that there exists a type of passion which consists precisely of the patience of* not going beyond the line; *and that this passion for balance is a strong passion and an enemy of all intoxication.*[3]

In 1926, Dalí made a brief trip to Brussels and Paris, where he visited Picasso's studio. Although Dalí's connection with advanced artists abroad was limited, he was a voracious reader and kept abreast of recent developments by combing through the pages of *L'Esprit Nouveau* and *La Révolution Surréaliste,* among numerous other publications. In September 1927, Dalí met Joan Miró (1893–1983) in Figueres. The older artist took a keen interest in his young protégé, facilitating his reception in Paris, where Dalí returned in April 1929 to film *Un chien andalou* with Buñuel. Over the course of 1927–29, Dalí also contributed a series of articles and chronicles to the Catalan review *L'Amic de les arts,* emerging as a significant voice among the Catalan literary avant-garde.

Following the filming of *Un chien andalou,* Dalí returned to Spain. That summer the artist, who now declared his adherence to the Surrealist movement, executed four of his most characteristic works, dreamscapes based on Freudian narratives. When Dalí returned to Paris the following autumn to celebrate his first exhibition in the French capital (Galerie Goemans, November 20–December 5) he was welcomed by André Breton (1896–1966) as Surrealism's newest member.

Surrealism provided Dalí with fertile ground for his visual and literary imagination.[4] In 1934 he illustrated the Comte de Lautréamont's *Les Chants de Maldoror* and exhibited his preparatory drawings and etchings for the publication in New York and Paris.[5] Although Dalí's artistic voice helped transform the Surrealist movement during the 1930s, the artist repeatedly found himself in conflict with Breton over the group's political (Marxist) commitment. As Dalí increasingly turned to commercial enterprises, producing work for the ballet, displays for department store windows, and advertisements for a range of products, he and Breton became estranged, leading to a definitive break by 1941.

With the outbreak of World War II, Dalí moved with his wife Gala, whom he had married in 1934, to the United States, where the couple remained from 1940 to 1948. During this period, Dalí became a kind of brand name, attracting such wealthy patrons as Caresse Crosby, executing numerous portrait commissions, producing commercial work for the designer Elsa Schiaparelli, and collaborating with Alfred Hitchcock on *Spellbound* and with Walt Disney on the animated film *Destino.* Dalí also published his extravagant autobiography, *The Secret Life of Salvador Dalí* (1942), in which he announced his break with Surrealism, his return to classicism and tradition, and his adherence to the apostolic faith of the Catholic Church.

Upon his return to Spain in 1948, Dalí continued to cultivate his reputation as an international celebrity. His developing interest in science and nuclear physics lead him to issue his "Mystical Manifesto" in 1951 and his "Anti-Matter Manifesto" in 1959, in which the artist advanced an unusual amalgam of science and intuition. Over the next three decades, Dalí produced paintings and drawings with historical subjects on a monumental scale, accepted numerous commissions for book illustrations that indulged his skills as a draftsman, and published several treatises. On September 28, 1974, he attended the inauguration of the Teatre-Museu Dalí in Figueres, testifying to his official status as one of the twentieth-century's most celebrated artists. Seven years later, on January 23, 1989, Dalí died at the age of eighty-five. He was laid to rest in the crypt of the Teatre-Museu three days later.

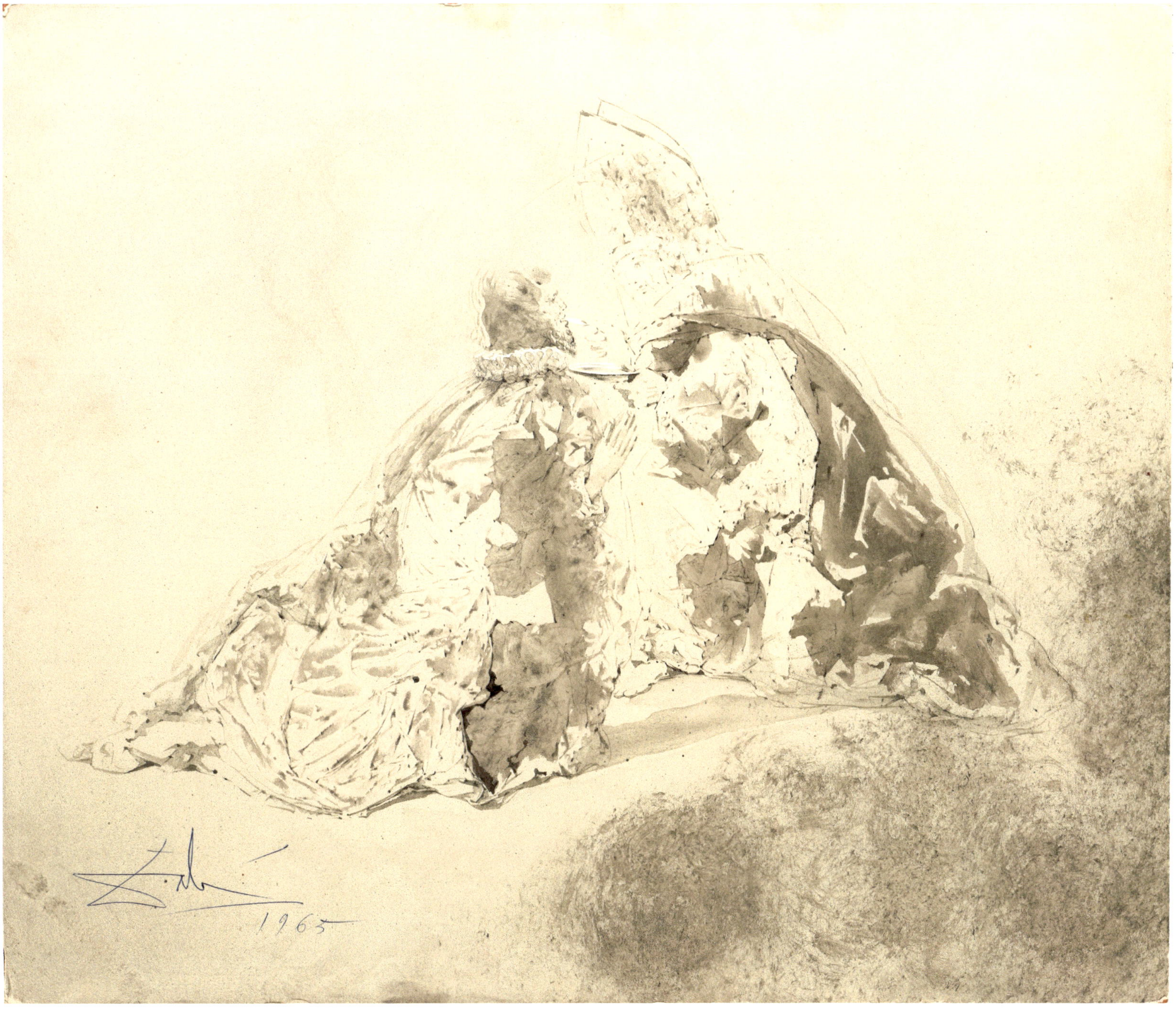

63. *Philip II Receiving Communion*, 1965

Verso (of mount): *Figure of Woman*

Brush and black and gray wash, with touches of white gouache, on cream wove paper, prepared with sprayed and scumbled gray tone, laid down on red-brown plied paper board; verso of mount: red chalk

45.7 x 54.5 cm. (18 x 21 7/16 in.)

Signed and dated in pen and blue ink on recto, lower left corner: *Dalí / 1965*

PROVENANCE: M. Knoedler & Co., New York; Mrs. Irving B. Kingsford Jr.

REFERENCE: Princeton 1970, 24

EXHIBITION: New York 1965

Gift of Mr. and Mrs. Irving B. Kingsford Jr., Class of 1942
x1969-2

Philip II Receiving Communion was featured in an exhibition at Knoedler Galleries, New York, that ran December 21–31, 1965, at which time it was purchased by Mrs. Irving B. Kingsford Jr. The delicate gray wash drawing shows Philip II during a characteristically pious moment, receiving communion from an archbishop. The monarch bows to the authority of the Catholic Church, prone before the mitered archbishop who offers him the sacrament. The drawing is related to a work listed in the Dalí catalogue raisonné simply as a "religious scene," dated 1963, suggesting that the Princeton drawing might have been postdated for the exhibition at Knoedler's. Characteristic of Dalí's bravura style at this time, the line is nervous but assured. A few summary details compose the outlines of the two figures while the voluminous folds of their costumes, offset by the application of thin washes of gray, are highlighted by the discrete presence of white to define the monarch's ruff collar and the eucharistic wafer in his mouth. This intimate scene suggests Philip's strong religious bond with the prelate, his role as defender of the faith against Protestantism in Northern Europe, and his divine right to rule.

Dalí's numerous references to Philip II at this time centered on the monarch's dual role as the self-appointed defender of the Catholic faith and as architect of the imperial expansion of the Spanish state. During Philip's reign, Spain emerged as the greatest power in Western Europe, with territories that extended to the Philippines, the Netherlands, Portugal, Naples, Sicily, and, for a brief period during his marriage to Queen Mary I, to England and Ireland. Philip II presided over the Golden Age in Spain, and literature and the arts flourished under his reign. In order to centralize his authority, Philip moved the Spanish court to its new capital in Madrid and successfully checked Ottoman expansion in the Mediterranean at the Battle of Lepanto in 1571. Plagued by disastrous economic expenditures, a war with France, and the defeat of the Spanish Armada in the English campaigns of 1588, 1596, and 1597, Philip's military legacy is mixed, although the Habsburg Dynasty reached the height of its ascendency in Europe under his rule.

Dalí's interest in historical themes paralleled his growing estrangement from the Surrealist movement. Toward the end of his eccentric autobiography of 1942, *The Secret Life of Salvador Dalí*, the internationally renowned Catalan artist proclaimed his allegiance to the classical tradition in painting and to the Catholic, apostolic faith of the Roman Church. Somewhat disingenuously closing the book on the Freudian narratives that had earned him worldwide celebrity, Dalí now championed the values of hierarchy, order, and obedience to authority. "Instead of automatism," Dalí declared, "style; "instead of nihilism, technique; instead of skepticism, faith; instead of promiscuity, rigor; instead of collectivism and uniformization—individualism, differentiation and hierarchization; instead of experimentation, tradition. Instead of Reaction or Revolution, RENAISSANCE!"[6] For an artist who had earned his reputation as one of the great avant-garde provocateurs of the twentieth century, this declaration signaled a kind of about-face in response to the forces of reaction against which the Surrealists had long militated: the Church, the bourgeois state, and traditional family values. After years of visual references to the work of artists like Giorgio de Chirico (1888–1978), Max Ernst (1901–1976), Pablo Picasso (1881–1973), Joan Miró (1893–1983), and René Magritte (1898–1967), Dalí now turned to Leonardo, Raphael, Bramante, Velázquez (1599–1660), and the sober, austere classicism of Juan de Herrera (ca. 1530–1597) for visual references. *Philip II Receiving Communion* fits squarely within Dalí's return to tradition and his new enthusiasm for history painting. RSL

64. *Female Nude*

Graphite applied with a soft applicator on machine-made blue laid paper

62 x 48 cm. ($24\frac{7}{16}$ x $18\frac{15}{16}$ in.)

Signed and dated in blue ballpoint pen, lower left: *Dalí / 1965*

Watermarks: INGRES D'ARCHES; M.B.M. (France) (see appendix)

Provenance: M. Knoedler & Co., New York; Mrs. Irving B. Kingsford Jr.

Reference: Princeton 1970, 24

Exhibitions: New York 1963; Birmingham 1964

Gift of Mr. and Mrs. Irving B. Kingsford, Jr., Class of 1942
x1969-3

This delicate drawing in black chalk on blue paper depicts a female nude in a contrapuntal pose, her right arm raised at the elbow and her left leg swinging backward. Signed and dated "Dalí 1965," the drawing was exhibited at Knoedler Galleries in an exhibition that ran from November 26 to December 26, 1963, and subsequently at the Birmingham Museum of Art from February 6 to March 5, 1964.[7] The drawing came to Knoedler's directly from the artist and likely was postdated when Mr. and Mrs. Irving B. Kingsford Jr. acquired it from the dealer in December 1965.

Typical of Dalí's later work, the nude is rendered in a quasi-academic style and positioned in a pose that recalls classical precedents. It is not known whether *Female Nude* was conceived as a preparatory study for an unfinished or lost work, or as an independent drawing. The relative non-finito of the drawing—particularly the summary treatment of the upper torso and the head—suggests that Dalí was working out a new composition. A related drawing of 1964, equally summary but executed in a more emphatic line, is identified by Robert Descharnes simply as "Female Nude on a Palette," but this and the Princeton drawing might be related to a more worked-up compositional sketch for *The Judgement of Paris* of 1964. RSL

1 The most comprehensive biography of Dalí is Gibson 1997.
2 Over the course of his long career Dalí often exhibited paintings and drawings together. He repeated this tactic in his second one-man show at the Galeries Dalmau (Dec. 31, 1926–Jan. 14, 1927), at the Zwemmer Gallery, London (Oct. 24–Nov. 10, 1934), at his first one-man show at New York's Museum of Modern Art (Nov. 19, 1941–Jan. 11, 1942), and at numerous exhibitions he celebrated at M. Knoedler and Co., New York, during the 1960s and 1970s.
3 Salvador Dalí, "Reflections," *L'Amic de les Arts* (Sitges) 2, no. 17 (Aug. 30, 1927): 69; as translated in Finkelstein 1998, 45.
4 Finkelstein 1998.
5 "Drawings and Etchings to illustrate Laudréamont's 'Les Chants de Maldoror' by Dalí," Julien Levy Gallery, New York, Apr. 3–28, 1934; "42 eaux-fortes et 30 dessins por Les Chants de Maldoror," Quatre Chemins, Paris, June 13–25, 1934.
6 Dalí 1942, 398.
7 *Dalí*, exh. cat., Knoedler Galleries, New York (Nov. 26–Dec. 26, 1963). The drawing is not listed in the catalogue. Birmingham 1964.

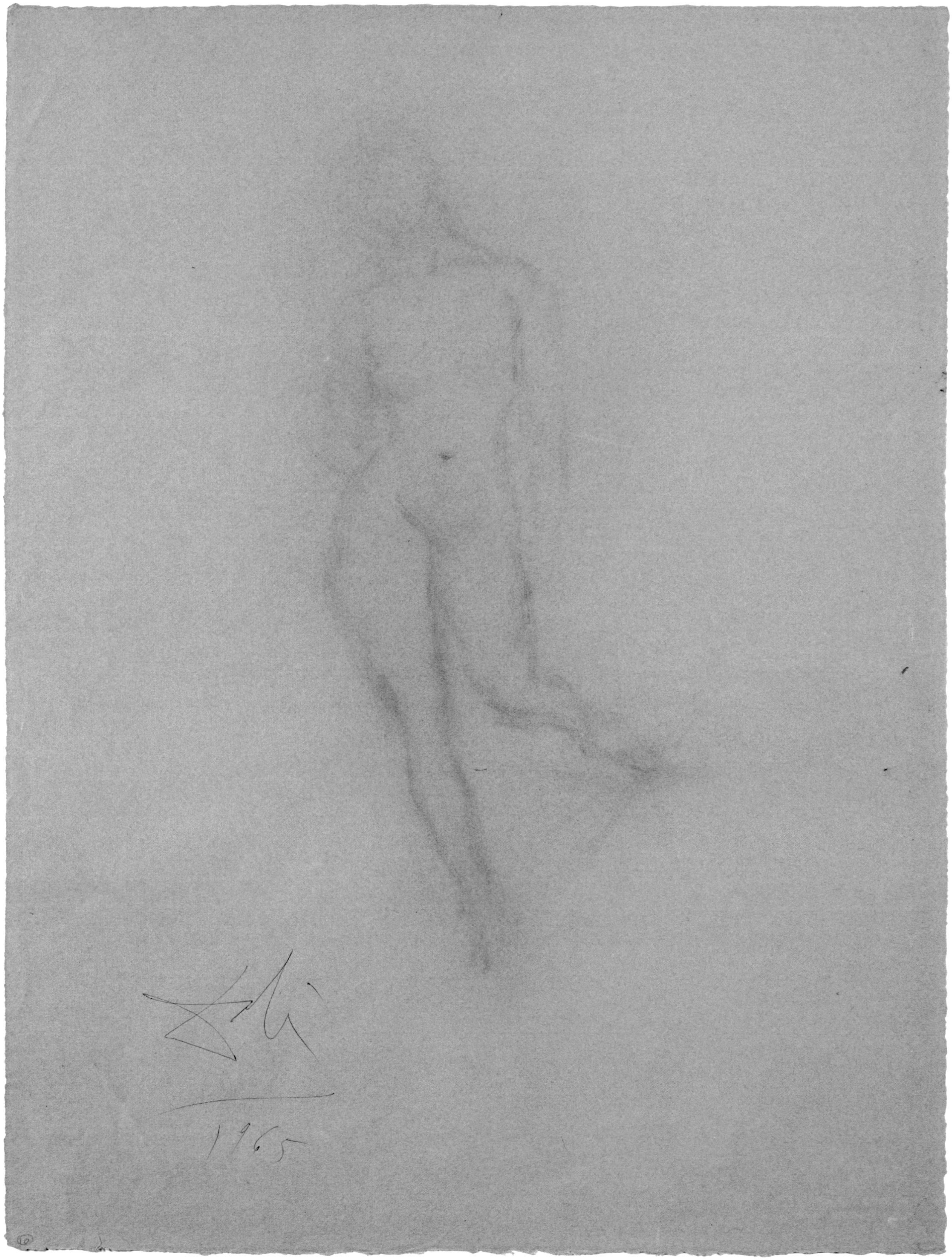
1965

ANDRÉS NAGEL

Donostia–San Sebastián, born 1947

Born in the Basque region of Spain, Andrés Nagel first exhibited in San Sebastián in 1968. He studied architecture at the Universidad de Navarra, Pamplona, before embarking on a career as an artist and sculptor. In 1972 he worked with the Grupo 15 in Madrid, and in his formative years his art was strongly influenced by fellow Basque sculptor Eduardo Chillida (1924–2002).

While Nagel creates in a variety of media, sculpture is a vital aspect of his work, with his works on paper incorporating sculptural or textural elements, particularly metals (such as lead) and metal threads or wires that bind these elements to heavy papers. In two recent series on paper, Nagel continued to make use of motifs from the natural world, combining assemblages of metal with animal and plant imagery in his sculptures and collages.[1] The proximity of the metal, an animated surface, and the natural forms of plants and people in motion, gives vibrancy to his collages.

Work by Nagel can be found in collections as widespread as the Museum of Contemporary Art, Tehran, Iran; the University of Iowa Museum of Art; the Calcografía Nacional, Madrid; the Hakone Open-Air Museum, Tokyo; the British Museum, London; the Banco de España Collection, Madrid; The Museo de La Habana, Havana, Cuba; Meadows Museum, Dallas; and the Fitzwilliam Museum, Cambridge, England. Nagel lives and works in San Sebastián, Spain.

65. *Indian – Mexico XVIII*, 1992

Graphite, color pencil, black ink, iridescent acrylic, gouache, paper and lead sheet collage, with metal wire, on heavy white wove paper

69.0 x 49.2 cm. (27 3/16 x 19 3/8 in.)

Signed in pencil, lower right, above the foot: *adenagel*; also scratched into lead, lower right: *6 de Junio 1000 / 900 / 90 Y 2*, with embossed mark at lower right: crowned escutcheon flanked by rampant lions

Provenance: Tasende Gallery, Los Angeles and La Jolla; Frank Ribelin, Texas

Exhibition: Tasende Gallery, La Jolla, California, 1992

Gift of Frank Ribelin
x1992-175

This collage of lead and paper is part of a numbered series entitled *Indian-Mexico*. Two collages from the series were sold to the same collector, who donated them to Princeton and to the Fitzwilliam Museum at Cambridge University (fig. 65.1).[2] On each of the works the artist has written the date in an unusual way, dividing the year into thousands, hundreds, and tens, followed by a "Y" (meaning "and" in Spanish) and a number for the year. Nagel's inscription on the Princeton collage indicates that it was created on June 6, 1992. The artist's signature appears above the foot at center right, one name overlaid on the other.

The collage comprises heavy paper and a lead plate across the bottom. The legs and feet of a figure in pants, presumably the Indian of the title, dominate the composition. Strips of torn paper are adhered to the center of the composition, slashes of white space across the figure's lifted leg and the space between his legs. A figure's leg appears in the same truncated fashion in several other works from the series, including *Indian-Mexico XVI*. A green plant fills the lower right corner of the Princeton composition and at left is a frieze of Indian figures, including a horse and a teepee, drawn in pencil on top of white gouache. The collage is painted in acrylic on paper in a predominantly gray and white palette; the irregular lead plate is attached across the bottom of the composition with metal staples and wires.

In Princeton's sheet, the shoe at the lower left is cut from a piece of lead while the shoe above the agave plant is suggested by exposed paper; perhaps Nagel planned to use lead here but did not, due to its weight. The pieces of paper that form the agave plant were left loose, as if to cover an intended shoe of lead. The mixture of paper and lead media is used here to convey the heaviness of the shoes, the

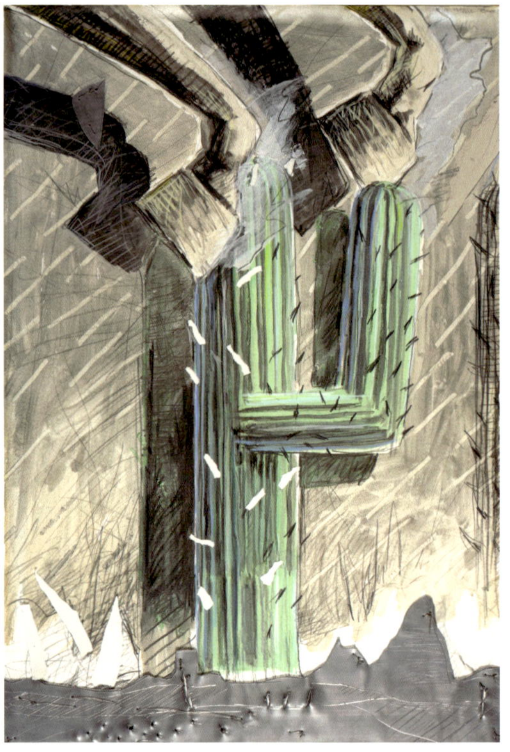

Fig. 65.1 Andrés Nagel, Spanish, born 1947: *Indian-Mexico XVI*. Collage and lead on paper, 69.0 x 47.0 cm. Fitzwilliam Museum, Cambridge, given by Frank Ribelin via the Jose Tasende Gallery through the American Friends of Cambridge University (PD.132-1992).

lightness and flexibility of the plants, and the crushing force of the feet. On the Cambridge collage, Nagel used a smaller lead sheet for the blade of an ax near the horse's hooves.

The artist used spray paint to create a glittery surface in some parts of the collage, which acts as a foil to the sheen of the lead plate at the bottom. Color is applied in jagged lines at the top and left sides and in the green of the plant, and additional color is lightly applied in the same manner in crayon along the pant legs.

Like the sculptor David Smith, who swept metal shavings from his sculptures into the ink that he applied to paper, giving it form and texture, Nagel uses sculptural techniques in his works on paper to achieve volume in his figures.[3] Nagel interrupts the sculptural elements with strokes that continue from one support medium to the other: his green crayon strokes, vigorously applied, cross over to the lead plate at bottom, leaving waxy lines on top of the plate and creating a transition from one surface to another.

The image of the heavy foot, stomping or stepping on something, is a subject that Nagel explored for several years prior to making this series. It can also be seen in sculptures like the *Step* (1988), of mixed media, oil on polyester, and fiberglass, in more light-hearted images, and in another sculpture depicting a foot kicking a can.[4] LAB

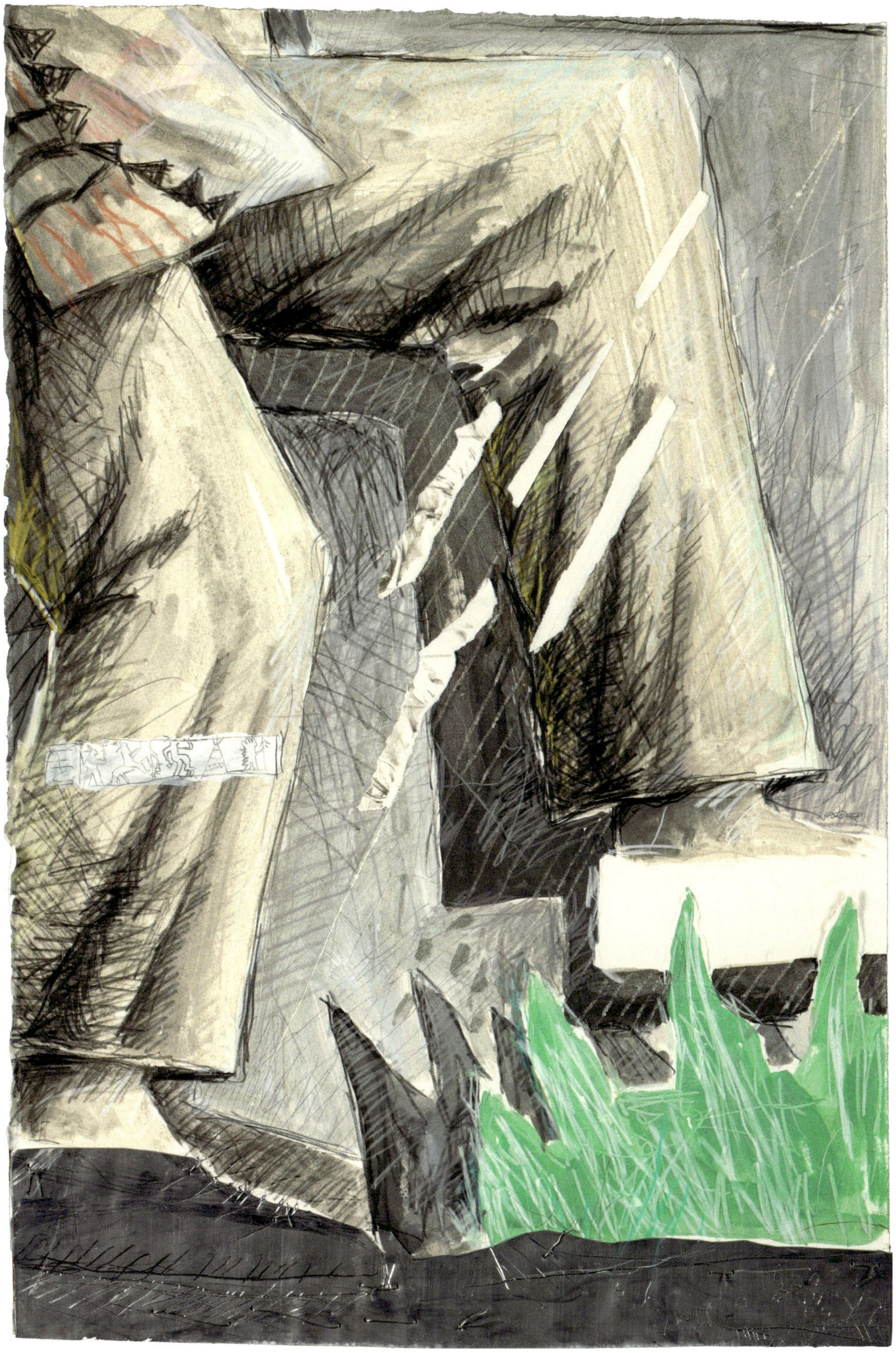

1 The *Misera* series from 2000, for example, depicted lobsters on paper, with metal attachments.

2 Aitor Tasende, Tasende Galleries, e-mail communication with author, January 15, 2008, and March 15, 2008. My thanks to Aitor Tasende.

3 Richard Mulholland (paper conservator at the Victoria and Albert Museum, London) presented the findings about David Smith's studio sweepings and his ink drawings in a symposium at the Metropolitan Museum of Art in July 2003. Richard Mulholland, "Multiplicar las asociaciones: David Smith y las pinturas modernas" in manuscript, 2012; "Postprints," 12e Jornada de Conservación de Arte Contemporáneo, IIC-GEC, Centro de Arte Reina Sofía, Museo Nacional Madrid, February 2011; Richard Mulholland, "Technique and Process in the papers of David Smith," *Study and Serendipity: Testimonies on Artists' Practice*, papers from the 3rd ICOM-CC Art Technological Source Research Center (ATSR) Symposium, University of Glasgow, June 2008.

4 Both sculptures are illustrated in the exhibition catalogue *Andrés Nagel: Mixed Media, Sculpture and Work on Paper* (Tasende Gallery, La Jolla, 1990). The first, *Step*, is cat. no. 11, the second is illustrated on the eighth page of the same catalogue (not paginated).

UNKNOWN ARTIST, ARAGON SCHOOL?

late 16th–early 17th century

66. *Half-Length Portrait of Monk Holding a Crucifix, with Sketches of Decorative Motifs*

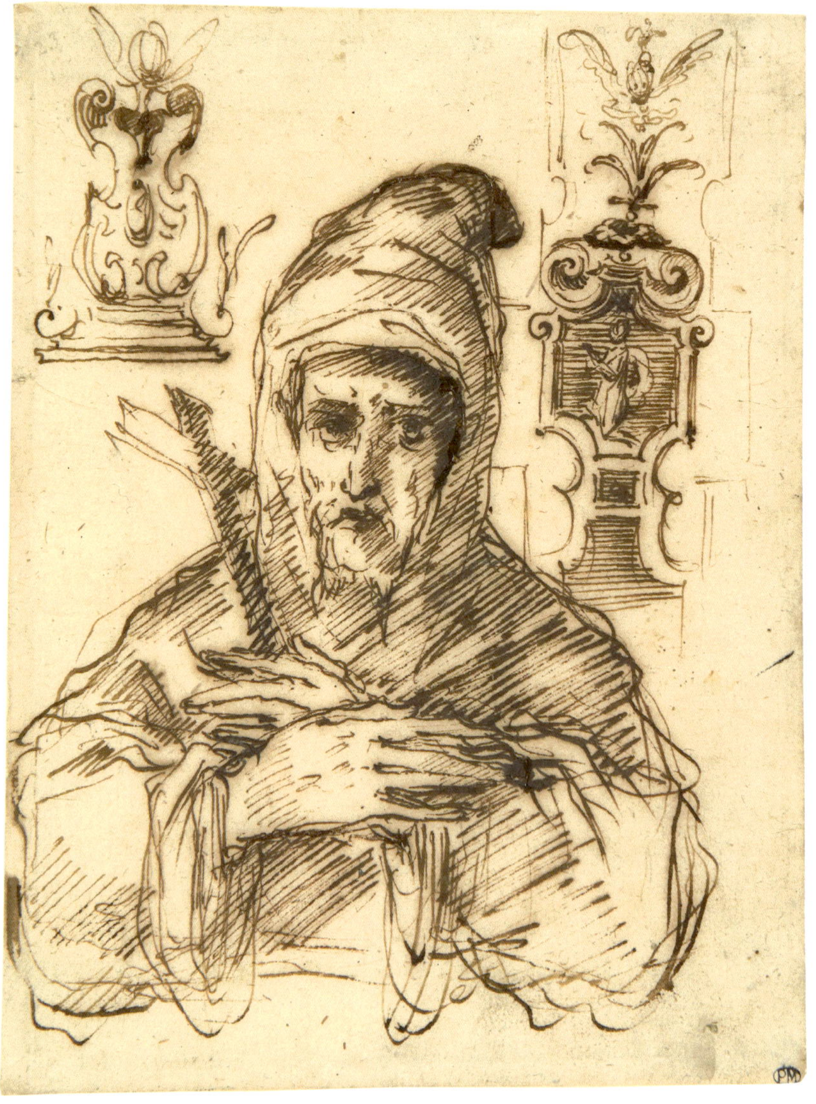

Pen and dark brown ink on beige laid paper, edge mounted to heavy cream card

15.4 x 11.7 cm. (6 1/16 x 4 9/16 in.)

WATERMARK: Shield or star in shield (partial)

PROVENANCE: Mathias Polakovits, Paris and New York, stamp (Lugt 3561) recto, lower right

REFERENCE: Princeton 2003, 115, as "Spanish, Anonymous, 17th century"

EXHIBITIONS: Princeton 1995; Princeton 1997

Museum purchase, Laura P. Hall Memorial Fund and Fowler McCormick, Class of 1921, Fund 2002-104

This half-length figure of a monk holding a crucifix loosely resembles late sixteenth-century sketches of mystical saints. The two smaller sketches above the monk's shoulders seem to be designs that would be carved or made from plaster.

The draftsman for the Princeton sheet might be from the circle of artisans working for Philip II at the Escorial, whose individual contributions and personal histories have yet to be studied fully. An example is Pedro Sánchez de Ezpeleta, a miniaturist, calligrapher, and illuminator from Zaragoza[1] who was described by Jusepe Martínez in the mid-1670s as a great illustrator who decorated choir books for Philip II at the Escorial.[2] The only drawing by him known to survive appears to be a presentation drawing that includes ornamental strapwork and his signature (ca. 1580–85, Juan Abelló Collection, Madrid). That drawing, possibly sent as a demonstration of draftsmanship to the king's personal secretary, Mateo Vázquez de Leca, remained in Seville and eventually entered the Alcubierre Album. Princeton's small drawing, in pen and dark brown ink, shows an artist who is more at home making grotesque ornament, as described in the left and right background of the sheet, than in depicting the figure that dominates the center. Like Ezpeleta's drawing, this sheet might have served to demonstrate the artist's abilities to a potential client or patron.

The angled cross, close parallel hatch marks, and inclusion of decorative motifs in the background recall the playful intermingling of decorative and figurative elements in the sheet attributed to Ezpeleta, adding stylistic support to a sixteenth-century date for this sheet. While Ezpeleta used wash to fill shadows on his small sketch, creating a more careful and finished appearance, the artist of Princeton's sheet employed closely spaced strokes and hatching from the upper right to the lower left. The artist also used horizontal strokes in the decorative cartouches, similar to this effect in the decorative forms on Ezpleta's drawing. LAB

1 Martínez 1988, 287, as *"grande iluminador."*
2 Navarrete Prieto and Pérez Sánchez 2009, 52–53.

UNKNOWN ARTIST, CATALAN SCHOOL

17th century

67. *Three Friars: Two Seated and One Standing*

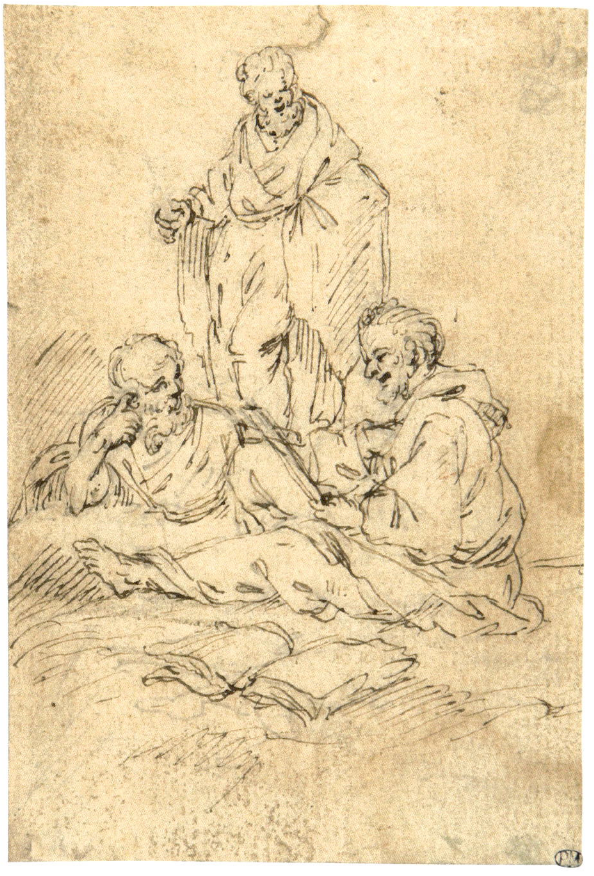

Pen and brown ink over traces of graphite (?) on tan laid paper, lined

11.5 x 8.1 cm. ($4\frac{1}{2}$ x $3\frac{3}{16}$ in.)

PROVENANCE: Mathias Polakovits, Paris and New York, stamp (Lugt 3561) recto, lower right, in black

Museum purchase, Laura P. Hall Memorial Fund and Fowler McCormick, Class of 1921, Fund 2002-118

At first glance the figures in this drawing appear to be apostles. They wear robes, and the figure seated at front seems to represent a friar or monk, with a hood folded onto his shoulders. He contemplates the crucifix in his hand, with his legs outstretched in front of him, and seems disengaged from the figure behind him, who holds a finger pointing to his ear. The figure standing at back could be leaning on something, but his left hand is not visible. The three figures, arranged together, are disengaged from each other.

The group is reminiscent of paintings of Camaldolese friars, or hermits, often depicted in threes in such a gathering. They are together but active or lost in their own pursuits. Founded by Saint Romuald in the eleventh century in the bishopric of Arezzo, Camaldolese monastic houses followed Benedictine rule. Additional houses were later founded in Turin, Padua, and Rome, as well as San Michele di Murano and Venice. Camaldolese houses encouraged individual spiritual pursuit as a reflection of the Holy Trinity, with cenobites (communal monks) and hermits living together under the same rule.

The tradition was established in Spain in the sixteenth century, when a Camaldolese hermitage was established at Montecorona near San Miguel de Cuixá in Catalonia. El Greco's intriguing *Allegory of the Camaldolese Order* (1599–1600, Colegio del Patriarca, Valencia) likely was painted for that hermitage. The symbolism of the three friars here, together but disengaged, refers to the simultaneous diversity and unity of the Holy Trinity, reflecting the Order's central belief. LAB

UNKNOWN ARTIST, SEVILLE SCHOOL

17th century

68. *God the Father*

Verso: *God the Father*

Pen and brown ink over red chalk, on circular shaped tan laid paper

11.6 cm. diam. (4 9/16 in. diam.)

PROVENANCE: Mathias Polakovits, Paris and New York, stamp (Lugt 3561) recto, lower right, in black

Museum purchase, Laura P. Hall Memorial Fund and Fowler McCormick, Class of 1921, Fund 2002-116

This fragmentary drawing has been cut out from a larger sheet and trimmed within a circle. On the verso is a partial larger study of God the Father, drawn inside a circle of clouds. God the Father is often represented swathed in clouds and extending a hand over a scene below, inferring his agency in scenes of the Annunciation and the Nativity or supporting the dead Christ in allegories of the Trinity. The extremely large hands of God the Father are exaggerated in order to convey the magnitude of that gesture of intervention.

The repetition of the theme on both sides of the paper and the handling of the pen and brown ink are reminiscent of drawings by Seville School artists from the 1660s and 1670s, dispersed among a variety of institutions by Mr. and Mrs. William B. Jaffe in the 1950s (Metropolitan Museum of Art, New York; Peddie School, Hightstown, N.J.; Hood Museum of Art, Dartmouth College, Hanover, N.H.; private collection on loan to Yale University Art Gallery).[1] LAB

1 Princeton 1976–77, 44–48; Peter Cherry, "Murillo's Drawing Academy," in *Bartolomé Esteban Murillo (1617–1682)* (New York: H. N. Abrams, 2002), 47–60; and Brown 2012, 27–29.

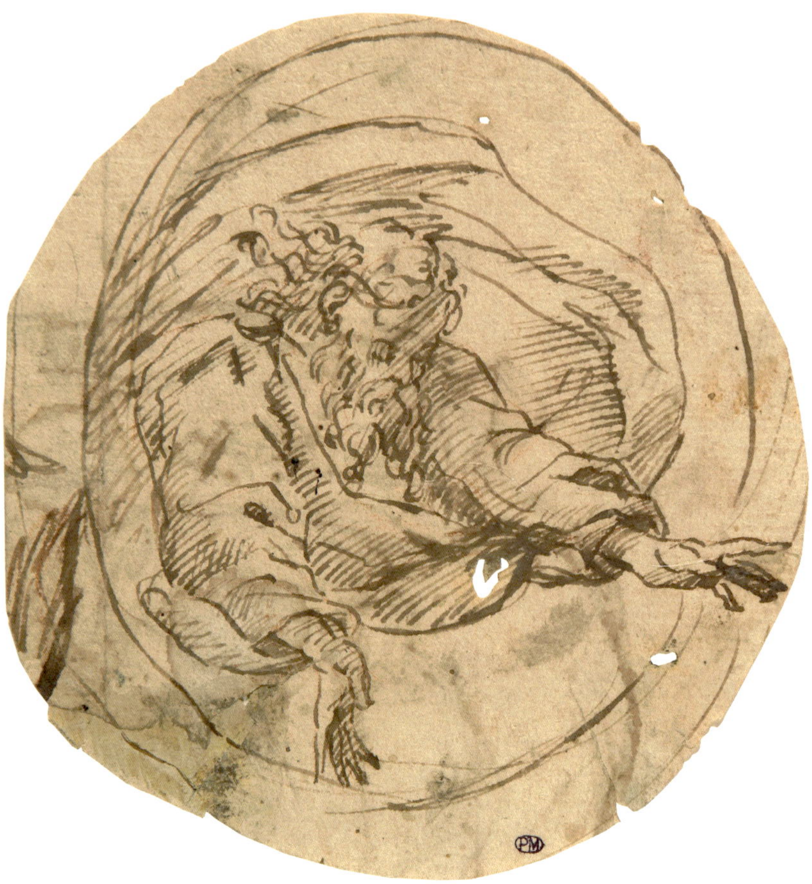

UNKNOWN ARTIST, SEVILLE SCHOOL

mid-17th century

69. *Saint Roch*

Pen and brown ink with brush and brown wash over graphite on light tan laid paper, squared in graphite; verso: red chalk partial sketch of concentric circles and red chalk grid

28.1 x 11.8 cm. (11 1/16 x 4 5/8 in.)

PROVENANCE: Mathias Polakovits, Paris and New York, stamp (Lugt 3561) recto, lower right, in black

EXHIBITIONS: Princeton 1995; Princeton 1997; Princeton 2001

Museum purchase, Laura P. Hall Memorial Fund and Fowler McCormick, Class of 1921, Fund 2002-100

70. *Saint Sebastian*

Pen and brown ink with brush and brown wash over graphite on light tan laid paper, squared in graphite

28.5 x 10.2 cm. (11 3/16 x 4.0 in.)

PROVENANCE: Mathias Polakovits, Paris and New York, stamp (Lugt 3561) recto, lower right, in black

EXHIBITIONS: Princeton 1995; Princeton 1997; Princeton 2001

Museum purchase, Laura P. Hall Memorial Fund and Fowler McCormick, Class of 1921, Fund 2002-99

This pair of drawings depicting Saints Roch and Sebastian shares the light application of wash and loose outlines of the figures of those saints by Pedro Núñez de Villavicencio (1635–1695) now in the collection of the Hamburger Kunsthalle (fig. 69–70.1). This similarity in execution suggests that the Princeton drawings may have been made around the same time for a religious client in Andalusia, perhaps by an artist who was familiar with Villavicencio's technique. The schematic rendering of the bodies also suggests

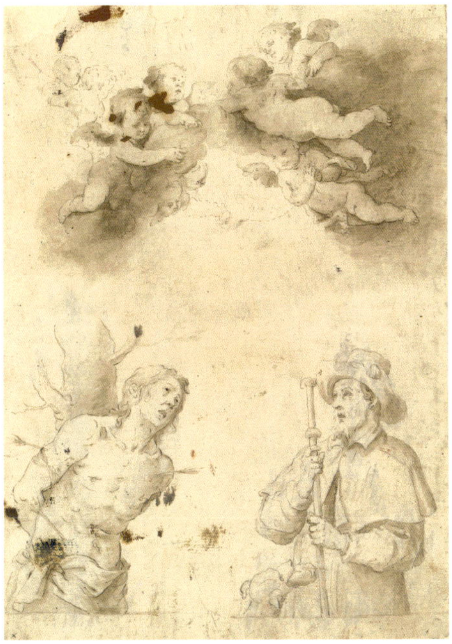

Fig. 69–70.1 Pedro Núñez de Villavicencio, Spanish, 1644–1695: *Angels, Saint Sebastian, and Saint Roch.* Pen and ink, 29.2 x 20.7 cm. Hamburger Kunsthalle (38637).

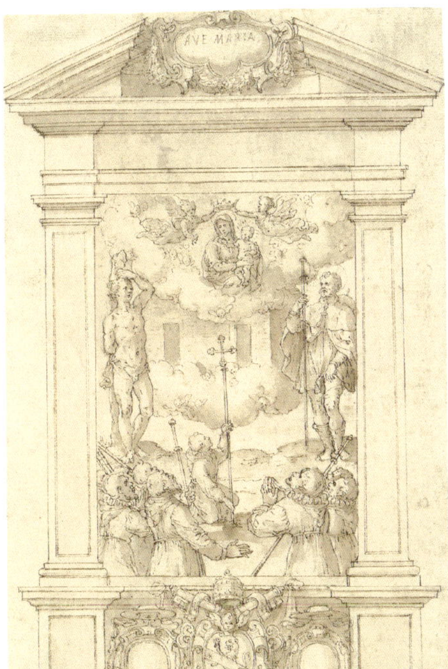

Fig. 69–70.2 Italian: altarpiece design with the Madonna of Loreto. 28.4 x 17.6 cm. Museo Nacional del Prado, Madrid (D01601).

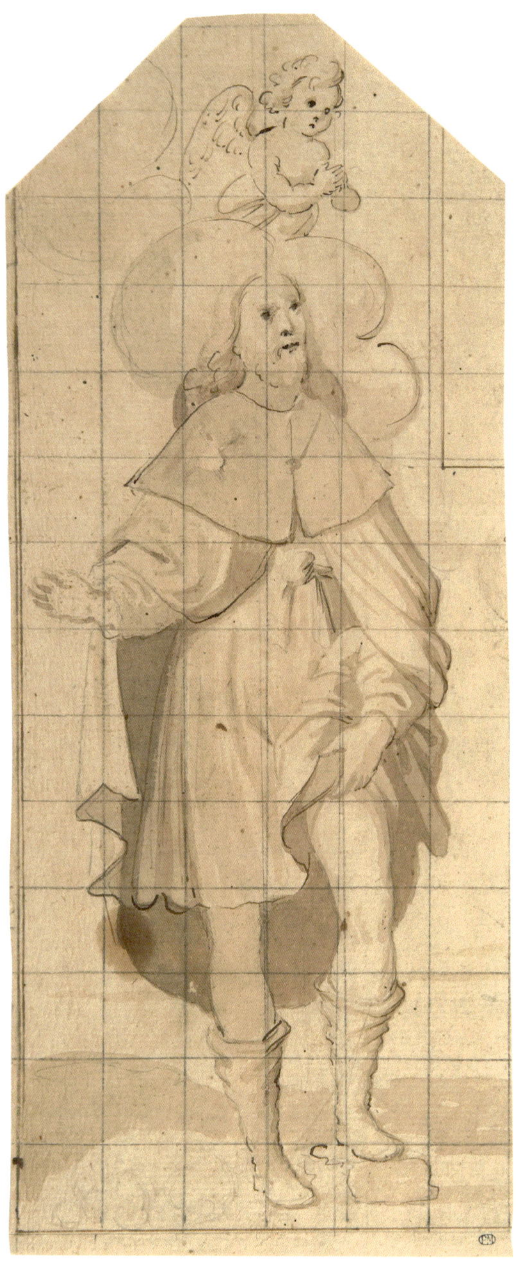

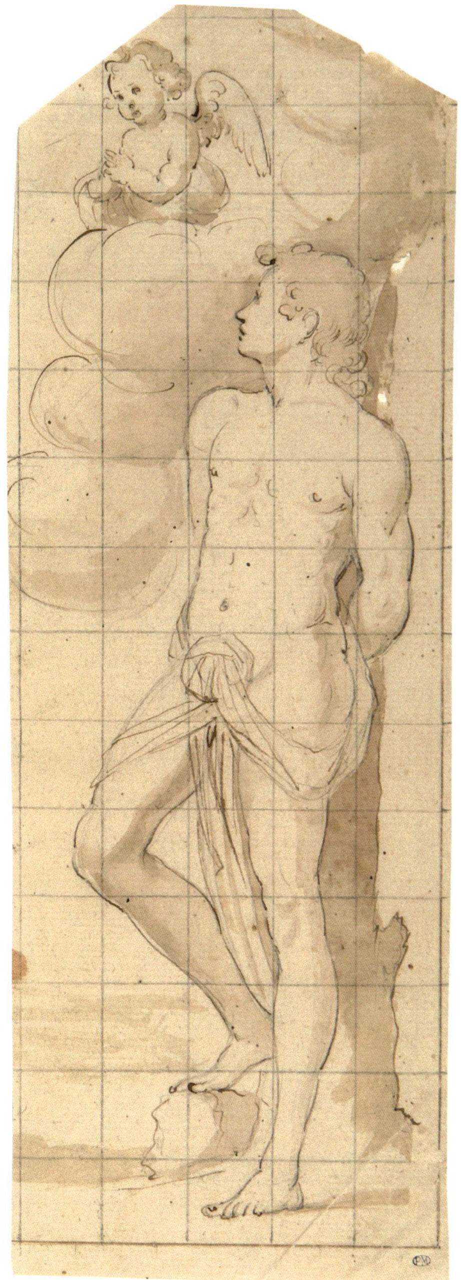

that the drawings may have been first ideas in preparing an altarpiece commission.

Frequently paired, Roch and Sebastian are often associated with port cities like Seville, Valencia, and Barcelona that were especially vulnerable and sought divine protection from the scourge of the plague. A typical presentation of the two plague saints in the company of the Virgin (*sacra conversazione*) is demonstrated in an anonymous Italian altarpiece design with the Madonna of Loreto (fig. 69–70.2) in the Prado's collection. LAB

UNKNOWN ARTIST, SPANISH SCHOOL

17th century

71. *St. Peter in Landscape*

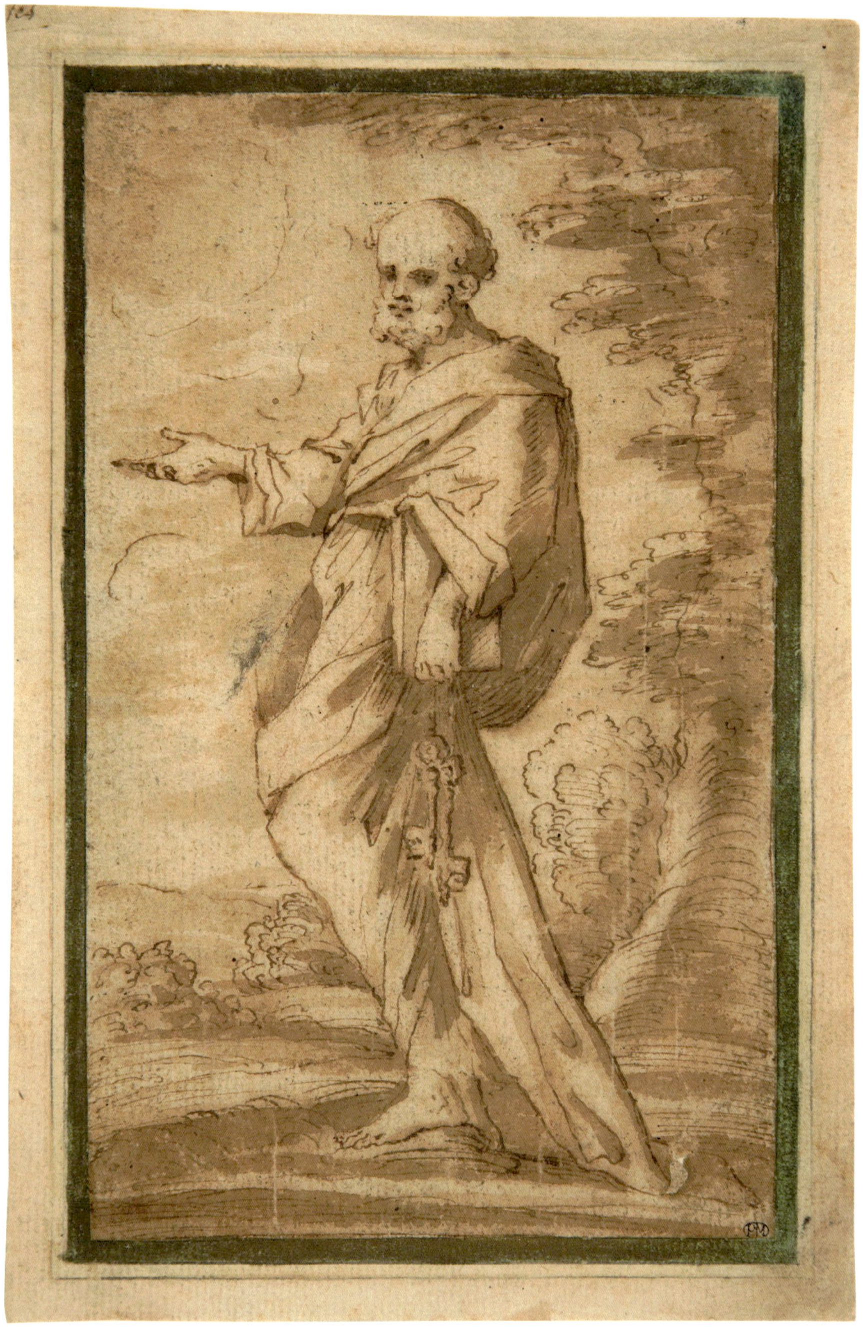

Pen and brown ink with brush and brown wash, over traces of red chalk, on light tan laid paper, lined

17.5 cm x 10.8 cm. (6⅞ x 4¼ in.)

Inscribed verso on mount, in black chalk, upper right: *St Peter*

PROVENANCE: Mathias Polakovits, Paris and New York, stamp (Lugt 3561) recto, lower right, in black

REFERENCE: Princeton 2003, 115

Museum Purchase, Laura P. Hall Memorial Fund and Fowler McCormick, Class of 1921, Fund 2002-108

This finished study of Saint Peter focuses closely on the figure, suggesting that the drawing might have been part of a larger series of saints, perhaps studies intended for an *apostolado*, where the figure of the saint was more important than its context. The attributes of Saint Peter—the keys to Heaven and the rock—derive from Christ's appointment of Peter as the foundation upon which he would build the church (Matthew 16:18) and his intention to give to Peter the keys to the kingdom of Heaven (Matthew 16:19).

UNKNOWN ARTIST, SPANISH SCHOOL

mid-17th century

72. *Christ Blessing*

Pen and brown ink with brush and brown wash, over red chalk, on tan laid paper, lined

14.5 x 19.9 cm. (5 11/16 x 7 13/16 in.)

Inscribed in graphite (illegible) on verso of mount

PROVENANCE: A. Chariatte (Lugt 88a); sale, Sotheby's, London, April 30, 1923, lot 17, as "Spanish School, Alonzo Cano, 17. Christ and Two Saints bistre pen and wash, and Seven others"; Parsons & Sons, London; Alfred Aaron de Pass (1861–1953), stamp (Lugt 108a) verso; gift to Cornwall County Museum, Truro, England, stamp (Lugt 2014e) verso; sale, Christie's, London, November 30, 1965, possibly part of lot 133; Mathias Polakovits, Paris and New York, stamp (Lugt 3561) recto, lower right, in black

REFERENCES: *Catalogue of Old Master Drawings and Modern Etchings, from the collection of the late Monsieur A. Chariatte*, April 30, 1923, lot 17; Penrose 1936, as "Spanish School," no. 122; London/Truro 1994, as "Spanish School, 122," former acc. no. 1928–316; Princeton 2003, 119, as "José Jiménez Donoso"

EXHIBITIONS: Penrose 1936, as "Spanish School," no. 122; Princeton 2001

Museum purchase, Laura P. Hall Memorial Fund and Fowler McCormick, Class of 1921, Fund 2002-88

This drawing was part of South African collector Alfred Aaron De Pass's gift to the Cornwall County Museum of Art in 1928 and bears the stamp that was used to indicate De Pass's donation to that institution.

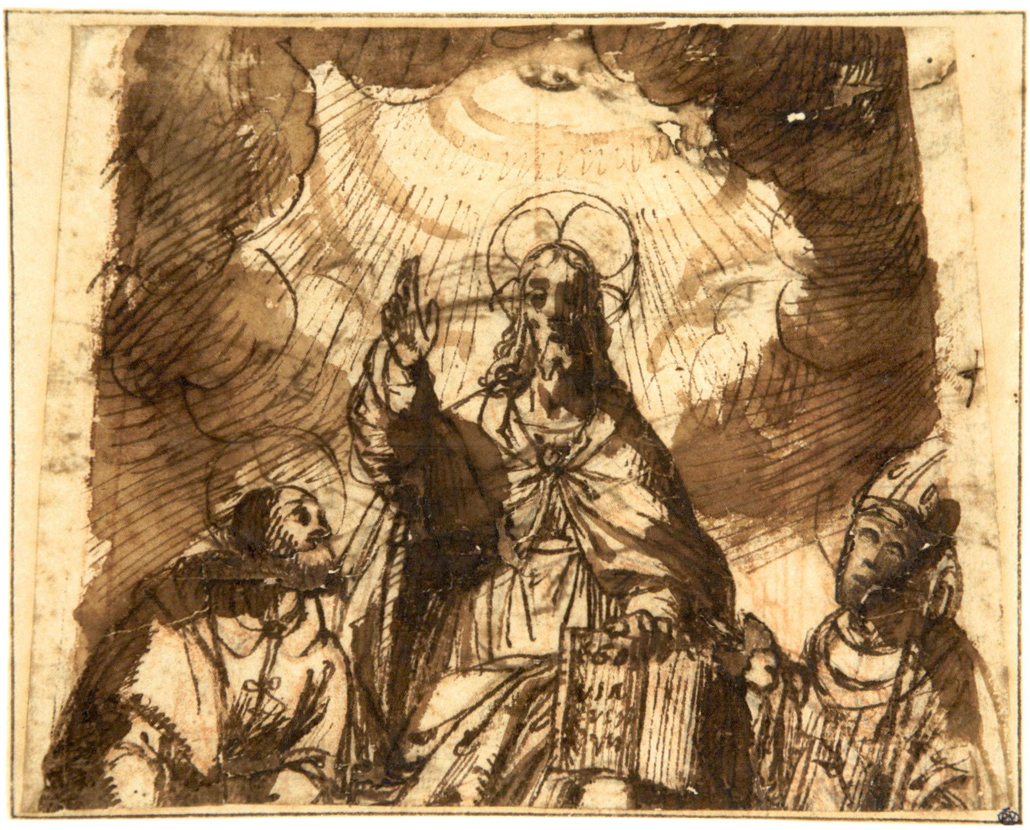

In Cornwall County Museum records the drawing was reattributed to El Greco; however, that attribution was changed after A. E. Popham wrote in 1957: "I see no reason for attributing this to El Greco. It is one of Parsons' ingenious ideas. I should call it Spanish School, 17th century."[1]

Deaccessioned from the Cornwall County Museum of Art, the drawing, with several others from the De Pass collection, appeared in one of two sales between 1965 and 1966. Among the group sold in 1965 were several important Spanish drawings, including a sketch by Murillo for the *Virgin and Child in Glory Adored by Saints* (The Wallace Collection, London) and a rare sheet by Romulo Cincinnato.[2]

Although skillfully restored, Princeton's sheet has suffered significant losses, notably in the faces of the two saints on the register below Christ and around the head of Christ, making a definitive attribution especially difficult. Despite stylistic affinities with drawings by Madrid school artists of the mid-seventeenth century, notably Mateo Cerezo Delgado (1637–1666), by whom there are only a scant few wash drawings, Popham's declaration seems to be the most apt. LAB

1 London/Truro 1994, "Spanish school, 122." Parsons & Sons was the dealer who sold it to De Pass before 1928. This drawing was not included in Popham's 1957 catalogue, although that was likely the year when he made this comment. London 1957.

2 The subsequent history of the drawings can be pieced together from a variety of sources. Marianne Joannides's 1994 study of the collection offers the most complete view to date. Priscilla Muller discussed the Murillo drawing and its provenance in Madrid 2006–7a, 167–69; Alfonso Pérez Sánchez discussed the provenance and attribution of the Cincinnato in Angulo Íñiguez and Pérez Sánchez 1975–88, vol. 2, 49, no. 265. The Cornwall Museum kept no records on the drawings beyond the time of their sale at Christie's, according to curator Lucinda Middleton in correspondence with the author, March 31, 2008. Princeton's sheet may have been part of lot 133, sold to Rudolf, as noted in London/Truro 1994.

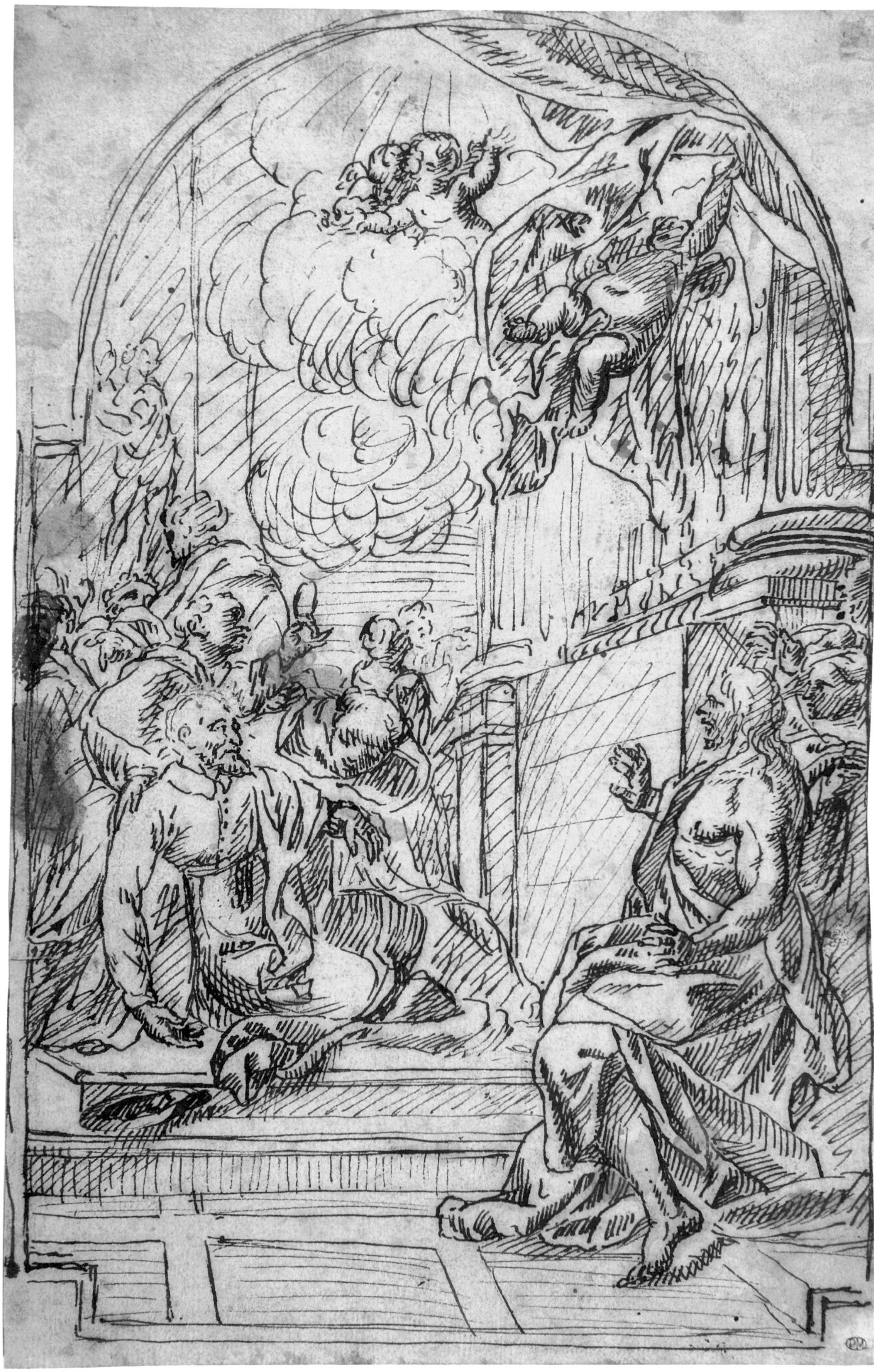

UNKNOWN ARTIST, SPANISH SCHOOL

mid-17th century

73. *The Vision of Saint Ignatius*

Verso: *Figure Sketch*

Pen and brown ink over traces of red chalk on tan laid paper; verso: red chalk

25.8 x 17.0 cm. (10³⁄₁₆ x 6¹¹⁄₁₆ in.)

PROVENANCE: Mathias Polakovits, Paris and New York, stamp (Lugt 3561) recto, lower right

REFERENCE: Princeton 2003, 115, as "Spanish, Anonymous, 17th century, *Death of a Saint*"

Museum purchase, Laura P. Hall Memorial Fund and Fowler McCormick, Class of 1921, Fund 2002-111

While the author of this sheet remains unknown, the scene that it depicts relates to the life of Saint Ignatius (1491–1556), representing a moment when he experienced a mystical vision of Christ. Traveling to see the pope in Rome with two companions, James Lainez (or Diego Laynez) and Peter Faber, Ignatius of Loyola stopped at a chapel in La Storta, Italy, and experienced the second of his important visions: God told him that he would work with Christ.

Supporting the fainting Saint Ignatius in Princeton's drawing are the two companions and standing behind is a man who holds what appears to be the Host while resting his hand on Ignatius's shoulder. The presence of God is indicated by the cloud of glory and the putti with rays of light at the upper right of the composition. An apparition of a bearded Christ, in a long robe and with a naked chest, is at right; he is represented without his customary cross, signifying his resurrected state. The chapel's tiled floor leads the viewer's eye to a series of steps before the altar; columns appear at the sides of the altar to indicate its grandeur.

The composition might have been intended for an altarpiece dedicated to the life of Saint Ignatius, the founder of the Jesuit Order, or a cycle of paintings representing his life for a Jesuit church. The artist's careful pen strokes resemble the technique of Antonio de Pereda (1611–1678), whose best-known series of drawings illustrated the "Good Death" of a just man (Musée du Louvre, Paris), a topos frequently represented in the seventeenth century.[1] Pereda's most important work reflects the influence of such Jesuits as Jerome Nadal, whose *Evangelicae historiae imagines* (1593) was readily available in Spain. Its importance as a source was noted by Francisco Pacheco in his *Arte de la pintura* of 1649,[2] and the artist of Princeton's sheet may have consulted the text. LAB

1 Pérez Sánchez 1986, 170–71; Angulo Íñiguez and Pérez Sánchez 1975–1988, vol. 2, nos. 296–324.

2 Boubli 2002, 116.

UNKNOWN ARTIST, VALENCIAN SCHOOL

late 17th century

74. *Assumption of the Virgin*

Verso: *Sketch of the Assumption of the Virgin*

Pen and brown ink on tan laid paper

16.8 x 13.5 cm. (6⁵⁄₈ x 5⁵⁄₁₆ in.)

Inscribed verso, in blue crayon, lower edge: *323*

PROVENANCE: Mathias Polakovits, Paris and New York, stamp (Lugt 3561) recto, lower right, in black

REFERENCE: Princeton 2003, 122

EXHIBITIONS: Princeton 1995; Princeton 1997

Museum purchase, Laura P. Hall Memorial Fund and Fowler McCormick, Class of 1921, Fund 2002-94

Nervous slashing lines impart a tremendous amount of energy to this sketch of the Assumption of the Virgin. The verso features a smaller version of the subject, with angels supporting the rising Virgin amid clouds. The image is enclosed by border lines on three sides, as if the artist roughly selected the boundaries of the composition on the verso of the sheet and developed the idea more fully on the recto.

When it was acquired by Princeton the drawing was attributed to Francisco de Herrera the Younger, but comparisons of the work's frenetic energy to his signed design for a processional sculpture (The Morgan Library, New York) reveal this drawing to be closer in technique to a drawing of *The Vision of Saint Anthony of Padua* (fig. 74.1).[1] Although signed "Saura" at lower left, that sheet is attributed to Vicente Salvador Gómez, a better-known Valencian school draftsman who used dense hatching and shading with tiny parallel lines and screens of hatchmarks to form swirling clouds composed of short strokes (see cat. 13).

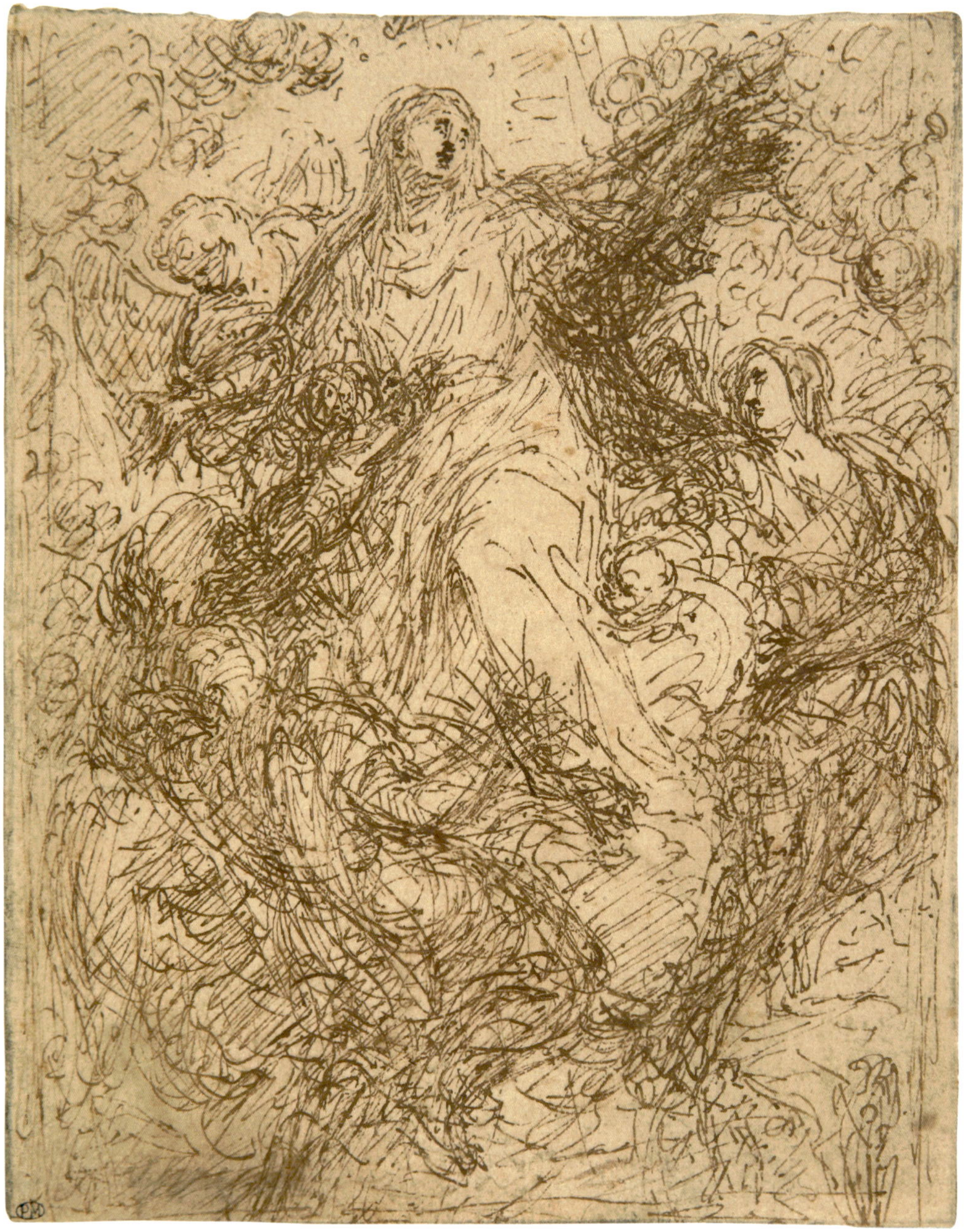

Another drawing to which the technique in Princeton's sheet might be compared is *Priest Celebrating Mass* (fig. 74.2). Recently the drawing has been attributed to Vicente Salvador Gómez,[2] and the general similarities between that drawing and Princeton's suggest that both artists were Valencian and trained in the same techniques. There is more work to be done on the influence of Vicente Salvador Gómez's *Cartilla y fundamentals reglas de Pintura* on the artists in and around Valencia who might have been affected by Salvador Gómez's distinctive hatching and energetic lines.[3] LAB

1 Mosén Domingo Saura was active in Valencia in the late seventeenth century and died there in the early eighteenth century. Of the four drawings associated with this artist, two are in the British Museum (1846-5-9-202, 1846-5-9-203). A black chalk drawing in the Prado, from the Fernando Durán collection, is attributed to Saura twice in an eighteenth-century hand (Madrid, Prado, F.D. 2011); another drawing in the Prado, *Vision of Saint Teresa*, also came from that collection (Madrid, Prado, F.D. 1155). The artist was described by Ceán Bermúdez as an avid draftsman whose drawings were "kept by the professors" of the Academy of San Carlos in Valencia. Saura's paintings, on the other hand, in churches of Lucena, San Esteban in Valencia, and San Pascual in Villarreal, mostly remain in situ, and his work is not well known outside the region.

2 Dallas/Ocala/Rotterdam 2003–4.

3. Espinós Díaz 1997, 160–62.

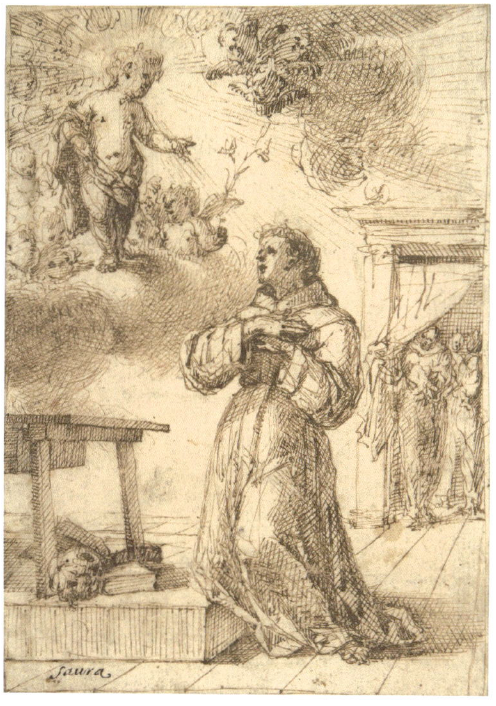

Fig. 74.1 Vicente Salvador Gómez, Spanish, 1637–ca. 1700: *The Vision of Saint Anthony of Padua*. Pen and brown ink over traces of leadpoint (?), 17.8 x 12.8 cm. The Metropolitan Museum of Art, Van Day Truex Fund, 2003 (2003.92).

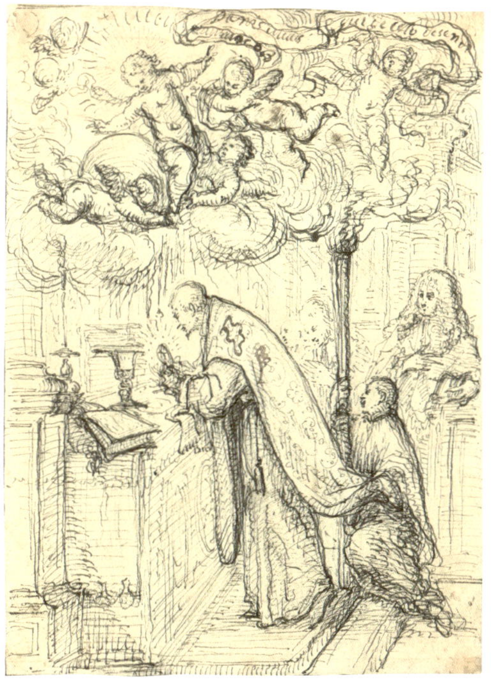

Fig. 74.2 Attributed to Vicente Salvador Gómez, Spanish, 1637–ca. 1700: *Priest Celebrating Mass*, 1650–1700. Pen and brown and black ink on paper, 20.8 x 15.2 cm. Collection Rijksprenten-kabinet Rijksmuseum, Amsterdam, purchase from F. G. Waller Fund (RP-T-1957-176).

Verso cat. 74

UNKNOWN ARTIST, SPANISH?

late 17th century

75. *Saint Januarius*

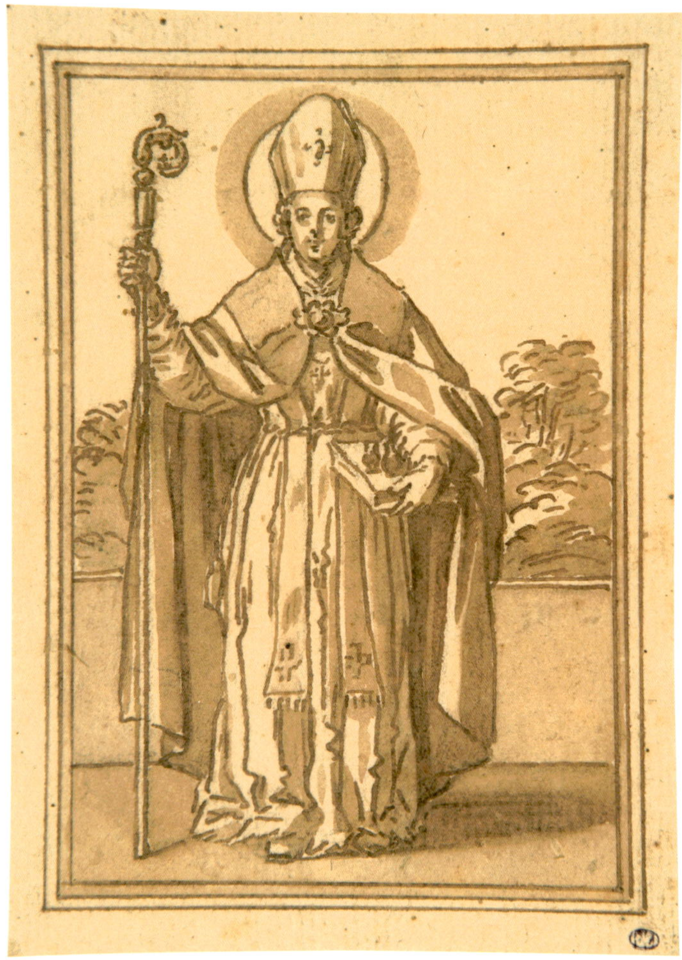

Pen and brown ink with brush and brown wash, over traces of black chalk, on tan laid paper, lined

12.4 x 9.0 cm. (4⅞ x 3 9/16 in.)

PROVENANCE: Mathias Polakovits, Paris and New York, stamp (Lugt 3561) recto, lower right, in black

REFERENCE: Princeton 2003, 115, as "Spanish, Anonymous, 17th century"

EXHIBITION: Princeton 2001, as "Spanish, Anonymous, 17th century"

Museum purchase, Laura P. Hall Memorial Fund and Fowler McCormick, Class of 1921, Fund 2002-102

This drawing and cat. 76 clearly were executed by the same hand, probably as finished ideas for the same commission. Saint Januarius—or San Gennaro, as he is called in Naples—was martyred for hiding Christians who were persecuted by Emperor Diocletian. He often is depicted with a book and two vials of his blood, which are believed to liquefy annually on his feast day, September 19. As he is patron saint of Naples, few representations of him are found outside of a Neapolitan context. LAB

UNKNOWN ARTIST, SPANISH?

late 17th century

76. *Saint Cecilia*

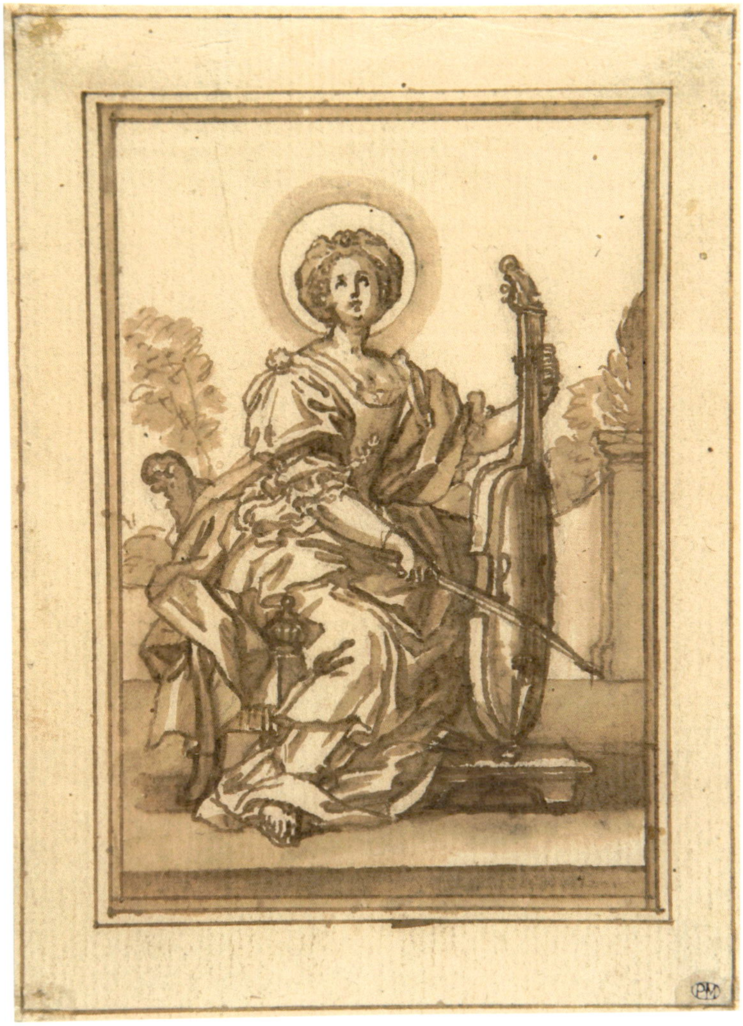

Pen and brown ink with brush and brown wash over traces of black chalk, on tan laid paper

13.6 x 10.2 cm. (5⅜ x 4.0 in.)

PROVENANCE: Mathias Polakovits, Paris and New York, stamp (Lugt 3561) recto, lower right, in black

REFERENCE: Princeton 2003, 115, as "Spanish, Anonymous, 17th century"

Museum purchase, Laura P. Hall Memorial Fund and Fowler McCormick, Class of 1921, Fund 2002-106

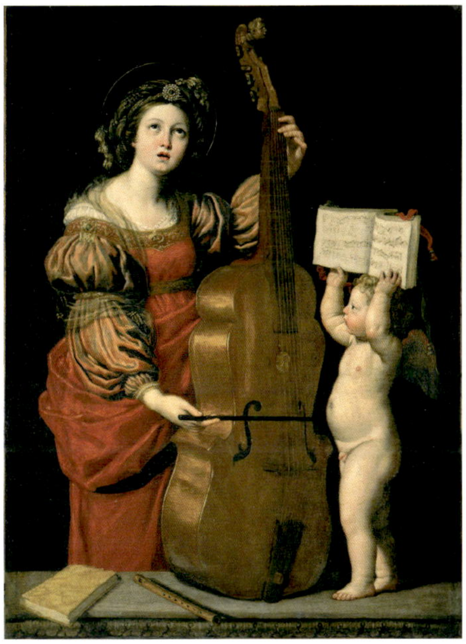

Fig. 76.1 Domenichino, Italian, 1581–1641: *Saint Cecilia with an Angel Holding a Musical Score*, ca. 1617–18. 160 x 120 cm. Musée du Louvre (793).

As the patron saint of music, Cecilia is usually depicted playing an instrument, often visited by an angel, and with her eyes lifted to heaven. At times she is shown with Saint Valerian, the bridegroom whom she converted to Christianity and who was also martyred for his faith.

This seated figure seems related to Domenichino's painting of about 1617–18 (fig. 76.1). Believed to have been commissioned by Cardinal Ludovico Ludovisi in Rome, that painting was taken to France between 1650 and 1660 and was acquired by Louis XIV in 1662.[1]

LAB

1 Louvre online database, "Saint Cecilia with an angel holding a musical score," written by Speranza Bastien. Richard Spear, *Domenichino*, 2 vols. (New Haven and London: Yale University Press, 1982), no. 53, pl. 176.

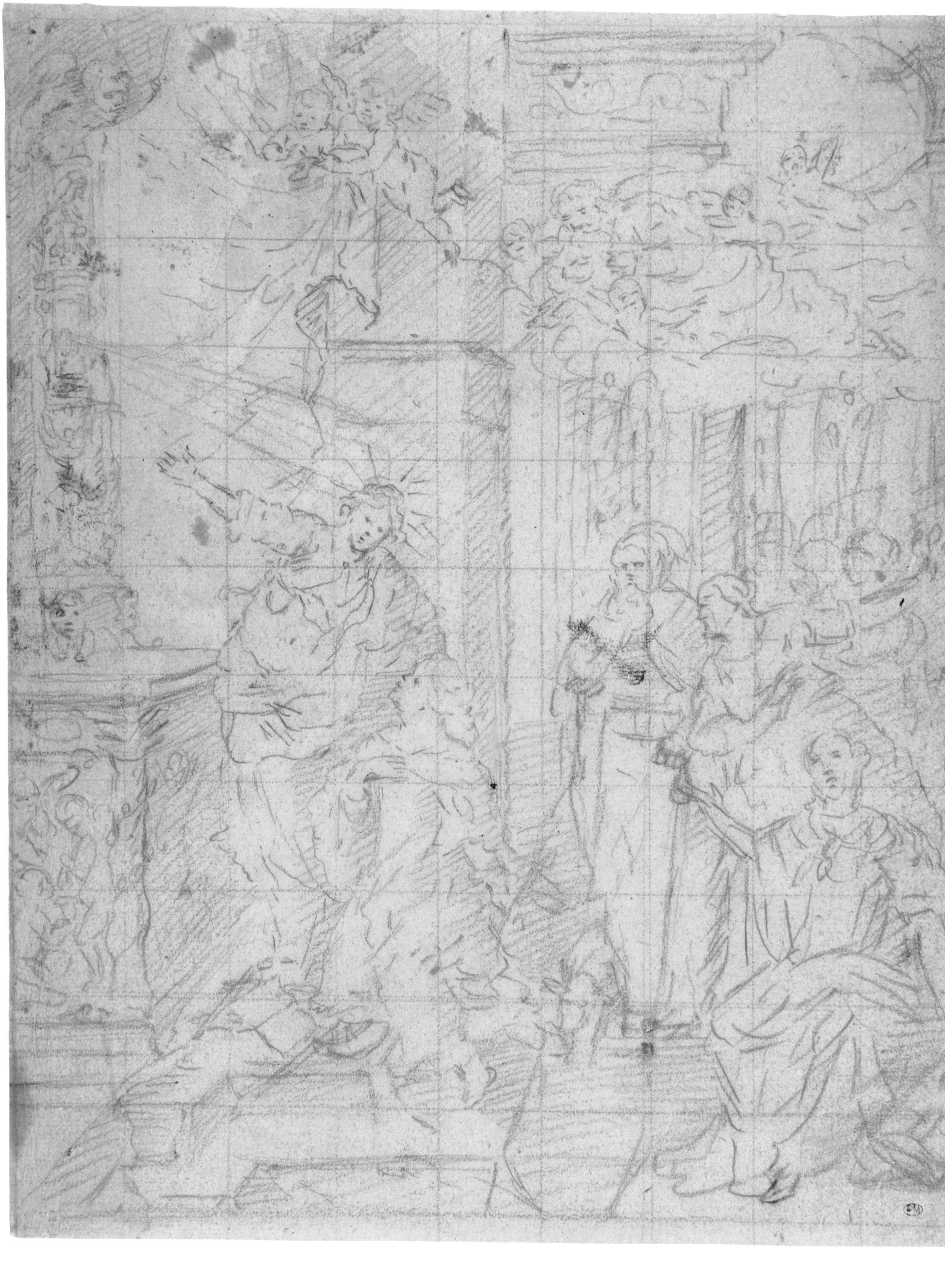

UNKNOWN ARTIST, SPANISH SCHOOL

last third of the 17th century

77. *Vision of Female Saint Kneeling Before Altar (Saint Claire's Conversion?)*

Verso: *Sketch of Half-Length Figure of Christ Crowned with Thorns*

Red chalk on tan laid paper, squared in red chalk; verso: red chalk

24.2 x 19.2 cm. (9⁹⁄₁₆ x 7⁹⁄₁₆ in.)

PROVENANCE: Mathias Polakovits, Paris and New York, stamp (Lugt 3561) recto, lower right, in black

REFERENCE: Princeton 2003, 116, as "Spanish, Anonymous, 17th century"

Museum purchase, Laura P. Hall Memorial Fund and Fowler McCormick, Class of 1921, Fund 2002-113

The subject of this drawing, like its authorship, is unclear. The scene might represent the conversion of Saint Claire. The daughter of a nobleman who heard Saint Francis preaching one Palm Sunday, Claire later experienced a vision of the risen Christ with the wounds inflicted by Longinus. Her younger sister, who followed Saint Claire into religious life, appears to be represented at the lower right of the scene, also dressed as a noblewoman and pointing to the conversion of Claire, represented at the left. A hooded figure, perhaps Saint Francis,[1] stands in the middle background. Above his head, God the Father appears in clouds, with cherubim, at the upper right. The sketch's architectural details suggest the interior of the church and the altar where the scene took place. The carved altar frontal, perhaps decorated with figures of the Baptism, can be seen at the left side of the sheet.

The sketch is detailed and squared for transfer, suggesting that a painting was made from this initial idea. The composition and the dress of the two female figures suggest a date in the last third of the seventeenth century, based on comparison with the dress depicted in court portraits of the period. LAB

1 According to Saint Claire's hagiography, Saint Francis was present at her conversion.

Verso cat. 77

UNKNOWN ARTIST, MADRID SCHOOL

late 17th century

78. *Figure Seated, Holding Staff*

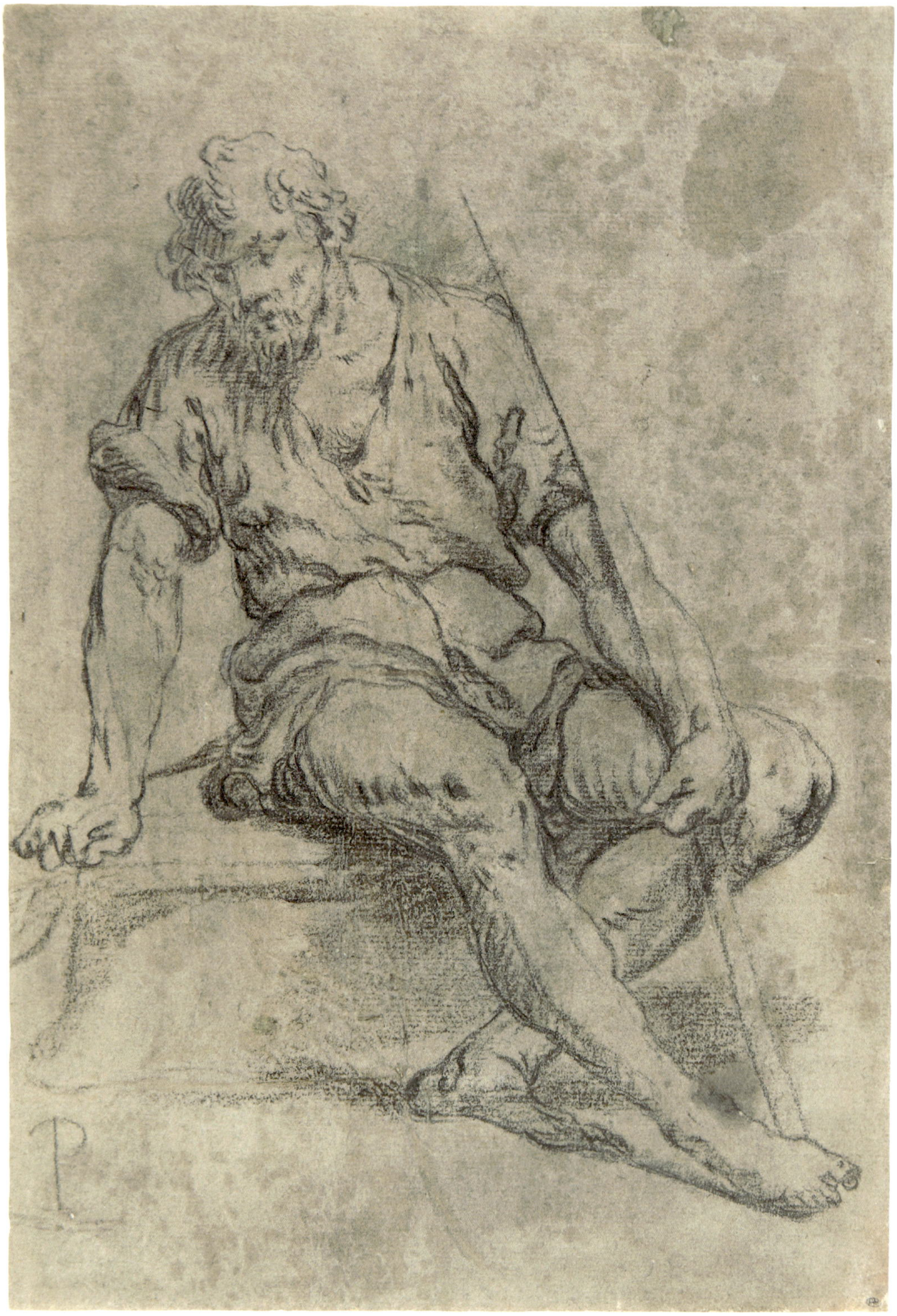

Black chalk on beige laid paper prepared with transparent gray watercolor wash

34.2 x 23.8 cm. ($13\frac{7}{16}$ x $9\frac{5}{16}$ in.)

Inscribed in black chalk, lower right: *P*

PROVENANCE: Mathias Polakovits, Paris and New York, stamp (Lugt 3561) recto, lower right, in black

REFERENCE: Princeton 2003, 116

Museum purchase, Laura P. Hall Memorial Fund and Fowler McCormick, Class of 1921, Fund 2002-115

This drawing represents a man, perhaps a shepherd, seated and resting, holding a staff. A large P of unknown meaning appears at lower left in the same black chalk as the drawing, suggesting that it could be an artist's monogram. The preparation of the sheet suggests that the draftsman wanted the effects given by a smooth gray gouache ground surface in contrast to the rough quality of the black chalk. Princeton's drawing of a posed figure and large monogram might be a student effort executed in an academy. LAB

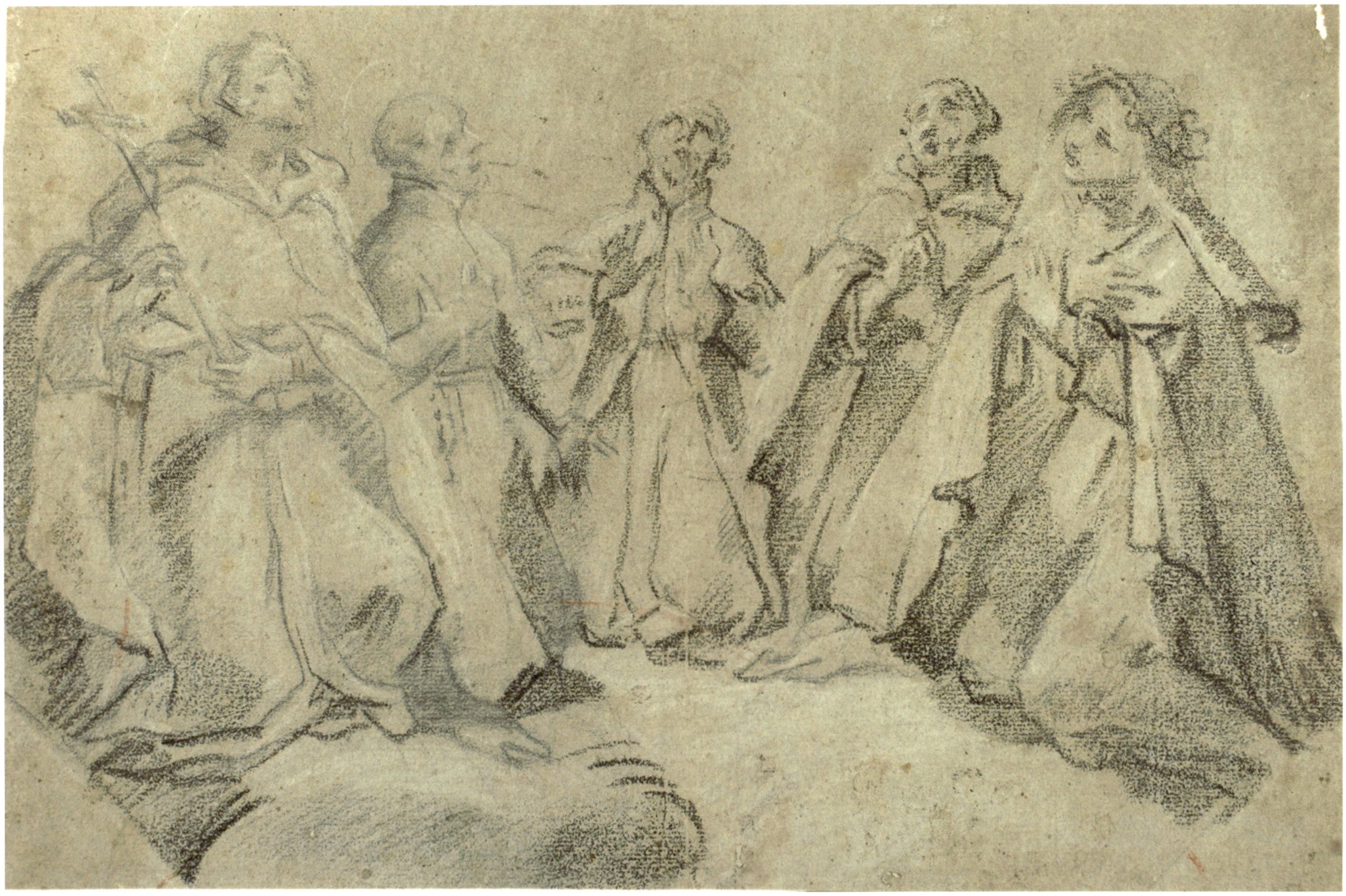

UNKNOWN ARTIST,
MADRID SCHOOL

late 17th century

79. *Five Kneeling Saints*

Black chalk on blue laid paper, lined

25.1 x 38.9 cm. (9 7/8 x 15 5/16 in.)

Watermark: Fleur-de-lis in circle

Provenance: Frank Jewett Mather Jr.

Gift of Frank Jewett Mather Jr.
x1976-77

Five Saints—Saint Ignatius of Loyola, Saint Teresa of Ávila, Saint Francis Xavier, Saint Philip Neri, and Saint Isidore, patron saint of Madrid—kneel and look heavenward. The five saints were canonized together in 1622 and were depicted together frequently in altarpieces, especially those for Jesuit churches; in the lower register of a painting of *Five Saints Adoring the Trinity*; or in Assumption of the Virgin pictures divided into heavenly and earthly registers. The suggestion of an angle at the left and right sides of this drawing, however, could also suggest that the composition was intended for a spandrel supporting a ceiling painting.

Saint Teresa of Ávila, the only female in the group, appears at the right. She is crowned with thorns on top of her wimple, a reference to her devotion to the image of Christ Crowned with Thorns, as described in her autobiography. The stiff and heavy depiction of the drapery on the kneeling figures is

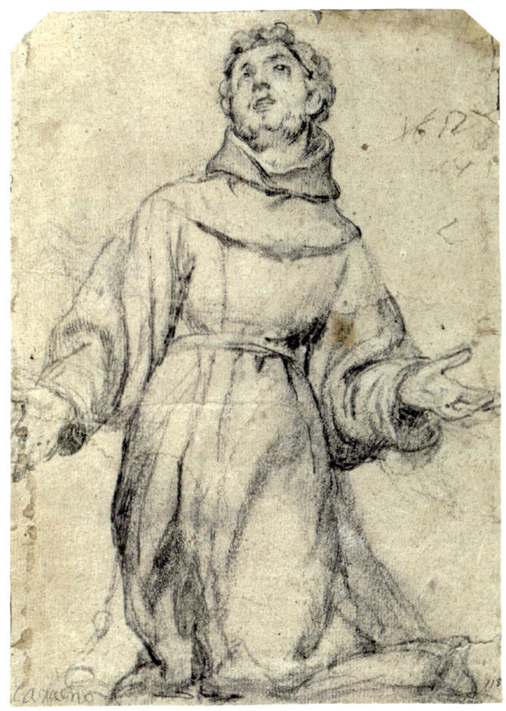

Fig. 79.1 Juan Carreño de Miranda, Spanish, 1614–1685: *Kneeling Saint Francis*. 25 x 18.4 cm. Museo Nacional del Prado, Madrid (D02127).

emphasized with strong, descending strokes and quick horizontal hatching to form shadows. The absence of defining attributes for Saint Ignatius (IHS), or Saint Isidore (a plow), for example, suggests a rough first sketch or a quick copy to remember an existing painting.

The artist seems to be familiar with Juan Carreño de Miranda's working method, using the broad side of the black chalk to make large strokes and the point to define details. The sheet lacks the finesse and subtlety that define Carreño's drawings, however (fig. 79.1). The blunt understanding of volume in Princeton's drawing instead seems informed by a loose and confident manner of sweeping the chalk across the sheet to suggest bodies underneath drapery, creating a summary of forms while leaving details undefined. LAB

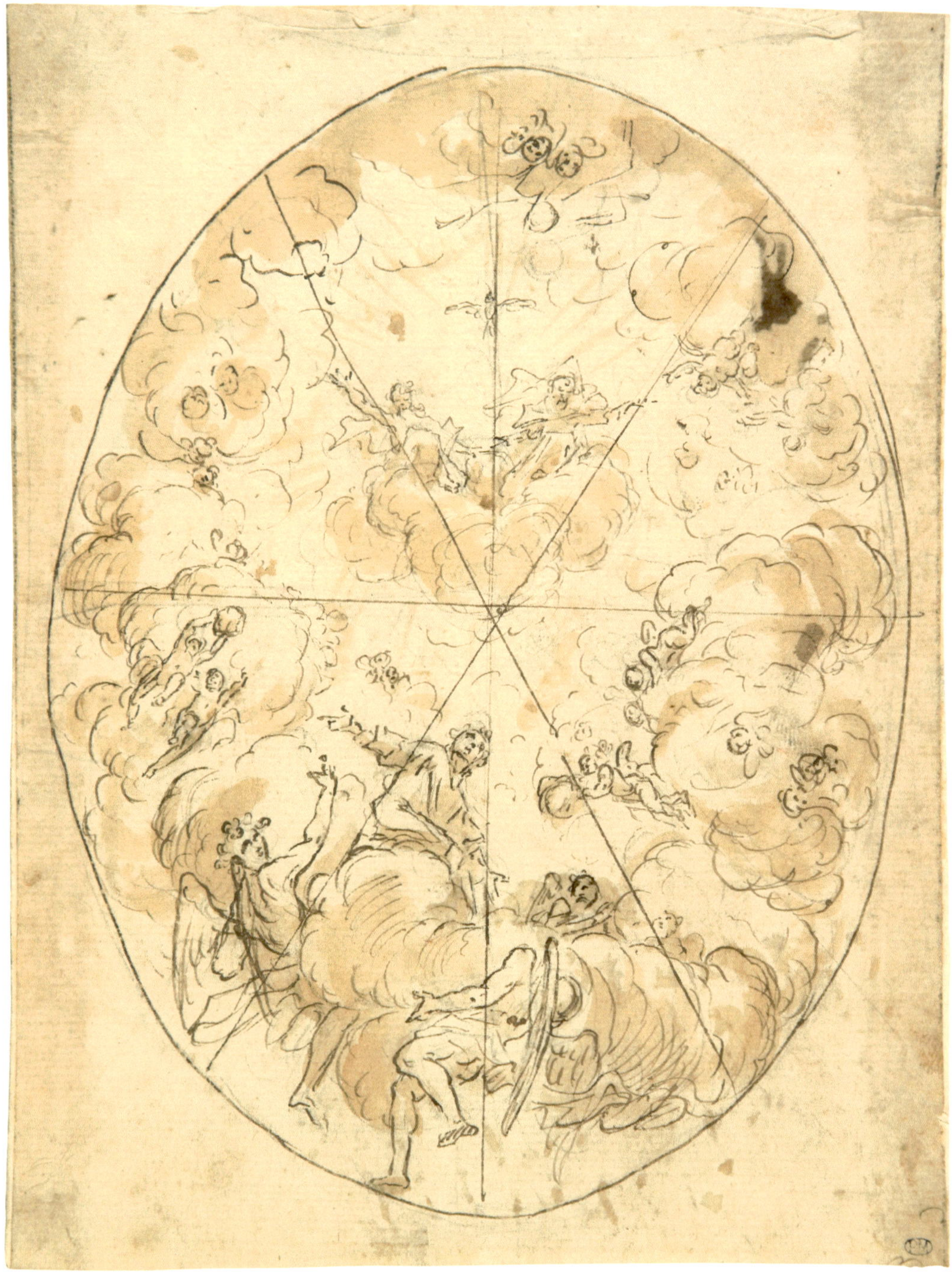

UNKNOWN ARTIST, MADRID SCHOOL

late 17th century–early 18th century

80. *Ascension of a Saint*

Pen and brown ink with brush and brown wash, over traces of graphite, on light tan laid paper, edge mounted to light tan laid paper

18.1 x 13.7 cm. (7⅛ x 5⅜ in.)

Inscribed in red chalk on verso, upper center: *G740*; lower right: *10-* and *48*

PROVENANCE: Mathias Polakovits, Paris and New York, stamp (Lugt 3561) recto, lower right, in black

EXHIBITIONS: Princeton 1995; Princeton 1997

Museum purchase, Laura P. Hall Memorial Fund and Fowler McCormick, Class of 1921, Fund 2002-105

A quick first sketch for a ceiling painting of the ascension of a saint, perhaps Saint Francis, this work features an oval composition first drawn in black chalk and later gone over with pen and ink and light wash. The schematic nature of the drawing and the indistinct figures make it difficult to ascertain which saint is depicted. However, the division of the oval with additional lines suggests that it might have been painted into an oval recession or dome (if indeed it was executed). The Trinity is visible at the middle of the top half of the oval, and the outstretched arm of Christ is echoed by the rising saint below, seated on a cloud held by two seraphim. Because many important Madrid school commissions of the second half of the seventeenth century are now destroyed and known only through descriptions—and because so few details in this drawing are suggestive of a specific saint's iconography—further study is needed.

Numbering in red crayon on the verso of the secondary support of this drawing, "G 740," is possibly the lot number from an auction house sale. Such crayon numbering was typically used in Parisian auction houses, although no such records were acquired with the drawing from the Polakovits collection. LAB

UNKNOWN ARTIST, PORTUGUESE?

late 17th–early 18th century

81. *Cadmus Killing the Dragon*

Verso: *Sketches of Saint Peter and Male Saint*

Red chalk on light tan laid paper; verso: pen and brown ink

24 x 18 cm. (9⁷⁄₁₆ x 7¹⁄₁₆ in.)

PROVENANCE: Mathias Polakovits, Paris and New York, stamp (Lugt 3561) recto, lower right, in black

Museum purchase, Laura P. Hall Memorial Fund and Fowler McCormick, Class of 1921, Fund 2002-110

The strong red chalk drawing on the recto of this sheet likely illustrates a scene from the Greek myth of Cadmus killing the dragon. The King of Phoenicia, Agenor, sent his son Cadmus to find his daughter Europa, who had been abducted by Zeus. The Oracle of Delphi instructed Cadmus to abandon the quest and instead to found a city. The site of that city, which was later known as Thebes, would be determined by the location where a cow collapsed in exhaustion. On that site Cadmus made a sacrifice to Athena and sent his followers to retrieve water from the nearby sacred spring of Dirce, which was guarded by a dragon, beloved of the god Ares. The dragon ate all of Cadmus's men, and in killing the creature Cadmus was protected by Athena, whose shield, with the gorgon's head at center, appears in the hand of Cadmus at the left of Princeton's drawing.

The artist of the sheet might be from the circle of the Portuguese draftsman Francisco Vieira, known as Vieira Lusitano (1699–1783), whose distinctive red chalk style was similar to that in this sheet. Vieira's demonstrated affinity for Roman, rather than Greek, mythological subjects and his confident red chalk drawing technique are no less interesting than "the spectacular drama of Vieira's private life."[1] His pupils included the artist biographer Cyrillo Volkmar Machado (1748–1823), whose own red chalk drawings demonstrate accomplished neoclassical drawing technique. The artist of this sheet was well versed in Greek mythology and had trained in an academy, perhaps in Rome.

In Princeton's drawing, Cadmus holds Athena's shield in his left hand as he raises his right to kill the serpent that winds around his foot at the base of the tree. His curved sword might be taken for a Phoenician curved-blade scimitar or short-sword. Wisps of curly hair fly out behind his head, and drapery loosely falls behind him and discreetly across his loins. The oak tree, symbolized by loopy leaves dripping from branches, stands at the visual border of the composition, on the right. Stylized treatment of leaves and trees is found in the drawings of Spanish artist Antonio del Castillo (1616–1668), an attribution that was rejected by Priscilla Muller.[2]

A drawing of two standing saints on the verso is likely by the same hand but in a different medium. The pen and ink sketches bleed through to the front of the sheet where the red chalk sketch does not hide them, implying that the pen and ink sketches were made after the red chalk drawing was discarded, perhaps by the same artist who made the drawing of Cadmus. One of the two saints dangles keys and must be Peter; the other, speaking and walking forward with his hand raised and without other attributes, may be Paul, who is often paired with Peter. The use of the sheet to doodle the two small saints might seem at odds with the highly finished red chalk study on the recto, but it is not uncommon to see sheets reused by an artist for another purpose. LAB

1 Nicholas Turner, "New Light on Vieira Lusitano as a Draftsman," *Master Drawings* 45, no. 3 (2007): 367–86.

2 Conversation with the author in May 2007.

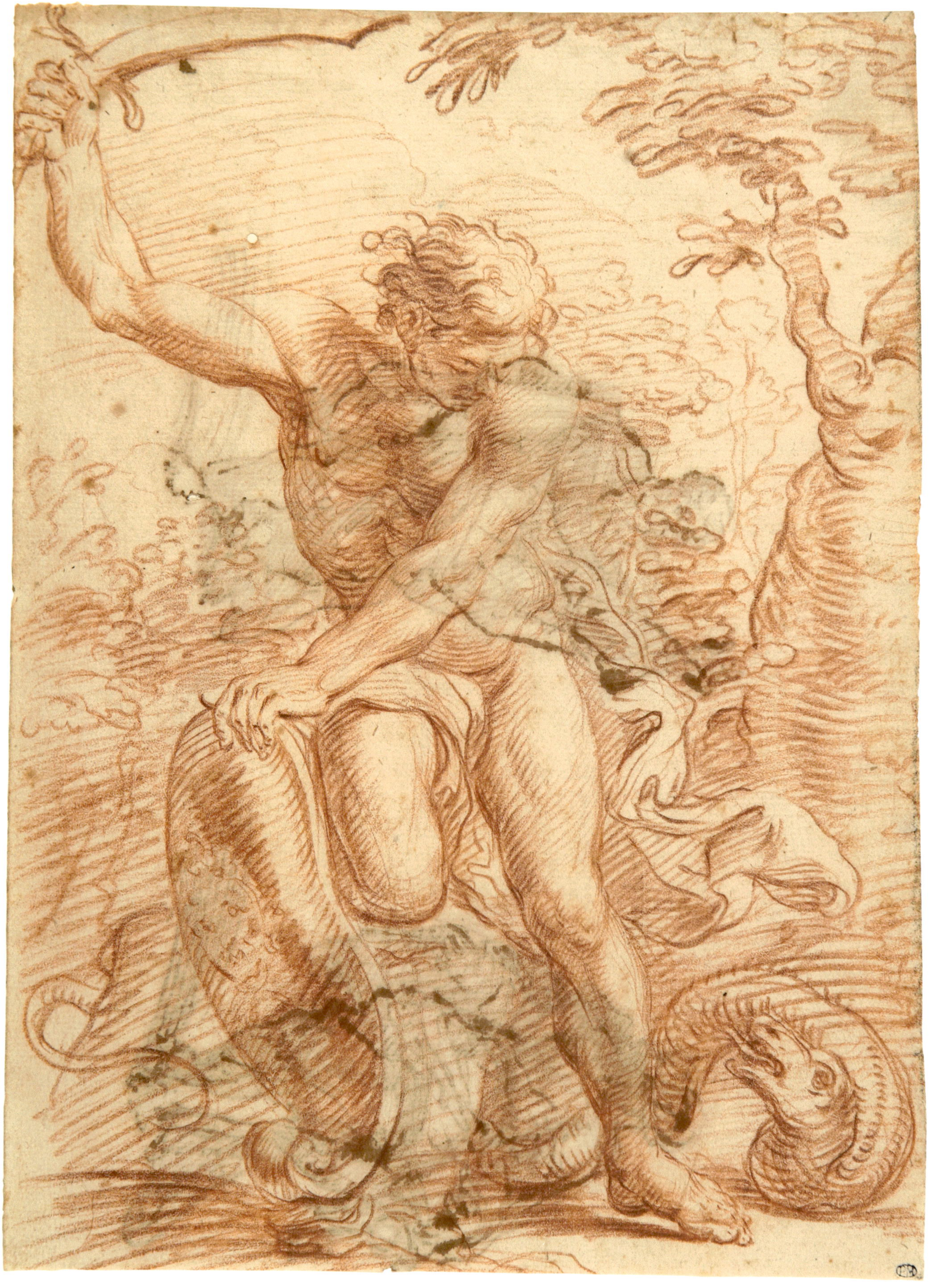

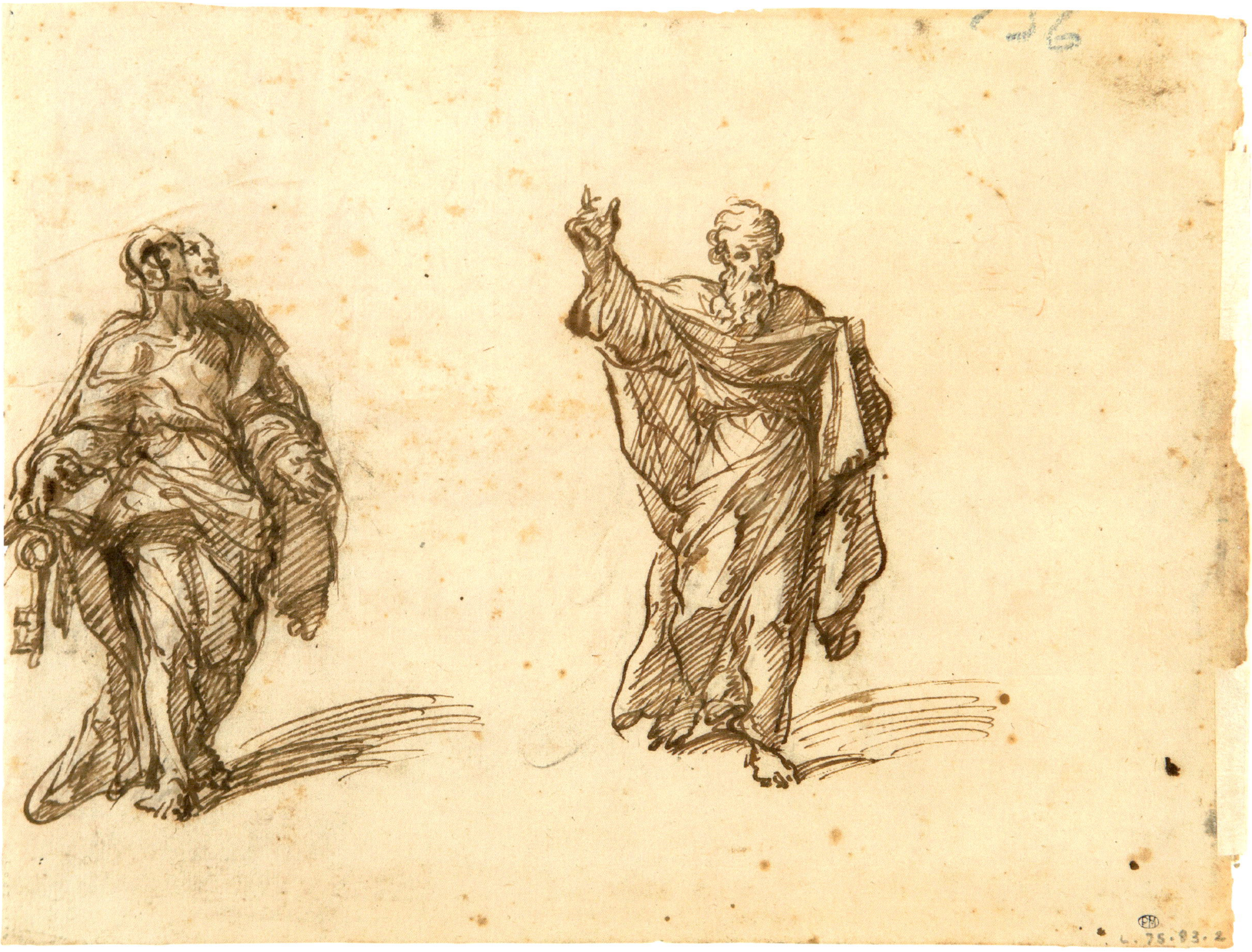

Verso cat. 81

UNKNOWN ARTIST, MADRID SCHOOL?

late 17th–early 18th century?

82. *Annunciation and Partial Sketch of Figure*

Pen and brown ink with brush and brown wash over graphite on light tan laid paper, lined

11.0 x 21.5 cm. ($4\frac{5}{16}$ x $8\frac{7}{16}$ in.)

Provenance: Ludwig Zatzka, Vienna (Lugt 2672); Mathias Polakovits, Paris and New York (Lugt 3561), no stamp

Reference: Princeton 2003, 118, as "Circle of Sebastián de Herrera Barnuevo"

Exhibition: Princeton 2001

Museum purchase, Laura P. Hall Memorial Fund and Fowler McCormick, Class of 1921, Fund 2002-81

The artist of this unusual combination of finished and unfinished sketches used a compass to draw circles around the figure groups. The roundel at left features a graphite sketch of Christ Ecce Homo; at right is a more finished sketch of the Virgin and the angel Gabriel, with the dove of the Holy Spirit above, in graphite reinforced with pen and ink and wash. The top of a third roundel is visible at the lower center of the sheet. The sketches might have been intended for paintings to be inset at the top left and right sides of an altarpiece.

The angel Gabriel holds a lily and touches his other hand to his breast as he bends his head. The brown ink and wash technique used in this sheet resembles that of Madrid School painters of the mid-century, but the use of ink wash was a pan-European drawing technique especially in the late seventeenth and early eighteenth centuries. An attribution to the circle of painter and sculptor Sebastián de Herrera Barnuevo (1619–1671) was once suggested, but this drawing lacks the specificity and definition found in his drawings.

The finely modeled features of the faces in Herrera Barnuevo's wash sketches are completely lacking in the Princeton sheet, as are that artist's careful shaping of fingers and arms. A sketch for *A Female Personification of Abundance* (see fig. 14.2) is a perfect example of Herrera Barnuevo's controlled and delicate use of wash as well as his reliance on variation in the tone and thickness of his lines. The loose application of wash on the figure of Gabriel and along the side of the Virgin's face offers a distinct contrast to the careful and controlled manner in which Herrera Barnuevo applied wash to his figures, removing the possibility of such an attribution.

This particular drawing once belonged to Viennese architect Ludwig Zatzka (1857–1925), whose collection was described in 1916 by Leo Planiscig and largely consisted of Dutch, Flemish, German, and Austrian drawings acquired in Viennese sales between 1870 and 1890 and dispersed in several sales after his death.[1] Zatzka's collection also included the eighteenth-century collection of Italian Count Gianazei, acquired over a number of years at sales in Udine, with additional sheets from the Baron Adalbert Freiherr von Lanna collection (Lugt 2672; Lugt 2773), largely consisting of German, Dutch, Italian, and Austrian drawings. LAB

1 Leo Planiscig, *Der Cicerone* 8 (1916): 343. Lugt Supplément, 2672. Sales at Paris (expert Max Bine), June 19, 1925, drawings; also less important drawings at Vienna, Nov. 8–9, 1926 (expert Leo Schidlof).

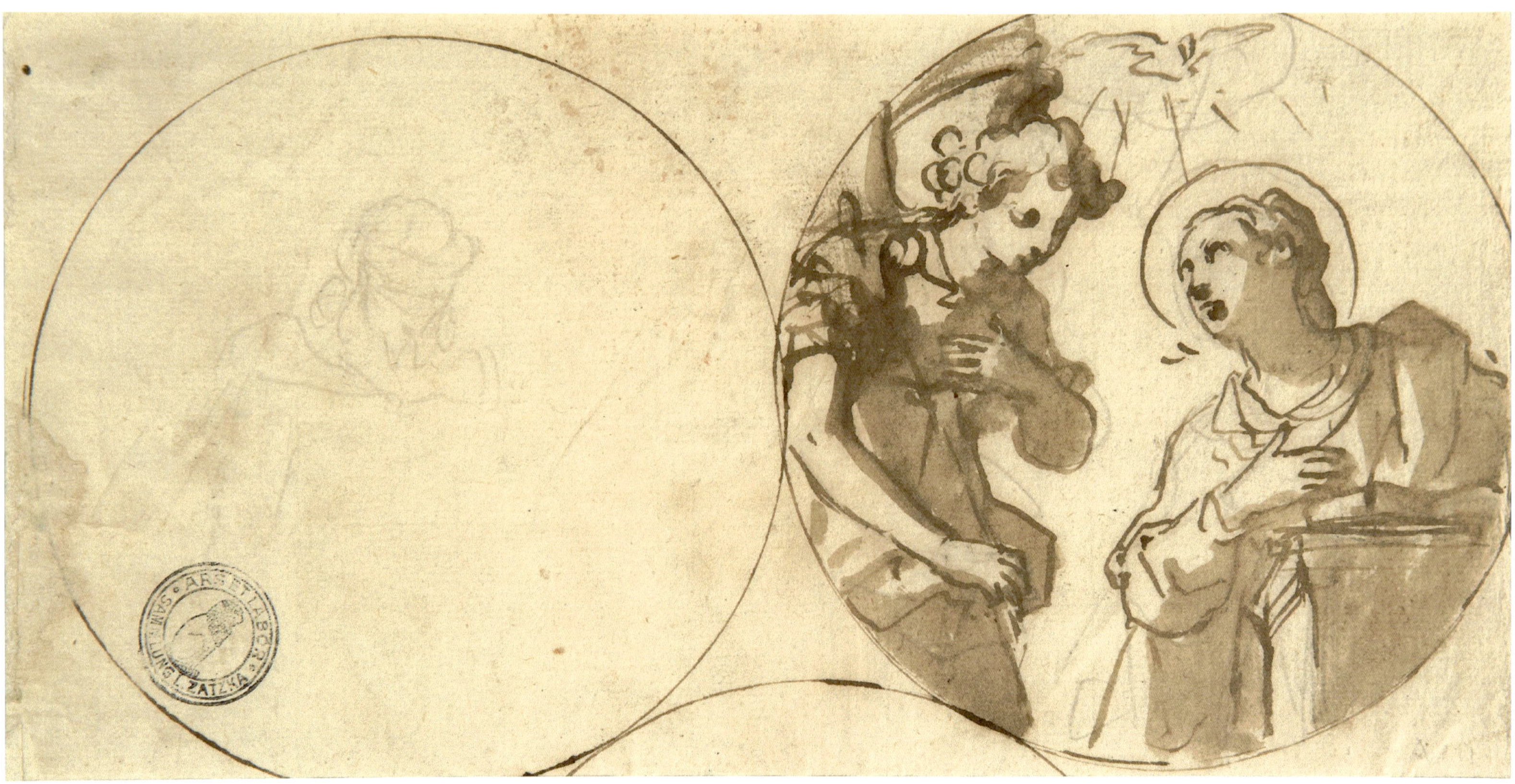

UNKNOWN ARTIST, SPANISH?

18th century?

83. *Saint Anthony of Padua Holding a Lily*

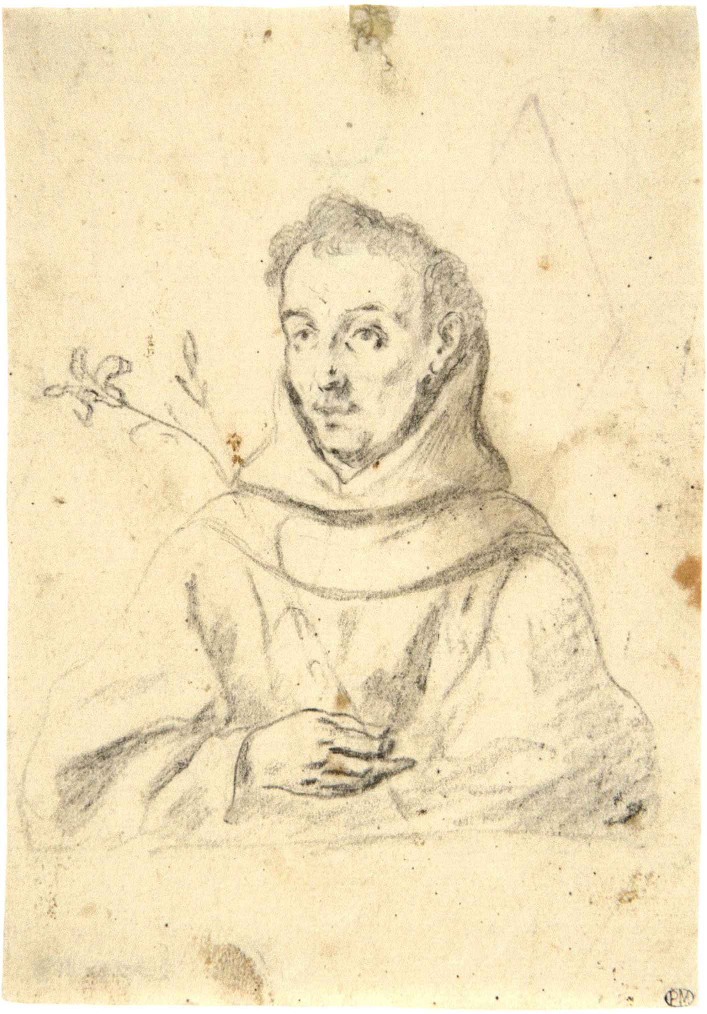

Black chalk on beige laid paper

13.5 x 9.8 cm. (5 5/16 x 3 7/8 in.)

Inscribed on verso, in graphite: *20426*; in pen and brown ink: *144 or L14*

Watermark: Boot in circle. [The watermark in this sheet, a boot in a circle, suggests the paper may be Genoese. See Churchill 551 (18th c. Genoese).]

Provenance: Private collection, Rome; Mathias Polakovits, Paris and New York, stamp (Lugt 3561) recto, lower right, in black

Museum purchase, Laura P. Hall Memorial Fund and Fowler McCormick, Class of 1921, Fund 2002-117

Saint Anthony of Padua gazes serenely to the left, holding the stem of a lily in his proper right hand. Most often in the seventeenth century, Saint Anthony of Padua was shown holding the Christ child, but in this case he holds the lily to indicate his purity, a more symbolic representation of the saint.

A purple stamp from the Ufficio Esportazione Artistica Roma indicates that this drawing was given an export permit to leave Italy, implying that it was in an Italian collection prior to its acquisition by Mathias Polakovits. The inscription on the verso, in pen and brown ink, evaluating the drawing at fourteen *lire*, also suggests an Italian provenance. A Spanish drawing by Vicente Carducho, *The Lion Hunt*, has the same export stamp.[1]

The blackening of the pupils of Saint Anthony's eyes in the Princeton drawing was done using a sharpened point, in a technique that draws attention to the widespread eyes and the delicacy of the other facial features. LAB

1 Carducho's *The Lion Hunt* was sold at Sotheby's in July 1976 and was acquired by the National Gallery in 1977. This drawing does not appear among the Spanish drawings in that sale, however, so it is unclear where Polakovits may have acquired it, or whether it was exported from Rome in the 1970s as well.

UNKNOWN ARTIST, MADRID SCHOOL

mid-18th century

84. *Seated Virgin with Angels*

Black chalk heightened with white gouache, on tan laid paper prepared with gray ground

25.1 x 18.7 cm. (9⅞ x 7⅜ in.)

Inscribed on verso in graphite, center: *7 dibujos*; at upper left corner on verso in black chalk: *1852*; in pen and brown ink and again in pen and brown ink: *3*; in pen and brown ink: *53*; in black chalk: *No 14*

Provenance: Mathias Polakovits, Paris and New York, stamp (Lugt 3561) recto, lower right, in black

Museum purchase, Laura P. Hall Memorial Fund and Fowler McCormick, Class of 1921, Fund 2002-119

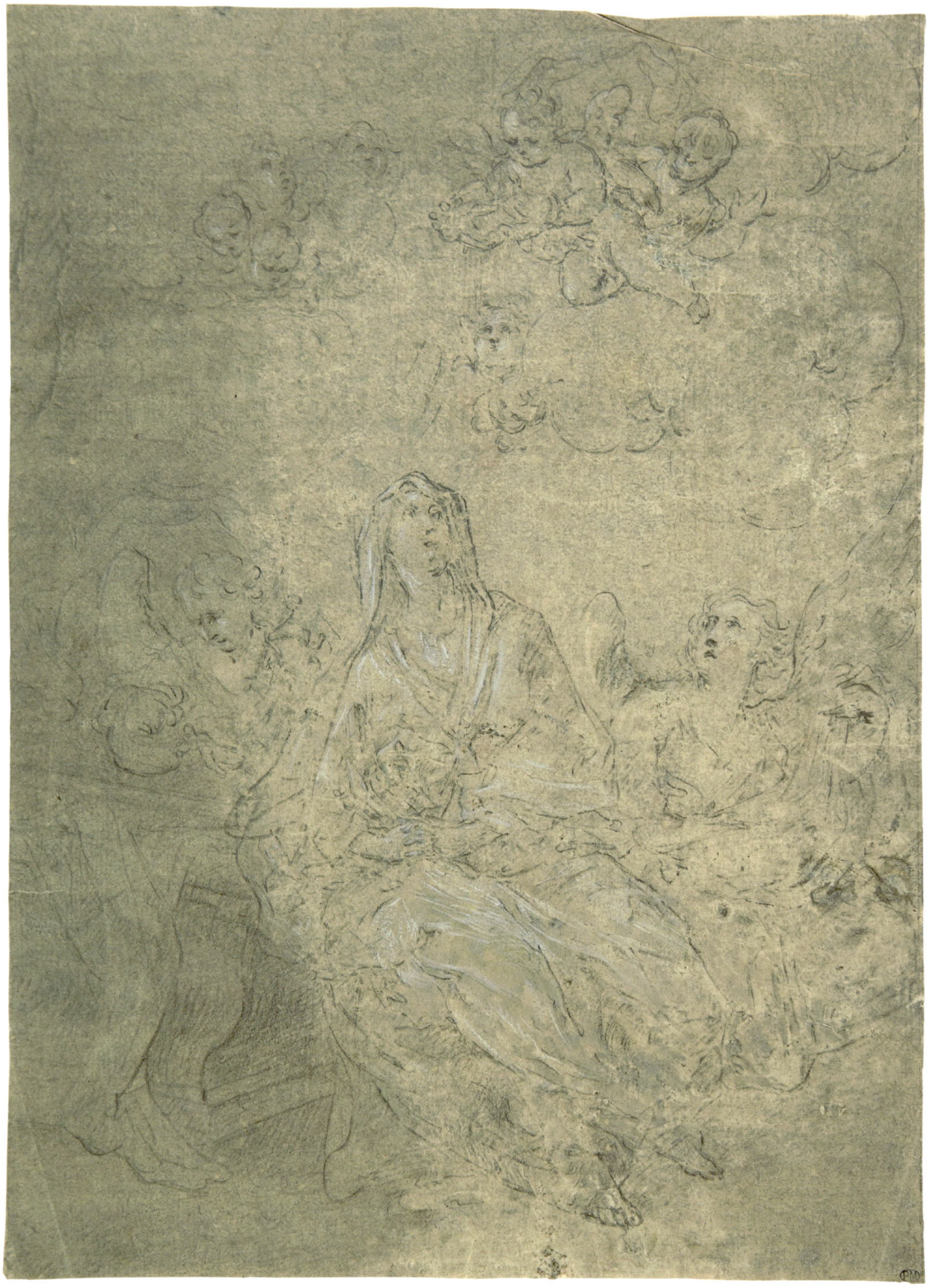

The graceful Virgin twists slightly and looks to the cloud appearing above her, with faces of cherubs along its lower edge. Although the drawing has suffered some rubbing—revealing a lighter colored beige paper under the preparation layer of gray wash, especially around the head of the Virgin—its delicacy remains. Faintly rendered in black chalk, angels on either side of the central figure gesture toward her. Her skirt and veil have been touched with white gouache highlighting, applied with point of brush. This sophisticated technique, and the delicacy of the figures, suggests an artist with academic training, working at court, who was aware of Corrado Giaquinto's (1703–1766) allegorical paintings for the royal palace, in which angels in such poses support cloud-borne figures.

The artist of Princeton's drawing used the delicate figure types with long limbs that Giaquinto taught to his pupils. Such artists as Zacarías González Velázquez (1763–1834) adapted this technique, using prepared papers with black and white chalk drawing, especially on a series of preparatory drawings he made for the commission at San Francisco el Grande.

An inscription on the verso, "7 dibujos," implies that this sheet was once part of a group of seven drawings, which may one day shed light on its original provenance or attribution. Additional numbers on the verso in a variety of media—"No 14," "53," "1852," and "3"—probably indicate lot numbers annotated when the drawing was sold at auction. LAB

UNKNOWN PORTUGUESE ARTIST (CARV.º NEGREIROS?)

active 1770

85. *Head and Torso of Man*, 1770

Black chalk on beige laid paper, inlaid in heavy light tan wove card

19.7 x 27 cm. (7¾ x 10⅝ in.)

Inscribed in pen and brown ink, upper left: *di Carv.º Negreiros, 20º iiº, 1770*

Watermark: vertical orientation parallel with the chain lines, 6.5 cm in height: Crowned shield with letters: "F G" over "G L" (see appendix)

Provenance: Joseph F. McCrindle, New York and Princeton

Gift of the Joseph F. McCrindle Foundation
2009-51

This drawing—by an artist with the Portuguese surname Negreiros (which is visible in the annotation at the upper left in an abbreviated form of Cavaliero Negreiros)—appears to be a student work, perhaps executed while the artist was studying in Rome in 1770; the date annotated at the top of the drawing seems to be October 2, 1770. Although we know of Portuguese artists with the surname Negreiros—including Manuel da Costa Negreiros (1701–1750), artist and architect for King João V—the Portuguese chronicler Cyrillo Volkmar Machado (1748–1823) does not mention an artist with the surname Negreiros active in 1770 in his *Collecção de memorias relativas ás vidas dos pintores, e escultores, architetos e gravadores portuguezes, e dos estrangeiros, que estiverão em Portugal.*[1]

In the eighteenth century many Portuguese artists began their studies at the academy in Lisbon and continued, with the king's patronage, at various academies in Rome. For example, a Portuguese artist who was in Rome slightly later, Domingos António Sequeira (1768–1837), studied in Rome with Antonio Cavalucci (1752–1795) on a pension from the Portuguese royal academy; he distinguished himself through his study there such that in 1794 he was made a member of the Academia de San Luca. Sequeira, who taught at least one Brazilian studio assistant who later studied in Lisbon, also created connections to the New World. The surname of the artist who made Princeton's drawing, "Negreiros," might also be that of an unknown Brazilian artist working in such circumstances in Rome.

LAB

1 See entry on "José da Costa Negreiros," in Cyrillo Volkmar Machado, *Collecção de memorias relativas ás vidas dos pintores, e escultores, architetos e gravadores portuguezes, e dos estrangeiros, que estiverão em Portugal* (Coimbra: Imprensa da Universidade, 1922), 89–90.

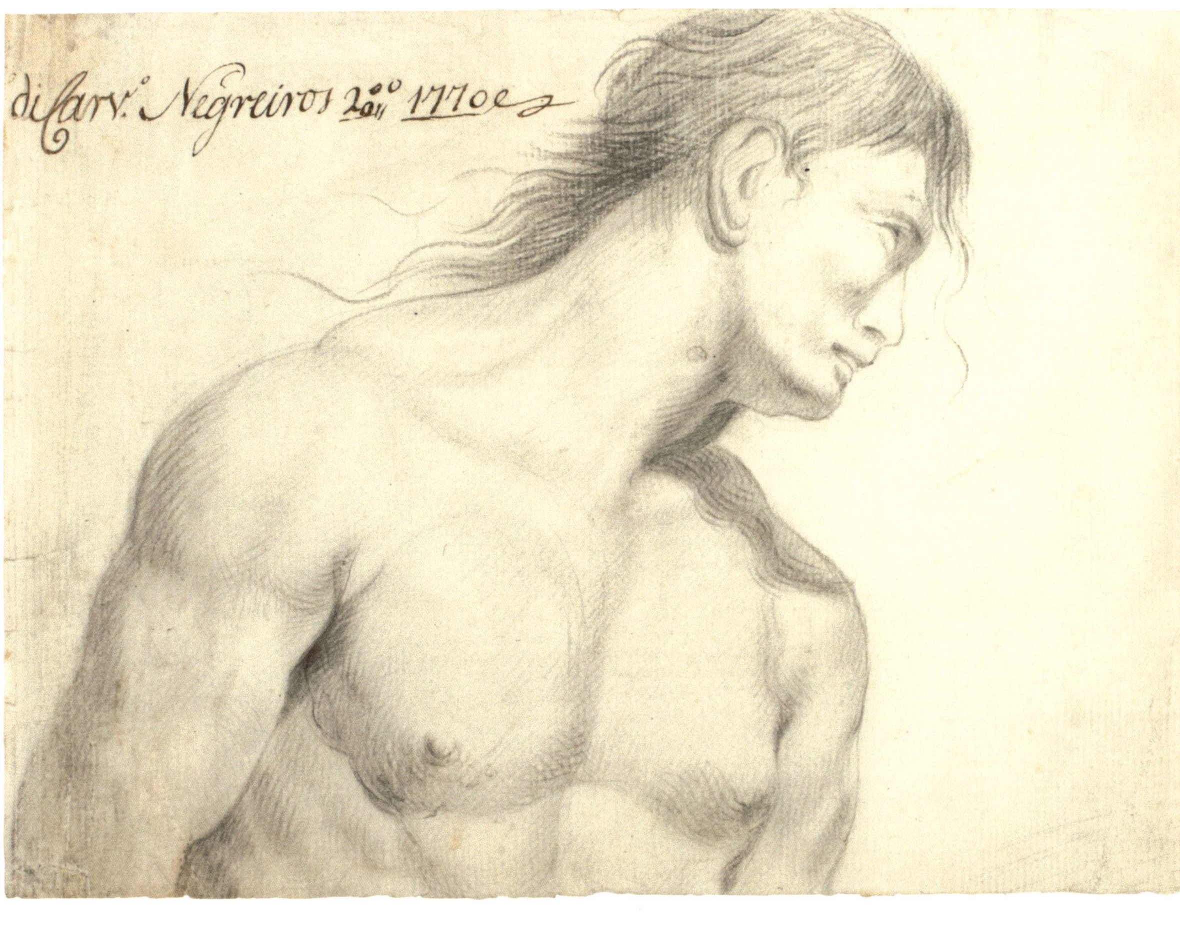

UNKNOWN ARTIST, MADRID SCHOOL

late 18th–early 19th century

86. *Battle between Greeks and Trojans*

Black chalk (or charcoal), heightened with white, on heavy gray-brown laid paper, lined

34.5 x 52.2 cm. (13 9/16 x 20 9/16 in.)

PROVENANCE: Mathias Polakovits, Paris and New York, stamp (Lugt 3561) recto, lower right, in black

REFERENCE: Princeton 2003, 116, as "Spanish, Anonymous, 17th century"

Museum purchase, Laura P. Hall Memorial Fund, and Fowler McCormick, Class of 1921, Fund 2002-114

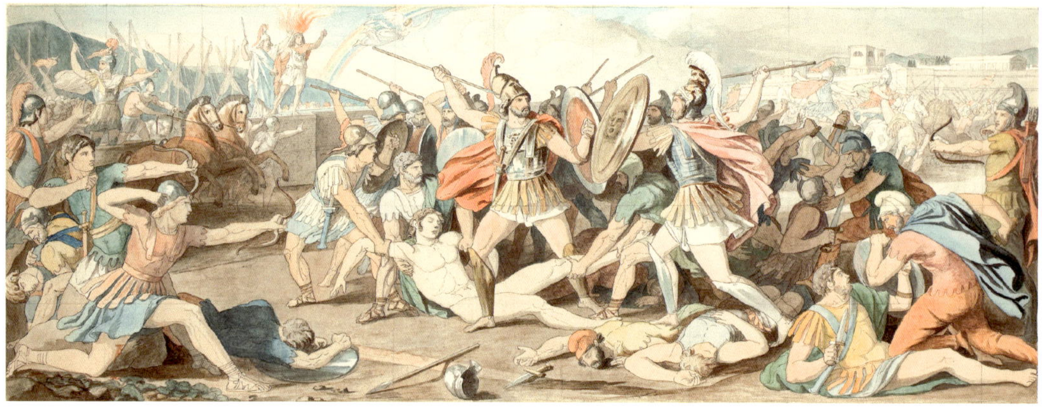

Fig. 86.1 José de Madrazo y Agudo, Spanish, 1781–1859: *Battle between the Greeks and the Trojans,* ca. 1812. 42 x 95 cm. Museo Nacional del Prado, Madrid (D06937).

This drawing depicts a scene from Homer's *Iliad*—retold by the Roman poet Virgil in Book II of the *Aeneid*—of the battle between the Greeks and the Trojans in which Pyrrhus killed Priam. Recently, such scholars as Navarrete Prieto have attributed other drawings depicting Homeric and Virgilian scenes to Juan Carreño de Miranda (1614–1685), based on comparisons with drawings in the Alcubierre Album (Juan Abelló Collection, Madrid).[1] Much more likely, however, the Princeton drawing was made by a student at the Real Academia.

A frequently assigned subject, the battle for the palace served as a source for many Spanish academic competitions of the mid to late eighteenth century.[2] One of the great Spanish interpreters of Homeric themes, José de Madrazo y Agudo (1781–1859) was the director of the Prado from 1838 to 1857. Father to a dynasty of important artists, curators, and dealers, José de Madrazo became interested in classical themes taken from the ancient texts while studying in Paris from 1801 to 1803.[3] Under the patronage of Charles IV and Don Fernando La Serna, ambassador to France, Madrazo entered the studio of Jacques-Louis David and began to focus on neoclassical subjects and themes. José de Madrazo's preparatory drawing of the battle between Greeks and Trojans (fig. 86.1) depicted the sort of multifigured confusion, classical armor, and battling figures found in abundance in his final 1812 painting for the pontifical palace of Monte Cavallo, Quirinal, in Rome, made on the occasion of Napoleon's visit.[4] Upon returning home to Madrid in 1819, Madrazo brought his interest with him, inculcating students with classical literary themes.

Certain unresolved details on Princeton's sheet—the barely indicated legs of the man reclining on the ground at center and the extravagance of the armor—demonstrate that the drawing is student work, possibly unfinished. The greasy black chalk used with white highlighting and the unspecific, awkward anatomy of the figures also suggest the hand of a student sketching an assigned multifigure composition in some haste. One of the tests at the Real Academia was to complete just such an assignment—a complex history subject—in a two-hour time frame. LAB

1 Navarrete Prieto and Pérez Sánchez 2009, 98–99ff.
2 Enrique Arias Anglés y Aurora Gil Serrano, "Temas homéricos en la pintura española del siglo XIX," *Archivo Español de Arte* 75, no. 299 (2002): 237–53.
3 Ibid., p. 238.
4 Ibid. The painting is considered lost and the drawing was only recently rediscovered, having been described in the catalogue of the Sociedad Española de Amigos del Arte en 1913, *Exposición de Pinturas Españolas de la primera mitad del siglo XIX,* reproduced on p. 135. For full discussion of the lost painting, see ibid., 238–39.

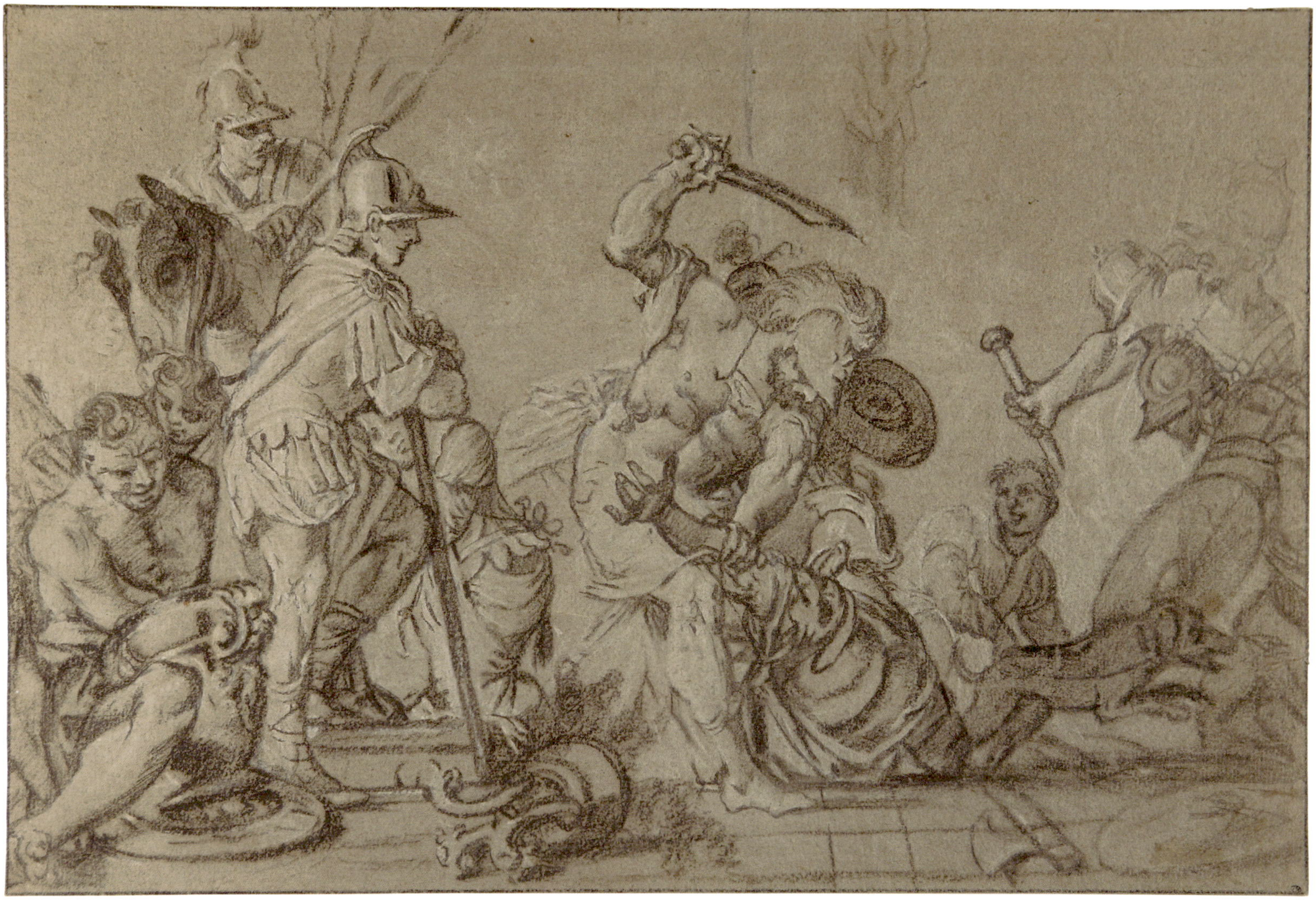

APPENDIX OF WATERMARKS

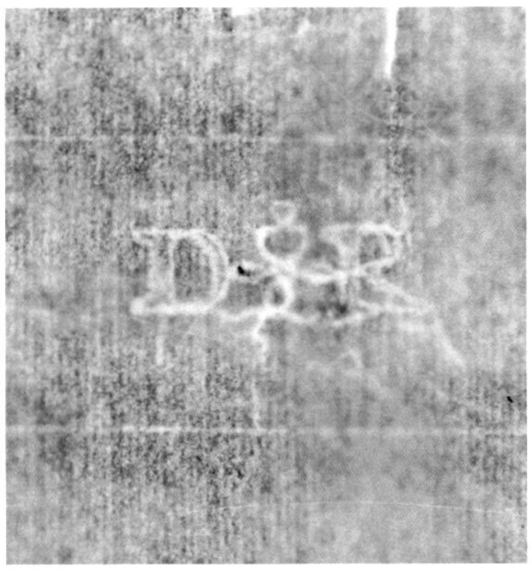

Cat. 2

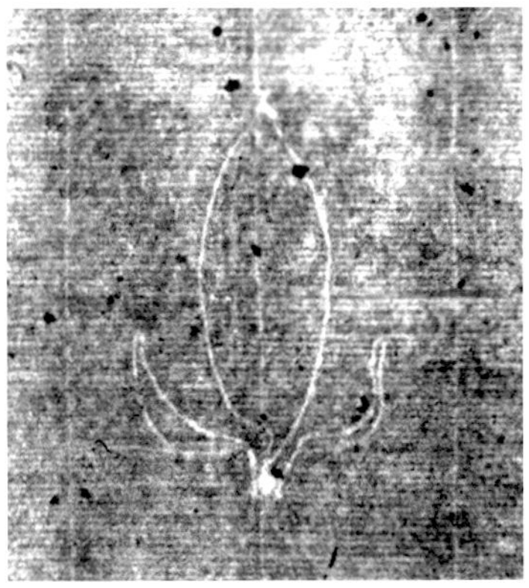

Cat. 14

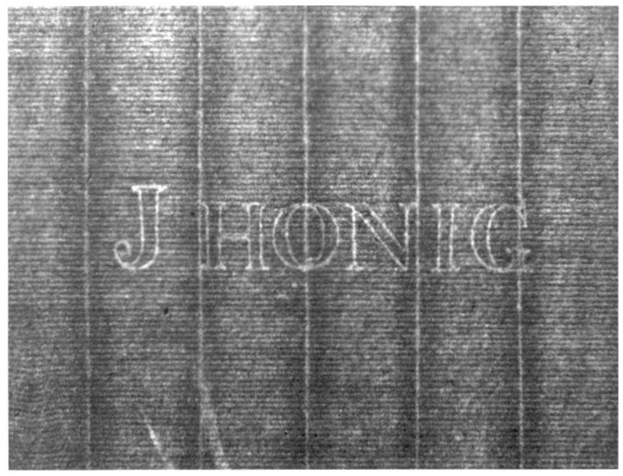

Cat. 23

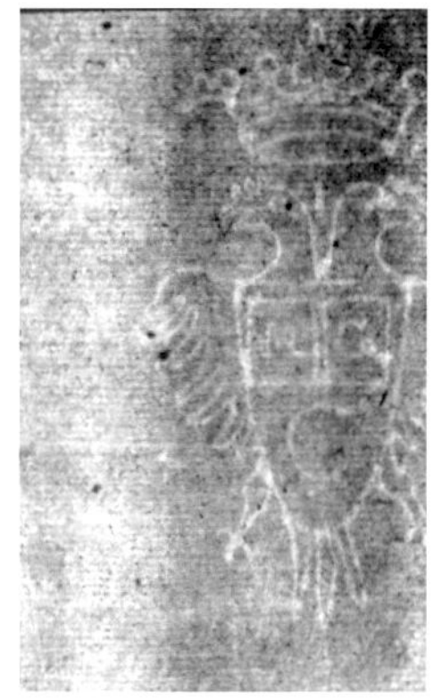

Cat. 30

Cat. 50

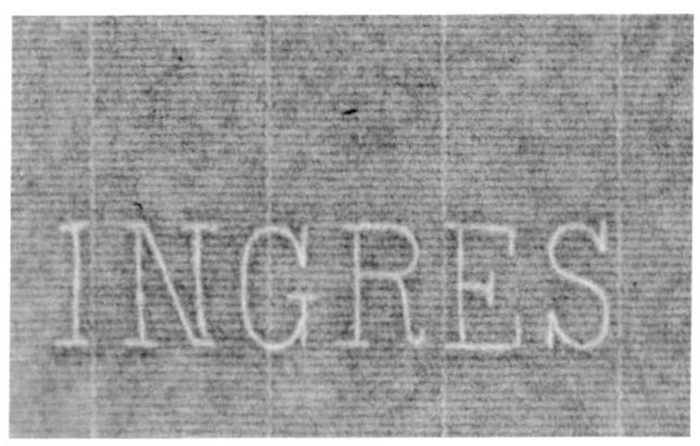

Cat. 55

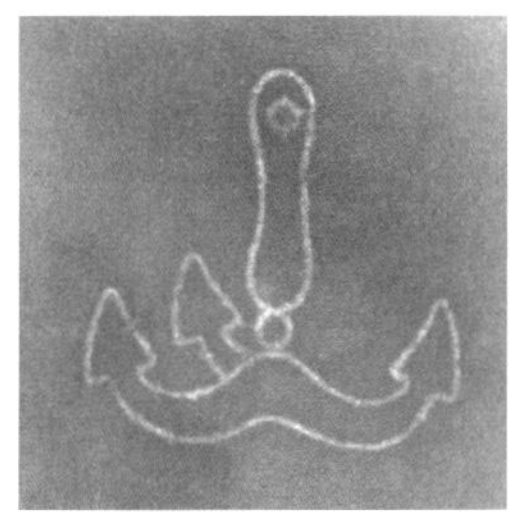

Cat. 57

Cat. 64

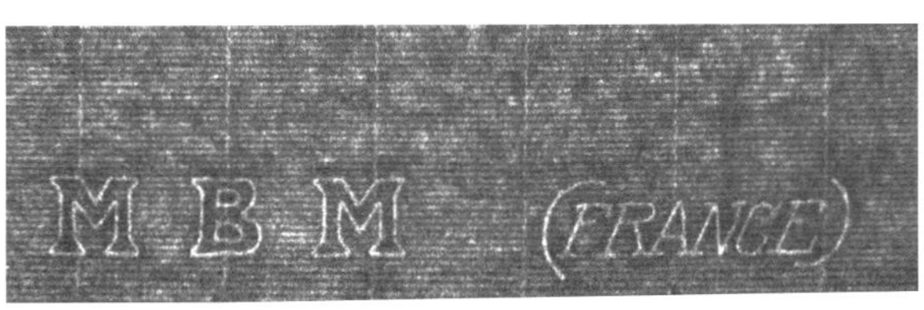

Cat. 64

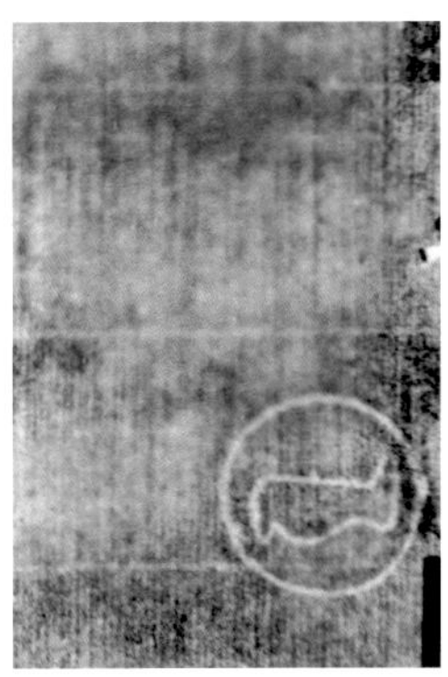

Cat. 83

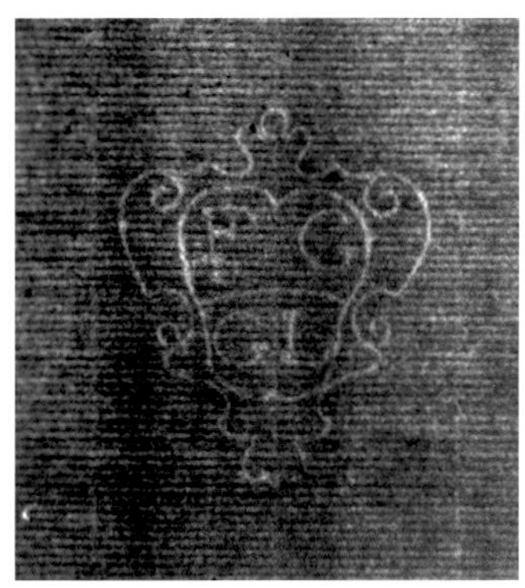

Cat. 85

BIBLIOGRAPHY

Adams and Seilern 1961
Adams, Frederick B., Jr., and Antoine Seilern. *Eleventh Report to the Fellows of the Pierpont Morgan Library, 1961*. New York: Pierpont Morgan Library, 1961.

Aguerri Martínez and Salas Vázquez 1989
Aguerri Martínez, Ascención, and Eduardo Salas Vázquez. *Catálogo del Gabinete de Estampas del Museo Municipal de Madrid/Estampas Extranjeras*. Vol. 2. Madrid: Museo Municipal, 1989.

Agulló y Cobo 1987
Agulló y Cobo, Mercedes. "El pintor madrileño Jerónimo Ezquerra." *Villa de Madrid* 25, no. 93 (1987): 3–24.

Agulló y Cobo 1994
Agulló y Cobo, Mercedes. *Documentos para la Historia de la Pintura Española*. Vol. 1. Madrid: Museo del Prado, 1994.

Agulló y Cobo 1996
Agulló y Cobo, Mercedes. *Documentos para la Historia de la Pintura Española*. Vol. 2. Madrid, Museo del Prado, 1996.

Agulló y Cobo 2003
Agulló y Cobo, Mercedes. "El Convento de San Diego de Alcalá." *Cuadernos de Arte e Iconografía* 12, no. 23 (2003): 3–76.

Agulló y Cobo 2005
Agulló y Cobo, Mercedes. *Documentos para la Historia de la Escultura Española*. Madrid: Fundación de Apoyo a la Historia del Arte Hispánico, 2005.

Agulló y Cobo 2006
Agulló y Cobo, Mercedes. *Documentos para la Historia de la Pintura Española*. Vol. 3. Madrid: Fundación de Apoyo a la Historia del Arte Hispánico, 2006.

Alcolea Blanch 1990
Alcolea Blanch, Santiago. "Fortuny: puntualizaciones al catálogo de una exposición." *Archivo español de arte* 63, no. 249 (1990): 43–58.

Angulo Íñiguez 1957
Angulo Íñiguez, Diego. *José Antolínez*. Madrid: Instituto Diego Velázquez, del Consejo Superior de Investigaciones Científicas, 1957.

Angulo Íñiguez 1959
Angulo Íñiguez, Diego. "Francisco Camilo." *Archivo Español de Arte* 32, no. 126 (1959): 89–108.

Angulo Íñiguez 1965
Angulo Íñiguez, Diego. "Nuevas obras de Francisco Camilo." *Archivo Español de Arte* 38, no. 149 (1965): 59–61.

Angulo Íñiguez 1974
Angulo Íñiguez, Diego. "Algunos dibujos de Murillo." *Archivo Español de Arte* 47, no. 186 (1974): 97–108.

Angulo Íñiguez and Pérez Sánchez 1975–88
Angulo Íñiguez, Diego, and Alfonso E. Pérez Sánchez. *A Corpus of Spanish Drawings*. 4 vols. London: Harvey Miller, 1975–1988.

Ansón Navarro 2007
Ansón Navarro, Arturo, ed. *Francisco Bayeu y sus discípulos*. Zaragoza: Cajalón, 2007.

Arnáez 1975
Arnáez, Rocío. *Catálogo de Dibujos: Dibujos Españoles, siglo XVIII, A–B*. Vol. 2. Madrid: Museo del Prado, 1975.

Arnáiz 1981
Arnáiz, José Manuel. *Eugenio Lucas. Su Vida y su Obra*. Madrid: M. Montal, 1981.

Arnáiz 1988
Arnáiz, José Manuel. "El Album de Vicente Camarón y otros dibujos españoles inéditos." *Academia* 67 (1988): 181–209.

Arnáiz, López Jiménez, and Merchán Díaz 1992
Arnáiz, José Manuel, Javier López Jiménez, and Manuel Merchán Díaz, eds. *Cien Años de Pintura en España y Portugal (1830–1930)*. Vol. 9. Madrid: Antiqvaria, 1992.

Azcárate Luxan 1994
Azcárate Luxan, Isabel, et al. *Historia y Alegoría: Los Concursos de Pintura de la Real Academia de Bellas Artes de San Fernando (1753–1808)*. Madrid: Real Academia de Bellas Artes de San Fernando, 1994.

Bambach 1999
Bambach, Carmen C. "Recently Acquired Spanish Baroque Drawings at The Metropolitan Museum of Art." *Master Drawings* 37, no. 4 (winter 1999): 407–15.

Bambach 2009
Bambach, Carmen C. "A New Ribera Drawing Among Michelangelos." *Apollo Magazine* 170, no. 568 (September 2009): 50.

Banner 1999
Banner, Lisa A. "A Selection of Spanish Drawings from The Metropolitan Museum of Art." *Master Drawings* 37, no. 4 (winter 1999): 394–406.

Banner 2006
Banner, Lisa A. "Review of *Catálogo de la Colección de Dibujos del Instituto Jovellanos de Gijón*, by Alfonso E. Pérez Sánchez." *caa.reviews* (Mar. 30, 2006), DOI: 10.3202/caa.reviews.2006.36, http://www.caareviews.org/reviews/831.

Banner 2007
Banner, Lisa A. "Francisco de Solís: A Seventeenth-Century Artist-Collector in Madrid." *Master Drawings* 45, no. 3 (2007): 359–66.

Banner 2009
Banner, Lisa A. *The Religious Patronage of the Duke of Lerma, 1598–1621*. Farnham, U.K.; Burlington, Vt.: Ashgate, 2009.

Banner 2010a
Banner, Lisa A. "Review of *Álbum Alcubierre: Dibujos de la Sevilla ilustrada del Conde del Águila a la Colección Juan Abelló*, by Benito Navarrete Prieto and Alfonso E. Pérez Sánchez." *Master Drawings* 48, no. 4 (2010): 544.

Banner 2010b
Banner, Lisa A. "Francisco Bayeu's Drawing of the Dove of the Holy Spirit for El Pilar." In *Art in Spain and the Hispanic World: Essays in Honor of Jonathan Brown.* Edited by Sarah Schroth, pp. 129–42. London: Paul Holberton Publishing, in association with Centro de Estudios Europa Hispánica, 2010.

Barcelona 1937
Meridià presenta Exposició de Dibuixos sobre la Guerra presos directament del Natural per Luis Quintanilla. Barcelona, 1937. Exh. cat. Hotel Ritz, Barcelona, Dec. 25–31, 1937.

Barcelona 1974
Mariano Fortuny. Barcelona, 1974. Exh. cat. Museo de Arte Moderno, Barcelona, Nov. 1974; Salas de Exposiciones de la Dirección General de Bellas Artes, Madrid, Dec. 1974.

Barcelona 1993
Cercle Artístic de Sant Lluc, 1893–1993: Cent Anys. Barcelona: Generalitat de Catalunya, Departament de Cultura, 1993.

Barcelona 1997
Carbonell, Jordi A., et al., eds. *Marià Fortuny: Dibuixos i Gravats al Museu Salvador Vilaseca.* Barcelona, 1997. Exh. cat. Fundaciò Caixa Penedès, Barcelona, 1997.

Barcelona 2002
Arnáiz, José Manuel. *Eugenio Lucas Velázquez (1817–1870): Dibujos y pinturas de un visionario.* Madrid, 2002. Exh. cat. Artur Ramon Col. leccionsme, Barcelona, Jan. 10–Feb. 16, 2002; Jorge Juan Galería de Arte, Madrid, Feb. 25–Mar. 23, 2002.

Barcelona 2003–4
Doñate, Mercé, Cristina Mendoza, and Francesc Quílez i Corella. *Fortuny (1838–1874).* Barcelona, 2004. Exh. cat. Museu Nacional d'Art de Catalunya, Barcelona, Oct. 17, 2003–Jan. 18, 2004.

Barcelona 2006–7
Clair, Jean. *Picasso i el circ.* Barcelona, 2006. Exh. cat. Museu Picasso, Barcelona, 2006–2007.

Barcelona 2008–9
Quílez i Corella, Francesc M. *L'imaginari d'Eugenio Lucas: La influència de Goya a la poètica romàntica.* Barcelona, 2008. Exh. cat. Museu Nacional d'Art de Catalunya, Barcelona, Nov. 4, 2008–Feb. 1, 2009.

Barrio Moya 1982
Barrio Moya, José Luis. "Pedro de Villafranca y Malagón, Pintor y grabador manchego del siglo XVII." *Cuadernos de Estudios Manchegos,* no. 13 (1982): 107–22.

Bassegoda i Hugas 1994
Bassegoda i Hugas, Bonaventura. "Noves dades sobre el canonge Vicente Vitoria (Dénia, 1650–Roma, 1709), tractadista, pintor, gravador i col.leccionista." *Butlletí del Museu Nacional d'Art de Catalunya* 2 (1994): 37–62.

Baticle and Marinas 1981
Baticle, Jeannine, and Cristina Marinas. *La Galerie Espagnole de Louis-Philippe au Louvre, 1838–1848.* Paris: Éditions de la Réunion des musées nationaux, 1981.

Bayer 1995
Bayer, Andrea. "A Note on Ribera's Drawing of Niccolò Simonelli." *Metropolitan Museum Journal* 30 (1995): 73–80.

Bédat 1989
Bédat, Claude. *La Real Academia de Bellas Artes de San Fernando (1744–1808).* Madrid: Fundación Universitaria Español, 1989.

Beutler 1997
Beutler, Werner. *Vicente Carducho: Der Grosse Kartäuserzyklus in El Paular.* Salzburg: Institut für Anglistik und Amerikanistik, 1997.

Bielefeld 2011–12
Kellein, Thomas, and David Riedel, eds. *Picasso 1905 in Paris.* Munich, 2011. Exh. cat. Kunsthalle Bielefeld, Sept. 20, 2011–Jan. 15, 2012.

Bilbao 2005
Viar, Javier. *Artearen Papera–El Papel del Arte: Dibujos y grabados, siglos XV–XVIII.* Bilbao, 2005. Exh. cat. Colección Museo de Bellas Artes de Bilbao, June 11–Sept. 4, 2005.

Birmingham 1964
American Painters of the Precise Image. Birmingham, Ala., 1964. Exh. cat. Birmingham Museum of Art, Feb. 6–Mar. 5, 1964.

Birmingham 1971
The Art of Spain. Birmingham, Ala., 1971. Exh. cat. Birmingham Museum of Art, Mar. 19–Apr. 4, 1971.

Bofarull y Sans 1910
Bofarull y Sans, Francisco de A. de. *Los Animales en las Marcas del Papel.* Barcelona: Villanueva y Geltrú, 1910.

Boubli 1994
Boubli, Lizzie. "'Magnífico maestre Alonso Berruguete': Introduction à l'étude de son oeuvre graphique." *Revue de l'Art* 103 (1994): 11–32.

Boubli 1999
Boubli, Lizzie. "The State of Scholarship of Sixteenth and Seventeenth-Century Spanish Drawings." *Master Drawings* 37, no. 4 (winter 1999): 349–64.

Boubli 2002
Boubli, Lizzie. *Inventaire Général des Dessins: École Espagnole, XVIe–XVIIIe siècle.* Paris: Musée du Louvre, 2002.

Bray 1996
Bray, Xavier. "Bayeu Drawings at the Prado, Madrid." *Burlington Magazine* 138, no. 1114 (January 1996): 54–55.

Bray 1997
Bray, Xavier. "The Iconography of Francisco Bayeu's Frescoes for the Colegiata at La Granja de San Ildefonso." *Burlington Magazine* 139, no. 1133 (August 1997): 543–47.

Bray 1999
Bray, Xavier. "Drawings by Giaquinto's Spanish Followers: Antonio González Velázquez and José del Castillo." *Master Drawings* 37, no. 4 (winter 1999): 416–28.

Breunig 1988
Breunig, Leroy C., ed. *Apollinaire on Art: Essays and Reviews, 1902–1918.* New York: Da Capo Press, 1988.

Brown 1972
Brown, Jonathan. "Notes on Princeton Drawings 6: Jusepe de Ribera." *Record of the Art Museum, Princeton University* 31, no. 2 (1972): 2–7.

Brown 1973
Brown, Jonathan. "Spanish Baroque Drawings in the Sperling Bequest." *Master Drawings* 11, no. 4 (winter 1973): 377.

Brown 1973a
Brown, Jonathan. "Notes on Princeton Drawings 9: Bartolomé Esteban Murillo." *Record of the Art Museum, Princeton University* 32, no. 2 (1973): 28–33.

Brown 1974
Brown, Jonathan. "Pen Drawings by Herrera the Younger." In *Hortus Imaginum: Essays in Western Art*. Edited by Robert Enggass and Marilyn Stokstad, pp. 129–38. Lawrence: University of Kansas, 1974.

Brown 1975a
Brown, Jonathan. "Drawings by Herrera the Younger and a Follower." *Master Drawings* 13, no. 3 (autumn 1975): 235–40.

Brown 1975b
Brown, Jonathan. "Exhibition Review: Spanish Baroque Drawings in North American Collections." *Master Drawings* 13, no. 1 (spring 1975): 60–63.

Brown 1976
Brown, Jonathan. "A Portrait Drawing by Velázquez." *Master Drawings* 14, no. 1 (spring 1976): 46–51.

Brown 1978
Brown, Jonathan. *Images and Ideas in Seventeenth-Century Spanish Painting*. Princeton: Princeton University Press, 1978.

Brown 1980
Brown, Jonathan. "Eighteenth-Century Spanish Drawings." *Master Drawings* 18, no. 3 (autumn 1980): 270–74.

Brown 1983a
Brown, Jonathan. "Drawings by Andalusian Masters." *Apotheca* 3 (1983): 9–13.

Brown 1983b
Brown, Jonathan. "Murillo: New Drawings, Old Problems." *Master Drawings* 21, no. 2 (summer 1983): 160–62.

Brown 1983c
Brown, Jonathan. "Selected Drawings by Spanish Baroque Masters." *Master Drawings* 21, vol. 4 (winter 1983): 401–7.

Brown 1991
Brown, Jonathan. *Zurbarán*. London: Thames and Hudson, 1991.

Brown 1998
Brown, Jonathan. *Painting in Spain, 1500–1700*. New Haven: Yale University Press, 1998.

Brown 2009
Brown, Jonathan. "Precisiones sobre la capilla de San Diego de Alcalá, en Santa María de Jesús de Alcalá de Henares." *Archivo Español de Arte* 82, no. 327 (2009): 316.

Brown 2012
Brown, Jonathan. *Murillo: Virtuoso Draftsman*. New Haven: Yale University Press, 2012.

Brown and Mann 1990
Brown, Jonathan, and Richard Mann. *The Collections of the National Gallery of Art, Systematic Catalogue: Spanish Paintings of the Fifteenth through Nineteenth Centuries*. Washington, D.C.: National Gallery of Art; Cambridge, U.K.: Cambridge University Press, 1990.

Burdett 1935
Burdett, Basil. "The Drypoints of Luis Quintanilla." *Print Collector's Quarterly* 22, no. 3 (July 1935): 265–78.

Burgos 2006
García de la Torre, Fuensanta. *Dibujar la Mirada: Fondos del Museo de Bellas Artes de Córdoba*. Burgos, 2006. Exh. cat. Centro Cultural, Casa del Cordón, Feb. 16–Apr. 16, 2006.

Buser 1976
Buser, Basil. "Jerome Nadal and Early Jesuit Art in Rome." *Art Bulletin* 58, no. 3 (September 1976): 424–33.

Byrne 1981
Byrne, Janet S. *Renaissance Ornament Prints and Drawings*. New York: The Metropolitan Museum of Art, 1981.

Cadena 2004
Cadena, Josep M., ed. *El Dibuix a Catalunya: 100 Dibuixants que cal Conèixer*. Barcelona: Pòrtic, 2004.

Caparrós Masegosa 1999
Caparrós Masegosa, Lola. *Prerrafaelismo, Simbolismo y Decadentismo en la Pintura Española de Fin de Siglo*. Granada: Universidad de Granada, 1999.

Carducho 1633
Carducho, Vicente. *Diálogos de la Pintura*. Madrid: Martínez, 1633.

Carducho 1979
Carducho, Vicente. *Diálogos de la Pintura*. Edited by Francisco Calvo Serraller. Madrid: Turner, D. L., 1979.

Carrete Parrondo 1981
Carrete Parrondo, Juan. "Grabados alegóricos del siglo XVII." *Goya: Revista de arte* 161–162 (1981): 346–49.

Carrete Parrondo, De Diego, and Vega 1985
Carrete Parrondo, Juan, Estrella de Diego, and Jesusa Vega. *Catálogo del Gabinete de Estampas del Museo Municipal de Madrid/Estampas Españoles*. Vol. 1. Madrid: Ayuntamiento de Madrid, Concejalía de Cultura, 1985.

Carroll and Fernández 2007
Carroll, Peter N., and James D. Fernández. *Facing Fascism: New York & the Spanish Civil War*. New York: Museum of the City of New York and New York University Press, 2007.

Casado Cimiano 2006
Casado Cimiano, Pedro. *Diccionario Biográfico de Ilustradores Españoles del siglo XIX*. Madrid: Ollero y Ramos, 2006.

Casal 2006
Casal, Marta Cacho. "Gonzalo Argote de Molina and his museum in Seville." *Burlington Magazine* 148, no. 1243 (October 2006): 689–93.

Caturla 1968–69
Caturla, María Luisa. "Documentos en torno a Vicencio Carducho." *Arte Español* 26, no. 3 (1968–1969): 145–21.

Ceán Bermúdez 1800
Ceán Bermúdez, Juan Agustín. *Diccionario Histórico de los Mas Ilustres Profesores de las Bellas Artes en España.* Madrid: Real Academia de San Fernando, 1800.

Cepeda 1670
Cepeda, Gabriel de. *Historia de la milagrosa y venerable Imagen de N. S. de Atocha, patrona de Madrid: discurrese sobre su antiguedad, origen y prodigios, etc.* Madrid: Imprenta Real, 1670.

Cirici Pellicer 1951
Cirici Pellicer, A. *El Arte Modernista Catalán.* Barcelona: Aymá, 1951.

Cleveland/New York 2006–7
Robinson, William H., Jordi Falgàs, and Carmen Belén Lord. *Barcelona and Modernity: Picasso, Gaudí, Miró, Dalí.* New Haven, 2006. Exh. cat. Cleveland Museum of Art, Oct. 15, 2006–Jan. 7, 2007; The Metropolitan Museum of Art, New York, Mar. 7–June 3, 2007.

Colomer Amat 1998–99
Colomer Amat, Emilia. "Libros de horas impresos en España en el primer tercio del siglo XVI." *Locus Amoenus* 4 (1998–1999): 127–35.

Copenhagen 2006
Fischer, Chris, and Joachim Meyer. *Neapolitan Drawings: Italian Drawings in the Department of Prints and Drawings.* Copenhagen, 2006. Exh. cat. Statens Museum for Kunst, Copenhagen, 2006.

Cordero de Ciria 2003
Cordero de Ciria, Enrique. "Mostrar el arte: consideraciones sobre la cuestión del desnudo en España en los siglos XVI y XVII." *Boletín del Museo e Instituto Camón Aznar* 92 (2003): 29–65.

Cornudella i Carré 1997
Cornudella i Carré, Rafael. *Para una Revisión de la Obra Pictórica de Francisco Preciado de la Vega.* Barcelona: Universitat Autònoma, 1997.

Córdoba 1997–98
García de la Torre, Fuensanta. *Dibujos del Museo de Bellas Artes de Córdoba.* Córdoba, 1997. Exh. cat. Museo de Bellas Artes de Córdoba, 1997–1998.

Cornejo 2006
Cornejo, Francisco J. "Noticias de Francisco de Herrera el Viejo en Madrid y del Retablo Mayor del Colegio de San Basilio, de Sevilla." *Archivo Español de Arte* 79, no. 316 (2006): 355–70.

Cuartero y Huerta 1951
Cuartero y Huerta, Baltasar. *Relación descriptiva de los Cincuenta y Seis cuadros pintados por Vicencio Carduchi para el Claustro Grande de la Cartuja del Paular.* Madrid: Imprenta y Editorial Maestre, 1951.

Dacos 1997
Dacos, Nicole. "Giulio Aquili, Andrés de Melgar et leurs grotesques." *Dialoghi di Storia dell'Arte* 4/5 (December 1997): 24–33.

Dalí 1942
Dalí, Salvador. *The Secret Life of Salvador Dalí.* New York: Dial Press, 1942.

Dallas 2012
Finaldi, Gabriele, ed. *Jusepe de Ribera's Mary Magdalene in a New Context. The Prado at the Meadows.* Vol. 2. Dallas, Tex., 2012. Exh. cat. Meadows Museum, Southern Methodist University, Dallas, Sept. 18, 2011–Jan. 15, 2012.

Dallas/Ocala/Rotterdam 2003–4
Tatsakis, Sandra, and Mark Roglán. *Spanish Master Drawings from Dutch Public Collections (1500–1900).* Rotterdam, 2003. Exh. cat. Meadows Museum, Dallas, Sept. 14–Nov. 9, 2003; Appleton Museum of Art, Ocala, Fla., Nov. 21, 2003–Jan. 18, 2004; Museum Boijmans van Beuningen, Rotterdam, May 21–Aug. 1, 2004.

Danesi Squarzina 2006
Danesi Squarzina, Silvia. "New Documents on Ribera, *'pictor in Urbe,'* 1612–1616." *Burlington Magazine* 148, no. 1237 (April 2006): 244–51.

Dansey Smith 1978
Dansey Smith, Hilary. *Preaching in the Spanish Golden Age: A Study of Some Preachers of the Reign of Philip III.* Oxford: Oxford University Press, 1978.

Davillier 1875
Davillier, Baron Charles. *Fortuny: sa vie, son oeuvre, sa correspondance.* Paris: Aubry, 1875.

DeWald 1948
DeWald, Ernest T. "A Drawing by Picasso." *Record of the Art Museum, Princeton University* 7, no. 2 (1948): 10.

Díaz Gallegos 1999
Díaz Gallegos, Carmen. "Dibujos de Maella para las decoraciones alegóricas de los Palacios Reales." *Reales Sitios* 36, no. 140 (1999): 25–34.

Drake and Drake 1971
Drake, Maurice, and Wilfred Drake. *Saints and Their Emblems.* Detroit: Gale Research Company, 1971.

Dufour 2008
Dufour, Lydia. "Some Little-known drawings by Eugenio Lucas at the Morgan Library & Museum." *Master Drawings* 46, no. 2 (summer 2008): 175–86.

Echeverría Goñi 1995
Echeverría Goñi, Pedro Luis. "La policromía del retablo calceatense." In *Damián Forment, escultor renacentista: Retablo Mayor de la Catedral de Santo Domingo de la Calzada*, pp. 215–30. San Sebastián: Catedral de Santo Domingo de la Calzada, 1995.

Edinburgh 1994
From Leonardo to Manet: Ten Years of Collecting Prints and Drawings. Edinburgh, 1994. Exh. cat. National Gallery of Scotland, Edinburgh, Feb. 11–Apr. 17, 1994.

Edinburgh/Glasgow 1999–2000
Clifford, Timothy. *Designs of Desire: Architectural and Ornament Prints and Drawings, 1500–1850.* Edinburgh, 1999. Exh. cat. The Burrell Gallery, Glasgow, Nov. 18, 1999–Jan. 10, 2000; National Gallery of Scotland; Edinburgh, Mar. 31–June 18, 2000.

Eitner, Fryberger, and Osborne 1993
Eitner, Lorenz, Betsy G. Fryberger, and Carol M. Osborne. *Stanford University Museum of Art, The Drawing Collection.* Stanford, Calif.: Stanford University Museum of Art, 1993, cat. no. 84.

Enciclopedia 2006
Enciclopedia del Museo del Prado. Edited by Miguel Zugaza and Francisco Calvo Serraller. Madrid: Fundación Amigos del Museo del Prado, 2009.

Espinós Díaz 1975
Espinós Díaz, Adela. "Dibujos de los siglos XVI y XVII en el Museo de San Carlos de Valencia." *Archivo de arte valenciano* 46 (1975): 72–84.

Espinós Díaz 1978
Espinós Díaz, Adela. "Un dibujo inédito de Juan Antonio Conchillos y Falcó (1641–1711)." *Archivo de arte valenciano* 49 (1978): 57–59.

Espinós Díaz 1987
Espinós Díaz, Adela. "Nuevos datos sobre la colección de dibujos del Museo de San Pío V de Valencia." *Archivo Español de Arte* 60, no. 237 (1987): 17–34.

Espinós Díaz 1994
Espinós Díaz, Adela. *Dibujos Valencianos del siglo XVII.* Valencia: Museo de Bellas Artes, 1994.

Espinós Díaz 1997
Espinós Díaz, Adela. *Dibujos Valencianos del siglo XVII.* Seville: Fundación el Monte, 1997.

Fabre 1829
Fabre, Francisco José. *Descripción de las alegorías pintadas en las Bóvedas del Real Palacio de Madrid.* Madrid: Eusebio Aguado, 1829.

Falomir Faus 1999
Falomir Faus, Miguel. "La construcción de un mito: Fortuna crítica de Juan de Juanes en los siglos XVI y XVII." *Espacio, tiempo y forma, serie VII, Historia del arte* 12 (1999): 123–48.

Farmer 1997
Farmer, David Hugh. *The Oxford Dictionary of Saints.* 4th ed. New York: Oxford University Press, 1997.

Fernández López 2003
Fernández López, José. *Lucas Valdés (1661–1725).* Seville: Diputación Provincial de Sevilla, 2003.

Fernández-Santos Ortiz-Iribas 2005
Fernández-Santos Ortiz-Iribas, Jorge. "Entre Agostino Carracci y Veronese: apuntes sobre el aprendizaje italiano de Francisco de Herrera 'el Mozo.'" *Archivo Español de Arte* 78, no. 311 (2005): 245–61.

Finaldi 2005
Finaldi, Gabriele. "Dibujos inéditos y otros poco conocidos de Jusepe de Ribera." *Boletín del Museo del Prado* 23, no. 41 (2005): 24–44.

Finkelstein 1998
Finkelstein, Haim. *The Collected Writings of Salvador Dalí.* Cambridge, U.K.: Cambridge University Press, 1998.

Florence 1967
Vitzthum, Walter, and Anna Maria Petrioli, eds. *Cento disegni napoletani: sec. XVI–XVIII.* Florence, 1967. Exh. cat. Gabinetto disegni e stampe degli Uffizi, Florence, 1967.

Florence 1972
Pérez Sánchez, Alfonso E. *Mostra di Disegni Spagnoli.* Florence, 1972. Exh. cat. Galleria degli Uffizi, Florence, 1972.

Fontbona et al. 2002
Fontbona, Francesc, et al. *Repertori de Catàlegs d'Exposicions Col.lectives d'Art a Catalunya (Fins a l'Any 1938).* Barcelona: Institut d'Estudis Catalans, 2002.

Fort Worth 1982–83
Felton, Craig, and W.B. Jordan, eds. *Jusepe de Ribera lo Spagnoletto, 1591–1652.* Fort Worth, Tex., 1982. Exh. cat. Kimbell Art Museum, Fort Worth, Dec. 4, 1982–Feb. 6, 1983.

Fuendetodos 2009
Lambán, Javier. *La estela de Goya: Discípulos y Seguidores Interpretan la Obra del Maestro.* Zaragoza, 2009. Exh. cat. Museo del Grabado, Fuendetodos, Mar. 30–May 31, 2009.

Gállego 1984
Gállego, Julián. *Visión y Símbolos en la pintura española del Siglo de Oro.* Madrid: Cátedra, 1984.

Gallego Gallego 1990
Gallego Gallego, Antonio. *Historia del Grabado en España.* Madrid: Ediciones Cátedra, 1990.

García Cueto 2005
García Cueto, David. "Don Diego de Aragón, IV Duque de Terranova, y el envío de esculturas para Felipe IV durante su Embajada en Roma (1654–1657)." *Archivo Español de Arte* 78, no. 311 (2005): 317–22.

García de la Torre 2001
García de la Torre, Fuensanta. *Homenaje a Alonso Cano. Dibujos.* Seville: Consejería de Cultura, 2001.

Garvey 1978
Garvey, Eleanor M. "Francisco Herrera the Younger: A Drawing for a Spanish Festival Book." *Harvard Library Bulletin* 26, no. 1 (January 1978): 28–37.

Gassier 1972
Gassier, Pierre. "Une source inédite de dessins de Goya en France au XIXe siècle." *Gazette des Beaux-Arts* 80 (July–August 1972): 109–20.

Gassier 1973
Gassier, Pierre. *The Drawings of Francisco Goya: The Complete Albums.* New York: Praeger, 1973.

Gassier and Wilson 1971
Gassier, Pierre, and Juliet Wilson. *Goya: His Life and Work.* London: Thames and Hudson, 1971.

Gaya Nuño 1961
Gaya Nuño, Juan Antonio. *La arquitectura española en sus monumentos desaparecidos.* Madrid: Espasa-Calpe, 1961.

Gibbons 1977
Gibbons, Felton. *Catalogue of Italian Drawings in the Art Museum, Princeton University.* Princeton: Princeton University Press, 1977.

Gibson 1997
Gibson, Ian. *The Shameful Life of Salvador Dalí.* London: Faber and Faber, 1997.

Glimcher and Glimcher 1986
Glimcher, Arnold, and Marc Glimcher, eds. *Je Suis le Cahier: The Sketchbooks of Picasso.* New York: The Pace Gallery, 1986.

González García 1999
González García, Juan Luis. "'Ut Pictura Rhetorica': Juan de Juanes y el retablo de San Esteban de Valencia." *Boletín del Museo del Prado* 17, no. 35 (1999): 21–56.

González López and Martí Ayxelá 1989
González López, Carlos, and Montserrat Martí Ayxelá. *Mariano Fortuny Marsal, 1838–1874.* Barcelona: Diccionari Ràfols, 1989.

Green 1992
Green, Christopher. *Juan Gris.* New Haven and London: Yale University Press, 1992.

Hamburg 1966
Stubbe, Wolf. *Spanische Zeichnungen von El Greco bis Goya.* Hamburg, 1996. Exh. cat. Aus den Sammlungen des Prado-Museums, der Nationalbibliothek und der Akademie San Fernando in Madrid, ergänzt mit Blättern der Hamburger Kunsthalle, Oct.–Nov. 1966.

Harris 1964
Harris, Tomás. *Goya: Engravings and Lithographs.* Oxford: B. Cassirer, 1964.

Heredia Moreno 2005
Heredia Moreno, María del Carmen. "Dibujos de Alonso Berruguete, Julio de Aquilis y Andrés de Melgar en la Fundación Lázaro Galdiano." *Goya: Revista de arte* 306 (2005): 132–44.

Herrera-Dávila 1832
Herrera-Dávila, José. *Guia de Forasteros de la Ciudad de Sevilla* (Seville, 1832).

Iowa 1951
Six Centuries of Master Drawings. Iowa City, Iowa, 1951. Exh. cat. University of Iowa, School of Fine Arts, summer 1951.

Indianapolis 2009–10
Kasl, Ronda, et al. *Sacred Spain: Art and Belief in the Spanish World.* Indianapolis, Ind., 2009. Exh. cat. Indianapolis Museum of Art, Oct. 11, 2009–Jan. 3, 2010.

Jardí 1976
Jardí, Enric. *Història del Cercle Artístic de Sant Lluc.* Barcelona: Ediciones Destino, 1976.

Karmel 2003
Karmel, Pepe. *Picasso and the Invention of Cubism.* New Haven and London: Yale University Press, 2003.

Kinkead 1982a
Kinkead, Duncan T. "Francisco de Herrera and the Development of the High Baroque Style in Seville." *Record of the Art Museum, Princeton University* 41, no. 2 (1982): 12–23.

Kinkead 1982b
Kinkead, Duncan T. "'The Triumph of St. James,' by Matías de Arteaga y Alfaro." *Master Drawings* 20, no. 3 (autumn 1982): 257–58, 300.

Konečný 1985
Konečný, Lubomír. "A New Drawing by Jusepe de Ribera." *Burlington Magazine* 127, no. 985 (April 1985): 226–27, 229.

Kubler 1965
Kubler, George. "Vicente Carducho's Allegories of Painting." *Art Bulletin* 47, no. 4 (December 1965): 439–45.

Lafuente Ferrari 1980
Lafuente Ferrari, Enrique. *Goya Drawings.* Bilbao: Silex, 1980.

La Jolla/Chicago 1990
Andrés Nagel: Mixed Media, Sculpture and work on paper. La Jolla, Calif., 1990. Exh. cat. Tasende Gallery, La Jolla, Mar. 10–Apr. 22, 1990; Chicago International Art Exposition, May 10–15, 1990.

Lanchner 1993
Lanchner, Carolyn. *Joan Miró.* New York: The Museum of Modern Art, 1993.

Lawrence 1958
Masterworks from University and College Art Collections: An Exhibition of Works of Art Lent by Forty-two American Colleges and Universities to Celebrate the Anniversary of the Museum of Art. Checklist. The University of Kansas Museum of Art, Feb. 22–Mar. 30, 1958.

Lawrence 1974
McKim-Smith, Gridley. *Spanish Baroque Drawings in North American Collections.* Lawrence, Kans., 1974. Exh. cat. University of Kansas Museum of Art, Oct. 19–Nov. 24, 1974.

Lebensztejn 1990
Lebensztejn, Jean-Claude. *L'art de la tache: Introduction à la Nouvelle méthode d'Alexander Cozens.* Paris: Éditions du Limon, with The Getty Grant Program and the Centre National des Lettres, 1990.

Le Fell 2004
Turner, Nicholas, and Xavier Bray. *An Important Collection of Late Eighteenth-Century Valencian Drawings: José Camarón Boronat, 1731–1803, Rafael Ximeno y Planes, 1759–1807, José Camarón y Meliá, 1760–1819, Vicente López y Portaña, 1772–1850.* Paris, 2004. Exh. cat. Galerie Jean-Marie Le Fell, Paris, 2004.

Lefort 1869
Collection de M. Paul Lefort, Dessins Anciens, principalement de l'École Espagnole eaux-fortes et lithographies de Goya. Paris, 1869.

Le Harivel 1992
Le Harivel, Adrian. *Nathaniel Hone the Elder, 1718–1784.* Dublin: Town House in association with the National Gallery of Ireland, 1992.

London 1954
Goya: Drawings from the Prado Museum and the Lazaro Galdiano Museum, Madrid; Etchings from the Lazaro Galdiano Museum and the Collection of Tomas Harris, Esq.; Lithographs from the Lazaro Galdiano Museum. London, 1954. Exh. cat. The Arts Council of Great Britain, London, June 12–July 25, 1954.

London 1957
An Exhibition of Drawings from the Alfred A. de Pass Collection, belonging to the Royal Institution of Cornwall, Truro. London, 1957. Exh. cat. Nottingham University Gallery, Jan. 19–Feb. 9, 1957, and 4 other English galleries through June 1957.

London 1973
Master Drawings presented by Adolphe Stein. London, 1973. Exh. cat. Terry-Engell Gallery, London, July 3–9, 1973.

London 1986
Old Master Drawings. London, 1986. Exh. cat. P. & D Colnaghi & Co., Ltd., London, July 1–19, 1986.

London 2001
Wilson-Bareau, Juliet. *Goya: Drawings from His Private Albums.* London, 2001. Exh. cat. Hayward Gallery, London, Feb. 22–May 13, 2001.

London/Truro 1994
Joannides, Marianne. *Exhibition Catalogue of Master Drawings from the De Pass Collection, Royal Cornwall Museum, Truro.* London, 1994. Exh. cat. Phillips, London, Aug. 2–Sept. 4, 1994; Royal Cornwall Museum, Truro, Sept. 10–Oct. 31, 1994.

López Navío 1961
López Navío, José. "Testamento de Francisco de Herrera, el joven." *Archivo Hispalense* 35, no. 110 (1961): 261–74.

López-Rey 1953
López-Rey, José. *Goya's Caprichos: Beauty, Reason, and Caricature.* Princeton: Princeton University Press, 1953.

López Sobrado 1992
López Sobrado, Esther. "Sobre la Pintura Mural de Luis Quintanilla." *Boletín del Seminario de Estudios de Arte y Arqueología* 58 (1992): 511–20.

López Torrijos 1987
López Torrijos, Rosa. "Los grutescos de Rafael y Udine en la pintura española. La estufa y la logia de Carlos V." *Storia dell'Arte* 60 (1987): 171–77.

López Vizcaíno and Carreño 2007
López Vizcaíno, Pilar, and Ángel Mario Carreño. *Juan Carreño Miranda: Vida y Obra.* Madrid: Cajastur, 2007.

Los Angeles 1976
Feinblatt, Ebria. *Old Master Drawings from American Collections.* Los Angeles, 1976. Exh. cat. Los Angeles County Museum of Art, Apr. 29–June 13, 1976.

Los Angeles 1997
Turner, Nicholas, Lee Hendrix, and Carol Plazzotta. *European Drawings: Catalogue of the Collections.* Vol. 3. Los Angeles, 1997. Exh. cat. The J. Paul Getty Museum, 1997.

Lucie-Smith 1992
Lucie-Smith, Edward. *Andrés Nagel.* New York: Rizzoli, 1992.

Luna 1980
Luna, Juan J. "Jean Ranc: ideas artísticas y métodos de trabajo, a través de pinturas y documentos." *Archivo español de arte* 53, no. 212 (1980): 449–65.

Lunn and Espinosa-Carrión 1979
Lunn, M.R., and V. Espinosa-Carrión. "Los dibujos de Juan Carreño de Miranda." *Archivo Español de Arte* 52, no. 207 (1979): 281–306.

Madrid 1928
Centenario de Goya. Exposición de Pinturas. Madrid, 1928. Exh. cat. Museo del Prado, Madrid, 1928.

Madrid 1980
Pérez Sánchez, Alfonso E. *El Dibujo Español de los Siglos de Oro.* Madrid, 1980. Exh. cat. Salas de Exposiciones del Palacio de Bibliotecas y Museos, Madrid, May 1980.

Madrid 1992
Pérez Sánchez, Alfonso E., and Nicola Spinosa. *Ribera: 1591–1652.* Madrid, 1992. Exh. cat. Museo del Prado, Madrid, June 2–Aug. 1, 1992.

Madrid 1992–93
El dibujo en España. Madrid, 1992. Exh. cat. Caylus Anticuario, Madrid, Dec. 1992–Jan. 1993.

Madrid 1993
La colección Raimon Casellas: dibujos y estampas del Barroco al Modernismo del Museu Nacional d'Art de Catalunya. Madrid, 1993. Exh. cat. Museo del Prado, Madrid, 1993.

Madrid 1994
Obras Maestras de la Real Academia de San Fernando: su primer siglo de historia, Exposición conmemorativa del 250 aniversario de su fundación. Madrid, 1994. Exh. cat. Museo de la Real Academia de Bellas Artes de San Fernando, Madrid, May 31–Aug. 28, 1994.

Madrid 1997
Leonardo Alenza (1807–1845): Dibujos y Estampas, Museo Romántico. Madrid, 1997. Exh. cat. Museo Romántico, Madrid, 1997.

Madrid 2001
Véliz, Zahira. *Alonso Cano: Dibujos.* Madrid, 2001. Exh. cat. Museo Nacional del Prado, Madrid, Apr. 2–June 24, 2001.

Madrid 2001–2
Schroth, Sarah, Alejandro Vergara, and Thea Vignau-Wilberg. *Rubens: Dibujos para el retrato ecuestre del Duque de Lerma.* Madrid, 2001. Exh. cat. Museo Nacional del Prado, Madrid, Nov. 7, 2001–Jan. 6, 2002.

Madrid 2002a
Sonseca Mas, Yara, ed. *Dibujos: Colección Rodríguez Moñino-Brey, Real Academia Española.* Madrid, 2002. Exh. cat. Real Academia Española, Madrid, 2002.

Madrid 2002b
Henares Cuéllar, Ignacio L. *Alonso Cano: La Modernidad del Siglo de Oro Español.* Madrid, 2002. Exh. cat. Sala de Exposiciones de la Fundación Santander Central Hispano, Madrid, Apr. 1–May 26, 2002.

Madrid 2005
Juan Gris: Paintings and Drawings, 1910–1927. Madrid: Museo Nacional Centro de Arte Reina Sofía, 2005.

Madrid 2005–6
Blas, Javier, José Miguel Medrano, et al. *Daniel Urrabieta Vierge (1851–1904): creador de imágenes, ilustrador gráfico.* Madrid, 2005. Exh. cat. Centro Cultural del Conde Duque, Madrid, Oct. 4, 2005–Jan. 8, 2006.

Madrid 2006–7a
Muller, Priscilla E. *Dibujos españoles en la Hispanic Society of America: del Siglo de Oro a Goya.* Madrid, 2006. Exh. cat. Museo Nacional del Prado, Madrid, Dec. 5, 2006–Mar. 4, 2007.

Madrid 2006–7b
Navarrete Prieto, Benito. *El Papel del Dibujo en España.* Madrid, 2006. Exh. cat. Caylus, Madrid, Nov. 2–Dec. 15, 2006; Artur Ramon Col. leccionisme, Barcelona, Feb. 1–Mar. 2, 2007.

Madrid 2011a
Matilla, José Manuel. *No solo Goya: Adquisiciones para el Gabinete de dibujos y estampas del Museo del Prado, 1997–2010.* Madrid, 2011. Exh. cat. Museo Nacional del Prado, Madrid, May 5–Aug. 28, 2011.

Madrid 2011b
Milicua, José, and Javier Portús Pérez, eds. *El Joven Ribera.* Madrid, 2011. Exh. cat. Museo Nacional del Prado, Madrid, Apr. 4–July 31, 2011.

Madrid/Boston/New York 1988–89
Pérez Sánchez, Alfonso E., and Eleanor A. Sayre. *Goya and the Spirit of the Enlightenment.* Boston,

1989. Exh. cat. Museo Nacional del Prado, Madrid, Oct. 6–Dec. 18, 1988; Museum of Fine Art, Boston, Jan. 18–Mar. 26, 1989; The Metropolitan Museum of Art, New York, May 9–July 16, 1989.

Madruga Real 1999
Madruga Real, Ángela. "Arquitectura y espectáculo: los Teatros del Palacio de Aranjuez." *Reales Sitios* 36, no. 140 (1999): 14–24.

De la Mano 1998
De la Mano, José Manuel. "Nuevas Aportaciones a la intervención de Maella en la decoración de la colegiata de La Granja." *Archivo Español de Arte* 71, no. 284 (1998): 375–90.

De la Mano 2002
De la Mano, José Manuel. *Trazos de las Luces: Dibujos Españoles del siglo XVIII.* Madrid: José de la Mano Galería de Arte, 2002.

De la Mano 2006
De la Mano, José Manuel. "Mariano Maella y la decoración de la Casa del Labrador: Programas pictóricos para una villa rural de Carlos IV." *Reales Sitios* 170 (2006): 20–41.

De la Mano 2010a
De la Mano, José Manuel. *Fecit: Spanish Old Master & Modern Drawings.* Madrid: José de la Mano Galería de Arte, 2010.

De la Mano 2010b
De la Mano, José Manuel. *Fecit II: Spanish Old Master & Modern Drawings.* Madrid: José de la Mano Galería de Arte, 2010.

De la Mano 2011
De la Mano, José Manuel. *Mariano Salvador Maella (1739–1819): Dibujos catálogo razonado.* Santander: Fundación Botín, 2011.

Marco García 2006
Marco García, Víctor. *El Pintor Vicente Salvador Gómez: Valencia, 1637–1678.* Valencia: Institució Alfons el Magnànim. Diputaciò de Valencia, 2006.

Marías Franco 2007
Marías Franco, Fernando. "Estudiando dibujos; falseando atribuciones: un Joan de Joanes y un Greco." In *In Sapientia Libertas: Escritos en Homenaje al Profesor Alfonso E. Pérez Sánchez*, pp. 216–22. Madrid: Museo Nacional del Prado; Seville: Fundación Focus-Abengoa, 2007.

Martínez 1988
Martínez, Jusepe. *Discursos practicables del nobilísimo arte de la pintura.* Edited by Julián Gállego. Madrid: Akal, 1988.

Martínez Escudero 1900
Martínez Escudero, Antonio. *Historia del convento de Santo Tomás de Madrid del Orden de Predicadores.* Vol. 1, pt.1. Madrid: Francisco Viñals, 1900.

Martínez Ripoll 1978
Martínez Ripoll, Antonio. *Francisco de Herrera "el Viejo."* Seville: Excma, 1978.

Mayor 1977
Mayor, A. Hyatt. "Review. Jonathan Brown, *Murillo and His Drawings." Master Drawings* 15 (1977): 184–85.

McDonald 1998
McDonald, Mark P. "Some Drawings by Jusepe de Ribera." *Storia dell'Arte* 78 (1993): 156–61.

McDonald 1998a
McDonald, Mark P. "A drawing by Antonio del Castillo y Saavedra in the British Museum." *Melbourne Art Journal* 2 (1998): 15–22.

McDonald 1998b
McDonald, Mark P. "Ribera's Earliest Drawing?" *Master Drawings* 37, no. 4 (winter 1999): 368–92.

McDonald 2007
McDonald, Mark P. "Italian, Dutch, and Spanish Pattern Prints and Artistic Education in Seventeenth-Century Madrid." *Storia dell'Arte* 98 (2000): 76–87.

McDonald 2007
McDonald, Mark P. "Spanish drawings." *Burlington Magazine* 149, no. 1248 (March 2007): 205–6.

McKim-Smith 1980
McKim-Smith, Gridley. "The Problem of Velázquez's Drawings." *Master Drawings* 18, no. 1 (spring 1980): 3–24.

McKim-Smith 1984
McKim-Smith, Gridley. "Dibujos pocos conocidos de Vicente Carducho." *Archivo Español de Arte* 57, no. 225 (1984): 92–95.

Meder 1978
Meder, Josef. *The Mastery of Drawing.* 2 vols. Translated by Winslow Ames. New York: Abaris Books, 1978.

Moffitt 1990
Moffitt, John F. "Francisco Pacheco and Jerome Nadal: New Light on the Flemish Sources of the Spanish 'Picture-within-the-Picture.'" *Art Bulletin* 72, no. 4 (December 1990): 631–38.

Mollinedo 1973
Mollinedo, Dolores. "Algunos Dibujos de Mariano Salvador Maella." *Archivo Español de Arte* 46, no. 182 (1973): 145–58.

Morales y Marín 1995
Morales y Marín, José Luis. *Francisco Bayeu: vida y obra.* Zaragoza: Ediciones Moncayo 1995.

Morales y Marín 1996
Morales y Marín, José Luis. *Mariano Salvador Maella: vida y obra.* Zaragoza: Ediciones Moncayo, 1996.

Moreno Villa 1926
Moreno Villa, José. *Dibujos del Instituto Jovellanos de Gijón. Catálogo.* Madrid, 1926.

Moyssén 1985
Moyssén, Xavier. *El Pintor Rafael Ximeno y Planes: su libreta de dibujos.* Mexico: Sociedad de Exalumnos de la Facultad de Ingeniería, 1985.

Muller 1963
Muller, Priscilla E. "The Drawings of Antonio del Castillo y Saavedra." Ph.D. diss., New York University, 1963.

Muller 1976
Muller, Priscilla E. "Juan de Juanes: un dibujo problemático." *Archivo Español de Arte* 49, no. 194 (1976): 176–79.

Muller 1984
Muller, Priscilla E. *Goya's "Black" Paintings: Truth and Reason in Light and Liberty.* New York: The Hispanic Society of America, 1984.

Muller 1989
Muller, Priscilla E. "Review of *Goya y el Espíritu de la ilustración. Goya and the Spirit of the Enlightenment*." *Master Drawings* 27, no. 4 (winter 1989): 374–77.

Muller 1990
Muller, Priscilla E. "Francisco de Herrera the Younger, Bartolomeo Salvestrini, and 'The Angel with a Censer' or 'The Archangel Sealtiel.'" *Master Drawings* 28, no. 3 (autumn 1990): 290–95.

Munich 2008–9
100 Master Drawings from the Morgan Library & Museum. Munich, 2008. Exh. cat. Staatliche Graphische Sammlung, Munich, Dec. 11, 2008–Mar. 1, 2009.

Nancarrow and Navarrete Prieto 2004
Nancarrow, Mindy, and Benito Navarrete Prieto. *Antonio del Castillo*. Madrid: Fundación de Apoyo a la Historia del Arte Hispánico, 2004.

Navarrete Prieto 1998
Navarrete Prieto, Benito. *La Pintura andaluza del siglo XVII y sus fuentes grabadas*. Madrid: Fundación de Apoyo a la Historia del Arte Hispánico, 1998.

Navarrete Prieto and García de la Torre 2008
Navarrete Prieto, Benito, and Fuensanta García de la Torre. *Antonio del Castillo, 1616–1668: Dibujos: catálogo razonado*. Santander: Fundación Marcelino Botín, 2008.

Navarrete Prieto and Pérez Sánchez 2009
Navarrete Prieto, Benito, and Alfonso E. Pérez Sánchez. *Álbum Alcubierre: Dibujos: De la Sevilla del Conde del Águila a la colección Juan Abelló*. Madrid: Fundación de Apoyo a la Historia del Arte Hispánico, 2009.

Navarrete Prieto, Zapata Fernández de la Hoz, and Martínez Ripoll 2008
Navarrete Prieto, Benito, Teresa Zapata Fernández de la Hoz, and Antonio Martínez Ripoll. *Fuentes y Modelos de la Pintura barroca Madrileña*. Madrid: Arco/Libros, 2008.

New York 1930
Drawings by Old Masters from the Private Collection of Prof. Frank Jewett Mather, Jr. New York, 1930. Exh. cat. Roerich Museum, New York, Dec. 18–31, 1930.

New York 1934
Hemingway, Ernest, and John Dos Passos. *Quintanilla*. New York, 1934. Exh. cat. Pierre Matisse Gallery, New York, Nov. 20–Dec. 4, 1934.

New York 1938
Hemingway, Ernest, and Alfred H. Barr, Jr. *Quintanilla: An Exhibition of Drawings of the War in Spain*. New York, 1938. Exh. cat. The Museum of Modern Art, New York, Mar. 16–Apr. 18, 1938.

New York 1944
Totalitarian Europe interpreted in watercolor and black and white by Luis Quintanilla. New York, 1944. Exh. cat. Knoedler Galleries, New York, May 15–June 2, 1944.

New York 1963
Dali. New York, 1963. Exh. cat. Knoedler Galleries, New York, Nov. 26–Dec. 26, 1963.

New York 1965
Dali's Drawings and Watercolors. New York, 1965. Exh. cat. Knoedler Galleries, New York, Dec. 21–31, 1965.

New York/San Francisco/Baltimore 1970
Four Americans in Paris: The Collections of Gertrude Stein and Her Family. New York, 1970. Exh. cat. The Museum of Modern Art, Dec. 1970; San Francisco Museum of Art, Sept. 9–Oct. 31, 1971; Baltimore Museum of Art, Apr. 4–June 13, 1971.

New York 1992
Pérez Sánchez, Alfonso E., and Nicola Spinosa. *Jusepe de Ribera, 1591–1652*. New York, 1992. Exh. cat. The Metropolitan Museum of Art, New York, Sept. 18–Nov. 29, 1992.

New York 2006
Brown, Jonathan, and Susan Grace Galassi. *Goya's Last Works*. New York, 2006. Exh. cat. The Frick Collection, New York, Feb. 22–May 14, 2006.

New York 2010–11
Brown, Jonathan, Lisa A. Banner, Susan Grace Galassi, et al. *The Spanish Manner: Drawings from Ribera to Goya*. New York, 2010. Exh. cat. The Frick Collection, New York, Oct. 5, 2010–Jan. 9, 2011.

New York 2011
Umland, Anne. *Picasso: Guitars, 1912–14*. New York, 2011. Exh. cat. The Museum of Modern Art, New York, Feb. 13–June 6, 2011.

New York/Washington, D.C. 2011–12
Galassi, Susan Grace, and Marilyn McCully. *Picasso's Drawings, 1890–1921: Reinventing Tradition*. New Haven, 2011. Exh. cat. The Frick Collection, New York, Oct. 4, 2011–Jan. 8, 2012; the National Gallery of Art, Washington, D.C., Feb. 5–May 6, 2012.

Núñez Vernis 1998
Núñez Vernis, Bertha. "En torno a la obra pictórica de Zacarías González Velázquez." *Goya: Revista de arte* 262 (1998): 37–51.

Núñez Vernis 1999
Núñez Vernis, Bertha. "Once escenas franciscanas de Zacarías González Velázquez en el Museo Lázaro Galdiano." *Goya: Revista de arte* 268 (1999): 30–39.

Orcaña 1995
Orcaña, María Teresa. *Picasso y Els 4 Gats: La Llave de la modernidad*. Barcelona: Museu Picasso, 1995.

Orellana 1967
Orellana, Marcs Antonio de. *Biografía pictórica valentina: o vida de los pintores, arquitectos, escultores y grabadores valencianos*. Edited by Xavier de Salas. Valencia, 1967.

Orso 1989
Orso, Steven N. *Art and Death at the Spanish Habsburg Court: The Royal Exequies for Philip IV*. Columbia, Mo.: The University of Missouri Press, 1989.

Orso 1990
Orso, Steven N. "Praising the Queen: The Decorations at the Royal Exequies for Isabella of Bourbon." *Art Bulletin* 72, no. 1 (March 1990): 51–73.

Oviedo 2002
Véliz, Zahira. *Dibujos Españoles del Siglo de Oro, The Apelles Collection*. Oviedo, 2002. Exh. cat. Museo de Bellas Artes de Asturias, Palacio de Velarde, Oviedo, July 4–Sept. 1, 2002.

Páez Ríos 1982
Páez Ríos, Elena. *Repertorio de Grabados Españoles en la Biblioteca Nacional.* Vol. 2. Madrid: Secretaría general técnica, 1982.

Palencia Tubau 192–?
Palencia Tubau, Ceferino. *Leonardo Alenza.* Madrid: Estrella, [192–?].

Palomino 1987
Palomino de Castro y Velasco, Antonio. *Lives of the Eminent Spanish Painters and Sculptors.* Edited and translated by Nina Ayala Mallory. New York: Cambridge University Press, 1987.

Papi 2007
Papi, Gianni. *Ribera a Roma.* Soncino: Edizioni dei Soncino, 2007.

Paris 1842
Catalogue des Tableaux, Dessins et Gravures de la Collection Standish, légués au Roi par M. Franck Hall Standish. Paris, 1842.

Paris 1852
Catalogue de Livres Provenant des Bibliothèques du Feu Roi Louis-Philippe. Paris: L. Potier, Libraire, 1852.

Paris 1912
Exposition Daniel Vierge. Paris, 1912. Exh. cat. Union central des arts décoratifs, Palais du Louvre, Pavillon de Marsan, Paris, Jan. 11–Feb. 12, 1912.

Paris 1935
Lemoisne, Paul-André, and Jean Adhémar. *Goya: Exposition de l'Oeuvre Gravé, de Peintures, de Tapisseries et de Cent dix Dessins du Musée du Prado.* Paris, 1935. Exh. cat. Bibliothèques Nationales de France, Paris, 1935.

Paris 1979
Goya, 1746–1828: Peintures, Dessins, Gravures. Paris, 1979. Exh. cat. Centre culturel du Marias, Paris, Mar. 13–June 16, 1979.

Paris 1991
Boubli, Lizzie, and Alfonso E. Pérez Sánchez. *Dessins espagnols: Maîtres des XVIe et XVIIe siècles.* Paris: Réunion des musées nationaux, 1991.

Parrado del Olmo 1998
Parrado del Olmo, Jesús María. "Andrés de Melgar en el Retablo de Pozuelo de la Orden: Las relaciones entre pintores en el medio Castellano del primer tercio del siglo XVI." *Boletín del Seminario de Estudios de Arte y Arqueología* 64 (1998): 255–76.

Pascual Chenel 2009
Pascual Chenel, Álvaro. "Sebastián de Herrera Barnuevo y los retratos ecuestres de Carlos II durante su minoría de edad, fortuna iconográfica y propaganda política." *Reales Sitios* 182 (2009): 4–26.

Pascual Chenel 2010
Pascual Chenel, Álvaro. *El retrato de estado durante el reinado de Carlos II: imagen y propaganda.* Madrid: Fundación Universitaria Española, 2010.

Paul 1939
Paul, Elliot. *Luis Quintanilla.* New York, 1939. Exh. cat. Associated American Artists' Galleries, New York, Nov. 6–25, 1939.

Penrose 1936
Penrose, George. *Catalogue of paintings, drawings and miniatures in the Alfred A. de Pass collection, Truro, Cornwall City Museum and Art Gallery.* Truro: Cornish Riviera Press, 1936.

Percy and Cazort 2004
Percy, Ann, and Mimi Cazort. *Italian Master Drawings at the Philadelphia Museum of Art.* Philadelphia: Philadelphia Museum of Art, 2004.

Pérez Sánchez 1972
Pérez Sánchez, Alfonso E. *Jerónimo Jacinto de Espinosa.* Madrid: Instituto Diego Velázquez, 1972.

Pérez Sánchez 1979
Pérez Sánchez, Alfonso E. "Juan de Juanes, en su Centenario." *Archivo de Arte Valenciano* 50 (1979): 5–16.

Pérez Sánchez 1985
Pérez Sánchez, Alfonso E. *Juan Carreño de Miranda, 1614–1685.* Avilés: Ayuntamiento de Avilés, 1985.

Pérez Sánchez 1986
Pérez Sánchez, Alfonso E. *Historia del dibujo en España: de la Edad Media a Goya.* Madrid: Ediciones Cátedra, 1986.

Pérez Sánchez and Navarrete Prieto 1996
Pérez Sánchez, Alfonso E., and Benito Navarrete Prieto. "Sobre Herrera 'el Viejo.'" *Archivo Español de Arte* 69, no. 276 (1996): 365–88.

Pérez Sánchez and Lafuente Ferrari 2003
Pérez Sánchez, Alfonso E., and Enrique Lafuente Ferrari. *Catálogo de la colección de dibujos del Instituto Jovellanos de Gijón.* Gijón: Ayuntamiento, 2003.

Poitiers 2006–7
Boubli, Lizzie et al. *Splendeurs baroques de Naples: dessins des XVIIe et XVIIIe siècles.* Montreuil, 2006. Exh. cat. Musée Sainte-Croix, Poitiers, Oct. 25, 2006–Feb. 25, 2007.

Poggi 1992
Poggi, Christine. *In Defiance of Painting: Cubism, Futurism and the Invention of Collage.* New Haven and London: Yale University Press, 1992.

Ponz 1947
Ponz, Antonio. *Viaje de España (1772–1794).* Edited by Casto María del Rivero. Madrid: M. Aguilar, 1947.

Preciado de la Vega 1789
Preciado de la Vega, Francisco. *Arcadia pictórica.* Madrid: Sancha, 1789.

Princeton 1948
"Recent Accessions." *Record of the Art Museum, Princeton University* 7, no. 2 (1948): 11.

Princeton 1949
Loan Exhibition of Picasso Drawings. Exh. cat. The Art Museum, Princeton University, Jan. 10–31, 1949.

Princeton 1953
"Recent Acquisitions." *Record of the Art Museum, Princeton University* 12, no. 1 (1953): 38–39.

Princeton 1970
"Acquisitions 1969." *Record of the Art Museum, Princeton University* 29, no. 1 (1970): 16–27.

Princeton 1972
Morrin, Peter, ed. *19th and 20th Century French Drawings from the Art Museum, Princeton University: An Introduction.* Exh. cat. The Art Museum, Princeton University, Mar. 4–Apr. 9, 1972.

Princeton 1973
Brown, Jonathan. *Jusepe de Ribera: Prints and Drawings.* Princeton, 1973. Exh. cat. The Art Museum, Princeton University, Oct.–Nov. 1973.

Princeton 1973a
"Acquisitions 1972." *Record of the Art Museum, Princeton University* 32, no. 1 (1973): 20–30.

Princeton 1976–77
Brown, Jonathan. *Murillo and His Drawings.* Princeton, 1976. Exh. cat. The Art Museum, Princeton University, Dec. 12, 1976–Jan. 30, 1977.

Princeton 1980
"Acquisitions of the Art Museum 1979." *Record of the Art Museum, Princeton University* 39, nos. 1–2 (1980): 40–63.

Princeton 1987
"Acquisitions of the Art Museum 1986." *Record of the Art Museum, Princeton University* 46, no. 1 (1987): 18–52.

Princeton 1995
Spanish Drawings. The Art Museum, Princeton University, Oct. 17 –Nov. 13, 1995.

Princeton 1997
Spanish Drawings. The Art Museum, Princeton University, Nov. 4 –Dec. 5, 1997.

Princeton 2001
Spanish Drawings in the Collection of and on Loan to The Art Museum, Princeton University. The Art Museum, Princeton University, Mar. 27–June 10, 2001.

Princeton 2003
"Acquisitions of the Princeton University Art Museum 2002." *Record of Princeton University Art Museum* 62 (2003): 107–61.

Princeton 2007
Princeton University Art Museum: Handbook of the Collections. Princeton: Princeton University Art Museum, 2007.

Prokop 2007
Prokop, Ellen. "Fray Juan Ricci, Mateo Cerezo the Younger, and the Commission to Complete the Retrochoir of the Cathedral of Burgos." *Hispanic Research Journal* 8, no. 5 (December 2007): 409–23.

Providence 1979
Festivities: Ceremonies and Celebrations in Western Europe, 1500–1790. Providence, R.I., 1979. Exh. cat. Bell Gallery, Brown University, Providence, Mar. 2–25, 1979.

Quevedo 1882
Quevedo, Francisco de. *Histoire de Pablo de Ségovie (El gran Tacaño).* Paris: León Bonhoure, 1882.

Quevedo 1892
Quevedo, Francisco de. *Pablo de Segovia.* London: T. Fisher Unwin, 1892.

Quiles García 2005
Quiles García, Fernando. *Alonso Miguel de Tovar (1678–1752).* Seville: Diputación de Sevilla, 2005.

Quimper/Paris 1994
Max Jacob et Picasso. Paris, 1994. Exh. cat. Musée des beaux-arts, Quimper, June 21–Sept. 4, 1994; Musée Picasso, Paris, Oct. 4–Dec. 12, 1994.

Quintanilla 1938–39
War In Spain: Pen and Ink Drawings by Luis Quintanilla. Exh. cat. Philadelphia Art Alliance, Brown University, Oct. 1–22, 1938; Middlebury College, Oct. 29–Nov. 19, 1938; Dartmouth College, Feb. 18–Mar. 11, 1939.

Quintanilla 1939
Quintanilla, Luis, and Elliot Paul. *All the Brave.* Introduction by Ernest Hemingway. New York: Modern Age Books, 1939.

Quintanilla 2003
Quintanilla, Paul. *Waiting at the Shore: Art, Revolution, War and Exile in the Life of the Spanish Artist Luis Quintanilla.* Lulu Press, 2003.

Quintanilla 2004
Quintanilla, Luis, ed. *"Pasatiempo," La Vida de un Pintor: Memorias.* Introduction by Esther López-Sobrado. Alborelle: Ediciós do Castro, 2004.

Ramírez Pascual 1995
Ramírez Pascual, Tomás. "La construcción del retablo mayor de Santo Domingo de la Calzada." In *Damián Forment, escultor renacentista: Retablo Mayor de la Catedral de Santo Domingo de la Calzada,* pp. 49–72. San Sebastián: Catedral de Santo Domingo de la Calzada, 1995.

Reff 1971
Reff, Theodore. "Harlequins, Saltimbanques, Clowns and Fools." *Artforum* 10, no. 2 (October 1971): 31–43.

Richardson 1991
Richardson, John. *A Life of Picasso, 1888–1906.* New York: Random House, 1991.

Richardson 2007
Richardson, John. *A Life of Picasso: The Triumphant Years, 1917–1932.* New York, Alfred A. Knopf, 2007.

Rivera Blanco and Rodicio Rodríguez 1977
Rivera Blanco, José Javier, and María Cristina Rodicio Rodríguez. "Un lienzo de Francisco Camilo en el Museo Diocesano de León." *Archivo Español de Arte* 50, no. 198 (1977): 159–60.

Rodríguez Rebollo 2007
Rodríguez Rebollo, Ángel. "A propósito de Alonso Cano: el dibujo para el retablo de San Diego de Alcalá y su homónimo para San Andrés." In *In Sapientia Libertas: Escritos en Homenaje al Profesor Alfonso E. Pérez Sánchez,* pp. 452–58. Madrid: Museo Nacional del Prado; Seville: Fundación Focus-Abengoa, 2007.

Rodríguez Ruiz and García-Toraño Martínez 2009
Rodríguez Ruiz, Delfín, and Isabel Clara García-Toraño Martínez. *Dibujos de Arquitectura y Ornamentación de la Biblioteca Nacional, Siglo XVIII.* Madrid: Biblioteca Nacional de España, Fundación Banco Santander, Fundación Arquitectura COAM, 2009.

Román 2000
Román, Dulce María. "Rubens and the Emergence of High Baroque Style at the Court of Madrid." *Athanor* 18 (2000): 45–53.

Ross 1996
Ross, Barbara. "The Prints and Drawings Collection: The Early Years." *Record of The Princeton University Art Museum* 55, no. 1–2 (1996): 135–55.

Sáenz Terreros 1981–82
Sáenz Terreros, María Victoria. "Pinturas y pintores de la primera mitad del siglo XVI en Santo Domingo de la Calzada." *Boletín de la Institución Fernán González* 60, no. 197 (1981–1982): 395–415.

Salort Pons, López Azorín, and Navarrete Prieto 2001
Salort Pons, Salvador, María José López Azorín, and Benito Navarrete Prieto. "Vicente Salvador Gómez, Alonso Cano y la pintura valenciana de la segunda mitad del siglo XVII." *Archivo Español de Arte* 74, no. 296 (2001): 393–424.

Sambricio 1955
Sambricio, Valentín de. *Francisco Bayeu.* Madrid: Instituto Diego Velázquez, 1955.

Sánchez Cantón 1930
Sánchez Cantón, Francisco J. *Dibujos Españoles, siglos X–XVII.* 5 vols. Madrid: Hauser y Menet, 1930.

Sánchez Cantón 1964
Sánchez Cantón, Francisco J. *Great Drawings of the World: Spanish drawings of the 10th to the 19th century.* New York: Shorewood Press, 1964.

Sancho 1997
Sancho, José Luis. "Mengs at the Palacio Real, Madrid." *Burlington Magazine* 139, no. 1133 (August 1997): 515–28.

San Francisco/Paris/New York 2011–12
Bishop, Janet, Cécile Debray, and Rebecca Rabinow, eds. *The Steins Collect: Matisse, Picasso, and the Parisian Avant-Garde.* San Francisco/New Haven, 2011. Exh. cat. San Francisco Museum of Modern Art, May 21–Sept. 6, 2011; Grand Palais, Paris, Oct. 3, 2011–Jan. 20, 2012. The Metropolitan Museum of Art, Feb. 21–June 3, 2012.

Santander 2005
López Sobrado, Esther. *Luis Quintanilla (1893–1978): Estampas y Dibujos en el legado de Paul Quintanilla.* Santander, 2005. Exh. cat. Paraninfo de la Universidad de Cantabria, Santander, May 26–July 16, 2005.

Santander 2009
Véliz, Zahira. *Alonso Cano, 1601–1667: Dibujos.* Santander, 2009. Exh. cat. Sala de exposiciones Fundación Marcelino Botín, Santander, Apr. 3–May 17, 2009.

Santander 2012
Mena, Manuela. *Bartolomé Esteban Murillo (1617–1682).* Santander, 2012. Exh. cat. Sala de Exposiciones Fundación Botín, Santander, Mar. 30–May 27, 2012.

Santiago Páez 1966
Santiago Páez, Elena. *Catálogo de las Estampas de Goya en la Biblioteca Nacional.* Madrid: Biblioteca Nacional, 1966.

Santiago Páez 1997
Santiago Páez, Elena. *El Gabinete de Ceán Bermúdez: Dibujos, Estampas y Manuscritos de la Biblioteca Nacional.* Gijón: Museo-Casa Natal de Jovellanos, 1997.

Sanz-Pastor y Fernández de Piérola 1976
Sanz-Pastor y Fernández de Piérola, Consuelo. *Museo Cerralbo: Catálogo de Dibujos.* Madrid: Comisaría Nacional de Museos y Exposiciones, 1976.

Sarró 2005
Sarró, Miguel, *Pinturas de Guerra: Dibujantes antifascistas en la Guerra Civil española.* Madrid: Traficantes de sueños, 2005.

Sayre 1958
Sayre, Eleanor. "An Old Man Writing: A Study of Goya's Albums." *Museum of Fine Arts Bulletin* 56, no. 305 (autumn 1958): 116–36.

Schrader 2006
Schrader, Jeffrey. *La Virgen de Atocha: Los Austrias y las imágenes milagrosas.* Translated by Teresa Sans y Fabián Chueca. Madrid: Ayuntamiento de Madrid, 2006.

Schroth 2010
Schroth, Sarah, ed. *Art of Spain and the Hispanic World: Essays in Honor of Jonathan Brown.* London: Paul Holberton Publishing, in association with Center for Spain in America, 2010.

Seville 1995–96
Pérez Sánchez, Alfonso E., and Benito Navarrete Prieto. *Tres Siglos de Dibujo Sevillano.* Seville, 1995. Exh. cat. Hospital de los Venerables, Seville, Nov. 30, 1995–Feb. 11, 1996.

Seville 1997
Dibujos Valencianos del siglo XVII. Seville, 1997. Exh. cat. Sala Villasís, Seville, Apr. 29–June 22, 1997.

Seville/Bilbao 2005–6
Pérez Sánchez, Alfonso E., and Benito Navarrete Prieto. *De Herrera a Velázquez: el primer naturalismo en Sevilla.* Seville, 2005. Exh. cat. Hospital de los Venerables, Seville, Nov. 29, 2005–Feb. 28, 2006; Museo de Bellas Artes de Bilbao, Mar. 20–May 28, 2006.

Spinosa 2008
Spinosa, Nicola. *Ribera: La Obra completa.* Madrid: Fundación Arte Hispánico, 2008.

Stampfle 1974
Stampfle, Felice. *Drawings: Major Acquisitions of the Pierpont Morgan Library, 1924–1974.* New York: Pierpont Morgan Library, 1974.

Steinberg 1996
Steinberg, Leo. *The Sexuality of Christ in Renaissance Art and in Modern Oblivion.* Chicago: University of Chicago Press, 1996.

Stepanek 1978
Stepanek, Pavel. "Un dibujo inédito de Mariano Salvador Maella en Checoslovaquia." *Archivo de Arte Valenciano* 49 (1978): 54–56.

Stratton 1994
Stratton, Suzanne L. *The Immaculate Conception in Spanish Art.* New York: Cambridge University Press, 1994.

Stratton-Pruitt et al. 2002
Stratton-Pruitt, Suzanne, et al. *Bartolomé Esteban Murillo (1617–1682): Paintings from American Collections.* New York: H.N. Abrams, 2002.

Sullivan 1986
Sullivan, Edward J. *Baroque Painting in Madrid: The Contribution of Claudio Coello, with a Catalogue Raisonné of His Work.* Columbia, Mo.: University of Missouri, 1986.

Sullivan 2010–11
Sullivan, Edward J., ed. *Nueva York, 1613–1945.* London, 2010. Exh. cat. El Museo del Barrio, New York, Sept. 17, 2010–Jan. 9, 2011.

Summa Artis 1987–88
Carrete Parrondo, Juan, et al. *Summa Artis: Historia General del Arte.* Vol. 31, *El Grabado en España.* Madrid: Espasa Calpe 1987–88.

Thacher 1937
Thacher, John S. "The Paintings of Francisco de Herrera, the Elder." *Art Bulletin* 19, no. 3 (September 1937): 325–80.

Tomlinson 1989
Tomlinson, Janis A. *Francisco Goya: The Tapestry Cartoons and Early Career at the Court of Madrid.* New York: Cambridge University Press, 1989.

Tomlinson 1992
Tomlinson, Janis A. *Goya in the Twilight of the Enlightenment.* New Haven: Yale University Press, 1992.

Tomlinson 1994
Tomlinson, Janis A. *Francisco Goya y Lucientes, 1746–1828.* London: Phaidon, 1994.

Tomlinson 1996
Tomlinson, Janis. "Evolving Concepts: Spain, Painting, and Authentic Goyas in 19th Century France." *Metropolitan Museum of Art Journal* 31 (1996): 189–202.

Tormo 1927
Tormo, Elías. "Mateo Cerezo." *Archivo Español de Arte y Arqueología,* no. 8 (May–August, 1927): 113–29; and "Mateo Cerezo Continuación." *Archivo Español de Arte y Arqueología,* no. 9 (September–December 1927): 245–74.

Tormo 1949
Tormo, Elias. "Los Cuatro grandes crucifijos de bronce dorado en El Escorial. Obra de Pompeo Leoni, Pietro Tacca, Lorenzo Bernini y Domenico Guidi." In *Pintura, escultura y arquitectura en España: Estudios dispersos,* 355–79. Madrid: Instituto Diego Velázquez de Arte y Arqueología, 1949.

Trapier 1940
Trapier, Elizabeth du Gué. *Eugenio Lucas y Padilla.* New York: The Hispanic Society of America, 1940.

Trapier 1941
Trapier, Elizabeth du Gué. "Notes on Spanish Drawings." *Notes Hispanic* 1 (1941): 1–61.

Trapier 1942
Trapier, Elizabeth du Gué. "The Use of the Reed Pen by the Artists of Andalucía." *Notes Hispanic* 2 (1942): 1–14.

Trapier 1943
Trapier, Elizabeth du Gué. "A Sketch by José Antolínez." *Notes Hispanic* 3 (1943): 135–38.

Trapier 1963
Trapier, Elizabeth du Gué. "Unpublished Drawings by Goya in the Hispanic Society of America." *Master Drawings* 1, no. 1 (spring 1963): 11–20.

Trapier 1970
Trapier, Elizabeth du Gué. "Algunos dibujos valencianos (de los siglos XVII–XVIII) en la colección de la Hispanic Society." *Archivo Español de Arte,* no. 171 (1970): 348–51.

Turner 2002
Turner, Nicholas. *Dibujos de Maestros Europeos en las Colecciones Portuguesas, 1500–1800.* Madrid: Museo Nacional del Prado, 2002.

Valdivieso 1982
Valdivieso, Enrique. "Obras inéditas de Francisco Camilo." In *Miscelánea de Arte,* pp. 155–58. Madrid: Instituto Diego Velázquez, 1982.

Valencia 1999
La luz de las imágenes: Catedral de Valencia. Valencia, 1999. Exh. cat. Catedral de Valencia, Feb. 4–June 30, 1999.

Valencia 2000
Pérez Sánchez, Alfonso E. *Jerónimo Jacinto de Espinosa (1600–1667).* Valencia, 2000. Exh. cat. Museo de Bellas Artes de Valencia, Sept. 8–Nov. 12, 2000.

Valencia 2010
Espinós Díaz, Adela. *Líneas Maestras: Dibujos del Museo de Bellas Artes de Valencia.* Burgos, 2010. Exh. cat. Cultural Cordón, Burgos, Mar. 25–May 23, 2010.

Véliz 1986
Véliz, Zahira. *Artists' Techniques in Golden Age Spain: Six Treatises in Translation.* New York: Cambridge University Press, 1986.

Véliz 1999
Véliz, Zahira. "Quotation in the drawing practice of Alonso Cano." *Master Drawings* 37, no. 4 (winter 1999): 373–39.

Véliz 2007
Véliz, Zahira. "Alonso Cano's Drawings for the Life of St. Dominic in Santa Cruz la Real, Granada." *Master Drawings* 45, no. 3 (2007): 325–44.

Véliz 2011
Véliz, Zahira. *Alonso Cano (1601–1667): Dibujos: catálogo razonado.* Santander: Fundación Marcelino Botín, 2011.

Véliz 2012
Véliz, Zahira. *Spanish Drawings in the Courtauld Gallery: Complete Catalogue.* London: The Courtauld Gallery and Centro de Estudios Europa Hispánica, in association with Paul Holberton Publishing, 2012.

Vey and Salas 1965
Vey, Horst, and Xavier de Salas. *German and Spanish Art to 1900.* New York: F. Watts, 1965.

Vigo 1994
Pintores del Reinado de Felipe IV. Vigo, 1994. Exh. cat. Museo Nacional del Prado, Madrid, Sept.–Oct. 1994.

De la Viñaza 1887
De la Viñaza, Conde. *Goya, Su Tiempo, Su Vida, Sus Obras.* Madrid: Tipografía de Manuel G. Hernández, 1887.

Watrous 1957
Watrous, James. *The Craft of Old Master Drawings.* Madison: University of Wisconsin Press, 1957.

Wethey 1952
Wethey, Harold E. "Alonso Cano's Drawings." *Art Bulletin* 34, no. 3 (September 1952): 217–34.

Wethey 1954
Wethey, Harold E. "Herrera Barnuevo's Work for the Jesuits of Madrid." *Art Quarterly* 17 (1954): 335–44.

Wethey 1958
Wethey, Harold E. *Alonso Cano, pintor.* Madrid: Instituto Diego Velázquez, 1958.

Wethey 1966
Wethey, Harold E. "Herrera Barnuevo and His Chapel in the Descalzas Reales." *Art Bulletin* 48, no. 1 (March 1966): 15–34.

Wilson-Bareau 1996a
Wilson-Bareau, Juliet. "Goya in The Metropolitan Museum." *Burlington Magazine* 138, no. 1115 (February 1996): 95–103.

Wilson-Bareau 1996b
Wilson-Bareau, Juliet. "Goya and the X Numbers: The 1812 Inventory and Early Acquisitions of Goya Pictures." *Metropolitan Museum Journal* 31 (1996): 159–74.

Zapata Fernández de la Hoz 2010
Zapata Fernández de la Hoz, Teresa. "Unpublished Drawings by Matías de Torres (1635–1711)." *Master Drawings* 48, no. 4 (2010).

Zervos 1954
Zervos, Christian. *Pablo Picasso.* Vol. 6 (Supplément aux volumes 1 à 5). Paris: Cahiers d'Art, 1954.

PHOTOGRAPHY CREDITS

Figs. 1.1, 21.1, 21.2, 22.1, 22.2, 26.1, 69–70.2, 79.1, 86.1 © Museo Nacional del Prado - Madrid - (España)

Figs. 2.1, 2.2, 4.1, 14.1, 14.2, 15.2, 24.2, 74.1 Image copyright © The Metropolitan Museum of Art. Image source: Art Resource, NY

Fig. 2.3 Hill-Stone Incorporated

Fig. 5.1 © The Cleveland Museum of Art

Fig. 5.2 © C. Lancien, C. Loisel / Musées de la Ville de Rouen

Fig. 9.1 Scala / Art Resource, NY

Fig. 10.1 Instituto dos Museus e da Conservação, I. P. / Divisão de Documentação Fotográfica

Fig. 10.2 bpk, Berlin / Alte Pinakothek / Art Resource, NY

Fig. 15.1 Photograph © 2012 Museum of Fine Arts, Boston

Fig. 16.1 Courtesy National Gallery of Art, Washington

Figs. 18.1, 31.1 Courtesy Real Academia de Bellas Artes de San Fernando

Fig. 19.1 Museo de Bellas Artes, Valencia

Figs. 20.1, 69–70.1: bpk, Berlin / Hamburger Kunsthalle / Christoph Irrgang / Art Resource, NY

Fig. 23.2 Courtesy of the Hispanic Society of America, New York

Fig. 23.3 Erich Lessing / Art Resource, NY

Figs. 24.1, 48.1, 48.2 © Museu Nacional d'Art de Catalunya, Barcelona / Photographers: Calveras/ Mérida/Sagristà

Fig. 31.2 Réunion des Musées Nationaux / Art Resource, NY / Photograph by Michèle Bellot

Fig. 31.3 Réunion des Musées Nationaux / Art Resource, NY / Photograph by Thierry Le Mage

Fig. 37.2 Réunion des Musées Nationaux / Art Resource, NY / Photograph by Madeleine Coursaget

Cats. 56–57 © 2012 Estate of Pablo Picasso / Artists Rights Society (ARS), New York

Fig. 56.1 CNAC/MNAM/Dist. Réunion des Musées Nationaux / Art Resource, NY / © 2012 Estate of Pablo Picasso / Artists Rights Society (ARS), New York

Fig. 56.2 Scala / Art Resource, NY / © 2012 Estate of Pablo Picasso / Artists Rights Society (ARS), New York

Fig. 57.1 CNAC/MNAM/Dist. Réunion des Musées Nationaux / Art Resource, NY / Photograph by Christian Bahier / © 2012 Estate of Pablo Picasso / Artists Rights Society (ARS), New York

Fig. 57.2 © 2012 Estate of Pablo Picasso / Artists Rights Society (ARS), New York / Photography Gassull Fotografia

Fig. 58.1 © Stichting Kröller-Müller Museum

Cats. 59–61 © Estate of Luis Quintanilla

Fig. 62.1, 62.2, 62.3 © The Museum of Modern Art/Licensed by SCALA / Art Resource, NY/ © 2012 Successió Miró / Artists Rights Society (ARS), New York /ADAGP, Paris

Cat. 62 © 2012 Successió Miró / Artists Rights Society (ARS), New York /ADAGP, Paris

Cats. 63–64 © Salvador Dalí, Fundació Gala-Salvador Dalí, Artists Rights Society (ARS), New York 2012

Cat. 65 © 2012 Artists Rights Society (ARS), New York / VEGAP, Madrid

Fig. 65.1 © Fitzwilliam Museum, Cambridge / Art Resource, NY / © 2012 Artists Rights Society (ARS), New York / VEGAP, Madrid

Fig. 74.2 Courtesy Rijksmuseum, Amsterdam

Fig. 76.1 Erich Lessing / Art Resource, NY